RESPONSIVE HUMAN RIGHTS

This open access book asks, who is a vulnerable person in human rights law?

It assesses the treatment of vulnerability by the European Court of Human Rights, an area that has been surprisingly underexplored by European human rights law to date. It explores legal-philosophical understandings of the topic, providing a theoretical framework that can be used when examining the question. Not confining itself to the abstract, however, it provides a bridge from the theoretical to the practical by undertaking a comprehensive examination of the Court's approach under Article 3 ECHR. It also pays particular attention to the concept of human dignity.

Well written and compellingly argued, this is an important new book for all scholars of European human rights.

Volume 106 in the Series Modern Studies in European Law

Modern Studies in European Law
Recent titles in this series:

Citizenship, Crime and Community in the European Union
Stephen Coutts

Critical Reflections on Constitutional Democracy in the European Union
Edited by Sacha Garben and Inge Govaere

Constitutional Law of the EU's Common Foreign and Security Policy: Competence and Institutions in External Relations
Graham Butler

The Juridification of Individual Sanctions and the Politics of EU Law
Eva Nanopoulos

Sixty Years of European Integration and Global Power Shifts: Perceptions, Interactions and Lessons
Edited by Julien Chaisse

Fundamental Rights and Mutual Recognition in the Area of Freedom, Security and Justice: A Role for Proportionality?
Ermioni Xanthopoulou

Law and Judicial Dialogue on the Return of Irregular Migrants from the European Union
Edited by Madalina Moraru, Galina Cornelisse and Philippe De Bruycker

Framing Convergence with the Global Legal Order: The EU and the World
Edited by Elaine Fahey

EU Citizenship at the Edges of Freedom of Movement
Katarina Hyltén-Cavallius

The Internal Market 2.0
Edited by Sacha Garben and Inge Govaere

New Directions in European Private Law
Edited by Mateja Durovic and Takis Tridimas

Standing to Enforce European Union Law before National Courts
Hilde Ellingsen

The Relative Authority of Judicial and Extra-Judicial Review: The EU Courts, the Boards of Appeal and the Ombudsman
Michal Krajewski

For the complete list of titles in this series, see 'Modern Studies in European Law' link at www.bloomsburyprofessional.com/uk/series/modern-studies-in-european-law

Responsive Human Rights

Vulnerability, Ill-treatment and the ECtHR

Corina Heri

•HART•
OXFORD • LONDON • NEW YORK • NEW DELHI • SYDNEY

HART PUBLISHING

Bloomsbury Publishing Plc

Kemp House, Chawley Park, Cumnor Hill, Oxford, OX2 9PH, UK

1385 Broadway, New York, NY 10018, USA

29 Earlsfort Terrace, Dublin 2, Ireland

HART PUBLISHING, the Hart/Stag logo, BLOOMSBURY and the Diana logo are trademarks of Bloomsbury Publishing Plc

First published in Great Britain 2021

A catalogue record for this book is available from the British Library.

ISBN: HB: 978-1-50994-123-0
ePDF: 978-1-50994-125-4
ePub: 978-1-50994-124-7

Typeset by Compuscript Ltd, Shannon

This monograph has been adapted from (but is not identical to) PhD research conducted by the author at the University of Zürich. That research was funded by the Swiss National Science Foundation and the Janggen-Pöhn Foundation. An open access version of this book was made possible through the support of the Swiss National Science Foundation

ACKNOWLEDGEMENTS

In late 2012, this book began life as a PhD research proposal at the University of Zurich. Since then, it has taken me to different institutions and countries, brought me joy as well as sleepless nights, and accompanied me on a now almost decade-long career as a scholar. During that time, I have had the good fortune of being surrounded by people who have continually encouraged and supported me, and to whom I owe a tremendous debt of gratitude.

First and foremost, I am immensely grateful to Helen Keller, who supervised my doctoral research at the University of Zurich with tremendous brilliance, insight, wisdom and kindness. I am also grateful to my co-supervisor, Daniel Moeckli, who read the manuscript with a critical eye and whose feedback made this a better book. Thanks also go to Cedric Marti and Lea Raible, for fruitful discussions and for showing me the ropes at the RWI.

From Zurich, I went to the Human Rights Centre at Ghent University, where I spent time as a visiting scholar thanks to the support of the Swiss National Science Foundation and the Janggen-Pöhn Foundation. In Ghent, I joined 'the Strasbourg Club' and the wonderful group of colleagues so inspiringly led by Eva Brems, including Laurens Lavrysen, Stijn Smet, Saïla Ouald-Chaib, Abdi Jibril Ali, Eline Kindt, Pieter Cannoot, Katrijn Vanhees, Evelyn Merckx, Martine Dewulf, and too many others to name.

As a postdoctoral researcher at the University of Amsterdam, I turned my PhD into a monograph while surrounded by another group of brilliant colleagues and students. Thanks go especially to Kevin Jon Heller, who went out of his way to help me navigate this process, and Yvonne Donders and Jackson Oldfield, who broadened my horizons. At various points during my research, I also benefited from insightful discussions on the Court's vulnerability reasoning with Nesa Zimmermann, Alexandra Timmer and Lourdes Peroni, among others, and received helpful questions and comments from participants at various workshops and conferences.

I owe a debt of gratitude to Hart Publishing, and especially Sinead Moloney, for believing in this book and for their editorial support. I am also thankful to the two anonymous referees who provided generous feedback on the manuscript. The open-access publication of this volume was made possible by a grant from the Swiss National Science Foundation.

Research can be a lonely endeavour, and I am deeply grateful to my friends and family for their support. To my parents, Michael and Eveline, thank you for being my first and biggest fans and for celebrating the fact that I was born with a book under my arm. To Sebastian, thank you for sharing big ideas and for challenging me to be more critical. A mi abuela Sorne, la persona más fuerte que conozco, gracias por haberme tenido siempre entre algodones. To my Grosi Dora, who left us while I was working on this book, for believing in it even before I did. To Peter and Francine (and the whole *kroost*), for opening your home to me and treating me like one of your own. To Evelyn, Alfie, Marco, Keerti, Ellen, Jeroen, Nora, Lore, and others (you know who you are), for the laughs and warmth and drinks. And last but most certainly not least, from the first blueberry to the surprise defence, neither this book nor anything else would have been possible without Joke. Thank you for making it fun.

CONTENTS

LIST OF FIGURES

LIST OF ABBREVIATIONS

CAT	UN Committee against Torture
CCPR	Human Rights Committee
CEDAW	Convention on the Elimination of all Forms of Discrimination Against Women, 1249 UNTS 13, 18 December 1979, New York, in force since 3 September 1981, 189 states parties
CESCR	Committee on Economic, Social and Cultural Rights
CETS	Council of Europe Treaty Series
CIA	United States Central Intelligence Agency
CPT	European Committee for the Prevention of Torture and Inhuman or Degrading Treatment or Punishment
CRC	Convention on the Rights of the Child, 1577 UNTS 3, 20 November 1989, New York, in force since 2 September 1990, 196 states parties
CRPD	Convention on the Rights of Persons with Disabilities, 2515 UNTS 3, 13 December 2006, New York, in force since 3 May 2008, 167 states parties
CSCE	Conference on Security and Co-operation in Europe
ECHR	Council of Europe, European Convention for the Protection of Human Rights and Fundamental Freedoms, as amended by Protocols nos. 11 and 14, supplemented by Protocols nos. 1, 4, 6, 7, 12 and 13, ETS 5, Rome, 4 November 1950, entered into force 3 September 1953, 47 states parties
ECRI	European Committee against Racism and Intolerance
ECSR	European Committee of Social Rights
ECtHR	European Court of Human Rights (also termed 'the Court')
ESC	European Social Charter
ETS	European Treaty Series
EU	European Union

FCNM	Framework Convention for the Protection of National Minorities, ETS 157, Strasbourg, 1 February 1995, in force since 1 February 1998, 39 states parties
GC	Grand Chamber
HRC	UN Human Rights Committee
ICC	International Criminal Court
ICCPR	International Covenant on Civil and Political Rights, 999 UNTS 171, New York, 16 December 1966, in force since 23 March 1976, 168 states parties
ICESCR	International Covenant on Economic, Social and Cultural Rights, 993 UNTS 3, New York, 19 December 1966, in force since 3 January 1976, 164 states parties
ICJ	International Court of Justice of the United Nations
ICTR	International Criminal Tribunal for Rwanda
ICTY	International Criminal Tribunal for the former Yugoslavia
IDT	Inhuman and degrading treatment
ILC	International Law Commission
OAS	Organization of American States
OAU	Organization of African Unity
OHCHR	Office of the High Commissioner for Human Rights
OSCE	Organization for Security and Co-operation in Europe
PACE	Parliamentary Assembly of the Council of Europe
UDHR	UN General Assembly, Universal Declaration of Human Rights, UNGA Res. 217 A (III) 10 December 1948
UNCAT	UN Convention Against Torture and Other Cruel, Inhuman or Degrading Treatment or Punishment, 1465 UNTS 85, 10 December 1984, in force since 26 June 1987, 160 states parties
UNGA	General Assembly
UNTS	United Nations Treaty Series
WHO	World Health Organization

Introduction

Chapter Summary

The aim of this book is to analyse the doctrine of vulnerability, a relatively new yet already well-established concept that affects the interpretation of the European Convention on Human Rights (ECHR). By applying the concept of vulnerability, the European Court of Human Rights (ECtHR) tailors the Convention's standards to the needs of specific individuals and groups, and therefore ensures context-responsive rights protection. This introductory chapter outlines the key topics discussed in the book. First, it presents the ways in which the Court responds to specific circumstances and thereby moves between universality and relativism and between formal and substantive equality. Secondly, it introduces the concept of vulnerability in terms of the persons or groups thus described by the Court, its reasons for deploying the concept, and the forms and effects of its use. Thirdly, it explores the reasons for and urgency of examining vulnerability specifically from the perspective of the prohibition of torture and inhuman and degrading treatment in Article 3 ECHR. Finally, it outlines the theoretical backdrop for studying the Court's vulnerability concept, and how this will be integrated with an analysis of the Court's practice.

Keywords: European Convention on Human Rights; European Court of Human Rights; vulnerability; prohibition of torture and inhuman and degrading treatment; substantive equality.

PART I

Legal and Conceptual Foundations

1

Substantive Scene-Setting – The Prohibition of Torture and Inhuman and Degrading Treatment

Chapter Summary

Evaluating the impact of the Court's vulnerability concept on its case law under Article 3 ECHR requires, as its basis, an understanding of that provision itself and of its application by the Court. The present chapter provides just that. It will first sketch the general background against which the prohibition of torture – and its definition – evolved, and then turn specifically to the approach of the ECtHR. In particular, it will touch on three aspects of the Court's approach that are of relevance of the further analysis: first, that the prohibition of torture and inhuman and degrading treatment (IDT) is (relatively) absolute; secondly, that the concept of what constitutes proscribed ill-treatment has evolved over time, and adapts to changing circumstances and understandings; and, thirdly, that the ECtHR takes a context-responsive approach to the severity test under Article 3 that determines whether a given treatment is compatible with respect for human dignity.

Keywords: Article 3 ECHR, prohibition of torture, inhuman and degrading treatment, evolutive interpretation, relativity and absoluteness, history of torture, threshold of severity test, positive obligations.

I. The Evolving Prohibition of Torture

In order to analyse the effects of vulnerability reasoning on the ECtHR's approach to the prohibition of torture and inhuman and degrading treatment, the following will explore key aspects of the scope of this prohibition, and how it came to be.

What constitutes prohibited ill-treatment has continually changed and expanded over time, and acts understood as torture have been inflicted, discussed, and legally defined for millennia.[1] For example, Ancient Greek, Roman and Egyptian civilisations allowed such treatment to be inflicted on persons lacking

[1] Manfred Nowak and Elizabeth McArthur, *The United Nations Convention against Torture: A Commentary* (OUP, 2008), 1–2.

full legal personality, such as foreigners and slaves.[2] In Europe, torture was notoriously commonplace until the Enlightenment, when increasing respect for human dignity and recognition of the unacceptable brutality and doubtful efficacy of torture coincided with its prohibition in many parts of Europe.[3]

Moral disgust with the idea of torture was revived after the Second World War.[4] Those experiences meant that the nascent international protection of human rights concerned itself extensively with the prohibition of torture and inhuman and degrading treatment. A corresponding provision was integrated first into the Universal Declaration of Human Rights of 1948.[5] This was soon followed by the ECHR, which in its Article 3 created the first binding human rights norm prohibiting torture and IDT, stating succinctly that '[n]o one shall be subjected to torture or to inhuman or degrading treatment or punishment.' Similar prohibitions in other regional and international human rights instruments followed.[6]

The scope of what constitutes torture has evolved dramatically over time and continues to be controversial. At the same time, the relevant regional and international adjudicators and bodies have regularly referred to and drawn upon each other's work and on that of the Special Rapporteur on Torture and Other Cruel, Inhuman and Degrading Treatment, in effect creating a certain convergence in how they interpret and expand the scope of the prohibition. For example, when the Special Rapporteur first asserted, in 1986, that rape can constitute torture,[7] this idea was quickly taken up by other bodies. Twelve years later, the ICTY, the ICTR, the IACHR and the ECtHR had all found that the prohibition of torture and ill-treatment had been violated by acts of rape.[8] In this sense, while it may be

[2] Nigel S Rodley and Matt Pollard, *The Treatment of Prisoners under International Law*, 3rd edn (OUP, 2009), 8.

[3] Rodley and Pollard (n 2), 8–9.

[4] Fatima Kola, 'Assessing and Revising the Absolute Prohibition of Torture: An Examination of Its Purpose, Philosophical Justification and Structural Elements' (Dissertation, University College London, 2011), 44.

[5] UDHR, Art 5.

[6] Selected examples include Art 7 ICCPR; Art 5 of the American Convention on Human Rights, adopted on 22 November 1969, in force since 18 July 1978, OAS Treaty Series No 36, 1144 UNTS 123, 25 states parties; Organization of African Unity, African Charter on Human and Peoples' Rights, 27 June 1981, entered into force on 21 October 1986, CAB/LEG/67/3 rev 5 (1982) 21(1) *International Legal Materials* 58–68, 53 states parties, Art 5; Organization of American States, Inter-American Convention to Prevent and Punish Torture, 9 December 1985, in force since 28 February 1987, OAS Treaty Series, No 67, 18 states parties; and Council of Europe, European Convention for the Prevention of Torture and Inhuman or Degrading Treatment or Punishment, 26 November 1987, in force since 1 February 1989, ETS 126, 47 states parties.

[7] Manfred Nowak, 'What Practices Constitute Torture?: US and UN Standards' (2006) 28(4) *Human Rights Quarterly* 809–41, citing Peter Kooijmans, 'Torture and Other Cruel, Inhuman or Degrading Treatment or Punishment', UN Doc E/CN.4/1986/15, 19 February 1986, para 119.

[8] Nowak (n 7), 3–4; citing *Aydin v Turkey* App no 23178/94, Judgment (GC) of 25 September 1997, Reports 1997-VI; Inter-American Commission on Human Rights, *Martín de Mejía v Peru*, Case 10.970, Report No 5/96, 1 March 1996; ICTY, *Prosecutor v Furundžija* (Judgment), ICTY IT-95-17/1-T, 10 December 1998 (1999) 38(2) *International Legal Materials* 317–393, paras. 163, 171; ICTR, *Prosecutor v Akayesu* (Judgment), ICTR-96-4-T, 2 September 1998 (1998) 37(6) *International Legal Materials* 1399–1410, para 597. See also Clare McGlynn, 'Rape, Torture and the European Convention on Human Rights' (2009) 58(3) *International and Comparative Law Quarterly* 565–95, 565.

difficult to identify a single definition of torture and IDT, the relevant international standards have nevertheless converged significantly to date.

II. The ECtHR's Interpretation of Article 3 ECHR

Article 3 ECHR was the first binding, albeit regional, prohibition of torture under international human rights law. The provision is succinct, and does not define torture or IDT. Today, by means of the Court's jurisprudence, it has become a multifaceted set of state obligations, which are affected by the vulnerability of an individual applicant or a group to which they belong. To preface the discussion of what vulnerability does here, the following will detail certain aspects of the evolution of that provision and its scope as it currently stands.

A. The Threshold of Severity Test

The test for determining whether Article 3 ECHR has been violated, as created and applied by the Court, is one of degree and of circumstance. To violate Article 3, ill-treatment must reach a 'minimum level of severity'. Because of the absolute nature of the provision, there can be no justification of ill-treatment that passes this threshold.

The de minimis threshold is relative: as the Court found in the 1978 *Ireland v United Kingdom* judgment, 'it depends on all the circumstances of the case, such as the duration of the treatment, its physical or mental effects and, in some cases, the sex, age and state of health of the victim, etc.'[9] Although Article 3 standards have continued to evolve since then, the *Ireland* judgment indicates that – as early as 1978 – the Court was prepared to adopt a differentiated and victim-specific or contextual understanding of the provision.

This 'de minimis' rule has been reiterated countless times in the Court's subsequent jurisprudence.[10] In *Soering v United Kingdom*, the Court supplemented it by finding that the severity of ill-treatment depends not only on the factors listed in *Ireland*, but also on 'all the circumstances of the case, such as the nature and context of the treatment or punishment, the manner and method of its execution'.[11] This has continued to evolve, and the Court has now developed a standard formula for applying the threshold of severity. This describes a test that is 'relative; it depends on all the circumstances of the case, such as the nature and context of

[9] *Ireland v United Kingdom* App no 5310/71, Judgment of 18 January 1978, Series A, No 25, para 162.

[10] Aisling Reidy, 'The Prohibition of Torture: A Guide to the Implementation of Article 3 of the European Convention on Human Rights' 6 *Human Rights Handbooks* (Council of Europe 2002), 10–11.

[11] *Soering v United Kingdom* App no 14038/88, Judgment of 7 July 1989, Series A161, para 100; Reidy (n 10), 10.

the treatment, the manner and method of its execution, its duration, its physical or mental effects and, in some instances, the sex, age and state of health of the victim.'[12] In addition, as clarified in *Khlaifia and Others* in 2016, the Court takes into consideration three factors: 1) the purpose of ill-treatment and the intention and motivation behind it, 2) its context, 'such as an atmosphere of heightened tension and emotions', and 3) the vulnerability of the victim.[13]

In other words, the Court takes the whole context of a given act of ill-treatment into account, and its assessment is relative to the situation, to the ill-treatment, and to traits specific to the victim. Vulnerability reasoning informs this context-sensitive assessment because it relates to the situation concerned (for example, detention), to the ill-treatment (with some acts, for example rape, exploiting vulnerability or causing victims to feel particularly vulnerable), and to the traits of a given victim (for example, young age or disability). Chapter four will show that vulnerability can also have various other effects, but its ability to affect the threshold of severity test, and thereby the scope of Article 3, is certainly a key one.

B. A Typology of Prohibitions under Article 3

Article 3 textually prohibits different types of acts. It can, strictly speaking, be dissected into five possible prohibitions, namely the prohibitions of torture, of inhuman treatment, of inhuman punishment, of degrading treatment and of degrading punishment. While the Court does not always make clear distinctions between these different prohibited behaviours, it has established criteria for distinguishing three types of acts.

i. The Court's Early Case-Law: Torture versus Inhuman and Degrading Treatment and Punishment

Although the Court long shied away from defining torture itself, and instead referred to the definition in Article 1 UNCAT,[14] it did develop its own case law, including its own standards for delimiting torture from other types of ill-treatment. Already in the 1969 '*Greek Case*', the Commission delineated the levels of severity of the different types of ill-treatment under Article 3 into a hierarchy by stating that 'all torture must be inhuman and degrading treatment, and inhuman treatment also degrading.'[15] It then defined these concepts for the first time.

[12] See *Bouyid v Belgium* App no 23380/09, Judgment (GC) of 28 September 2015, Reports 2015, para 78.

[13] *Khlaifia and Others v Italy* App no 16483/12, Judgment (GC) of 15 December 2016, Reports 2016 (extracts), para 160.

[14] *Gäfgen v Germany* App no 22978/05, Judgment (GC) of 1 June 2010, Reports 2010, para 90.

[15] *Governments of Denmark, Norway, Sweden and the Netherlands v Greece ('the Greek Case')* App nos 3321/67 …, Report of 5 November 1969, part II, *Yearbook of the ECHR*, 12 (1969), 186, para 2.

In doing so, it specified that 'inhuman treatment' means 'at least such treatment as deliberately causes severe suffering, mental or physical, which, in the particular situation, is unjustifiable'.[16] It also held that 'torture' was an aggravated form of inhuman treatment because it has an added element, and namely a specific purpose, 'such as the obtaining of information or confession, or the infliction of punishment'.[17] Degrading treatment or punishment, it held, 'grossly humiliates [the affected individual] before others or drives him to act against his will or conscience'.[18]

The next important milestone came in 1978, with the above-mentioned *Ireland* case. There, the Court examined whether five techniques of interrogation employed by the United Kingdom's government had violated the rights of the suspected terrorists on whom they were inflicted.[19] In light of the particular stigma attached to a finding of torture, and the insufficient intensity of the victims' suffering, the Court found that the treatment in question did not constitute torture, but was instead inhuman treatment.[20] The Court also elaborated on the meaning of 'inhuman' and 'degrading' treatment, emphasising 'intense physical and mental suffering' in regard of the former and 'feelings of fear, anguish and inferiority capable of humiliating and debasing [its victims] and possibly breaking their physical or moral resistance' in regard of the latter.[21]

With this judgment, the Court indicated that the decisive issue in differentiating between torture and inhuman and degrading treatment is the intensity of the suffering caused, and not the purpose of the acts concerned. The severity criterion has been repeated countless times in the jurisprudence that followed, although the Court's approach has been contested as overemphasising the outcomes of torture and failing to appreciate its qualitative and relational wrongfulness.[22]

With time, the Court began to expand the scope of what constitutes torture, as it predicted that it would do in *Selmouni v France*.[23] However, the elements of intent and purpose were not erased from the Court's jurisprudence, neither by *Ireland* nor by the Court's later case law. For example, in *Aksoy v Turkey*, in 1996, when the Court found that an act had constituted torture for the first time in its history, it based its reasoning on those elements. It accordingly held that a 'deliberately inflicted' act of 'Palestinian hanging' perpetrated with premeditation in order to extract information from the victim was so serious and cruel that it could only be described as torture.[24]

[16] Ibid.

[17] Ibid.

[18] Ibid.

[19] *Ireland* (n 9), paras 165–68. See also Anja Katarina Weilert, *Grundlagen und Grenzen des Folterverbotes in verschiedenen Rechtskreisen* (Springer, 2009), 18.

[20] *Ireland* (n 9), paras 167–68.

[21] Ibid, para 167.

[22] Natasa Mavronicola, *Torture, Inhumanity and Degradation under Article 3 of the ECHR: Absolute Rights and Absolute Wrongs* (Hart, 2021), 71.

[23] *Selmouni v France* App no 25803/94, Judgment (GC) of 28 July 1999, Reports 1999-V, para 101.

[24] *Aksoy v Turkey* App no 21987/93, Judgment of 18 December 1996, Reports 1996-VI, para 64.

In general terms, a finding of torture under the ECHR is understood as entailing a special stigma and requires, in addition to an element of severity, an element of intent and one of purpose to this day.[25] However, there have been some divergent strands of case law in this regard.[26] In some instances, the Court has focused more on the gratuitous nature of the violence used, rather than on a particular intent.[27] In others, it has focused on the severity and type of suffering inflicted.[28] In yet other cases, the Court has taken as a primary consideration whether the ill-treatment had long-lasting after-effects for the health of the victims.[29]

ii. Inhuman versus Degrading

Situations that do not meet the definition of torture may nevertheless fall under Article 3 by constituting inhuman or degrading treatment. Some of the Court's early case law indicated a hierarchy between these two, with degrading treatment being described as the less severe form of ill-treatment.[30] This distinction may not be all that relevant anymore. For one, Natasa Mavronicola has made a convincing argument for the fact that the distinction is qualitative one.[31] In addition, the Court does not make an explicit distinction between inhuman and degrading treatment in every case. It sometimes contents itself with a finding that a given treatment has 'at least' constituted inhuman treatment[32] or that treatment has been inhuman and degrading.[33] Sometimes it fails even to indicate anything beyond the fact that a violation of Article 3 has taken place.[34]

That is not to say that inhumanity is indistinguishable from degradation. In defining inhuman treatment or punishment, the Court has referred to treatment that 'was premeditated, was applied for hours at a stretch and caused either actual bodily injury or intense physical or mental suffering.'[35] By contrast, degrading treatment or punishment is 'such as to arouse in [its] victims feelings of fear, anguish and inferiority capable of humiliating and debasing them and possibly breaking their physical or moral resistance'.[36] However, in both cases, the de

[25] *El-Masri v the former Yugoslav Republic of Macedonia* App no 39630/09, Judgment (GC) of 13 December 2012, Reports 2012, para 197. See also *İlhan v Turkey* App no 22277/93, Judgment (GC) of 27 June 2000, ECHR 2000-VII, para 85.

[26] Mavronicola (n 22).

[27] *Cestaro v Italy* App no 6884/11, Judgment of 7 April 2015, para 174.

[28] *Erdal Aslan v Turkey*, nos 25060/02 and 1705/03, Judgment of 2 December 2008, para 73.

[29] *Cestaro* (n 27), paras 176, 178.

[30] *Tyrer v the United Kingdom* App no 5856/72, Judgment of 25 April 1978, Series A26, para 29; *The Greek Case* (n 15), para 2.

[31] Mavronicola (n 22), 90.

[32] *Süheyla Aydın v Turkey* App no 25660/94, Judgment of 24 May 2005, para 197.

[33] *Ribitsch v Austria* App no 18896/91, Judgment of 4 December 1995, Series A336, para 39; *Algür v Turkey* App no 32574/96, Judgment of 22 October 2002, para 46.

[34] *Ayse Tepe v Turkey* App no 29422/95, Judgment of 22 July 2003, para 42.

[35] See, for example, *Kudła v Poland* App no 30210/96, Judgment (GC) of 26 October 2000, Reports 2000-XI, para 92; *Gäfgen* (n 14), para 89.

[36] *Ireland* (n 9), para 167.

minimis threshold must be reached and 'the suffering and humiliation involved must in any event go beyond that inevitable element of suffering or humiliation connected with a given form of legitimate treatment or punishment.'[37]

In addition, in order to determine whether a treatment or punishment is degrading, the Court often examines the object of the alleged ill-treatment in order to determine whether it aimed to 'humiliate and debase' the victim – even though the lack of such an intention does not rule out a violation of Article 3[38] – and whether 'it adversely affected his or her personality in a manner incompatible with Article 3'.[39] Publicity is not a precondition here: 'it may well suffice that the victim is humiliated in his or her own eyes, even if not in the eyes of others'.[40]

iii. Treatment versus Punishment

In the past, the Court has occasionally taken the distinction between 'treatment' and 'punishment' very seriously. For example, in one case, it held that the findings on inhuman and degrading treatment made in *Ireland* did not apply to a case on 'punishment'.[41] However, this rigid distinction seems to have softened with later case law. In many cases, the Court now makes general findings about treatment *and* punishment.[42] At the same time, there is a conceptual specificity to 'punishment', which requires the distinction of legitimate punishment and that which goes beyond. In the detention context, the Court has issued extensive jurisprudence on the suffering and humiliation that goes beyond what is necessarily involved in a carceral sentence.[43] This is discussed more in depth in the context of the vulnerability of detainees.

C. Types of State Obligations Regarding Ill-treatment

Along with prohibiting different types of ill-treatment, Article 3 also imposes different types of obligations on states, namely both positive and negative ones.[44]

[37] *Kudła* (n 35), para 92.

[38] *Price v United Kingdom* App no 33394/96, Judgment of 10 July 2001, Reports 2001-VII, para 24.

[39] *Raninen v Finland* App no 20972/92, Judgment of 16 December 1997, Reports 1997-VIII, para 55.

[40] Ibid.

[41] *Tyrer* (n 30), para 29.

[42] *Keenan v United Kingdom* App no 27229/95, Judgment of 3 April 2001, Reports 2001-III, para 116.

[43] Mavronicola (n 22), 113–25.

[44] See Stijn Smet, 'The "Absolute" Prohibition of Torture and Inhuman or Degrading Treatment in Article 3 ECHR: Truly a Question of Scope Only?' in Eva Brems and Janneke H Gerards (eds), *Shaping Rights in the ECHR: The Role of the European Court of Human Rights in Determining the Scope of Human Rights* (CUP, 2013) 273–93, 278. On positive obligations under Art 3 and the Convention in general, see Lavrysen Laurens, *Human Rights in a Positive State: Rethinking the Relationship Between Positive and Negative Obligations under the European Convention on Human Rights* (Intersentia, 2016).

In general terms, the negative obligations require states to refrain from subjecting anyone to torture and inhuman or degrading treatment. As a complement to this, the positive and investigative obligations under Article 3 require states to protect and fulfil individual rights or, in other words, to prevent a risk of ill-treatment from materialising.[45]

The positive limb of Article 3 applies where 'the authorities knew or ought to have known at the time of the existence of a real and immediate risk of ill-treatment of an identified individual from the criminal acts of a third party', and failed to take reasonable measures.[46] The fact that states can violate their positive obligations under Article 3 where they *should have known* of a risk of ill-treatment, ie where knowledge can be imputed, implies that they should conduct due diligence to identify such risks.[47] Additionally, Article 3 does not require proof that ill-treatment would not have happened 'but for' a state failure to take measures. It is sufficient to prove that the state failed to take measures that were reasonably available, and which had 'a real prospect of altering the outcome or mitigating the harm.'[48]

Positive obligations on the part of the state may have socio-economic implications. Budgetary considerations cannot, however, a priori free states from their obligations under Article 3 ECHR. For while these obligations should not place a disproportionate burden on states, they must at least provide 'effective protection' to vulnerable individuals and 'include reasonable steps to prevent ill-treatment of which the authorities had or ought to have had knowledge'.[49] In short, the Court has held that the allocation of limited state resources should prioritise the needs of those deemed most vulnerable. While this provides a certain minimum content of states' positive obligations, even this is limited – in light of 'the difficulties in policing modern societies, the unpredictability of human conduct and the operational choices which must be made in terms of priorities and resources' – so as not to create 'an impossible or disproportionate burden' on the state.[50] Furthermore, as discussed in chapter eight of this volume, this raises questions about whether prioritising the protection of certain individuals over those of others on the basis of generalised attributes or dependencies generates new inequalities.

States' positive obligations under Article 3 have also given rise to the provision's procedural aspect. In order to satisfy these procedural obligations, states must institute 'an effective official investigation … capable of leading to the identification and punishment of those responsible.'[51] However, the investigative obligation

[45] *Đorđević v Croatia* App no 41526/10, Judgment of 24 July 2012, Reports 2012, para 138.

[46] Ibid, para 139.

[47] Lavrysen (n 44), 169, with further references.

[48] *E and Others v United Kingdom* App no 33218/96, Judgment of 26 November 2002, para 99.

[49] *O'Keeffe v Ireland* App no 35810/09, Judgment (GC) of 28 January 2014, Reports 2014 (extracts), para 144.

[50] Ibid.

[51] *Assenov and Others v Bulgaria* App no 24760/94, Judgment of 28 October 1998, Reports 1998-VIII, para 102.

under Article 3, which has evolved into a separate and autonomous duty, is 'not an obligation of result, but of means'.[52] Accordingly, an investigation need not be successful in order to satisfy state obligations, but it should be *capable* of succeeding. In other words, it must make 'a serious attempt' to establish the facts, identify the responsible parties and lead to their punishment.[53] It should also enjoy independence from the executive in institutional and practical terms, and should permit the victim to participate effectively.[54]

D. The Court's Contextual Severity Assessment

Both the de minimis threshold that determines the applicability of Article 3 and the thresholds between the various categories of proscribed ill-treatment are responsive to the facts of a case and to victim-specific circumstances, and have been for decades. Nevertheless, the Court's case law under Article 3 has not always been characterised by the same context-sensitivity as it displays today. While the Court already used the 'level of severity' test in 1978, holding that this level was relative and dependent on the circumstances and specifics of a case,[55] the level of context-responsiveness used by the Court today did not evolve until later.

Beginning with *Selmouni*, in 1999, the Court clarified that Article 3 must be understood in light of modern-day conditions, and also explained that the severity of violence inflicted on an alleged victim is relative, finding that it 'depends on all the circumstances of the case, such as the duration of the treatment, its physical or mental effects and, in some cases, the sex, age and state of health of the victim, etc.'[56] *Selmouni* thus meant that the Court would not bind itself to its own previous interpretations of the threshold of severity, and carved out room for flexibility in future cases. At the same time, the Court found that the treatment at issue 'would be heinous and humiliating for anyone, irrespective of their condition'[57] – a characterisation it later used as a basis for its finding that Mr Selmouni had been tortured.[58] In this regard, Aisling Reidy observed two decades ago that while the 'subjective' criteria of gender, age and health 'are relevant' in determining the intensity of suffering, 'the mitigating weight that such relative factors are given … must be minimal. Acts which objectively inflict sufficient severity of pain will be considered torture, whether or not a person is male or female, or of particularly strong constitution or not.'[59]

[52] *Stanimirovic v Serbia* App no 26088/06, Judgment of 18 October 2011, para 28.
[53] *Aslakhanova and Others v Russia* App nos 2944/06 …, Judgment of 18 December 2012, para 144; *El-Masri* (n 25), paras 182–85.
[54] *El-Masri* (n 25), paras 182–85.
[55] *Ireland* (n 9), para 162.
[56] *Selmouni* (n 23), para 100.
[57] Ibid, para 103.
[58] Ibid, para 105.
[59] Reidy (n 10), 12.

Reidy's analysis might look a bit different if conducted today. Regard for context in the Court's ill-treatment jurisprudence has evolved from a mitigating factor to the core of the test that determines whether Article 3 has been violated. Contextual severity assessment has allowed the Court to move past definitional straitjackets and towards a holistic test that determines when a given treatment or punishment is incompatible with human dignity.

This approach is, however, not without its critics.[60] This has been due to the difficulty of measuring the intensity of a victim's suffering and the fact that using a flexible diagnostic standard might undermine the significance of the fact that all of the categories of treatment proscribed under Article 3 are absolutely prohibited.[61] These criticisms are particularly acute in the vulnerability context, and will be taken up in the fifth chapter of this volume.

E. Article 3 between Absoluteness and Relativity

Article 3 ECHR is famously an absolute right. This distinguishes it from, for example, the right to respect for private and family life under Article 8 ECHR, which guarantees physical and psychological integrity and can thus potentially overlap with Article 3, or cover situations where Article 3 leaves off.[62] In other words, and as made clear by its text, Article 3 ECHR does not permit limitations. This is true for acts amounting to torture but also for inhuman and degrading treatment or punishment.[63] Thus, the provision does not permit a balancing of interests: it demands absolute application, even in the presence of important reasons relating to the maintenance of law and order.[64] In this sense, the Court has held that Article 3's protection may not be waived 'under any circumstances, even the most difficult', and that its 'philosophical basis … does not allow for any exceptions or justifying factors or balancing of interests, irrespective of the conduct of the person concerned and the nature of the offence at issue.'[65]

[60] For an incisive discussion of the relative and absolute approaches to Art 3, see Natasa Mavronicola and Francesco Messineo, 'Relatively Absolute?: The Undermining of Article 3 ECHR in Ahmad v UK' (2013) 76(3) *Modern Law Review* 589–603; Mavronicola (n 22).

[61] Walter Kälin, 'Filling the Gaps: Contributions by the Human Rights Committee to the Fight Against Torture' in Walter Kälin et al (eds), *International Law, Conflict and Development: The Emergence of a Holistic Approach in International Affairs* (Martinus Nijhoff, 2010) 169–80, 178, referring to the ECtHR's judgment in *Ireland* (n 9), para 167. See also Nigel S Rodley, 'The Prohibition of Torture: Absolute Means Absolute' (2006) 34(1) *Denver Journal of International Law and Policy* 145–60, 154–57.

[62] See *Söderman v Sweden* App no 5786/08, Judgment (GC) of 12 November 2013, Reports 2013, paras 80–81; *Stubbings and Others*, Nos 22083/93 and 22095/93, Judgment of 22 October 1996, Reports 1996-IV, para 61.

[63] *Gäfgen* (n 14), para 107.

[64] *Tyrer* (n 30), para 38.

[65] *Gäfgen* (n 14), para 107.

This special 'philosophical basis' is evident not only in the Court's approach to the merits of complaints under Article 3, but also regarding the awards granted upon a finding of a violation.[66]

At the same time, there is certainly a degree of discretion and interpretation involved in the application of Article 3. This is true for the positive obligations contained in the provision, given that these are duties of means and not result, and also for the negative obligation under Article 3, given that the minimum level of severity is relative.[67] While the prohibition of torture and IDT does not permit any balancing of interests, a certain test of proportionality does enter into play here. This is the test that for example distinguishes legitimate uses of potentially lethal police force from ill-treatment, and requires an evaluation of whether the treatment was appropriate to its context.[68]

If we understand the assessment that takes place under Article 3 as context-responsiveness instead of as relativity, then this does not necessarily undermine the absolute nature of Article 3, but instead makes it possible to apply the provision to real-life situations. In this vein, Natasa Mavronicola and Francesco Messineo have argued that the Court's key concerns when determining whether a case falls under Article 3 are applicants' agency and dignity.[69] These concepts are key elements of personhood, which chapter four of the present volume will provide an opportunity to explore in greater depth.

In the same vein, Manfred Nowak has argued that the insidiousness of torture lies not or not only in the gravity of the force used and the injuries caused, but primarily in the victim's powerlessness and vulnerability.[70] That is why a use of force as light as a slap to the face of a detained suspect would violate Article 3,[71] though the provision would potentially not be violated by much more severe force applied under different circumstances. In other words, the threshold under Article 3 responds to context, and takes a victim's position vis-à-vis the perpetrator into account along with all of the circumstances of a case, including – as the Court has so often stated – 'the nature and context of the treatment, the manner and method of its execution, its duration, its physical or mental effects and, in some instances, the sex, age and state of health of the victim'.[72] Understanding this relativity is, in a sense, the purpose of the present volume.

[66] *Bureš v Czech Republic* App no 37679/08, Judgment of 18 October 2012, para 81.

[67] Natasa Mavronicola, 'Is the Prohibition Against Torture and Cruel, Inhuman and Degrading Treatment Absolute in International Human Rights Law? A Reply to Steven Greer' (2017) 17(3) *Human Rights Law Review* 479–98.

[68] *Torture and Other Cruel, Inhuman or Degrading Treatment*, Report of the Special Rapporteur on the Question of Torture, Manfred Nowak, UN Doc E/CN.4/2006/6, 23 December 2005, 14–15, fn 2.

[69] Mavronicola and Messineo (n 60), 594.

[70] Manfred Nowak, 'Challenges to the Absolute Nature of the Prohibition of Torture and Ill-Treatment' (2005) 23(4) *Netherlands Quarterly of Human Rights* 674–88, 678.

[71] *Bouyid* (n 12).

[72] *Kudła* (n 35), para 91; Smet (n 44), 276; Michael K Addo and Nicholas Grief, 'Does Article 3 of The European Convention on Human Rights Enshrine Absolute Rights?' (1998) 9(3) *European Journal of International Law* 510–24, 511, 522.

F. Attempts to Rationalise or Justify Ill-treatment

The ECtHR has unequivocally established that Article 3 is absolute. The right is also non-derogable as per Article 15 ECHR. At the same time, discussions about rationalising or justifying ill-treatment recur regularly. This includes debates about the *jus cogens* status of the prohibition of torture and IDT.[73] In this context, in recent years, states have overtly challenged the scope and application of the peremptory norm around torture.[74] The fact that inhuman and degrading treatment or punishment is considered to be less severe than torture has led to arguments that these types of ill-treatment can be justified or that their prohibition does not constitute *jus cogens*.[75]

Attempts to crack open the door to justifying ill-treatment are many, and they range from 'ticking bomb' scenarios – which portray torture as a moral necessity, for example to stop a terrorist's bomb from exploding or to save a child's life by torturing his abductor[76] – to ideas of punitive, educational, interrogational or voluntary torture as permissible in certain circumstances.[77]

Though these scenarios can be seductive, they are also misleading.[78] Torture is a question of extremes: either it is employed in a society or not, but it cannot be employed just a little bit under the perfect circumstances.[79] In the same vein, human dignity cannot be set aside only slightly. There is, in other words, a strict and necessary distinction to be made between contextually identifying ill-treatment and justifying that treatment. In this regard, consent and context matter – they can make the difference, for example, between voluntary extreme body modifications and ill-treatment, and between sexual violence and consensual sexual encounters.[80] Here, context reigns supreme: while consent matters, its ability to justify a given type of treatment should be approached with increasing caution as the treatment concerned becomes more painful, dehumanising, traumatising or terrifying.[81]

While consent, necessity and exigency thus all have the potential to appear to bring treatment below the threshold of severity in certain circumstances, these considerations also have the potential to hollow out the prohibition of ill-treatment. A contextual analysis must accordingly be applied in the awareness

[73] On this concept, see Rodley (n 61), 155–58; ICTY, *Prosecutor v Furundžija* (n 8), paras 153–57.

[74] Andrea Bianchi, 'Human Rights and the Magic of *Jus Cogens*' (2008) 19(3) *European Journal of International Law* 491–508, 505–06.

[75] Yuval Shany, 'The Prohibition Against Torture and Cruel, Inhuman and Degrading Treatment and Punishment: Can the Absolute Be Relativized under Existing International Law?' (2007) 56(3) *Catholic University Law Review* 837–70, esp 840.

[76] *Gäfgen* (n 14), paras 84, 95, 107, 175, 177.

[77] Peter Brian Barry, 'The Kantian Case Against Torture' (2015) 90(4) *Philosophy* 593–621, 597, 602–04.

[78] Henry Shue, 'Torture in Dreamland: Disposing of the Ticking Bomb' (2006) 37(2) *Case Western Reserve Journal of International Law* 231–39, 231.

[79] Ibid.

[80] Ibid, at 601 and throughout.

[81] Ibid, 606.

that, while some acts may not constitute ill-treatment, there can be no justification for those that do.[82] In this regard, the Court's practice indicates that ill-treatment must be absolutely prohibited because torture and ill-treatment violate inner life and deprive the victim of moral standing.[83] Even where the physical suffering inflicted is at a relatively low level, for example that of a slap in the face, it can show a fundamental disrespect for the dignity and worth of one's person in context, for example during an interaction with the police.[84] In this sense, ill-treatment dehumanises victims and removes barriers to further harming their agency and dignity.[85] This loss of moral standing can also stem from social processes such as dehumanisation, stereotyping and the objectification of an out-group, which can all make individuals more vulnerable to torture.[86]

III. Vulnerability and the Evolutive Interpretation of Article 3 ECHR

Making sense of how the Court interprets the standards outlined in the previous sections, especially the severity of a given treatment and the concept of vulnerability, means understanding the Court's approach to the interpretation of the ECHR overall, and Article 3 in particular.

One key element here is the living instrument approach. As mentioned above, in *Selmouni v France*, the Court applied that approach to find that the scope of what constitutes 'inhuman and degrading treatment' as opposed to 'torture' could grow in the future.[87] And indeed, over time, the scope of Article 3 has grown to include cases that the Court arguably would not have considered in violation of Article 3 in its early jurisprudence. Some scope-extending examples include a village public official who suffered injuries when a villager punched him in the face;[88] a detainee who had been granted access to inadequate heating and to only two showers per week;[89] and an injury caused by a negligent automobile accident, which some judges considered to highlight a 'drift into the trivialization of Article 3 rights'.[90] These cases might once ostensibly have fallen under the right to physical

[82] See Smet (n 44), 274, 276–77.

[83] *Bouyid* (n 12), paras. 3, 10–11, 87–90.

[84] Ibid.

[85] Herbert C Kelman, 'The Policy Context of Torture: A Social-Psychological Analysis' (2005) 87(857) *International Review of the Red Cross* 123–34, 123 and 126–33.

[86] Ibid, 133; Susan T Fiske, 'From Dehumanization and Objectification, to Rehumanization: Neuroimaging Studies on the Building Blocks of Empathy' (2009) 1167 *Values, Empathy, and Fairness Across Social Barriers: Annals of the New York Academy of Sciences* 31–34, 81–82.

[87] *Selmouni* (n 23), paras 95, 101.

[88] *İbrahim Demirtaş v Turkey* App no 25018/10, Judgment of 28 October 2014, paras 6 and 8. See also the Joint Dissenting Opinion of Judges Sajó and Keller, esp para 14.

[89] *Apostu v Romania* App no 22765/12, Judgment of 3 February 2015, paras 40, 44, 82.

[90] *Kraulaidis v Lithuania* App no 76805/11, Judgment of 8 November 2016, esp the Concurring Opinion of Judges Sajó, Tsotsoria, Wojtyczek and Kucsko-Stadlmayer, paras 2, 7.

and moral or psychological integrity under Article 8 ECHR, which applies to treatment that does not reach the threshold of Article 3.[91] Alternatively, in the past they might have been seen as falling outside the scope of the Convention altogether. Occasional though they may be, remarkable cases like these indicate that there may be a downward drift going on in relation to Article 3's threshold of severity.

George Letsas's account of the interpretation of the Convention as a whole can provide some clarification here. He argues that, by applying the 'living instrument' doctrine, the Court jettisons traditional forms of treaty interpretation, including the opinion of the Convention's drafters and the public and authorities in the Member States, and instead searches for the 'truth' of Convention rights.[92] In other words, he argues that the Court fleshes out legal human rights with new content derived from existing moral human rights.

By way of example, Letsas cites *Tyrer v United Kingdom*. That case concerned the issue of public birching, a punishment involving the beating of a victim's bare posterior with a birch rod. Although this treatment was endorsed by local law and public opinion, the Court held that this could not replace its own determination of whether birching constituted inhuman or degrading treatment. After all, the Court held, this treatment could potentially even be socially accepted *because* it was inhuman or degrading.[93] The Court ultimately found a violation of Article 3, given that birching assaulted 'precisely that which it is one of the main purposes of Article 3 … to protect, namely a person's dignity and personal integrity'.[94] The case thus not only marked the introduction of the living instrument approach, but also the Court's first reference to the concept of human dignity, which has since served to give content to Article 3.[95]

Since *Tyrer*, the Court has continued to flesh out the standards under Article 3 – in Letsas's terms, getting closer to the 'truth' of the provision.[96] The Court's interpretive techniques concerning Article 3 relate to the normative principles that underlie the right, as indicated by the Court's references to human dignity and personal integrity.[97] According to Letsas, the Court's method is furthermore justified by the counter-majoritarian nature of human rights.[98] A moral reading of the ECHR is therefore, he argues, indispensable if the Court is

[91] *Botta v Italy* App no 21439/93, Judgment of 24 February 1998, Reports 1998-I, para 32.

[92] George Letsas, *A Theory of Interpretation of the European Convention on Human Rights* (OUP, 2007), 74–76, esp 75; George Letsas, 'The ECHR as a Living Instrument: Its Meaning and Legitimacy' in Andreas Føllesdal, Birgit Peters and Geir Ulfstein (eds), *Constituting Europe: The European Court of Human Rights in a National, European and Global Context* (CUP, 2013) 106–41, 123.

[93] See *Tyrer* (n 30), para 31, as discussed in Letsas, *Theory of Interpretation* (n 92), 75.

[94] *Tyrer* (n 30), para 33.

[95] Ibid, paras 33 and 35.

[96] Letsas, *Theory of Interpretation* (n 92), 74–77, esp 75.

[97] George Letsas, 'Strasbourg's Interpretive Ethic: Lessons for the International Lawyer' (2010) 21(3) *European Journal of International Law* 509–41, 528.

[98] Letsas, 'Living Instrument' (n 92), 123–24, with further references to the Court's case aw.

to perform its function of protecting the human rights that people really have, as opposed to the ones that states consider them to have.[99]

Of course, the idea of the rights that citizens 'really' have is a polemic concept that leans towards natural law and is constantly in flux. From a positivist standpoint, this approach raises legitimacy problems and impinges on state sovereignty. Letsas counters this critique by arguing that, as the Convention's authoritative interpreter, the Court will not lose legitimacy as long as it reasons consistently and in good faith – thus, seeks to identify and apply the principles underlying human rights – and justifies its decisions according to principles that represent a vision of justice that is both intelligible and coherent.[100] While intelligibility, coherence, and good faith are certainly important, it is questionable whether this suffices to convince states and their polities to accept all developments in the Court's case law. However, at the same time, failing to adapt the Convention's requirements to present-day conditions would mean that the ECHR would lose relevance over time as its guarantees age; such a wooden approach to the Convention cannot be in the interest of effectively protecting human rights, either.

In short, the Court's interpretation of Article 3 ECHR operates between these poles. Its approach has not only caused the scope of the provision to grow over time, but it has also rendered the Court willing to consider a variety of circumstances in determining whether a violation has taken place, delving into assessments of the cumulative effect of various factors on applicants and on the emotional effect of a given treatment. *Ad absurdum*, though, Letsas's formula seems to imply that the Court can expand the scope of Article 3 to encompass any sort of treatment as long as it does so in adherence to the requirements he has identified. This is difficult to accept given that, in the particular context of Article 3 and in light of the provision's absolute nature, its scope must be not only clear but also relatively narrow.[101]

In most cases, lower-severity violations of the Convention patently offend modern conceptions of justice, equality, human dignity, and non-discrimination. However, there must be a threshold between these lower-severity violations of Article 3 and instances of injustice, inequality, indignity, and discrimination that do *not* fall under the provision, for example microaggressions between private parties.[102] In other words, Article 3 cannot be used to address human suffering

[99] Ibid, 124, citing Letsas, *Theory of Interpretation* (n 92).

[100] Letsas, 'Living Instrument' (n 92), 136–38, drawing on Ronald M Dworkin, *Law's Empire* (Belknap Press, 1986).

[101] Addo and Grief (n 72), 516; Alexander Green, 'An Absolute Theory of Convention Rights: Why the ECHR Gives Rise to Legal Rights That Cannot Conflict with Each Other' (2010) 16 *UCL Jurisprudence Review* 75–93, 78; Natasa Mavronicola, 'Güler and Öngel v Turkey: Article 3 of the European Convention on Human Rights and Strasbourg's Discourse on the Justified Use of Force' (2013) 76(2) *The Modern Law Review* 370–82, 374.

[102] Microaggressions are defined as subtle and often unconscious denigrating messages sent to members of minorities during commonplace exchanges. See Derald Wing Sue et al, 'Racial Microaggressions in Everyday Life: Implications for Clinical Practice' (2007) 62 *American Psychologist* 271–86, 273.

and injustice in its every permutation, not because this suffering and injustice is not morally wrong, painful, or unjust, but because a widely inclusive reading of the provision would deprive findings of a violation of their gravity and significance, and the provision of its authority; it would also make the provision unenforceable in practice.[103]

In this regard, it could be argued that Article 3 cannot be a panacea for omnipresent harms. To this, it can be replied that Article 3 violations are exceedingly common today. Indeed, in 2019, 19 per cent of the violations of the Convention found by the Court concerned Article 3.[104] At the same time, it is important to allow the prohibition to retain its contours while embedding it within broader efforts to combat the systems and situations that create, allow, foster and reinforce injustice.

Based on the case law evaluated by this analysis, it appears that fears about an excessive relaxing of standards under Article 3 due to vulnerability reasoning are misplaced. There undoubtedly comes a point when relaxing the standards under Article 3 – be it vis-à-vis all potential victims or only with regard to vulnerable individuals and groups – causes a loss of significance of the provision and creates setbacks for the seriousness with which findings of a violation are treated. However, generally speaking the Court maintains a relatively high severity threshold in vulnerability-related cases, albeit in a sometimes rather piecemeal fashion. Thus, vulnerability does not automatically mean that the threshold of severity has been met.[105] A more confusing strand of the Court's jurisprudence concerns cases in which it recognises the vulnerability of an applicant but then finds that, as the applicant was not particularly helpless, there has been no violation of Article 3.[106] This seems to introduce a further – and also vague – criterion into the Court's determination of what vulnerability means and what it does. The helplessness criterion may be used because the Court is apprehensive about the widescale effects that a case could otherwise have.

In this regard, and precisely given cases that, despite the application of a very low threshold of severity did not concern a vulnerable applicant, the standard required concerning vulnerable individuals and groups is in fact rather high. Any 'loosening' of standards under Article 3 cannot be traced to the introduction of vulnerability reasoning into the Court's case law. Quite to the contrary, vulnerability reasoning allows the Court to provide protection that is primarily more context-sensitive and inclusive, but not necessarily broader as concerns the severity aspect.

[103] *İbrahim Demirtaş* (n 88), Joint Dissenting Opinion of Judges Sajó and Keller, para 2.

[104] ECtHR, 'Annual Report 2019', www.echr.coe.int/Documents/Annual_report_2019_ENG.pdf, 131.

[105] *Kudła* (n 35), paras 99–100; *Zarzycki v Poland* App no 15351/03, Judgment of 12 March 2013, para 125; *Ostrowski v Poland* App no 26945/07, Decision of 1 September 2015, paras 76–77; *Mahamed Jama v Malta* App no 10290/13, Judgment of 26 November 2015, paras 100–01; *Giorgini v Italy* App no 20034/11, Decision of 1 September 2015, para 57.

[106] Compare, for example, *Jaeger v Estonia* App no 1574/13, Judgment of 31 July 2014, para 42, or *Julin v Estonia* App nos 16563/08 …, Judgment of 29 May 2012, para 189.

IV. Interim Conclusion

The above has shown that the prohibition of torture and degrading treatment and punishment is understood as a prohibition of the 'worst of the worst' – torture – along with less severe forms of ill-treatment, and has hinted that the prohibition protects two foundational elements of inner life, namely dignity and agency. Once considered a permissible form of treatment for persons with perceived reduced moral standing, such as slaves, non-citizens or traitors, torture today has emerged as an absolutely prohibited act that cannot be justified vis-à-vis any class of human individuals.

The understanding of what types of treatment can constitute torture – and what constitutes inhuman and degrading treatment and punishment – has evolved over time, as has the practical reality of ill-treatment, which today generally speaking no longer entails gruesome medieval forms of mutilation but takes subtler and often psychological forms. The potential for gradual adjustment of the prohibition of torture and inhuman and degrading treatment is also visible under Article 3 ECHR. Compliance with the article, which prohibits different types of treatment and punishment, is measured by means of the 'degree of severity' test. Certain factors – such as the age and state of health of the victim – may aggravate or mediate the type of ill-treatment at issue or raise treatment that would not otherwise fall under Article 3 to meet the threshold of severity for the provision's application.

Some commentators have argued that establishing whether Article 3 has been violated requires a degree of nuance and proportionality analysis that undermines its absolute nature. Others have contested the scope of Article 3 today as overly broad. Considering how ill-treatment works – namely the fact that it attacks the dignity and agency of the victim, who is likely othered and dehumanised in the eyes of the perpetrator – has here been suggested as an essential element of analysing whether that threshold has been met and countering these critiques to some degree. It has also been noted that many of the cases flagged for their excessively broad understanding of Article 3's scope are not vulnerability-related cases. Indeed, vulnerability reasoning levels the playing field for vulnerable applicants in this regard, but it has not led the charge in terms of lowering the threshold of severity.

2

Theoretical Scene-Setting – Vulnerability Theory

Chapter Summary

The concept of vulnerability has been the subject of extensive ethical, philosophical and legal-theoretical debates. In order to analyse the ECtHR's vulnerability jurisprudence, the present chapter discusses key philosophical and legal-theoretical approaches to vulnerability, along with the reception of this work by those scholars who have analysed the Court's approach to vulnerability to date. These theoretical perspectives push back against the liberal fiction of the legal subject and argue for community, state responsiveness and a universal but differentiated understanding of vulnerability related to human embodiment in a fragile physical form. These theoretical approaches are starkly different from the Court's approach to vulnerability, and can help to identify some shortcomings in how the Court applies this concept.

Keywords: vulnerability theory; legal subjectivity; vulnerability paradigm; substantive equality; equality of opportunity; Martha Albertson Fineman; the responsive state; sources of resilience.

I. A Primer on Vulnerability Theory

Vulnerability is often used – even in a legal context – in the sense of its common definition, and without clear legal consequences. However, this undiscriminating rhetorical use of the concept in practice stands in contrast to a growing body of work by philosophers, ethicists and legal theorists. These scholars have understood human vulnerability as justifying legal and moral obligations that range in scope from a basic 'natural' injunction on lethal violence[1] to a rich human rights discourse.[2]

[1] To HLA Hart, vulnerability engenders equality, as '[e]ven the strongest must sleep at times'. It is somewhat surprising that Hart's positivist thesis allows for obligations based on vulnerability and transcending the division between morality and law. He, however, considers vulnerability a 'truism' of human existence, and argues that the restriction of violence is therefore a necessary element of both law and morality, for '[i]f there were not these rules what point could there be for beings such as ourselves in having rules of any other kind?' (HLA Hart, *The Concept of Law*, 3rd edn (OUP, 2012), 194–95).

[2] Martha Albertson Fineman, 'Equality, Autonomy, and the Vulnerable Subject in Law and Politics' in Martha Albertson Fineman and Anna Grear (eds), *Vulnerability: Reflections on a New Ethical Foundation for Law and Politics* (Ashgate, 2013) 13–27, 13.

The idea that embodiment-related human vulnerability is a generative force – a source of inter-human bonds – has been explored for decades by a number of prominent scholars. Emmanuel Lévinas, for example, argued that the vulnerability that humans experience makes them into something other than a detached rational consciousness; he argued that the suffering of an individual physical body is the source of understanding and responsibility for the vulnerability of others – in other words, the source of sympathy.[3] This responsibility, he argued, is an ethical condition of existence, and one that pervades our human lives: '[l]e moi, de pied en cap, jusqu'à la moelle des os, est vulnérabilité'.[4]

Building on the idea that vulnerability generates obligations, Robert E Goodin has criticised the idea that our moral responsibilities towards other people are narrow in scope, due predominantly to those closest to us, and assumed voluntarily or based on family relationships.[5] Goodin instead argues for social justice and a community of caring on the basis that every human individual is embedded in a broad network of moral obligations towards those who are more vulnerable. Taking a consequentialist route, Goodin thereby argues, in other words, that the dependency of the vulnerable per se – and not charity or benevolence – compels care.[6]

Certain aspects of Goodin's approach are reflected in contemporary legal theory, particularly feminist legal theory.[7] Scholars in this field, for example Anna Grear, see vulnerability as a manner of revolutionising the architecture of law, which is constructed around the ideal of a rational subject excised from both embodiment and socio-cultural context.[8] That ideal, which has been traced back to the work of Kant, Rawls, and Descartes, provokes injustices and shortcomings in the legal system because it sees legal subjects as removed from their real bodies and contexts.[9] The vulnerable subject is advanced as a solution to this problem: as

[3] Emmanuel Lévinas, *Humanisme de l'autre homme* (Fata Morgana, 1972), 102–11

[4] Ibid, 104.

[5] Robert E Goodin, *Protecting the Vulnerable: A Reanalysis of Our Social Responsibilities* (University of Chicago Press, 1985).

[6] Ibid, xi, 11, 14–15; Catriona Mackenzie, Wendy Rogers and Susan Dodds, 'Introduction: What is Vulnerability and Why Does It Matter for Moral Theory?', in Catriona Mackenzie, Wendy Rogers and Susan Dodds (eds), *Vulnerability: New Essays in Ethics and Feminist Philosophy* (OUP, 2014) 1–29, 10. For a detailed critique of Robert E Goodin's work, see Ruth J Sample, *Exploitation: What It Is and Why It's Wrong* (Rowman & Littlefield, 2003), *passim*.

[7] Mackenzie, Rogers and Dodds (n 6), 10; Martha Albertson Fineman, 'The Vulnerable Subject: Anchoring Equality in the Human Condition' (2008) 20(1) *Yale Journal of Law and Feminism* 1–23; Lauren B Wilcox, *Bodies of Violence: Theorizing Embodied Subjects in International Relations* (OUP, 2015), 31–35; Eva Feder Kittay, *Love's Labor: Essays on Women, Equality and Dependency* (Routledge, 1999), 54–57; Anna Grear, *Redirecting Human Rights: Facing the Challenge of Corporate Legal Humanity* (Palgrave Macmillan, 2010).

[8] Anna Grear, 'Vulnerability, Advanced Global Capitalism and Co-Symptomatic Injustice: Locating the Vulnerable Subject', in Martha Albertson Fineman and Anna Grear (eds), *Vulnerability: Reflections on a New Ethical Foundation for Law and Politics* (Ashgate, 2013), 41–60, 43–44.

[9] Ibid.

a more realistic alternative to the autonomous liberal legal subject, it represents a way to reconceptualise the latter.[10]

Feminist theorists, in particular, criticise the liberal ideal of the legal subject as built on the presumption that legal subjects are self-sufficient, rational, independent, and arguably male. This is seen as removed from the reality of human embodiment in a needy body that is susceptible to harm.[11] Juxtaposed with the ideal of the autonomous subject, vulnerability appears to be a form of deviance; however, these scholars have also seen it as a realistic alternative to the liberal ideal and to its approach to equality, which is a purely formal one.[12]

This emphasis on formal equality arises because, when the idea of the legal subject is flattened, disembodied, and decontextualised, it is also homogenised, and formal equality – thus, in other words, equal treatment for all – appears as the only necessary form of equality.[13] In this regard it has been argued that, as no human individual is invulnerable or wholly independent from others, subjectivity should more adequately represent the lived experiences of human beings of all genders, abilities, and levels of privilege. The argument here is that, though emphasising formal equality, 'liberalism's best intentions can have the worst effects' by negating the inequalities that arise from differences between subjects and which need to be taken into consideration in order to ensure substantive equality.[14] It is thus necessary to take the reality of human physical embodiment and social context and the vulnerability that inevitably accompanies the existence of and dependence on the body into consideration when reinterpreting the legal subject.[15]

Others have also theorised vulnerability. Judith Butler, for example, has argued that, as the necessity of human embodiment in physical form renders all humans vulnerable, attention to and mindfulness of physical vulnerability may lead to the peaceful resolution of political problems.[16] Erinn C Gilson has further developed Butler's approach towards an argument for social justice similar to Robert E Goodin's by reasoning that humans are involuntarily responsible to each other in a community based on common vulnerability.[17] Of all of these scholars, however, Martha Albertson Fineman is the most prominent, and the most relevant for present purposes. Her work is discussed in the next section.

[10] Fineman (n 7), 10–11 and throughout; Wilcox (n 7), 32; Grear (n 7), 44; see also Otto Dianne, 'Lost in Translation: Re-Scripting the Sexed Subjects of International Human Rights Law' in Anne Orford (ed), *International Law and Its Others* (CUP, 2006) 318–56, 353, whose arguments follow a similar vein but who eschews the characterisation of women specifically as vulnerable and thus as victims.

[11] Fineman (n 7), 9–10.

[12] Ibid, 2–4.

[13] Grear (n 7), 44.

[14] Wilcox (n 7), 32.

[15] See Grear (n 7), esp 126–28.

[16] Judith Butler, *Precarious Life: The Powers of Mourning and Violence* (Verso, 2004), 29.

[17] Erinn C Gilson, *The Ethics of Vulnerability: A Feminist Analysis of Social Life and Practice* (Routledge, 2014), 55.

II. The Work of Martha Albertson Fineman

The most prominent modern vulnerability scholar, Martha Albertson Fineman, has gradually developed a concept of vulnerability using the idea of a vulnerable subject to enable 'a stealthily disguised human rights discourse' before United States audiences.[18] Her approach has evolved from those beginnings into 'an independent universal approach to justice, one that focuses on exploring the nature of the human, rather than the rights, part of the human rights trope'.[19] To Fineman, vulnerability captures the differences between individuals based on institutional and economic differences, and varies according to the quantity and quality of resources available to each individual in moments of crisis or opportunity.[20] Her theory of vulnerability seeks to address the disadvantage, inequality and injustice masked by ideas about individual responsibility and autonomy and the minimal state; she does so by employing the uniting and bonding force of our shared human vulnerability as beings embodied in a mortal form.[21]

Fineman's vulnerability is universal: she considers that using vulnerability to single out particular groups implies 'victimhood, deprivation, dependency or pathology'.[22] She rejects this approach, and sees vulnerability as 'a complement to the autonomous liberal subject' and as 'detached from specific subgroups', describing it as a constant and complex, universal part of the human condition.[23] In this sense, she sees vulnerability as '*the* primal human condition'.[24]

On this basis, Fineman has developed her vulnerability paradigm into two prongs. First, she emphasises the universality of vulnerability based on human embodiment – in the sense that, due to our fragile human bodies, no human individual is invulnerable. Secondly, she emphasises the differences among individuals that arise from embodiment's various manifestations and stages and the different ways in which we are societally and socially embedded.[25] Fineman's vulnerability thesis thus supports a move towards a more realistic view of the human subject and demands an explanation from the state when it confers privileges or advantages on certain groups.[26] Ultimately, it rejects the 'neoliberal fixation on personal

[18] Fineman (n 2), 13. See also Fineman (n 7), Martha Albertson Fineman, 'Elderly as Vulnerable: Rethinking the Nature of Individual and Societal Responsibility' (2012) 20(2) *Elder Law Journal* 71–111; Martha Albertson Fineman, 'Beyond Identities: The Limits of an Anti-Discrimination Approach to Equality' (2012) 92 *Boston University Law Review* 1713–70; Fineman (n 2).

[19] Fineman (n 2), 13.

[20] Fineman (n 7), 10, 13–15.

[21] Ibid, *passim*; Catriona Mackenzie, 'The Importance of Relational Autonomy and Capabilities for an Ethics of Vulnerability', in Catriona Mackenzie, Wendy Rogers and Susan Dodds (eds), *Vulnerability: New Essays in Ethics and Feminist Philosophy* (OUP, 2014) 33–59, 41.

[22] Fineman (n 7), 8.

[23] Fineman (n 2), 17, 20 and 22–24; Fineman (n 7), 1–3.

[24] Martha Albertson Fineman, 'Equality and Difference: The Restrained State' (2015) 66(3) *Alabama Law Review* 609–26, 614, emphasis in the original.

[25] Ibid, 613–14, 618–19.

[26] Martha Albertson Fineman, 'The Vulnerable Subject and the Responsive State' (2010) 60(2) *Emory Law Journal* 251–75, 274–75.

responsibility' in favour of rethinking the political subject in a way that recognises and incorporates differences.[27]

The antonym of Fineman's 'post-identity' vulnerability is not invulnerability, which she considers impossible in humans, but resilience.[28] She calls for a 'responsive' state that will abandon the liberal image of a strong, independent (male) citizen and instead build institutions that provide individuals with the assets they need in order to be resilient to human rights violations. Society cannot eradicate vulnerability, but it can mediate, compensate and lessen it and build resilience to prevent misfortune and help take advantage of opportunities.[29] Fineman's focus particularly lies on the pursuit of substantive equality in the socio-economic context. Notably, Fineman also points out the benefits individuals reap from their own vulnerability: unlike Turner, she does not identify vulnerability simply with suffering, but also sees it as generative of opportunities for 'innovation and growth, creativity, and fulfilment'.[30]

III. Theorising Human Rights through a Vulnerability Lens

Fineman's theoretical approach has been widely received by scholars whose work concerns human rights and vulnerability; in fact, most of the main analyses of the ECtHR's vulnerability case law mentioned below have made reference to her work.[31] In addition, Fineman's theory has also been decisively influential for authors outside of the ECtHR context.[32]

For example, Bryan S Turner has understood vulnerability as the foundation for universal human rights, for overcoming cultural relativism and, ultimately, seemingly for humanitarian intervention.[33] In his analysis, the frailty or vulnerability that is part of our existence as humans gives rise to a collective sympathy and

[27] Fineman (n 24), 616–17.
[28] Fineman (n 2), 20–24.
[29] Fineman (n 7), 10, 13–15.
[30] Fineman (n 18), 96.
[31] See Alexandra Timmer, 'A Quiet Revolution: Vulnerability in the European Court of Human Rights' in Martha Albertson Fineman and Anna Grear (eds), *Vulnerability: Reflections on a New Ethical Foundation for Law and Politics* (Ashgate, 2013) 147–70; Lourdes Peroni and Alexandra Timmer, 'Vulnerable Groups: The Promise of an Emerging Concept in European Human Rights Convention Law' (2013) 11(4) *International Journal of Constitutional Law* 1056–85; Ivona Truscan, 'Considerations of Vulnerability: From Principles to Action in the Case Law of the European Court of Human Rights' (2013) 36(3) *Retfærd* 64–83; Samantha Besson, 'La vulnerabilité et la structure des droits de l'homme: L'exemple de la jurisprudence de la Cour européenne des droits de l'homme', in Laurence Burgorgue-Larsen (ed), *La vulnérabilité saisie par les juges en Europe* (Editions Pedone, 2014), 59–85; Carolina Yoko Furusho, 'Uncovering the Human Rights of the Vulnerable Subject and Correlated State Duties under Liberalism' (2016) 5(1) *UCL Journal of Law and Jurisprudence* 175–205.
[32] Furusho (n 31).
[33] Bryan S Turner, *Vulnerability and Human Rights* (Pennsylvania State University Press, 2006), 6–9.

a range of rights, of which the prohibition of torture is the most fundamental.[34] Turner argues that vulnerability, understood as the experience of misery shared by all of humanity and as the foundation of human rights,[35] leads humans to form institutions intended to protect their vulnerable physical selves. These institutions, he notes, are often fragile themselves.[36]

The work of Anna Grear picks this up, arguing that the experiences of the Holocaust – particularly the publicly distributed images of the victims and survivors of the concentration camps – led to an increased sensitivity to the vulnerability of humanity as a whole.[37] Grear calls for human rights discourse to be redirected and reinvigorated by recognising human beings as fundamentally vulnerable 'body-persons'.[38] She considers that 'the most disempowered figure of humanity' is also the most vulnerable: this is 'the haunting figure of the refugee who lays bare the lacuna at the heart of international human rights law', who also represents 'an ethical summons' to redirect international human rights law and 'the bottom-line test for an adequate conception of international human rights subjectivity'.[39] Grear concludes that attention to human vulnerability would reinvigorate human rights and cause them to stand on a 'foundation of a deeply humanitarian response to human vulnerability as embodied (speaking) beings, directly challenging the overextension of human rights discourse'.[40]

Martha Nussbaum, too, has drawn on human vulnerability to develop a capabilities approach for exploring matters of social justice. She has explored the meaning of our shared human vulnerability, and found in its recognition a way to reaffirm the equal dignity of all human individuals and to move away from attitudes founded on shame and disgust against some.[41] To Nussbaum, the vulnerability of children in particular is a physical, emotional and cognitive immaturity that renders them dependent on adults and causes them to experience life in a manner unlike that of adults. The differences between children's rights as recognised in the Convention on the Rights of the Child (CRC) and the human rights of adults, she argues, arise from a desire to compensate for this vulnerability and to ultimately provide children with the same level of protection as that afforded to adults.[42] Children's lack of control over their own decisions – due to their lack of agency – means that the state has a special responsibility to ensure that they enjoy certain 'capabilities'.[43] The capabilities approach developed by Nussbaum, which

[34] Ibid, 9; Bryan S Turner, 'Outline of a Theory of Human Rights' (1993) 27(3) *Sociology* 489–512, 502.
[35] Ibid, 3 and 9.
[36] Ibid, 25 and 31–33.
[37] Grear (n 7), 142–47.
[38] Ibid, 41 and 202.
[39] Ibid. 165–16.
[40] Ibid. 167.
[41] Martha C.Nussbaum, *Hiding from Humanity: Disgust, Shame, and the Law* (Princeton University Press, 2004), esp 1–18.
[42] Rosalind Dixon and Martha C Nussbaum, 'Children's Rights and a Capabilities Approach: The Question of Special Priority' (2012) 97(3) *Cornell Law Review* 549–94, 574.
[43] Ibid, 559–60, 575, 579–81.

goes beyond children's rights and applies to all human individuals, draws on the work of Amartya Sen and responds to realities of dependency by encouraging a focus on specific capabilities to ensure that individuals are able to live as autonomously as possible in a manner conforming to human dignity.[44]

The work of these scholars, and of Martha Albertson Fineman, has informed several examinations of the ECtHR's approach to vulnerability. These authors have noted the various functions of vulnerability in the Court's case law, including its use in identifying additional groups protected by the prohibition of discrimination, in reinforcing the protection against indirect discrimination, and in expanding the state's positive obligations.[45] Scholars have discussed the various 'vulnerable groups' identified by the Court – namely the Roma community, asylum-seekers, people living with HIV, and people with cognitive disabilities[46] – as well as the case law that considers individual applicants to be in 'situations of vulnerability' due to factors such as their youth, detention, migration status, pregnancy, illness, proximity to death or LGBTQI identity.[47] In particular, Lourdes Peroni and Alexandra Timmer have argued that, in the case law of the ECtHR, vulnerability can serve as a heuristic device in order to identify flaws in what human rights law *is* like and prescribe what human rights law *ought* to look like.[48] In other words, vulnerability is a normative concept. Alexandra Timmer[49] has built on this, noting that vulnerability enables the Court to produce 'context-sensitive judgments' and prioritise certain interests over the state margin of appreciation.[50]

[44] Martha C.Nussbaum, *Women and Human Development: The Capabilities Approach* (CUP, 2001), *passim*; Martha C Nussbaum, *Frontiers of Justice: Disability, Nationality, Species Membership* (Belknap Press, 2007); Dixon and Nussbaum (n 42), 552–54. For an overview of Amartya Sen's approach, compare Amartya Sen, 'Equality of What?' (Tanner Lecture on Human Values, Stanford University, 22 May 1979), http://tannerlectures.utah.edu/_documents/a-to-z/s/sen80.pdf, 217–19.

[45] Dimitris Xenos, 'The Human Rights of the Vulnerable' (2009) 13(4) *International Journal of Human Rights* 591–614. See also Timmer (n 31), 150–51, 162–64, 165–67.

[46] Peroni and Timmer (n 31), 1063–64.

[47] Timmer (n 31), 150–51, 162 162–64, 169–70.

[48] Peroni and Timmer (n 31), 1061.

[49] Timmer (n 31).

[50] Ibid, 162–65.

PART II

Mapping the Court's Approach to Vulnerability

3

A Typology of the Court's Approach to Vulnerability under Article 3 ECHR

Chapter Summary

This chapter systematically examines the Court's Article 3 case law for references to vulnerability. Based on case law groups, it creates a typology of types of vulnerability recognised by the Court. The first category is dependency-based vulnerability, which concerns minors, the elderly, and those with psychosocial and cognitive disabilities. A related category, which accounts for the bulk of the Court's references to vulnerability under Article 3, concerns vulnerability due to state control. In addition, applicants may be considered vulnerable due to experiences of victimisation or a feeling of vulnerability, because of a context of migration, discrimination or marginalisation, or due to pregnancy or situations of precarious reproductive health, unpopular views, or the intersection of various sources of vulnerability. The chapter discusses the case law in relation to each of these categories in turn, provides a qualitative and quantitative overview of references, and discusses some underexplored sources of vulnerability that the Court could potentially consider in the future. It also provides the groundwork for an analysis of the effects and pitfalls of vulnerability reasoning under Article 3, as fleshed out in the chapters that follow.

Keywords: Vulnerability reasoning, vulnerable groups, marginalisation, othering, victimisation, dependency, detention, minors, psychosocial disability, migration.

I. Overview: A Typology and Distribution of References

In order to map the reasons why a given group or individual may be considered vulnerable by the Court, it is useful to create a typology of sources of vulnerability. There have been some proposals, made elsewhere, on how to go about creating such a typology. Proposals include dividing sources of vulnerability into 'etic' and 'emic' vulnerability, differentiating between vulnerable groups and vulnerable individuals, and creating a more detailed typology that lists all recognised sources of vulnerability separately.

The first proposed typology divides sources of vulnerability into 'etic' and 'emic' vulnerability. An 'etic' approach defines vulnerability as the existence of a risk that justifies intervention, while an 'emic' approach links it to a person's psycho-social cultural context, and sees vulnerability as an individual lived experience.[1] The Court's Article 3 jurisprudence recognises sources of vulnerability than can fall under one or the other of these types of vulnerability. It takes an 'etic' approach, for example, to the vulnerability of migrants in the State to which they are to be returned,[2] and it takes an 'emic' approach when it bases its finding of a violation of the provision on, for example, the subjective sense of violation experienced by applicants.[3] A division of vulnerability into these two categories shows the flexibility of the concept, underscores the resulting difficulties of definition, and highlights the importance of listening to and understanding the experiences of the individuals concerned.[4] The division into etic and emic sources of vulnerability does not, however, create a useful typology of vulnerability on its own.

To enrich this, a distinction can be made between vulnerable groups, on the one hand, and vulnerable individuals, on the other. This is also a distinction made by the ECtHR. As discussed below, under the prohibition of discrimination in Article 14 ECHR, the Court has defined vulnerable groups as 'historically subject to prejudice with lasting consequences', which results in social exclusion and can entail legislative stereotyping that precludes an individualised assessment of a person's capacities and needs.[5] The Court has considered that restrictions of the rights of vulnerable groups with a protracted history of discrimination, for example people with a cognitive disability, entail a narrow margin of appreciation on the part of the state, and must be justified by 'very weighty reasons'.[6]

Vulnerable groups identified by the Court to date include the Roma community, people living with HIV, asylum-seekers and people with cognitive disabilities.[7] This list likely does not represent a *numerus clausus*. For example,

[1] Michael C Dunn, Isabel CH Clare and Anthony J Holland, 'To Empower or to Protect? Constructing the "Vulnerable Adult" in English Law and Public Policy' (2008) 28(2) *Legal Studies* 234–53, 245–46; Jonathan Herring, 'Vulnerability, Children and the Law' in Michael Freeman (ed), *Law and Childhood Studies* (vol 14, OUP, 2012) 243–63 245–46.

[2] Such a risk must be proven and individualised in order for expulsion to conditionally violate Article 3 (see *I.I.N. v Netherlands* Apop no 2035/04, Decision of 9 December 2004; *N.M.B. v Sweden* App no 68335/10, Judgment of 27 June 2013, paras 32–33).

[3] On the sense of vulnerability as a violation of Art 3, see for example *Rachwalski and Ferenc v Poland*, no 47709/99, Judgment of 28 July 2009, para 61; *Ilaşcu and Others v Republic of Moldova and Russia* App no 48787/99, Judgment (GC) of 8 July 2004, Reports 2004-VII, para 446.

[4] Herring (n 1), 246–49.

[5] *Kiyutin v Russia* App no 2700/10, Judgment of 10 March 2011, Reports 2011, para 63; *Alajos Kiss v Hungary* App no 38832/06, Judgment of 20 May 2010, para 42, with references; Lourdes Peroni and Alexandra Timmer, 'Vulnerable Groups: The Promise of an Emerging Concept in European Human Rights Convention Law' (2013) 11(4) *International Journal of Constitutional Law* 1056–85.

[6] *Alajos Kiss* (n 5), para 42, with references.

[7] *D.H. and Others v Czech Republic* App no 57325/00, Judgment (GC) of 13 November 2007, Reports 2007-IV, para 182; *Kiyutin* (n 5), para 64; *M.S.S. v Belgium and Greece* App no 30696/09, Judgment (GC) of 21 January 2011, Reports 2011, para 251; *Alajos Kiss* (n 5), para 42. For a more comprehensive analysis, see Peroni and Timmer (n 5).

in *Kiyutin v Russia*, the Court held that groups can also be vulnerable on account of their sex, sexual orientation, race or ethnicity, mental faculties or disability.[8] The Court's understanding of group vulnerability also seems to be sensitive to, in addition to historical discrimination, the conditions facing the members of a given group as individuals today. Thus, in *I.B. v Greece*, the Court held that 'HIV-positive persons have to face up to a whole host of problems, not only medical, but also professional, social, personal and psychological ones, and above all to sometimes deeply rooted prejudices even among the most highly educated people.'[9] There, the Court went on to address the existence of prejudices which stigmatise or marginalise those living with the virus, and found that people living with HIV constitute 'a vulnerable group with a history of prejudice and stigmatization'.[10]

Individual vulnerability has been less clearly described and delimited by the Court than group vulnerability, and the former concept has also been used to encompass a wider range of applicants than the latter. In general terms, individual vulnerability can stem from an aspect of an individual's status or identity, or from powerlessness, dependence, and exposure to an increased risk of human rights violations. Alexandra Timmer, in her ground-breaking 2013 article,[11] created a more detailed typology that identified seven grounds that have thus far brought about the qualification of individuals as vulnerable, one of which is the above-mentioned ground of membership in a vulnerable group. These grounds are:

- the inherent vulnerability of children and persons with cognitive disabilities;
- vulnerability due to state control;
- vulnerability related to gender, as applies to victims of domestic violence and women in precarious situations of reproductive health;
- vulnerability due to a legal power imbalance, as experienced by persons accused of a crime and those who lack legal capacity;
- vulnerability due to the espousal of unpopular views, which can arise in demonstrators and journalists;
- vulnerability in the context of migration, as applies to the detention and expulsion of asylum-seekers; and
- vulnerability due to group membership, as applies to Roma, persons living with HIV/AIDS, and – to some extent – asylum-seekers.

Timmer also included the category of compounded vulnerability, which encompasses intersections of the above traits such as, for example, in the case of a detained

[8] *Kiyutin* (n 5), para 63, with further references.

[9] *I.B. v Greece* App no 552/10, Judgment of 3 October 2013, Reports 2013, para 80.

[10] Ibid, para 81, citing *Kiyutin* (n 5), para 64.

[11] Alexandra Timmer, 'A Quiet Revolution: Vulnerability in the European Court of Human Rights' in Martha Albertson Fineman and Anna Grear (eds), *Vulnerability: Reflections on a New Ethical Foundation for Law and Politics* (Ashgate, 2013) 147–70, 151–54, and the case law cited therein.

child who is also a migrant.[12] This responds to the fact that the Court's concept of vulnerability can accommodate the intersection of traits and statuses that make an individual vulnerable.

The concept of intersectionality was famously coined by critical race scholar Kimberlé Crenshaw to describe the discrimination experienced by African-American women, who suffer discrimination because of their race or their gender along with discrimination that is unique to the intersection of those two traits.[13] This idea seems to have resonated with the Court, at least to some extent. For example, in *B.S. v Spain*, the Court held that the applicant was vulnerable by virtue of not just one but a series of traits, namely her African origin, her gender, and the fact that she was a sex worker.[14] It thereby displayed at least a fledgling awareness of intersectionality, although it has refused to explicitly apply this concept, or even to engage with it, in many of its key non-discrimination cases.[15]

The Court's case law continues to show that it is easier to delineate vulnerability by examining the grounds that cause it than by attempting to create a *numerus clausus* of individuals who can be considered vulnerable, given that the individuals who can fall into this category are many: from military conscripts,[16] to detainees in a drunken state,[17] to victims of violations of Article 3[18] and terminally ill patients seeking access to an experimental medicine,[19] among many others. In other words, identifying the principles behind and reasons for vulnerability reasoning provides a better understanding of what the concept means than enumerating vulnerable groups and individuals. This however makes it particularly relevant to note that the Court has thus far failed to articulate those principles.

A noteworthy element of Timmer's framework for present purposes is that it does not make a rigid conceptual distinction between individual and group vulnerability. This is important here because while some scholars – including Timmer – do seem to consider that there is some conceptual distinction to be made,[20] it is not clear that this distinction is particularly useful for the purposes of Article 3 ECHR.

That is not to say that there is no distinction to be made. Vulnerable groups are, according to the Court's case law, rendered vulnerable by their history of

[12] Ibid.

[13] Kimberlé Crenshaw, 'Demarginalizing the Intersection of Race and Sex: A Black Feminist Critique of Antidiscrimination Doctrine, Feminist Theory and Antiracist Politics' (1989) 1989(1) *University of Chicago Legal Forum* 139–67, 149.

[14] *B.S. v Spain* App no 47159/08, Judgment of 24 July 2012, para 62.

[15] *Garib v the Netherlands* App no 43494/09, Judgment (GC) of 6 November 2017, Reports 2017, Dissenting Opinion of Judge Pinto de Albuquerque joined by Judge Vehabović, para 34. See also *S.A.S. v France* App no 43835/11, Judgment (GC) of 1 July 2014, Reports 2014, where the Court did not engage with the concept despite its invocation by multiple third-party interveners.

[16] *Placì v Italy* App no 48754/11, Judgment of 21 January 2014, paras 49, 58, 59.

[17] *Kummer v Czech Republic* App no 32133/11, Judgment of 25 July 2013, para 69.

[18] *Buzilo v Republic of Moldova* App no 52643/07, Judgment of 21 February 2012, para 29.

[19] *Hristozov and Others v Bulgaria* App nos 47039/11 and 358/12, Judgment of 13 November 2012, Reports 2012 (extracts), paras 112, 122.

[20] Contrast Timmer (n 11) and Peroni and Timmer (n 5).

discrimination, and vulnerable individuals are, as evident from the case law, rendered vulnerable by some other trait, condition or situation – for example, their dependency or the fact that they are under the sole authority of state authorities. There is thus a definitional difference between these two concepts, which may stem from the fact that the concept of vulnerable groups evolved largely under the auspices of Article 14 ECHR. Ultimately, though, there seem to be limited differences between the effects of membership in a vulnerable group and individual vulnerability, at least under Article 3. While membership in a vulnerable group has relevance in expulsion cases as concerns the burden of proving that an individual faces a risk of ill-treatment if returned,[21] group and individual vulnerability seem to overlap in all other regards.

This point is underscored by the fact that the Court itself does not always heed this distinction between group and individual vulnerability. For example, in *Centre for Legal Resources on behalf of Valentin Câmpeanu v Romania*, the Court examined an application brought on behalf of a young man of Roma ethnicity who suffered from a profound intellectual disability and who had been diagnosed with HIV as a child. Despite the intersection of multiple group-related grounds of vulnerability in this case (namely minor age, Roma ethnicity, intellectual disability and HIV/AIDS), the Grand Chamber did not consider Mr Câmpeanu to be a member of a vulnerable group – nor, *nota bene*, refer to the concept of intersectionality – instead referring to his 'heightened state of vulnerability', his 'state of extreme vulnerability' and the fact that he was a 'highly vulnerable person', respectively.[22] The Court's case law itself thus seems to indicate that there is no strict distinction to be made between group and individual vulnerability. This goes hand in hand with the fact that the Court can only consider cases concerning individual members of a vulnerable group, and not concerning a vulnerable group as a whole. While group membership may have certain evidentiary advantages or be otherwise relevant under Article 14 ECHR,[23] under other articles of the Convention it is generally the qualification as vulnerable that is decisive, independently of whether that vulnerability is individual or group-based.

It must be noted that the Court is, however, not particularly consistent in applying vulnerability reasoning. In cases concerning, for example, the alleged ill-treatment of detainees, it by turns emphasises the importance of their vulnerability,[24] merely pays lip service to the idea[25] or fails to mention it at

[21] *Gayratbek Saliyev v Russia* App no 39093/13, Judgment of 17 April 2014, para 62.

[22] *Centre for Legal Resources (CLR) on behalf of Valentin Câmpeanu v Romania* App no 47848/08, Judgment (GC) of 17 July 2014, Reports 2014, paras 143, 108 and 104.

[23] Under Art 14, membership in a vulnerable group narrows the state margin of appreciation and requires strict scrutiny (*I.B.* (n 9), paras 79, 81).

[24] *Aydin v Turkey* App no 23178/94, Judgment (GC) of 25 September 1997, Reports 1997-VI, paras 83–84.

[25] *Lipencov v Republic of Moldova* App no 27763/05, Judgment of 25 January 2011, para 32; *Gladović v Croatia* App no 28847/08, Judgment of 10 May 2011, para 37; *Oshurko v Ukraine* App no 33108/05, Judgment of 8 September 2011, para 69.

all.[26] Another source of uncertainty stems from the way in which the Court conceptualises vulnerability. For example, in one case, it found that an applicant military officer who had been sexually harassed at work was not vulnerable because the Court did not consider 'that the applicant's situation was akin to that of a child'.[27] This seems to imply that only extreme dependency engenders vulnerability. Yet, in other cases, the Court engages with the lived experiences of an individual applicant, and considers it decisive whether they *felt* vulnerable.[28] In yet other cases, vulnerability is considered the product of other feelings, including those of arbitrariness, inferiority and anxiety.[29] Though the determination that someone is vulnerable seems to be the outcome of an evaluative process, this process is usually not described in Strasbourg's judgments, making it difficult to determine how the Court reaches its conclusions about an applicant's vulnerability.

To shed some more light on this, and based on the methodology described in the annex,[30] the present chapter provides an in-depth and systematic overview of the Court's case law on vulnerability under Article 3 ECHR between the Court's first use of the concept and 28 February 2019. In doing so, this chapter will amend Alexandra Timmer's typology of the Court's uses of vulnerability,[31] tailoring that framework to the case law under Article 3. This is because the specificities of the Article 3 case law, combined with a systematic examination of hundreds of cases, mandate a series of departures from her original categories. For one, the distinction between vulnerable groups and individuals will not figure as prominently here, for the reasons just discussed. Furthermore, 'inherent vulnerability' will be reconceived as dependency-based vulnerability. This has a three-fold explanation: first, the amended term is considered more descriptive; secondly, it takes the often transitory nature of dependency-as-vulnerability more accurately into account; and thirdly, it may better serve to provoke a discussion about the ways in which the vulnerability of children and mentally disabled persons is constructed based on ideas about their dependency without regard for emancipatory or participatory interests. Psychosocial disability will be grouped into this category to reflect the Court's framing of it, although there are overlaps between this category and the category of discrimination-based vulnerability as discussed below. Despite its overlaps with dependency-based vulnerability, vulnerability due to state control will remain a separate category, as will vulnerability due to a legal power imbalance and vulnerability in the context of migration.

[26] For example *Nogin v Russia* App no 58530/08, Judgment of 15 January 2015 (where the judgment failed to mention the concept at all) and *Merezhnikov v Russia* App no 30456/06, Judgment of 12 November 2015 (where it was referred to by the parties (para 25) but not by the Court).

[27] *Reilly v Ireland* App no 51083/09, Decision of 23 September 2014, para 58.

[28] *Ülke v Turkey* App no 39437/98, Judgment of 24 January 2006, para 62.

[29] *M.S.S.* (n 7), para 233.

[30] See the 'Note on Methodology' at the end of this volume.

[31] Timmer (n 11), 151–54, and the case law cited therein.

Furthermore, gender-based vulnerability will be re-conceptualised for the purposes of the present volume. Although sex is one of the prohibited grounds for different treatment contained in the prohibition of discrimination in Article 14 ECHR, the Court does not consider women to be a vulnerable group as such. In other words, identifying as female does not automatically render applicants vulnerable in the case law studied. Instead, certain applicants may be considered vulnerable due to a particular situation in which they find themselves. This may be due to an experience of victimisation in the form of gender-based violence, as discussed below in section IV. It may also be due to various contexts that particularly affect women. An example is the existence of a local context hostile to women, as will be examined below in the section on vulnerability and migration (section V) and as was established for example in the *Opuz* case.[32] A further ground for vulnerability relates particularly to those who are pregnant, and their needs and the needs of their unborn children during pregnancy (section IV). Gender-based vulnerability as it relates to transgender or gender non-binary individuals will fall under the category on LGBTQI+ people (section VI).

When it comes to vulnerability due to victimisation, the present volume groups together cases concerning male and female victims of sexual violence, as well as those who experience a sense of vulnerability that causes suffering reaching the threshold of Article 3 due to victimisation. This moves the discussion away from the suggestion that all women are considered vulnerable in the Court's jurisprudence, for that is not the case. While, under Article 14, the Court does discuss domestic and gender-based violence as a problem of gender discrimination,[33] this is not reflected in its approach to Article 3. In this regard, it instead takes an inclusive approach to the types of violence concerned – be it physical or sexual, or constituting abuse in an economic, emotional or verbal sense – and to the possible victims, given that domestic violence 'affects different family members, although women make up an overwhelming majority of victims'.[34] This approach allows it to capture various types of violence, not just that against women, but also that against other victims, including against men and children, who may be directly or indirectly affected.[35]

A few additional amendments apply. What Timmer calls the espousal of unpopular views is relevant also under Article 3, but largely with respect to the risk of ill-treatment in expulsion cases. This source of vulnerability will therefore be considered together with migration-related cases. The section on vulnerability

[32] *Opuz v Turkey* App no 33401/02, Judgment of 9 June 2009, Reports 2009, para 160.
[33] *Volodina v Russia* App no 41261/17, Judgment of 9 July 2019.
[34] Ibid, para 71.
[35] *Opuz* (n 32), para 132.

due to discrimination and marginalisation will cover members of the LGBTQI community, religious and ethnic minorities, including Roma, and those living with HIV/AIDS. A penultimate section will have regard to intersecting sources of vulnerability and include comments on the intersection of poverty and vulnerability. The last section will explore some further applications of vulnerability to groups and individuals not yet (clearly) recognised as vulnerable.

This ultimately leads to the following typology of vulnerability under Article 3:

- dependency-based vulnerability, which concerns minors, the elderly, and those with psychosocial and cognitive disabilities (i.e. mental illness and intellectual disability);
- vulnerability due to state control, including that of detainees, military conscripts, and persons in state institutions;
- vulnerability due to victimisation, including by domestic and sexual abuse, other violations of Article 3, or because of a feeling of vulnerability;
- vulnerability in the migration context;
- vulnerability due to discrimination and marginalisation, which covers ethnic and religious minorities, LGBTQI people, and those living with HIV/AIDS;
- vulnerability due to pregnancy or situations of precarious reproductive health;
- vulnerability due to the espousal of unpopular views; and
- intersecting vulnerabilities.

Before exploring this amended typology in detail, Figure 3.1 provides a quantitative overview of the distribution of references to vulnerability under the various branches of the typology as of 28 February 2019. A more detailed quantitative exploration will follow below.

Figure 3.1 indicates that the various grounds for vulnerability are prevalent in the Court's case law to very different degrees. For example, the Court's case law concerning the vulnerability of detainees is perhaps the most differentiated of all sources of vulnerability, and the prevalence of references to the concept in its jurisprudence to date explains this to a certain extent. This overview also serves to highlight that some sources of vulnerability have only been discussed in rare cases, meaning that future case law will need to clarify or expand the Court's position.

With these figures in mind, the analysis will now turn to the typology of grounds for vulnerability, and explore these grounds in detail.

Figure 3.1 References to Vulnerability under Article 3 ECHR as of 28 February 2019

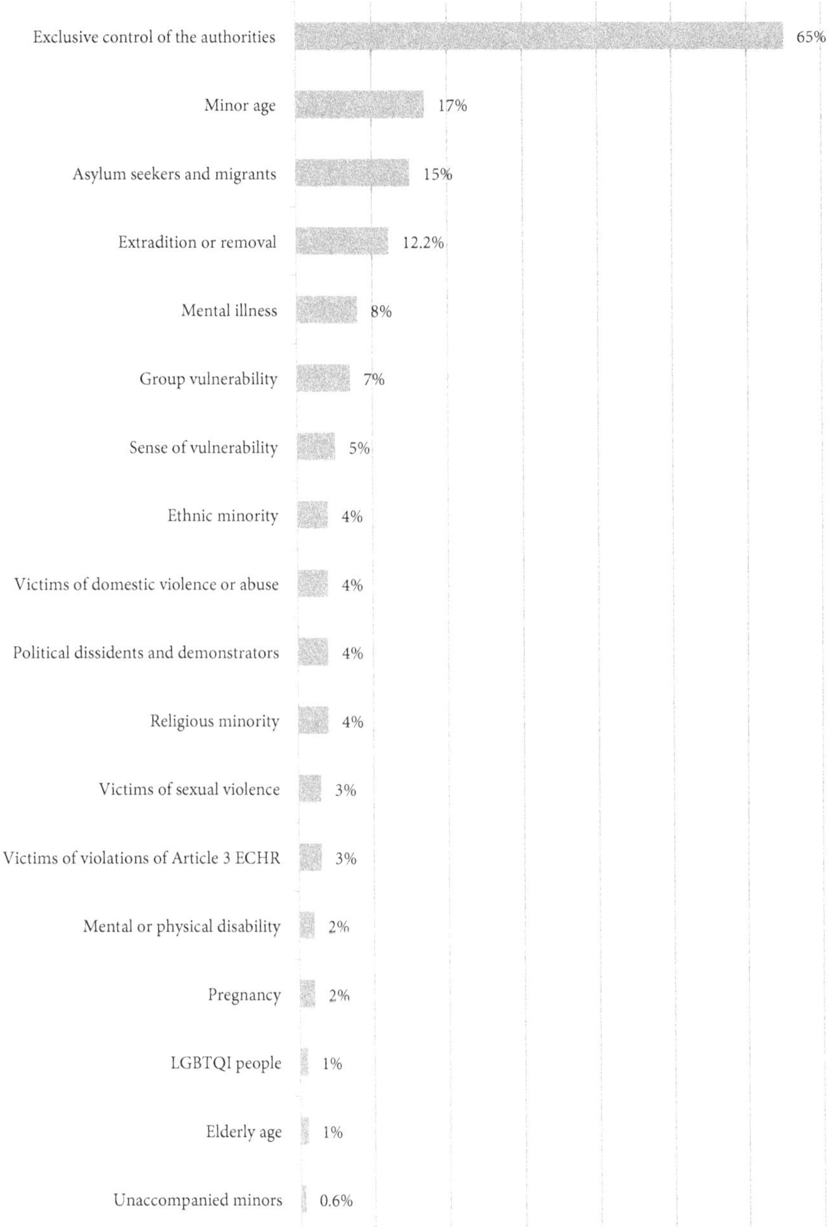

II. Dependency-based Vulnerability

A. Minors

The Court often refers to children as a paradigmatic example of who is vulnerable. This is true even in cases that do not actually concern minor applicants.[36] Children were also the first individuals considered vulnerable by the Court, with an early reference to their vulnerability being made under Article 3 in 1981.[37] Despite this initial reference, however, the Court's case law on the vulnerability of children did not take off until the late 1990s. The following will first summarise the early jurisprudence as concerns the vulnerability of children in general, and then differentiate specific constellations in which minors' vulnerability is often cited by the Court today, namely the contexts of sexual abuse, exclusive state authority, and childhood migration.

i. The Court's Early Case Law

The Court's current case law on the vulnerability of minors under Article 3 began in 1997, with *Aydin v Turkey*. That case concerned a 17-year-old girl who had been detained for three days by the authorities, during which time she was blindfolded, raped, paraded naked, and spun around in a tyre while sprayed with high-pressure water. In deciding the case, the Court referred to her overall sense of vulnerability and considered that she had been subjected to 'particularly terrifying and humiliating experiences … having regard to her sex and youth and the circumstances under which she was held.'[38]

A year later, in 1998, the Court went on to create its (now standard) language on the vulnerability of minors, when it held that '[c]hildren and other vulnerable individuals, in particular, are entitled to State protection, in the form of effective deterrence, against … serious breaches of personal integrity'.[39] This positive obligation to protect vulnerable individuals under Article 3 drew on past case law on the vulnerability and need for protection of children under Article 8 ECHR, specifically a case on the sexual abuse of a cognitively disabled girl in an institutional setting.[40] Contrasting this Article 8 case with the later case law on the vulnerability of children is a clear example of the Court's evolutive and expanding approach to Article 3. The type of treatment that violated Article 8 in the prior case, which was decided in 1985, would nowadays very likely be seen as reaching the threshold of Article 3, which requires more intense suffering. These cases thus

[36] *Opuz* (n 32), para 160; *M.B. v Romania* App no 43982/06, Judgment of 3 November 2011, para 52; *Đorđević* (n 45), para 138.

[37] *X. v Germany* (n 15), 165.

[38] *Aydin* (n 24), paras 83–84.

[39] *A. v United Kingdom* App no 25599/94, Judgment of 23 September 1998, Reports 1998-VI, para 22.

[40] Ibid, citing *X. and Y. v Netherlands* App no 8978/80, Judgment of 26 March 1985, Series A91, paras 21–27; *Stubbings and Others* (n 62), paras 62–64; CRC, Arts 19 and 37.

clearly illustrate the way in which a given treatment can pass from the scope of Article 8 to the scope of Article 3 with the passage of time.

In 1999, the Court again referred to its jurisprudence under Article 8 ECHR when it held that there is an obligation on states to provide effective deterrence against sexual abuse of children and other vulnerable individuals.[41] By 2001, the reference to Article 8 had fallen away, and the Court held that Articles 1 and 3 ECHR together obligate states

> to take measures designed to ensure that individuals within their jurisdiction are not subjected to torture or inhuman or degrading treatment, including such ill-treatment administered by private individuals … These measures should provide effective protection, in particular, of children and other vulnerable persons and include reasonable steps to prevent ill-treatment of which the authorities had or ought to have had knowledge.[42]

This finding was reiterated various times in the course of the following year.[43]

In the years that followed, the Court often applied this formula, and increasingly noted the vulnerability of young people up to the age of 19 or 20.[44] It used vulnerability reasoning to require states to pay special attention to protecting children, given that their ability or willingness to complain of ill-treatment is often reduced[45] and that they are more susceptible to trauma.[46] States have positive obligations to give adequate weight to minors' vulnerability, protect them, and take adequate measures to ensure that they are not exposed to ill-treatment.[47] In short, this means taking special measures in the form of 'extra protection' of vulnerable minors.[48] The Court also takes the vulnerability of minors into account by finding that a given form of treatment may have a more severe impact on minors than on adults for the purposes of the threshold of severity under Article 3.[49]

From these beginnings, the Court's jurisprudence has continued to emphasise 'effective deterrence' of ill-treatment regarding minors and young people.[50]

[41] *Stuart v United Kingdom* App no 41903/98, Decision of 6 July 1999, para 1, citing *Stubbings and Others* (n 62), para 64 and *Aydin* (n 24), para 86 (*sic*).

[42] *Z. and Others v United Kingdom* App no 29392/95, Judgment (GC) of 10 May 2001, Reports 2001-V, para 73.

[43] *G.G. v Italy* App no 34574/97, Decision of 10 October 2002; *D.P. and J.C. v United Kingdom* App no 38719/97, Judgment of 10 October 2002, para 109; *E. and Others v United Kingdom* App no 33218/96, Judgment of 26 November 2002, para 88.

[44] *Menesheva v Russia* App no 59261/00, Judgment of 9 March 2006, Reports 2006-III, para 61; *Knox v Italy* App no 76577/13, Judgment of 24 January 2019, para 41.

[45] *B. v Romania* App no 42390/07, Judgment of 10 January 2012, para 50.

[46] *Slavov and Others v Bulgaria* App no 58500/10, Judgment of 10 November 2015, para 82.

[47] *Yazgül Yilmaz v Turkey* App no 36369/06, Judgment of 1 February 2011, para 42; *Rahimi v Greece* App no 8687/08, Judgment of 5 April 2011, para 87.

[48] *Ateşoğlu v Turkey* App no 53645/10, Judgment of 20 January 2015, para 27.

[49] *Bati and Others v Turkey* App no 33097/96 and 57834/00, Judgment of 3 June 2004, Reports 2004-IV (extracts), para 122.

[50] *Sultan Öner and Others v Turkey* App no 73792/01, Judgment of 17 October 2006, paras 133 and 134; *Muskhadzhiyeva and Others v Belgium* App no 41442/07, Judgment of 19 January 2010, para 55; *Đurđević v Croatia* App no 52442/09, Judgment of 19 July 2011, Reports 2011 (extracts), paras 102 and 109; *M. and Others v Italy and Bulgaria* App no 40020/03, Judgment of 31 July 2012, para 105; *O'Keeffe v Ireland* App no 35810/09, Judgment (GC) of 28 January 2014, Reports 2014 (extracts), paras 144–46.

This includes an obligation to ensure effective protection against ill-treatment inflicted by private parties and the procedural obligation to provide an effective investigation and prosecution of ill-treatment.[51]

ii. Sexual Abuse of Minors

Certain constellations of ill-treatment affecting children have received particular attention from the Court. This is particularly true of cases involving the sexual abuse of minors. The relevant case law relates to both sexual abuse in the institutional and the private setting, and requires a context-sensitive and proactive approach by the authorities.

In 2003, for example, the Court found an Article 3 violation by the Bulgarian authorities, who had 'attached little weight to the particular vulnerability of young persons and the special psychological factors involved in cases concerning the rape of minors'.[52] In 2011, the Court made the same finding regarding the Romanian authorities and the sexual assault of children.[53] In the *P. and S. v Poland* judgment of 2012, concerning a 14-year-old girl who had become pregnant as the result of rape, the Court found that the respondent state had not only failed to protect the applicant from rape, which had placed her in a situation of 'great vulnerability'; it had also compounded the situation by, via its officials, humiliating the applicant and frustrating her attempts to obtain an abortion. All in all, the state had failed to have proper regard to the applicant's vulnerability, her young age, and her own feelings and views.[54]

This guidance has become more concrete over time. In 2016, again considering the special psychological factors involved in the rape of minors, the Court took its previous case law a step further, into a fully child-sensitive assessment.[55] In that judgment, *M.G.C. v Romania*, it engaged in detail with the domestic response to the multiple rape of an 11-year-old girl. The perpetrators had received relatively light sentences, and the domestic instances had ignored the fact that the victim had not yet reached the domestic age of consent; instead, they considered that her lack of consent had not been proven, and that she may even have provoked the acts in question. The Court re-examined this domestic evaluation of the facts, displaying little understanding for the authorities' approach to the issue of consent. It noted that the domestic authorities had failed to consider the difference in age and physical strength between the applicant and the fifty-two-year-old principal perpetrator. The Court also noted that, in evaluating the applicant's demeanour, which was interpreted as a sign of consent, the domestic courts had failed to 'demonstrate a child-sensitive approach', and that they had 'held against the applicant facts that

[51] *Đurđević* (n 50), para 102; *M.P. and Others v Bulgaria* App no 22457/08, Judgment of 15 November 2011, para 108.

[52] *M.C. v Poland* App no 23692/09, Judgment of 3 March 2015, para 183.

[53] *M. and C. v Romania* App no 29032/04, Judgment of 27 September 2011, para 119. Similarly also in *C.A.S. and C.S. v Romania* App no 26692/05, Judgment of 20 March 2012, para 81.

[54] *P. and S. v Poland* App no 57375/08, Judgment of 30 October 2012, para 161–66.

[55] *M.G.C. v Romania* App no 61495/11, Judgment of 15 March 2016, para 73.

were, in reality, consistent with a child's possible reaction to a stressful event, such as not telling her parents.'[56] The Court thus not only addressed the domestic courts' failure to engage with the applicant's age and psychology and provided concrete guidance, including by challenging the failure to order a specialist psychological evaluation, but effectively also addressed the fact that she was revictimised by the general conduct and outcome of the proceedings.[57]

The approach taken by the domestic authorities regarding the alleged rape of a minor, this time in a family setting, was criticised also in *G.U. v Turkey* in 2016.[58] After the victim was forced to give evidence in open court – a request to the contrary having been ignored – the alleged perpetrator, her stepfather, was acquitted due to a lack of proof and to medical evidence that he was impotent. In examining the case, the Court noted that neither the investigating authorities nor the domestic judges had taken the particular vulnerability of the victim, as a minor, into consideration. In doing so, they had also ignored the 'special psychological factors involved in the rape of minors committed in a family setting, which could have explained the victim's reluctance to report her rape and to describe the acts in question'.[59] The Court went on to recall that the authorities must display particular attention for vulnerable individuals, including children, and provide them with special protection given that their ability to complain about rights violations may be reduced.[60] In cases concerning the rape of minors, the Court held, the best interests of the child must predominate; respect for human dignity and psychological integrity require special attention when the victim of sexual violence is a child.[61] The Court also pointed out that the domestic authorities ignored evidence of trauma in the applicant, and instead focused on speculating about whether, given her 'corpulence', it would have been possible for her stepfather to rape her by force.[62] As a result, the Court found, the state had not complied with its positive obligations vis-à-vis the applicant under Articles 3 and 8 of the Convention.

Vulnerability may be particularly acute where minor age and intellectual disability or mental illness overlap. When it comes to sexual violence at the intersection of childhood age and intellectual disability, the Court considers that their disability puts minor applicants 'in a heightened state of vulnerability'.[63] The Court has been particularly exacting regarding states' obligations in this context, requiring the penalisation and effective prosecution of all non-consensual sexual acts, also absent physical resistance by the victim.[64] The Court furthermore requires consideration of victims' individual circumstances and the circumstances of the

[56] Ibid, para 70.
[57] Ibid, paras 70–75.
[58] *G.U. v Turkey* App no 16143/10, Judgment of 18 October 2016, paras 7–8.
[59] Ibid, para 72, translation by the author.
[60] Ibid.
[61] Ibid, para 73.
[62] Ibid, paras 75–76.
[63] *I.C. v Romania* App no 36934/08, Judgment of 24 May 2016, para 56.
[64] Ibid, para 52.

case in order to avoid misinterpretations of any failure to come forward and to allow for adequate and diligent analysis of the validity of consent.[65] Similarly, Court requires particular diligence from the state when it comes to sexual abuse at the intersection of mental illness and minor age. Where it can impute knowledge of a victim's mental illness to the authorities, the Court requires them to take the victim's particular moral and physical vulnerability into account, and take action to protect them.[66]

Below, in the discussion on minors in institutional settings, this analysis will discuss the *O'Keeffe v Ireland* case. That case is also relevant here, because it provides an example of the particularly stringent obligations on the state when it comes to sexual abuse of minors who are in its custody, albeit temporarily, ie for the purposes of schooling.[67] In *O'Keeffe*, the Court held, having regard to the fundamental nature of Article 3 and children's particular vulnerability, that the government had an 'inherent obligation' to protect these children, especially in primary schools, by taking special measures and adopting safeguards.[68] Because the applicant in *O'Keeffe* was vulnerable and in an institutional setting, the Court found that the state 'must be considered to have been aware of the sexual abuse of children by adults' – in other words, it imputed knowledge of a risk of ill-treatment to the state.[69]

To put it simply, this case law has crystallised into the finding that children are vulnerable to sexual abuse, and that for this reason they and other vulnerable persons are entitled to effective state protection.[70] This entails a range of overlapping state obligations: to provide for effective deterrence, to effectively protect, and to take reasonable steps to prevent ill-treatment.[71] The case law shows that the deterrence limb, or preventive obligation, means that the authorities must prevent sexual abuse of minors where they know or ought to know about relevant risks; this includes a requirement to deploy the criminal law, or what has elsewhere been called a 'coercive obligation'.[72] Known vulnerability (for example that of minors in the institutional setting) might contribute to imputing knowledge of a risk of ill-treatment, triggering the protective obligation.[73] And to effectively deter sexual abuse of minors, states must take measures aiming to ensure respect for victims' human dignity and protect the child's best interests; this means adequately investigating alleged sexual abuse, attaching sufficient weight to minors' vulnerability and their specific psychology,[74] and having regard for the

[65] Ibid, para 56.
[66] *V.C. v Italy* App no 54227/14, Judgment of 1 February 2018, paras 83/84, 99, 102, 110–11.
[67] *O'Keeffe* (n 50), para 145.
[68] Ibid, para 146.
[69] Ibid.
[70] *Talpis v Italy* App no 41237/14, Judgment of 2 March 2017, para 115.
[71] Corina Heri, 'Shaping Coercive Obligations through Vulnerability: The Example of the ECtHR', in Natasa Mavronicola and Laurens Lavrysen (eds), *Towards a Coercive Human Rights Law? Positive Duties to Mobilise the Criminal Law under the ECHR* (Hart, 2020).
[72] Laurens Lavrysen and Natasa Mavronicola, *Coercive Human Rights: Positive Duties to Mobilise the Criminal Law under the ECHR* (Hart, 2020), *passim*.
[73] *O'Keeffe* (n 50), paras 144–46, 168.
[74] *M.G.C.* (n 55), para 73.

fact that vulnerable minor victims' 'capacity or willingness to pursue a complaint' may be limited.[75]

iii. Physical Abuse of Minors

When minors are physically abused in non-sexual ways, the Court has taken a similar approach as described in the previous section. Its stance today is that the physical disciplining of children, though once widely accepted, has grown less acceptable in European societies to the point of becoming a violation of the victims' physical integrity. Two key cases in this progressive lowering of the threshold of severity, which represents a paradigmatic example of the evolutive interpretation of Article 3, were the 1998 judgment in *A. v United Kingdom*, concerning the caning of a boy by his stepfather,[76] and the previous 1978 case of *Tyrer v United Kingdom*, concerning public birching.[77]

Corporal punishment in the institutional setting will be discussed below.[78] When it comes to the corporal punishment of children in private contexts, in 2017, the Court held that Article 3 requires states to take measures to prevent such ill-treatment. It did so by holding that '[a]ssuring basic dignity to the child means that there can be no compromise in condemning violence against children, whether accepted as "tradition" or disguised as "discipline"'.[79] The Court held that children's uniqueness – which derives from 'their potential and vulnerability, their dependence on adults' – means that they must receive better, as opposed to less stringent, protection from violence, including from corporal punishment at home, which it described as 'being invariably degrading'.[80] Here, the Court displays no qualms about requiring the state to interfere in the sphere of relations between individuals, and instead makes clear demands on the kind of treatment to which children can be subjected in the home.

iv. Children under Exclusive State Authority

The Court has a long and consistent strain of case law considering children particularly vulnerable when they find themselves in the exclusive control of the authorities. This means that states must adhere to particular requirements when detaining minors or conducting police interviews or arrests involving them.[81] These requirements are additional to those concerning detention in general, which – as outlined below – make demands on safety from violence by other detainees and by staff, the provision of adequate medical care, and adequate conditions for those with special medical or physical needs.

[75] *I.C.* (n 63), para 51.
[76] *A. v United Kingdom* (n 39), paras 22–24.
[77] *Tyrer v United Kingdom* App no 5856/72, Judgment of 25 April 1978, Series A26, para 33.
[78] *V.K. v Russia* App no 68059/13, Judgment of 7 March 2017, paras 172 and 183.
[79] *D.M.D. v Romania* App no 23022/13, Judgment of 3 October 2017, para 50.
[80] Ibid.
[81] *Alkes v Turkey* App no 3044/04, Judgment of 16 February 2010, para 43; *Bati and Others* (n 49), especially para 122.

The Court's case law here is by now well-established. For example, in a series of 2016 judgments against France, the Court drew far-reaching consequences from the idea that children, in light of their vulnerability, need special protection when in the exclusive control of the authorities. There, the Court found that the immigration-related detention of very young children, even together with their parents, could prove traumatic to the point of violating Article 3.[82] These cases show that the Court is engaging in an increasingly detailed examination of whether the way states treat children in their care is compatible with those minors' rights under Article 3. In this regard, the Court consistently finds that children have specific needs given their age and dependence. In the French cases, the authorities had violated the ECHR by detaining small children; for example, in one of the cases, they interned a four-year-old boy for 18 days, albeit together with his parents.[83] The Court gave a detailed explanation of why detention had a negative impact on the children. It considered factors such as the presence of loud noise emissions from a nearby airport, which particularly affected the children given their need for outdoor recreation. It also noted that the fact that young children cannot be left unattended when their parents are interviewed means that they are repeatedly exposed to the presence of armed and uniformed police. The Court also noted the harmful effect of frequent loud-speaker announcements made at detention facilities.[84] Judgments like this can have potentially far-reaching effects because they imply that, under certain circumstances, the Convention could require that at least one parent be given their liberty so as to be with their child.

Before turning to the Article 3 obligations regarding minors in exclusive state control, it must be noted that the vulnerability of minors is equally relevant in other institutional contexts, such as for example the state schools. The Court has for example held that the positive obligation to protect vulnerable individuals from ill-treatment has particular importance 'in the context of the provision of an important public service such as primary education, school authorities being obliged to protect the health and wellbeing of pupils and, in particular, of young children who are especially vulnerable and are under the exclusive control of those authorities.'[85] In another case, ill-treatment in a nursery school was attributed to the state because it was inflicted in a state-supervised public nursery school during school hours.[86] The same findings have been made in the context of an orphanage.[87]

[82] *A.B. and Others v France* App no 11593/12, Judgment of 12 July 2016, paras 110–15; *A.M. and Others v France* App no 24587/12, Judgment of 12 July 2016, paras 47–53; *R.K. and Others v France* App no 68264/14, Judgment of 12 July 2016, paras 67–72; *R.C. and V.C. v France* App no 76491/14, Judgment of 12 July 2016, paras 35–40; *R.M. and Others v France* App no 33201/11, Judgment of 12 July 2016, paras 71–76.

[83] *A.B. and Others* (n 82), paras 110–11.

[84] Ibid, para 113.

[85] *O'Keeffe* (n 50), para 145.

[86] *V.K.* (n 78), paras 172 and 183.

[87] *X and Others v Bulgaria* App no 22457/16, Judgment (GC) of 2 February 2021.

But how precisely does vulnerability shape the rights of minors? For one, if the authorities inflict ill-treatment on a minor, particularly one who is under their exclusive authority, the Court has used vulnerability to pull that treatment under the scope of Article 3.[88] For example, in *Bouyid v Belgium*, a case concerning two brothers – one of whom was a minor – who were slapped by police officers during questioning, the Court found that the relevant officers had flouted their duty to protect these vulnerable individuals and to respect their human dignity.[89] The Court used this opportunity to hold that '[p]olice behaviour towards minors may be incompatible with [Article 3] simply because they are minors, whereas it might be deemed acceptable in the case of adults. Therefore, law-enforcement officers must show greater vigilance and self-control when dealing with minors'.[90] In other words, the vulnerability of minors when confronted with the authorities means that it may be incompatible with Article 3 to apply the same methods as one would to an adult. However, of course, this does not mean that any police investigative or criminal action against minors is per se incompatible with Article 3.

Two relevant cases in this regard were decided in 1999. They concerned criminal proceedings against two boys who were accused of murdering a toddler in the United Kingdom. There, the Court examined the compatibility with Article 3 of criminal proceedings conducted against the two perpetrators, who were aged 10 at the time of the crime and 11 during trial.[91] The representatives of the two boys, who had reached the domestic age of criminal responsibility and were tried in an adult court in a public trial, argued that the state had to 'ensure that the procedures adopted for the trial and sentencing of such young children were modified to reflect their age and vulnerability'.[92] The Court itself did not use vulnerability language, but went on to examine in substance whether this obligation had been complied with. In doing so, it noted that the authorities had not had any intention to cause the applicants suffering.[93] Furthermore, it found that any type of setting – be it formal or informal, public or private – would have caused the boys, who were suffering from post-traumatic stress disorder, great suffering, and that the circumstances did not go beyond what was strictly necessary in order for the authorities to deal with the crime committed.[94]

Today, such a case might be decided differently. States are obligated to provide extra protection to children in judicial proceedings, and treatment that may be permissible for adults can violate Article 3 when imposed on children.[95]

[88] *Iurcu v the Republic of Moldova* App no 33759/10, Judgment of 9 April 2013, para 38.

[89] *Bouyid v Belgium* App no 23380/09, Judgment (GC) of 28 September 2015, Reports 2015, paras 103, 107–11.

[90] Ibid, para 110.

[91] *V. v United Kingdom* App no 24888/94, Judgment [GC] of 16 December 1999, Reports 1999-IX, para 65; *T. v United Kingdom* App no 24724/94, Judgment (GC) of 16 December 1999, para 63.

[92] Ibid, paras 63–64 and 62–63, respectively.

[93] Ibid, paras 78 and 76, respectively.

[94] Ibid, paras 79 and 77, respectively.

[95] *Ateşoğlu* (n 48), para 27; *Zherdev v Ukraine* App no 34015/07, Judgment of 27 April 2017, para 86.

This obligation is particularly acute vis-à-vis children with special needs. For example, in a 2016 judgment concerning a minor who had been diagnosed with ADHD, the Court held that his Article 3 rights had been violated not only because he had lacked necessary medical treatment, but also because he had confessed under duress.[96] Criminal proceedings regarding juveniles, the Court held, should be oriented around the principle of respect for the best interests of the child and should guarantee, accordingly, that 'a child charged with an offence is dealt with in a manner which takes full account of his age, level of maturity and intellectual and emotional capacities, and that steps are taken to promote his ability to understand and participate in the proceedings'. This right of a minor defendant to participate effectively in his or her criminal trial requires the authorities to 'deal with him with due regard to his vulnerability and capacities' at every stage of criminal investigation, but especially during questioning.[97] The authorities must take steps to reduce children's feelings of inhibition and intimidation as much as possible, and to ensure that they have 'a broad understanding of the nature of the investigation, of what is at stake', and of their defence rights.[98]

These obligations are not limited to minors with special needs, however. Concerning a 16-year-old applicant, the Court held in 2017 that leaving him handcuffed and naked but for his underwear for hours, 'in a state of uncertainty and vulnerability', raised an issue under Article 3.[99] Placing the same applicant in a cell with adult detainees, it went on to note, 'must have contributed to creating in him feelings of fear, anguish, helplessness and inferiority, diminishing his dignity'.[100] In other words, the Court displays a great willingness to make inferences about the effects of a given treatment here. Increased awareness of the psychological vulnerability of children – including their inability to withstand the pressures associated with a criminal investigation – also means that, according to the Court, a minor's vulnerability can affect the assessment of evidence. In particular, considerations about their vulnerability can affect the evidentiary weight of police records signed by minors.[101]

It is not quite clear where the age ceiling for youth-related vulnerability in criminal proceedings lies. For example, in 2019, an applicant who was 20 years old when she was interrogated by Italian police regarding the death of her roommate submitted that she had been vulnerable because she was young, did not speak Italian well, and was in an extreme state of shock and confusion.[102] She argued that her incriminating statements were a result of the psychological pressure under which she was placed while in this state. Here, the Court found that the applicant

[96] *Blokhin v Russia* App no 47152/06, Judgment (GC) of 23 March 2016, Reports 2016, para 148.
[97] Ibid, para 195.
[98] Ibid.
[99] *Zherdev* (n 95), para 93.
[100] Ibid.
[101] *Volkan Özdemir v Turkey* App no 29105/03, Judgment of 20 October 2009, para 38.
[102] *Knox* (n 44).

was in an untenable psychological situation, and that her complaints about how she had been treated were not taken seriously. It went on to find a violation of Article 3 in its procedural limb. The emphasis on the applicant's youth evokes some of the case law discussed above, and indicates that this type of vulnerability is determined not by a fixed age limit, but by a contextual assessment. This, of course, raises questions of fairness, and it is not entirely clear how this situation is to be distinguished from the vulnerability in which people who are being interrogated by police generally find themselves.[103]

The vulnerability of children in detention also places the authorities under special investigative obligations. This may mean doing away with formal rules, for example when it comes to the lodging of complaints about sexual and physical abuse in detention by minor detainees.[104] In the same vein, delays in reporting ill-treatment in detention to the authorities should not be considered decisive for the legitimacy or admissibility of these claims, given the vulnerability of the minor detainees in question.[105]

Lastly, it should be noted that the obligation to provide special protection to children in the context of criminal proceedings goes beyond measures targeting them directly, and also requires the authorities to take minors' psychological vulnerability into consideration when they are indirectly affected by measures against their parents.[106] In 2016, the Court held that the manner in which an individual had been arrested in front of his children, aged four and eight, was incompatible with Article 3. In particular, the Court noted that while it could not prohibit the authorities from arresting suspects in front of their partners or children, there needed to be some consideration of the children and of possible alternative measures.[107] Removing arrested parents from their home without providing care and an explanation to their children can likewise violate Article 3.[108]

v. *Minors in the Migration Context*

The special vulnerability of minor migrants also has a considerable influence on the Court's reasoning under Article 3. In this regard, the Court has repeatedly held that minor asylum-seekers are 'a category of vulnerable persons particularly requiring the authorities' attention' and that children have special needs due to their age and their dependence, both in and outside the context of migration detention.[109] However, vulnerability is not reserved to those minors who have attained the formal status of asylum-seekers.

[103] *Utvenko and Borisov v Russia* App no 45767/09 and 40452/10, Judgment of 5 February 2019, para 189 (regarding Art 6).

[104] *A.Ş. v Turkey* App no 58271/10, Judgment of 13 September 2016, paras 72–73.

[105] *Nalbandyan v Armenia* App no 9935/06 and 23339/06, Judgment of 31 March 2015, para 106.

[106] *Govedarski v Bulgaria* App no 34957/12, Judgment of 16 February 2016, para 62.

[107] Ibid, para 62.

[108] *Ioan Pop and Others v Romania* App no 52924/09, Judgment of 6 December 2016, paras 61 and 63.

[109] *Popov v France* App no 39472/07 and 39474/07, Judgment of 19 January 2012, para 91; *Tarakhel v Switzerland* App no 29217/12, Judgment (GC) of 4 November 2014, Reports 2014 (extracts), para 99.

In the key 2006 *Mubilanzila Mayeka and Kaniki Mitunga v Belgium* judgment, the Court made clear that the vulnerability, dependence, and entitlement to protection of migrant children does not depend on whether they have attained asylum-seeker or refugee status.[110] In this judgment, the Court considered the case of an unaccompanied Congolese girl who, aged five, had entered Belgium illegally and who had then been detained and removed. In this context, the Court not only held that the young girl was extremely vulnerable due to her age, the fact that she had entered the country illegally and the fact that she was unaccompanied – a case of intersectionality further discussed below – but also that '[i]n view of the absolute nature of the protection afforded by Article 3 of the Convention, [the applicant's vulnerability] is the decisive factor and it takes precedence over considerations relating to [her] status as an illegal immigrant.'[111] Accordingly, she 'came within the class of highly vulnerable members of society to whom the Belgian State owed a duty to take adequate measures to provide care and protection'.[112]

The *Mubilanzila Mayeka and Kaniki Mitunga* judgment represented the clearest formulation of the Court's approach to the vulnerability of minors under Article 3 until that time. However, it is remarkable that the Court held that the young girl's vulnerability took precedence over her status as an illegal immigrant. This would make it seem that there is an element of balancing at play here, one that juxtaposes the interests of the child with the state's prerogative to expel non-citizens at its own discretion even under Article 3 ECHR.[113]

The same could be said of other examples of the Court's case law on the treatment of migrant children. In 2011, for example, in examining whether Article 3 had been violated in the case of three children who, together with their mother, had been detained in a closed transit centre for illegal aliens in Belgium, the Court held that the best interests of the child as per Article 3 CRC should take precedence in the context of expulsion. On that basis, the Court considered the three children vulnerable both by virtue of their age and due to their traumatising personal history, and found a violation of Article 3.[114] The reference to the CRC in that case was drawn from other case law brought under Article 8 ECHR, where the Court found that the state had exceeded its margin of appreciation and failed to adequately balance the interests at stake.[115] While the precedence of the child's best interests is a fixed feature of the Court's jurisprudence under Article 8, transplanting this standard into Article 3 must have due regard for the fact that states have no margin of appreciation under the latter.

[110] *Mubilanzila Mayeka and Kaniki Mitunga v Belgium* App no 13178/03, Judgment of 12 October 2006, Reports 2006-XI, para 55.

[111] Ibid.

[112] Ibid.

[113] Marie-Bénédicte Dembour, *When Humans Become Migrants: Study of the European Court of Human Rights with an Inter-American Counterpoint* (OUP, 2015), 3–5, 8 and 97; *Tatar v Switzerland* App no 65692/12, Judgment of 14 April 2015, para 39.

[114] *Kanagaratnam v Belgium* App no 15297/09, Judgment of 13 December 2011, para 67.

[115] *Nunez v Norway* App no 55597/09, Judgment of 28 June 2011, paras 9–12.

A different approach, truer to the absolute nature of Article 3, is the one taken in *Tarakhel v Switzerland*. There, the Court – although reiterating that a child's extreme vulnerability is decisive and takes precedence over their status as an illegal immigrant[116] – focused on concretising children's right to special protection and the threshold of severity under Article 3. It did so to rebut the presumption of compliance with the Convention by receiving states under the EU's Dublin Regulation.[117] It held that the 'requirement of "special protection" of asylum-seekers is particularly important when the persons concerned are children, in view of their specific needs and their extreme vulnerability.'[118] On this basis, it found that the reception conditions for children who seek asylum must be age-appropriate so as not to expose them to stress, anxiety, and trauma. Otherwise, Article 3's threshold of severity would be met. In other words, here, vulnerability was not used to balance different types of interests, but to provide a more complete understanding of the harms at stake. It is also notable that, expanding the finding made in *Mubilanzila Mayeka and Kaniki Mitunga*, even accompanied children were described as 'extremely vulnerable' here.[119]

In addition, the Court has set a clear standard as concerns the permissibility of detaining minors in the migration context. As discussed above, in a series of 2016 judgments against France, the Court found that the immigration-related detention of very young children, even together with their parents, could prove traumatic to the point of violating Article 3.[120] Given the impact of the detention conditions on the children, and the fact that they were confined together with their parents, which meant that they were exposed to the latter's suffering, the Court found a violation of Article 3 in these cases.[121] It held that the authorities must reserve immigration detention of children to a measure of last resort, and endeavour to keep it as short as possible. Beyond a brief period, detention of these very small children – and thus presumably also of their parents – is not permissible.[122] In addition, states have strict medical obligations towards vulnerable and very small children in their custody.[123]

These cases against France concerned children aged up to six years old. It is clear that the detention of children of this age is exceedingly difficult to reconcile with Article 3. However, the Court is more tolerant of detention measures ordered against teenagers in the migration context. A leading case in this regard is *Abdullahi Elmi and Aweys Abubakar v Malta*, concerning two unaccompanied teenagers who were detained for around eight months in a facility for adults

[116] *Tarakhel* (n 109), para 99.
[117] Council Regulation (EC) No 343/2003 of 18 February 2003, [2003] OJ L50/1–10, Now replaced by Regulation (EU) No 604/2013 of 26 June 2013, [2013] OJ L180/31–59.
[118] *Tarakhel* (n 109), para 119.
[119] Ibid.
[120] *A.B. and Others* (n 82), paras 110–15, esp 110, and the other four related cases cited in n 82.
[121] Ibid.
[122] Ibid, para 114.
[123] *Korneykova and Korneykov v Ukraine* App no 56660/12, Judgment of 24 March 2016, para 152.

while awaiting the outcome of a procedure to confirm their age. This case raised questions about who falls in the category of vulnerable minors. Here, the Court held that although the applicants were not small children, 'they still fell within the international definition of minors, in respect of which detention should be a last resort and which should be limited to the shortest time possible'.[124] Thus, the Court held, the detention conditions should have been adapted to their ages, which were later confirmed as being 16 and 17, respectively.[125] In particular, under Article 3, the Court highlighted that the applicants were provided with no counselling, educational assistance or other support from qualified personnel, nor with any entertainment facilities suitable to their age. In addition, the detention facility was characterised by appalling sanitary conditions and 'a tense and violent atmosphere', and the applicants reported being beaten and robbed by other detainees.[126] This, the Court held, was a violation of Article 3, even if the applicants' age had not yet been established at the outset.

This case shows two things in particular. First, although the requirements for the treatment of adolescents are not as strict as those concerning children, teens are still vulnerable and require special protection under Article 3. This allows for a portrayal of childhood vulnerability as a spectrum, which comes to an abrupt halt at the age of about 18 to 20. Secondly, in case of doubt about their age and therefore their vulnerability, the Article 3 rights of minors require states to err on the side of treating them as minors.

However, not all of the judges involved in deciding this case agreed. Judge Sajó, in a concurring opinion, argued not only against considering asylum-seekers as a vulnerable group, but also against the vulnerability of the applicants as minors on the basis that he did not 'consider that case-law based on the problems of small children is applicable to adolescents'.[127] In other words, Judge Sajó disagreed – not for the first time[128] – with the Court's approach to vulnerability, arguing that he would have 'preferred specifics' about why and how the applicants were vulnerable. Indeed, and although that may not be what Judge Sajó intended, greater engagement with why the applicants were vulnerable would have been preferable in this case, although its outcome and general approach are to be welcomed. Various complaints made by the applicants that were linked to their needs as vulnerable minors were lost in the judgment, for example their extremely limited ability to contact their families in Somalia.[129] Arguably, engaging with why and how the applicants were vulnerable – as unaccompanied minors lacking any kind of adult

[124] *Abdullahi Elmi and Aweys Abubakar v Malta* App nos 25794/13 and 28151/13, Judgment of 22 November 2016, paras 111 and 113.
[125] Ibid, paras 111 and 113.
[126] Ibid, paras 23, 110 and 111.
[127] Ibid, Concurring Opinion of Judge Sajó.
[128] *M.S.S.* (n 7), Partly Concurring and Partly Dissenting Opinion of Judge Sajó, and *Abdi Mahamud v Malta* App no 56796/13, Judgment of 3 May 2016, Partly Dissenting Opinion of Judge Sajó.
[129] *Abdullahi Elmi and Aweys Abubakar* (n 124), para 24.

support – may have meant engaging with the need to provide them with a meaningful opportunity to stay in touch with their families.

vi. Problems with Portraying Children as Vulnerable

Childhood age is the most consistently recognised source of vulnerability in the Court's case law. The Court's protection of children is comparatively well-developed, and it entails positive obligations on the part of states to take children's special needs into account and to advocate for their best interests. This child-friendly approach is certainly to be welcomed, and it has led to applicant-friendly results in many cases. For example, in *Tarakhel*, the Court focused on the vulnerability of the applicant family's children in order to overcome the requirement of a systemic deficiency in the Italian reception conditions, a requirement that had gone unmet in the preceding *Mohammed Hussein* case.[130] In *Blokhin*, the vulnerability of the minor involved was used to derive an obligation of the authorities to engage with his capacities, needs, and feelings.[131] The Court has furthermore recognised the vulnerability of children in many different contexts, and – in analogy to the best interests of the child principle under Article 8 – it gives precedence to the vulnerability of the child over other considerations.[132]

However, certain issues with the Court's approach remain. Indeed, while the Court often refers to children as a seemingly self-explanatory example of vulnerability, and uses respect for their vulnerability to lay the groundwork for protecting the rights of other vulnerable individuals and groups, the concept of a child's vulnerability is not as nuanced as that of the child's best interests. In other words, the Court's jurisprudence does not emphasise a transcendence of vulnerability in order to ensure respect for the capacities of children. To clarify: while the CRC emphasises procedural requirements such as hearing children and permitting them to participate in proceedings that concern them,[133] the Court's approach largely focuses on substantive outcomes, or on the requirement that states take children's vulnerability into consideration. Thus, the CRC guarantees a child 'not only rights derived from her or his vulnerability (protection) or dependency on adults (provision). The Convention recognises the child as a subject of rights.'[134] By contrast, in the Court's jurisprudence, the agency of children is not elevated in this manner. Instead, the Court's approach focuses largely on 'children's fragility and vulnerability and their dependence on adults for the [*sic*]

[130] Contrast *Tarakhel* (n 109), paras 119–22, and *Mohammed Hussein and Others v Netherlands and Italy* App no 27725/10, Decision of 2 April 2013, para 78.

[131] *Blokhin* (n 96), para 195.

[132] On the child's best interests, see, instead of many, *Mennesson v France* App no 65192/11, Judgment of 26 June 2014, Reports 2014 (extracts), paras 81 and 84; Helen Keller and Corina Heri, 'Protecting the Best Interests of the Child: International Child Abduction and the European Court of Human Rights' (2015) 84(2) *Nordic Journal of International Law* 270–96; *Tarakhel* (n 109), paras 119–22.

[133] Committee on the Rights of the Child, 'General Comment No 12 (2009): The Right of the Child to be Heard', UN Doc CRC/C/GC/12, 1 July 2009.

[134] Ibid, 6, para 18.

growth and development', which it has recognised as calling 'for greater investment in the prevention of violence and protection of children on the part of families, society and the state'.[135]

In some sense, the Court's understanding of Article 3 as providing protection, and not empowerment, to children is a direct outcome of its interpretation of that provision in general. However, this may not be the most child-friendly – or the most individual-friendly, or agency-friendly – manner to proceed. In 2012, Jonathan Herring examined claims that legal emphasis of the vulnerability of children results in a paternalistic system that denies their agency, exaggerates risks and downplays their abilities.[136] Herring employed a situational definition of vulnerability as exposure to a risk of harm, and found that this concept has been formative for the moral rhetoric of childhood.[137]

Herring's work cites the research of Anneke Meyer, who in turn considers that the ideas of vulnerability and innocence form the moral rhetoric of childhood in that they serve to explain and legitimise a wide variety of measures or ideas about children while doing away with the need to provide a justification: in her words, 'children are the reason'.[138] In so doing, Meyer has expressed a problem that lies at the very core of the Court's vulnerability jurisprudence. The Court often seems to permit vulnerability to suffice as the reason for a range of results under Article 3. A wide variety of reasons can be given to support the Court's reliance on vulnerability – for example, the idea that a society that fails to protect its weakest members destroys its own moral foundations, and thus itself, or the claim that we are all vulnerable and that a tailored response to the vulnerability inherent in each and every one of us is the foundational premise of human rights law – but the problem remains that the Court has not expressly acknowledged any one of them.

Herring criticises the approach to vulnerability employed regarding children today, arguing that it is selective regarding the risks it emphasises and homogenising – in other words, essentialising – as it negates the spectrum of childhood experiences and the diversity of children.[139] Herring also identifies a third risk by pointing out that vulnerability discourse may actually endanger children by emphasising their innocence and helplessness, which may attract abuse.[140] Emphasising innocence may also hamper the full human rights protection of those children and young adults who cannot be deemed innocent or helpless. Herring concludes by stating that while not wishing to overemphasise the resilience and capabilities

[135] Committee of Ministers of the Council of Europe, Recommendation CM/Rec(2009)10 on integrated national strategies for the protection of children from violence, adopted on 18 November 2009, preamble, 7th recital.

[136] Herring (n 1), 244.

[137] Ibid, 245–46, citing Anneke Meyer, 'The Moral Rhetoric of Childhood' (2007) 14(1) *Childhood* 85–104, 85.

[138] Meyer (n 137), 85.

[139] Herring (n 1), 249.

[140] Ibid, 250.

of children, he aims to show that the law 'exaggerates the vulnerability of children and exaggerates the capacity of adults'.[141]

To transfer these criticisms one-for-one onto the Court's child-related vulnerability reasoning as it stands today is perhaps overly harsh. Especially in recent cases, the Court has displayed an individual-sensitive and circumstance-responsive approach to childhood vulnerability. However, there is a salience to these concerns, and these authors' fears for the agency and independence of those labelled vulnerable are applicable to all of the applicants discussed in this volume, not just children. In particular, it is problematic to create a strict distinction between vulnerable children and invulnerable adults. Individual maturity covers a large spectrum, and it is largely artificial to assume that attaining the age of majority guarantees any particular level of development or independence. However, under the same argument it is also problematic to lump small children and adolescents together, and here the Court's judgments on the detention of children show an acute awareness of the differences between these two groups without negating the vulnerability of either. In recognising that young children are particularly impressionable and may suffer trauma as a result of experiences that would be considered bearable for adolescents,[142] it has thus paved the way for more individualised, context-sensitive vulnerability assessments in individual cases.

B. The Elderly

While vulnerability due to young age is a frequently cited component of the Court's case law under Article 3, as discussed in the previous section, the age-related vulnerability of the elderly has by contrast been paid less attention. In fact, there have only been a handful of relevant cases to date.

In two such cases, the Court recognised the vulnerability of elderly detainees. The first applicant was aged 63 at the time of his arrest[143] and the second was aged 77;[144] both had medical problems. The combination of advanced age and poor state of health rendered the applicants vulnerable, the Court held in both cases, and detention may have exacerbated their feelings of distress. In both cases, however, it took into consideration the authorities' responses to the applicants' vulnerability, including the medical assistance received, and found no violation of Article 3.[145]

By contrast, the Court did find a violation in *Cestaro v Italy*, where it considered the applicant, a 62-year-old demonstrator at a G8 summit who was severely injured by police, 'physically vulnerable' due to his age.[146] *Cestaro* showed that

[141] Ibid, 250.
[142] *A.B. and Others* (n 82), paras 110–15, esp 110, and the remaining case law in (n 82).
[143] *Stoyan Mitev v Bulgaria* App no 60922/00, Judgment of 7 January 2010, para 73.
[144] *Giorgini v Italy* App no 20034/11, Decision of 1 September 2015, paras 52 and 57.
[145] Ibid, para 57; *Stoyan Mitev* (n 143), para 73.
[146] *Cestaro v Italy* App no 6884/11, Judgment of 7 April 2015, para 180.

the physical fragility of elderly people – though the applicant, at age 62, likely represents the lower limit of what might be considered an elderly person – must be taken into consideration by the domestic authorities in determining the level of force appropriate to use regarding that person.

In *Mudric v Republic of Moldova*, the Court examined a case concerning domestic violence, finding that the victim was particularly vulnerable to attacks by her ex-husband because she was 'a single woman aged 72'.[147] It is curious here that this vulnerability seems to be relative not just to the applicant's aggressor, who was mentally ill and characterised as dangerous, but also relative to the authorities and to methods for seeking protection. This seems to indicate an awareness by the Court of the fact that age, like all grounds for discrimination, is socially constructed, and that the elderly are not or not just vulnerable per se, but also because of stereotypes about them and because they lack access to sources of protection.

Lastly, in *Irina Smirnova v Ukraine*, the Court considered the case of a retired single woman who had been repeatedly assaulted by the co-owners of her flat.[148] The Ukrainian government did not contest that the applicant, as a 'retired single woman', was a vulnerable person, and that it accordingly had a positive obligation to protect her.[149] Even though the applicant was only in her early sixties when the ill-treatment began, here it appears to be the power difference between the applicant, as a single older woman, and the 'younger and stronger' men who harassed her that was decisive for finding an Article 3 violation.[150]

Elderly applicants have also sought assistance from the Court to gain or improve access to socio-economic benefits, specifically old-age pensions. So far, the Court has not found any violations of Article 3 by the failure of the state to provide an old-age pension that is sufficiently high to ensure a life in dignity, although several such applications have come before it.[151] The Court has dismissed these applications as manifestly ill-founded, without using vulnerability reasoning in its decisions. However, it has held that complaints concerning pensions or other social benefits that are 'wholly insufficient' may raise an issue under Article 3.[152] The Court went on to hold that it 'cannot exclude that State responsibility could arise for "treatment" where an applicant, in circumstances wholly dependent on State support, found herself faced with official indifference when in a situation of serious deprivation or want incompatible with human dignity'.[153] This indicates that, in future cases, the Court may consider the vulnerability of elderly individuals

[147] *Mudric v the Republic of Moldova* App no 74839/10, Judgment of 16 July 2013, para 51.

[148] *Irina Smirnova v Ukraine* App no 1870/05, Judgment of 13 October 2016, paras 9–18.

[149] Ibid, para 69.

[150] Ibid, para 72.

[151] *Budina v Russia* App no 45603/05, Decision of 18 June 2009; *Larioshina v Russia* App no 56869/00, Decision of 23 April 2002.

[152] *Larioshina* (n 151), para 3.

[153] *Budina* (n 151).

in a socio-economic context. If it does so, it may reverse the current requirement of proof of concrete suffering, which will be nigh impossible for many applicants to provide.[154]

In many ways, vulnerability due to advanced age is a continuation of the vulnerability of children. All humans experience dependency at the beginning of life, and many experience it near the end. However, the Court has not yet gone into much detail regarding the vulnerability of the elderly, and many questions regarding the obligations of states surrounding dignity, aging and death are unanswered at present. For example, the section in this chapter concerning persons interned in state institutions will not go into the situation of nursing home residents because there has been no case law in this regard. However, there are many similarities between these situations and those of individuals confined, for example, to psychiatric hospitals. In this area, it is necessary to await future developments in the Court's jurisprudence; however, it is difficult to imagine that persons in nursing homes would not be considered vulnerable and in need of special consideration if the question arose.

C. Intellectual and Psychosocial Disabilities

As concerns the vulnerability of intellectually or cognitively disabled persons and persons living with mental illness, also known as psychosocial disabilities, the Court has built up an extensive case law in both regards. There is however some overlap between the two groups. In particular, both factors can be stigmatising, and both fall under the definition of disability under the Convention on the Rights of Persons with Disabilities.[155]

In this regard, the Committee on the Rights of Persons with Disabilities defines disability as including 'those who have long-term physical, including psychosocial, intellectual or sensory impairments, and should include past, present, future and presumed disabilities, as well as persons associated with persons with disabilities'.[156] This definition is kept inclusive because those affected by disability-related discrimination should not be 'burdened by proving that they are "disabled enough" in order to benefit from the protection of the law'.[157]

The Court does not apply clear definitions of either intellectual disability or mental illness, and often relies on medical evidence submitted by the parties to find that a person falls under either group. In this regard, it does not seem to apply any requirement that applicants must reach a specific level or degree of disability

[154] Ibid.

[155] Committee on the Rights of Persons with Disabilities, 'General Comment No 6 (2018) on Equality and Non-discrimination', Doc CRPD/C/GC/6, 26 April 2018, para 73(b).

[156] Ibid.

[157] Ibid.

in order to be considered vulnerable.[158] The following will discuss both of these groups in turn.

i. Intellectual or Cognitive Disabilities

Along with children, the Court frequently mentions mentally disabled individuals as a prime example of vulnerability.[159] The Court requires states to pay intellectually disabled persons particular attention, provide a suitable environment if they are taken into state custody, and afford victims of attacks on their physical or mental integrity special protection in light of their reduced ability or willingness to seek redress themselves.[160] This latter finding has particularly been developed in the context of sexual violence against persons with intellectual disabilities, where the Court has held that the failure to properly investigate or provide an appropriate judicial response to such allegations risks creating a background of impunity and breaching the state's positive obligations.[161]

Perhaps the leading judgment when it comes to vulnerability and intellectual disability is *Đorđević v Croatia*. Mr Đorđević, who had been divested of legal capacity due to his mental and physical disability, had been exposed to ill-treatment by a group of school-aged children.[162] Here the Court reiterated the state's obligation to take measures to protect people in its jurisdiction from ill-treatment, also if administered by private individuals, and held that these measures 'should provide effective protection, in particular, of children and other vulnerable persons'.[163] The Court went on to hold that, as the authorities had not taken 'all reasonable measures to prevent abuse against the first applicant, notwithstanding the fact that the continuing risk of such abuse was real and foreseeable', there had been a violation of Article 3.[164]

When it comes to criminal proceedings against individuals with cognitive disabilities, the state's obligation to effectively protect children and other vulnerable persons is also part of its procedural obligations under Article 3.[165] Deficiencies in how proceedings are conducted become 'are all the more serious' if the person concerned is a vulnerable, cognitively disabled person.[166]

When a person with cognitive disabilities is detained, the authorities must 'demonstrate special care in guaranteeing such conditions as correspond to the person's individual needs resulting from his disability'.[167] One example here

[158] *E.B. v Romania* App no 49089/10, Judgment of 19 March 2019, paras 59–60.
[159] *M.B.* (n 36), para 52.
[160] Ibid; *B. v Romania* (n 45), para 50.
[161] *E.B.* (n 158), paras 59–60; *I.C.* (n 63), para 55.
[162] *Đorđević v Croatia* App no 41526/10, Judgment of 24 July 2012, Reports 2012, para 6.
[163] Ibid, para 138.
[164] Ibid, paras 149 and 150.
[165] *W. v Slovenia* App no 24125/06, Judgment of 23 January 2014, para 70.
[166] Ibid, para 70.
[167] *Z.H. v Hungary* App no 28973/11, Judgment of 8 November 2012, paras 7, 10 and 29.

is *Ţicu v Romania*, where the Court held vis-à-vis a detainee who suffered from a severe delay in his mental and physical development that, in order to determine whether the medical treatment he received in detention was compatible with Article 3, it was necessary to take into consideration his vulnerability and his incapacity to complain about the treatment received. The Court used three criteria to determine whether the treatment had been adequate: the applicant's state of health, the adequate character of the medical treatment he had received in detention and the feasibility of continued detention given the applicant's state of health.[168] Other, later cases have echoed this finding.[169] Intellectual disability and detention will be discussed in more detail below, in the section on vulnerability in detention, so for the purposes of this section it suffices to note that special vulnerability-based state obligations exist in this regard.

As discussed above, the Court appears to place persons with cognitive disabilities in a position analogous to that of children, mentioning both in the same breath and failing to make meaningful distinctions between them. This analogy is, in some ways, useful: like young age, intellectual disability may render those affected dependent on others – be it the state or others who provide them with support in exercising their legal capacity and going about their lives – to some extent, and may therefore attract abuse. The Court's case law captures various constellations in which persons living with intellectual disabilities have found it difficult to respond to or even protest against violations of their rights. In addition, persons with severe cognitive disabilities may experience a legal power imbalance because they do not enjoy legal capacity, although this can raise its own issues under the Convention.[170]

However, the Court is striking a balance here between protecting people with intellectual disabilities and empowering them, and as it does so it should be wary of the triple risk of paternalising and stigmatising the individuals concerned and of essentialising their needs and experiences. Focusing on the limitations of these individuals as a group negates the fact that the extent and iteration of cognitive disability varies between individuals, and that failing to consider the agency and abilities of affected individuals may result in discriminatory outcomes.[171] In particular, comparing intellectually disabled people to children negates all the ways in which they are unlike children – not least their potential ability to exercise at least some aspects of their legal capacity, but also for example their possible desire to engage in sexual relationships or start families. In addition, any approach to the vulnerability of disabled people should be aware of the danger of 'othering',

[168] *Ţicu v Romania* App no 24575/10, Judgment of 1 October 2013, para 59.
[169] *Drăgan v Romania* App no 65158/09, Judgment of 2 February 2016, para 91.
[170] *Shtukaturov v Russia* App no 44009/05, Judgment of 27 March 2008, para 90.
[171] See, for an example from the Art 8 context, *Kocherov and Sergeyeva v Russia* App no 16899/13, Judgment of 29 March 2016.

and seek to counter this risk by advancing inclusion and by incorporating an awareness of the social model of disability.[172]

ii. Mental Illness (Psychosocial Disability)

In addition to intellectual disability, the Court has recognised mental illness (also termed psychosocial disability) as a source of vulnerability. The relevant cases concern a range of different contexts, from detention and institutionalisation to military conscription and the expulsion of migrants.

When it comes to mental illness and detention, since *Kudła v Poland*, the Court has consistently acknowledged that detained persons suffering from a psychological condition or mental illness are more vulnerable than the average detainee.[173] Even where measures taken regarding mentally ill detainees serve to protect the safety of other detainees, this must not aggravate the mental state of the individual concerned.[174] Regarding individuals who are confined to psychiatric hospitals, the Court has held that the vulnerable position of these individuals, who experience feelings of inferiority and powerlessness, calls for 'increased vigilance' in reviewing whether the requirements of the ECHR have been met.[175] Measures taken concerning these individuals must be medically necessary.[176] The Court has also formulated special obligations for states regarding mentally ill military conscripts, finding for example that Italy had violated Article 3 by failing to provide a framework to detect and react to the vulnerability of conscripts with psychosocial disabilities in a timely manner.[177] In addition, as discussed below concerning vulnerability and migration, psychosocial disability is also a factor that influences the Court's determination of whether the expulsion or return of an applicant is compatible with Article 3, although it does not do so consistently.[178]

The vulnerability of mentally ill persons also has an effect under Article 3 when persons with a psychosocial disability are the victims of violence. For example, if a psychosocially disabled person makes allegations of rape, the authorities must pay particular attention, and pursue all available possibilities for establishing the facts.[179] In addition, when faced with victims whose psychological condition is vulnerable, for example due to trauma, the uncertainty brought

[172] As discussed in Domańska Monika, 'People with Disabilities as a Vulnerable Group: The Concept of Protection of the Rights of Vulnerable Groups', 4(23) *Białostockie Studia Prawnicze* (2018) 25–34.

[173] *Kudła v Poland* App no 30210/96, Judgment (GC) of 26 October 2000, Reports 2000-XI, para 99. *Renolde v France* App no 5608/05, Judgment of 16 October 2008, Reports 2008 (extracts), para 120, *Sławomir Musiał v Poland* App no 28300/06, Judgment of 20 January 2009, para 87.

[174] *G. v France* App no 27244/09, Judgment of 23 February 2012, para 44.

[175] *M.S. v Croatia (No. 2)* App no 75450/12, Judgment of 19 February 2015, para 98.

[176] Ibid, para 98.

[177] *Placì* (n 16), para 59.

[178] *Sufi and Elmi v the United Kingdom* App no 8319/07 and 11449/07, Judgment of 28 June 2011, paras 303 and 312.

[179] *M.B.* (n 36), para 57.

about by excessively long-lasting proceedings and the need to relive the events during repeated interrogations may particularly affect these victims in a manner incompatible with Article 3.[180]

One informative case here is *Bureš v Czech Republic*. The 22-year-old applicant, who suffered from a psychosocial disability, accidentally overdosed on prescribed medication and was picked up by police while partially naked in public. Police assumed that he was a drug addict, and he was transferred to a sobering-up centre, where he was restrained in a manner that caused nerve damage to his hands and later impacted his ability to exercise his profession as a musician. He was then involuntarily hospitalised for over two months. In considering the applicant's complaint under Article 3, the Court considered that he was 'a young man of a fragile build, suffering from a mental illness' who found himself in a particularly vulnerable position in the sobering-up centre while accidentally intoxicated.[181] The Court found a violation of Article 3 in the fact that the authorities – who, it held, knew or should have known about the applicant's mental illness – strapped him to a bed in a centre meant for treating persons under the influence of drugs without properly checking the necessity of such treatment.[182] This case not only highlights the fact that the necessity of a given treatment can make the difference between a violation of Article 3 and permissible treatment, but also that measures applied to mentally ill persons and their particular vulnerability must be considered and assessed in the individual case.

In other words, when making an arrest or otherwise depriving anyone of their liberty, the authorities must be sensitive to the possibility that the person concerned may suffer from a psychosocial disability, and respond accordingly. In one 2017 case, concerning a man with a serious psychiatric disorder who died while being arrested, the Court held that he was vulnerable because of his mental illness and that he 'clearly did not understand what the police officers were doing'.[183] Police lost control of the situation and, despite the applicant's double vulnerability as a detainee and a mentally ill person, he 'was literally trampled underfoot by the police'.[184]

The stigmatisation of persons with psychosocial disabilities affects perceptions of those affected. The Court's case law resolutely breaks from this stigma with its vulnerability reasoning, which assists it in evaluating cases from the perspectives of applicants. In particular, the Court has developed an awareness of the impaired ability of some mentally ill persons to complain about ill-treatment, and has also begun to deploy a nuanced understanding of the variety of psychosocial disabilities and the range of effects they may have, as well as requiring sensitivity to the

[180] *S.Z. v Bulgaria* App no 29263/12, Judgment of 3 March 2015, especially para 52.
[181] *Bureš v Czech Republic* App no 37679/08, Judgment of 18 October 2012, para 88.
[182] Ibid, paras 94 and 105.
[183] *Boukrourou and Others v France* App no 30059/15, Judgment of 16 November 2017, para 85.
[184] Ibid, para 86.

existence and exigencies of these conditions from State authorities.[185] In doing so, the Court is contributing to replacing damaging archetypes or ideas of mentally ill persons – those fuelling fear and discrimination – with new ones that funnel an understanding of their particular needs and humanity, as well as feelings of injustice, into heightened protection At the same time, the Court must be careful not to reinforce ideas about the powerlessness or otherness of the persons concerned. Like for the intellectually disabled persons discussed in the preceding section, the Court must strike a balance between protecting and empowering persons with psychosocial disabilities.

III. Vulnerability Due to State Control

The most commonly found source of vulnerability in the Court's Article 3 case law is that of persons under state control. This includes persons in detention, but also those who are institutionalised or otherwise under the sole authority of the state. When people are deprived of their liberty, they are vulnerable because they depend on the authorities both to guarantee their safety and to provide them with access to essential resources like food, hygienic conditions, and health care. As a result, the state has particular obligations under Article 3 to protect and provide for individuals in its custody. While all persons deprived of their liberty are vulnerable, some are particularly vulnerable, for example because they suffer from a psychosocial disability or are minors. In addition, the state often controls the flow of information and access to proof here, and so the Court applies a presumption of state responsibility when harm comes to those deprived of their liberty. The following sections will discuss some different situations in which the Court has concretised this.

A. Detainees

When it comes to detainees, which for present purposes includes persons under arrest, in pre-trial detention, or serving a prison sentence, the concept of vulnerability applies in two ways. First, they are vulnerable because they are under exclusive state authority. Secondly, some prisoners are more vulnerable than others due to specific factors, such as for example a disability or illness. The following will consider these two sources of vulnerability individually.

i. The Vulnerability of Detainees in General

Today, the vulnerability of detainees is the most commonly recognised form of vulnerability in the Court's Article 3 case law. The Court is guided here by the

[185] *Riviere v France* App no 33834/03, Judgment of 11 July 2006, para 63; *Dybeku v Albania* App no 41153/06, Judgment of 18 December 2007, para 41.

idea that all prisoners have the right to be detained under conditions compatible with human dignity, meaning that the manner and method in which measures are executed may not 'subject them to distress or hardship of an intensity exceeding the unavoidable level of suffering inherent in detention'.[186] Incarceration, the Court has held, does not lead to a loss of Convention rights, but – to the contrary – may lead to a need for increased human rights protection because prisoners are in a vulnerable situation and entirely under the authority of the state.[187] On this basis, the Court has established that the health and wellbeing of prisoners must, though taking into account the practical demands of imprisonment, be considered; in assessing whether the treatment or punishment inflicted in a given case is compatible with Article 3, the vulnerability of the detainee in question must be taken into account.[188]

The beginnings of this strain of case law can be traced back to the 1990 case of *Tomasi v France*. There, one Commission member argued that even slight injuries may meet the threshold of severity of Article 3 when 'the victim is deprived of his liberty, vulnerable and in a state of inferiority'.[189] The Commission itself, in that case, relied on a 'presumption of severity' in cases of ill-treatment in detention.[190] In 1992, in its judgment in the same case, the Court built on these arguments to create the basis of what would later become the modern-day reversal of the burden of proof that is now commonly applied to injuries suffered in detention. This presumption means that, because of the vulnerability of detainees, when a person enters the custody of the authorities in good health and leaves with injuries, the State carries the burden of proof for explaining those injuries.[191]

Since then, the Court has frequently used vulnerability to reverse the burden of proof where allegations of ill-treatment in detention were concerned, and accepted that all detainees are vulnerable by virtue of being under exclusive state authority.[192] This applies to alleged violence, but also to, for example, failure to provide adequate food or medical care to detainees.[193] Article 3 requires the state itself to provide for these basic needs, and so it cannot avoid its obligation by, for example, allowing detainees to purchase their own food.[194]

However, the Strasbourg jurisprudence regarding the vulnerability of detainees has multiple strands. Three of these are discernible in the *Aydin v Turkey*

[186] *Rezmiveş and Others v Romania* App no 61467/12 …, Judgment of 25 April 2017, para 72.

[187] Ibid, para 72.

[188] *Renolde* (n 173), para 120.

[189] *Tomasi v France* App no 12850/87, Report (Commission) of 11 December 1990, Dissenting Opinion of JC Soyer, para 30, translation from the original French by the author.

[190] *Tomasi* (n 189), paras 91 and 102.

[191] *Tomasi v France* App no 12850/87, Judgment of 27 August 1992, Series A241-A, para 110. This was later adapted to its current form in *Selmouni v France* App no 25803/94, Judgment (GC) of 28 July 1999, Reports 1999-V, para 87. See also *Sitnikov v Russia* App no 14769/09, Judgment of 2 May 2017, para 35.

[192] *Ribitsch v Austria* App no 18896/91, Judgment of 4 December 1995, Series A336, para 36; *Shlychov v Russia* App no 40852/05, Judgment of 9 February 2016, para 57.

[193] *Beketov v Ukraine* App no 44436/09, Judgment of 19 February, para 141; *Mammadov and Others v Azerbaijan* App no 35432/07, Judgment of 21 February 2019, para 120.

[194] *Mammadov and Others* (n 193), 142.

case discussed above, which concerned a 17-year-old girl who was exposed to severe ill-treatment in detention, including rape. In this case, the Court considered that rape by a state official 'must be considered to be an especially grave and abhorrent form of ill-treatment given the ease with which the offender can exploit the vulnerability and weakened resistance of his victim.'[195] This draws on a first strand of vulnerability reasoning in the detention context, concerning the control that the authorities have over detainees, which creates a special obligation to ensure their wellbeing.[196]

The second strand of case law relates to the fact that the Court noted the applicant's age and sex in *Aydin*.[197] Although the Court did not explicitly label this as a source of vulnerability at the time, this type of finding later evolved into the case law that recognises that certain detainees are more vulnerable than others because, for example, of their youth, disability, or some other factor. This is discussed in more detail in the next section.

Thirdly, the Court held that the applicant had suffered terrifying, disorienting, humiliating, painful, anguishing and bewildering experiences, which must have led her to experience an 'overall sense of vulnerability'.[198] The idea of vulnerability as an emotion evoked in response to victimisation will be touched upon again below. That idea has frequently been cited by the Court. In doing so, it examines whether detainees have been made to feel vulnerable, fearful or anxious.[199] Such feelings can lead the Court to find that an act of torture has taken place.[200]

In addition to these three strands, in later cases the Court has also inferred an individual's feeling of vulnerability from the circumstances of a case: in a 2016 judgment, it concluded from the fact that the applicant's son threw himself from a window during ill-treatment in police custody that his suffering had been particularly acute and had thus constituted torture.[201] In another case, the Court found that the very fact of an applicant's illegal detention while he was covertly removed from Italy by United States intelligence operatives meant that he must have been in a permanent state of anxiety and uncertainty about his future, and that he therefore found himself in a 'situation of total vulnerability'.[202]

In parallel, the idea that humiliation of someone who is under the control of the authorities can constitute ill-treatment has also gained traction. In *Bouyid v Belgium*, concerning two brothers who were slapped by police officers during questioning, the Court found that the officers concerned had flouted their duty

[195] *Aydin* (n 24), para 83.
[196] *Özen and Others v Turkey* App no 29272/08, Judgment of 23 February 2016, para 75.
[197] *Aydin* (n 24), para 84.
[198] Ibid.
[199] *Dikme v Turkey* App no 20869/92, Judgment of 11 July 2000, Reports 2000-VIII, para 91; *Doğanay v Turkey* App no 50125/99, Judgment of 21 February 2006, para 32.
[200] *Dikme* (n 199), para 91; *Hajrulahu v the Former Yugoslav Republic of Macedonia* App no 37537/07, Judgment of 29 October 2015, para 100.
[201] *Lykova v Russia* App no 68736/11, Judgment of 22 December 2015, para 126.
[202] *Nasr and Ghali v Italy* App no 44883/09, Judgment of 23 February 2016, para 286, translation by the author.

to protect these vulnerable individuals and had failed to respect their human dignity.[203] The Court held that even a single unpremeditated slap without serious or lasting effects can be humiliating to the victim.[204] In the context of detention, this is particularly acute because this type of behaviour 'highlights the superiority and inferiority which by definition characterise the relationship between [law-enforcement officers] and [detainees]'.[205] The Court also emphasised that, because victims know that such treatment is in breach of officers' moral, professional, and legal obligations, this may additionally 'arouse in them a feeling of arbitrary treatment, injustice and powerlessness'.[206]

The finding in *Bouyid* concerning the lack of respect for the applicants' dignity and their feelings of humiliation could have potentially far-reaching consequences given that many aspects of detention – and perhaps detention itself – may humiliate detainees. This is particularly true because, in *Bouyid*, the Court found it sufficient for detainees to be humiliated in their own eyes, and not necessarily those of others.[207] Admittedly, this case is not about the humiliations that necessarily accompany detention, but instead about the entirely unrelated infliction of police violence on persons under the complete control of the authorities. In this regard, the Court rightly noted the impermissibility of violence in the context of the resulting power imbalance, and did not allow arguments about the potentially provocative behaviour of the applicants to affect this.[208]

In other words, when persons are in state custody, the power imbalance that occurs affects whether a given treatment falls under Article 3. Still, not every humiliation will meet the Article 3 threshold. For example, in *Szafrański v Poland*, the Court examined a complaint about conditions of detention, including the authorities' failure to provide a proper separation between a toilet and the rest of a shared cell. The Court held that, although states are obligated to ensure the compatibility of detention with the human dignity of detainees, who are vulnerable given their detention, the cumulative effect of the conditions of detention in this case did not reach the requisite level of distress and hardship necessary for a violation of Article 3.[209] However, the Court did find a violation of the lower-threshold Article 8, noting that the European Committee for the Prevention of Torture (CPT) requires a proper separation of toilets and that the domestic authorities had violated their positive obligation to ensure a minimum level of privacy.[210]

[203] *Bouyid* (n 89), paras 107–11.
[204] Ibid, paras 105–06.
[205] Ibid.
[206] Ibid, para 106.
[207] Ibid, para 87.
[208] Ibid, para 108.
[209] *Szafrański v Poland* App no 17249/12, Judgment of 15 December 2015, paras 22 and 27–28.
[210] Ibid, para 40.

ii. Particularly Vulnerable Detainees

Early on in its vulnerability case law concerning detainees, the Court also began to take into consideration the special vulnerability of particular applicants. In other words, while all detainees are vulnerable by virtue of being under the sole control of the state, the Court has also identified detainees who, by virtue of some other trait, are more vulnerable than the average detainee. For example, it has found that a Chinese detainee awaiting deportation in the United Kingdom was particularly vulnerable due to his 'position as a foreigner in the prison'.[211] More commonly, detainees of young or advanced age have been qualified as particularly vulnerable, with the Court tailoring the level of suffering that detained individuals may be expected to bear to the special psychology of children[212] and likewise finding that advanced age and the medical issues that accompany it can make an individual particularly vulnerable.[213] The vulnerability of minor detainees has been covered above in section II.A.iv.

The following will focus on four main sources of particular vulnerability in detention: mental health problems (ie psychosocial disabilities) and intellectual disabilities, physical disabilities or illnesses, the risk of abuse by other detainees and the risk of abuse by the prison authorities. A short section noting some peculiarities of the Court's approach to strip-searches will follow.

a. Psychosocial or Cognitive Disabilities and Detention

As discussed above, the Court has held that states have special obligations regarding persons who suffer from intellectual disabilities and mental illness. In addition, these sources of vulnerability require special attention in the detention context, where they are not necessarily distinguished from each other. These cases can concern detention in the law-enforcement context, but also include confinement in psychiatric hospitals, which typically places individuals in a 'position of inferiority and powerlessness' much like detention.[214]

When it comes to the issue of whether Article 3 allows for the detention of someone with a psychosocial or cognitive disability at all, the Court considers three criteria. These include the individual's medical condition, the adequacy of the medical care and assistance provided in detention, and the advisability of maintaining them in detention in view of their state of health.[215] In applying these three criteria, the Court has required increased vigilance from the authorities in reviewing the permissibility of detention given '[t]he feeling of inferiority and powerlessness which is typical of persons who suffer from a mental disorder'.[216]

[211] *Zhu v United Kingdom* App no 36790/97, Decision of 12 September 2000.
[212] *Bati and Others* (n 49), para 122; *Yazgül Yilmaz* (n 47), para 42.
[213] *Stoyan Mitev* (n 143), para 73; *Giorgini* (n 144), paras 52 and 57 (concerning the detention of a 77-year-old woman).
[214] *M.S. (No 2)* (n 175), para 98.
[215] *Aswat v United Kingdom* App no 17299/12, Judgment of 16 April 2013, para 50.
[216] Ibid.

When deciding to detain a person with psychosocial or cognitive disabilities, states must take into account that these detainees are particularly vulnerable because they may experience particular feelings of distress, fear, and anguish in detention.[217] The authorities must 'demonstrate special care in guaranteeing such conditions as correspond to the person's individual needs resulting from his disability'.[218] The vulnerability of mentally unstable applicants means that the authorities must use 'special precautions against unnecessarily affecting their psychological state' when carrying out any actions in their respect, for example a search of their cell.[219] Furthermore, the Court has regard for the fact that individuals suffering from a cognitive disability or illness may be less able to formulate a coherent complaint against their ill-treatment.[220]

In some cases, the Court has found that the failure to provide a specific service tailored to the needs of an applicant may violate Article 3. In 2019, in *Rooman v Belgium*, it examined an application from a severely mentally ill applicant who was subjected to compulsory confinement in the French-speaking part of Belgium, but who exclusively spoke German. It found that the failure to provide the applicant with access to a German-speaking psychologist had violated the state's obligation of means under Article 3 because, in this case, it meant that necessary treatment was not adequately available.[221] Similarly, in a case concerning a detainee serving a life sentence and suffering from schizophrenia and paranoid delusions, the Court held, given his vulnerability, that the failure to place him in an facility providing suitable psychiatric services had exposed the applicant to a risk to his health and must have caused him stress and anxiety.[222] In other words, the failure to transfer this seriously mentally ill prisoner to a suitable facility had violated Article 3.

In addition, as noted in a preceding section, when it comes to criminal proceedings against individuals with cognitive disabilities, the state's procedural obligations under Article 3 are particularly strict.[223]

As concerns the imposition of unwanted medical treatment on patients with psychosocial disabilities, the Court considers the established principles of medicine to be decisive. Accordingly, it has held that 'it is for the medical authorities to decide, on the basis of the recognized rules of medical science, on the therapeutic methods to be used, if necessary by force, to preserve the physical and mental health of patients who are entirely incapable of deciding for themselves and for whom they are therefore responsible'.[224] At the same time, the Court requires

[217] See, for some of the earlier examples of this case law, *Kudła* (n 173), para 99; *Keenan v United Kingdom* App no 27229/95, Judgment of 3 April 2001, Reports 2001-III, paras 110–11; *Pantea v Romania* App no 33343/96, Judgment of 3 June 2003, Reports 2003-VI (extracts), para 192; *Slimani v France* App no 57671/00, Judgment of 27 July 2004, Reports 2004-IX (extracts), para 28.

[218] *Z.H.* (n 167), paras 7, 10 and 29.

[219] *Ciorap v Republic of Moldova (No 5)* App no 7232/07, Judgment of 15 March 2016, para 48.

[220] *Drăgan* (n 169), para 91; *Stepanian v Romania* App no 60103/11, Judgment of 14 June 2016, paras 64 and 73.

[221] *Rooman v Belgium* App no 18052/11, Judgment (GC) of 31 January 2019, paras 153–59.

[222] *Gömi v Turkey* App no 38704/11, Judgment of 19 February 2019, para 87.

[223] *W. v Slovenia* (n 165), para 70.

[224] *M.S. (No 2)* (n 175), para 98.

safeguards for such measures: Article 3 permits non-consensual measures against 'patients with psychological or intellectual disabilities' only when these measures are a means of last resort, and only to prevent imminent harm to the person concerned or to others.[225]

The special obligations that result from the vulnerability of detainees also apply if the detainee concerned is considered to be particularly dangerous.[226] In the 2015 *Bamouhammad v Belgium* judgment, for example, the Court held that the respondent state had violated Article 3 because the applicant, who was suffering from prison psychosis, had been continually transferred between prisons, which had exacerbated his condition. Even though the authorities had treated the applicant, who was considered dangerous, differently from ordinary detainees, they had failed to take his vulnerability sufficiently into account and to envisage his situation from a humanitarian perspective.[227] In particular, the Court found that the modalities of the applicant's detention, namely his repeated transfers between prisons, delays in providing medical treatment, and the refusal to consider a different form of executing his sentence, could have provoked distress exceeding the threshold of Article 3.[228]

b. Physical Disabilities or Illnesses and Detention

Regarding the detention of persons with a physical disability or illness, obligations similar to those described in the preceding section apply. In order to determine whether the conditions of detention and the medical treatment provided are compatible with Article 3, the Court considers applicants' vulnerability and (in)capacity to complain about their treatment. It has found that these situations require 'special care in guaranteeing conditions that correspond to their special needs'.[229] States must also prove that applicants alleging the contrary have received comprehensive and adequate medical care.[230] They are also under an obligation to provide disabled prisoners with 'organised assistance' capable of ensuring respect for their human dignity.[231]

The Strasbourg judges use the same three criteria as described in the preceding section to determine whether an ill or disabled detainee's treatment meets the threshold required for a violation of Article 3. These are the applicant's state of health or medical condition, the adequate character of the medical treatment

[225] Ibid, para 104.
[226] *Bamouhammad v Belgium* App no 47687/13, Judgment of 17 November 2015, paras 125–32.
[227] Ibid, paras 123, 148.
[228] Ibid, para 155.
[229] *Mircea Dumitrescu v Romania* App no 14609/10, Judgment of 30 July 2013, para 59.
[230] *Savinov v Ukraine* App no 5212/13, Judgment of 22 October 2015, para 50; *Barsukov v Russia* App no 51252/09, Judgment of 6 June 2017, para 32.
[231] *Semikhvostov v Russia* App no 2689/12, Judgment of 6 February 2014, para 84.

received in detention, and the feasibility of continued detention given the applicant's health.[232]

The Court has unequivocally held that dependency on cellmates for medical treatment and assistance creates feelings of vulnerability and humiliation in prisoners forced to avail themselves of such help. This places them in a position of inferiority vis-à-vis other prisoners, and states cannot absolve themselves of their obligations towards ill or disabled prisoners by shifting responsibility for their care to their cellmates.[233] In 2015, the Court summarised its previous findings on this matter, holding that the assistance provided by co-detainees, even voluntarily, does not mean that the special needs of a dependent applicant have been satisfied, and so neither have the state's obligations.[234]

The obligation to take the vulnerability of detainees into account begins at the time of their arrest. For example, in 2013, the Court considered the case of a man who died from the combination of the stress of being arrested and a pre-existing cardiovascular affliction. While recognising the possibility of state responsibility, however, the Court also held that, in order to find the state responsible for the individual's death, the authorities must have reasonably been able to be aware of his vulnerability.[235] It has continued this line of reasoning in later cases.[236]

To date, the Court has taken into consideration the vulnerability of detainees suffering from a range of conditions, disabilities, and illnesses. To name but a few examples, regarding a detainee who suffered from unstable type-II diabetes, chronic pancreatic inflammation and stomach ulcers, the Court found that the authorities had to balance the risks posed by incarceration with particular diligence, including by regularly reviewing the compatibility of his health with detention.[237] In *Taïs v France*, the Court rejected the government's submission that the applicants' son, who was found dead in his cell, had been in good health when detained, noting that the fragile and HIV-positive young man had been incarcerated while drunk and in 'a worrying physical and moral state'.[238] In *Grzywaczewski v Poland*, the Court held that the cumulative effects of detention in an overcrowded space under inadequate living conditions had violated Article 3. The applicant in that case, who suffered from diabetes, prostate cancer, and mild cardiac disorders, was characterised as 'in a vulnerable position vis-à-vis other prisoners', which in this specific context seems to mean not that he risked violence, but that he suffered

[232] *Ţicu* (n 168), para 59; *Babar Ahmad and Others v United Kingdom* App nos 24027/07 …, Judgment of 10 April 2012, para 215.

[233] *Kaprykowski v Poland* App no 23052/05, Judgment of 3 February 2009, para 74; *Grimailovs v Latvia* App no 6087/03, Judgment of 25 June 2013, paras 151 and 153; *Semikhvostov* (n 231), para 84.

[234] *Helhal v France* App no 10401/12, Judgment of 19 February 2015, para 62, translated from the original French by the author.

[235] *Yüksel v Turkey* App no 49756/09, Decision of 1 October 2013, para 71.

[236] *Vinogradov v Russia* App no 27122/10, Judgment of 7 March 2017, para 42.

[237] *Andrzej Wierzbicki v Poland* App no 48/03, Judgment of 19 January 2010, para 58.

[238] *Taïs v France* App no 39922/03, Judgment of 1 June 2006, para 89, translation by the author.

more acutely under the circumstances of detention.[239] In another case, *Wenner v Austria*, the Court found that the state had violated Article 3 by refusing to provide the applicant, a life-long heroin addict, with drug substitution therapy in detention.[240]

In the same vein, the Court has held that disability makes prisoners 'more vulnerable to the hardships of detention'.[241] The Court bases these judgments on the physical and mental effect of a lack of adequate treatment and care. Inadequate medical treatment causes detainees to suffer distress exceeding the inevitable level of suffering inherent in detention.[242] In 2017, regarding a terminally ill detainee who was suffering the effects of heavy medication in difficult prison conditions, the Court held that, in this context, any lack of diligence by the authorities exacerbated his vulnerability, making it impossible for him to retain his dignity.[243]

This jurisprudence is not without its inconsistencies, however. In 2012, the Court found regarding the detention of an individual with amputated forearms that, though he was vulnerable, the absence of any 'incident or positive intention to humiliate or debase the applicant' meant that Article 3 had not been violated.[244] This finding is a curious one, given that the element of intent is not a requirement for finding that Article 3, in its inhuman and degrading treatment or punishment limbs, has been violated. The Court corrected itself in 2015, finding that the fact that a wheelchair-bound detainee had to depend on his cellmates in order to access the showers meant that Article 3 had been violated despite the absence 'of elements that lead one to think that the authorities were acting with the intent to humiliate or degrade the applicant'.[245]

However, that was not the end of this inconsistency. The question of intent was picked up again in *Ostrowski v Poland*, concerning a detainee with a hearing impairment who sought to obtain a second hearing aid from the prison authorities.[246] Here, the Court considered the question of intent as part of determining whether adequate medical treatment had been provided. The Court held that there was no evidence that the applicant had been humiliated or ill-treated by other detainees, and no evidence of an 'incident or positive intention to humiliate or debase the applicant on the part of the State authorities', so that even though the applicant was more vulnerable to the hardships of detention given his special needs, the circumstances of the case had not violated Article 3.[247]

[239] *Grzywaczewski v Poland* App no 18364/06, Judgment of 31 May 2012, paras 5 and 102.
[240] *Wenner v Austria* App no 62303/13, Judgment of 1 September 2016, paras 38 and 58.
[241] *Zarzycki v Poland* App no 15351/03, Judgment of 12 March 2013, para 125.
[242] *Raffray Taddei v France* App no 36435/07, Judgment of 21 December 2010, para 63.
[243] *Dorneau v Romania* App no 55089/13, Judgment of 28 November 2017, para 99.
[244] *Zarzycki* (n 241), para 125.
[245] *Helhal* (n 234), para 63, translation by the author.
[246] *Ostrowski v Poland* App no 26945/07, Decision of 1 September 2015, para 76.
[247] Ibid, paras 75–77.

Ostrowski conflicts with other cases where the Court has found that humiliation in one's own eyes can violate Article 3.[248] In this context, humiliation primarily comes into play concerning dependency on cellmates, and the Court rather consistently finds a violation of Article 3 where disabled inmates' welfare is left up to other detainees. For example, in 2016, regarding a blind applicant, the Court held that Article 3 was violated 'where prison staff felt that they had been relieved of their duty to provide security and care to more vulnerable detainees by making their cellmates responsible for providing them with daily assistance or, if necessary, with first aid'.[249] In other words, the human dignity of vulnerable detainees means that they must be provided with organised assistance.[250]

The Court's case law in this context continues to evolve. In a 2016 decision, concerning a detainee with partially reduced hearing, the Court departed from the intent requirement of *Ostrowski*, albeit to a similar result.[251] Here the Court found that the applicant had insufficiently substantiated her claims of exclusion and ridicule by other inmates. Therefore, it held that it could not find that 'the delay in providing her with a hearing aid at the public's expense could be perceived as humiliating or debasing treatment', even though '[a] prisoner with special needs is more vulnerable to the hardships of detention in view of his or her health problems, and the applicant must have felt excluded due to her hearing difficulties.'[252]

In short, failure to provide assistance to an ill or physically disabled detainee is incompatible with Article 3 if one of three alternative conditions is fulfilled: either the detainee in question becomes dependent on the assistance of other prisoners, or the detainee, despite functioning normally, but can prove that the authorities had the intent to humiliate them, or the detainee can prove that they were ridiculed by other detainees on account of their disability. A fourth alternative condition, that the detainee was humiliated in their own eyes, does not yet seem to have trickled down to these particular types of cases.

Not only the failure to take a particular inmate's illness into account, but also the corralling together of ill inmates and the resulting exposure to further diseases has been found by the Court to constitute a violation of Article 3. In 2016, regarding an inmate who suffered from hepatitis, tuberculosis, and HIV, the Court held that the fact that he shared an overcrowded ward in close quarters with many 'sick and occasionally infected inmates' had constituted degrading treatment.[253] In early 2021, the Court made a similar finding based on this case law – although without making any explicit reference to vulnerability – concerning the Covid-19 pandemic.[254]

[248] *Bouyid* (n 89), para 105; *Svinarenko and Slyadnev v Russia* App nos 32541/08 and 43441/08, Judgment (GC) of 17 July 2014, Reports 2014 (extracts), para 115.
[249] *Butrin v Russia* App no 16179/14, Judgment of 22 March 2016, para 63.
[250] Ibid.
[251] *Stefaniak v Poland* App no 56941/11, Decision of 19 April 2016, para 38.
[252] Ibid, para 40.
[253] *Vidish v Russia* App no 53120/08, Judgment of 15 March 2016, para 29.
[254] *Feilazoo v Malta* App no 6865/19, Judgment of 11 March 2021, para 92.

Disabled inmates' vulnerability not only influences the Court's determination of whether their detention causes them to suffer in a manner incompatible with Article 3. Vulnerability reasoning has also been used to find that the domestic authorities were under an obligation to transfer a disabled applicant to another correctional facility.[255] Furthermore, it reverses the burden of proof in certain cases: for example, where an applicant alleges that the authorities have not provided prescribed medications, the fact that the detainee concerned is vulnerable and in the control of the authorities means that the state must prove that the medications were administered.[256]

How far can the Court go in ordering the state to take specific medical measures? One case in which the Court made a very specific order to the state – and did so, remarkably, at the stage of interim protection – was *G. v Russia*, which concerned a detainee who had been diagnosed with rectal cancer, among other conditions.[257] Suffering from a prolapsed colon and in a great degree of pain, the applicant obtained a consultation with two external specialist doctors who recommended immediate surgery, warning that failure to operate could result in complications or death. A prison doctor found, however, that surgery was not immediately necessary, and prescribed absorbent underwear, which the prison authorities did not provide. The applicant spent the following year unable to control his defecation and being transferred in and out of the prison hospital, showing signs of inflammation, aggravation of a heart condition, and the potential spreading of his cancer. The Court, faced with this situation, ordered interim protection under rule 39 of the Rules of Court and indicated to the government that the applicant should be allowed to have colorectal surgery and two diagnostic procedures on his liver.[258] The government complied with the order almost immediately. In its judgment, the Court described the domestic authorities' approach to the matter as 'unacceptable', and found two violations of Article 3, one due to the lack of medical treatment and the other due to the conditions of detention, which did not afford the applicant any privacy.

This finding is, given the Court's previous case law as summarised above, unsurprising. What is surprising about the case, however, is that the Court – which does not itself have any medical expertise – ordered specific medical procedures and diagnostic tests. In cases such as this one, where the Court's judgment ultimately came almost nine years after the corresponding application had been made before it, such a specific order of medical procedures may be the only way to minimise applicants' suffering and to guarantee that detainees can access the treatment due to them under Article 3 ECHR before their condition has irreparably worsened – in other words, to guarantee effective protection of individual rights.

[255] *Neshkov and Others v Bulgaria* App nos 36925/10 …, Judgment of 27 January 2015, para 292.
[256] *Kolesnikovich v Russia* App no 44694/13, Judgment of 22 March 2016, para 74.
[257] *G. v Russia* App no 42526/07, Judgment of 21 June 2016, paras 4 and 8.
[258] Ibid, paras 4, 53; see also r 39 (interim measures) of the Rules of the ECtHR of 1 January 2020.

However, it must be noted that, though rule 39 protection helped the applicant in *G. v Russia* to obtain speedy access to medical care, this approach is effective only if states comply with the Court's interim protection orders. This has not always been the case. In one case, the Court ordered rule 39 protection for an applicant with cervical cancer who was being denied necessary radiation treatment in a Russian prison. Here, the authorities apparently failed to comply with the interim measures order, and the applicant died in detention before the case was decided.[259] There are more such examples, even if looking only at Russia during a one-year period. One case concerned an applicant who died of prostate cancer in detention despite a rule 39 order to transfer him to a specialist hospital.[260] Another case concerned an applicant suffering from a number of conditions, including HIV/AIDS, tuberculosis and hepatitis C, who died after the authorities failed to comply with the Court's interim protection order to conduct an independent medical examination.[261] The same thing occurred in another case, concerning a detainee suffering from metastatic kidney cancer; the prison authorities did not consider the possibility of radiation therapy and did not comply with the rule 39 order to conduct an independent medical examination, and he died before the case ever reached the judgment phase.[262]

In this context, in addition to vulnerability language, the Court has also referred to the 'precariousness' of a detainee's health or the resulting 'defencelessness'. It has used 'precariousness' language, for example, concerning a Romanian man who, after an altercation with the mayor of his town, was handcuffed to a tree outside the village police station. The Court took into account that the applicant, who had been left handcuffed outdoors on a cold and wet day, suffered from a 'precarious state of health'; accordingly, it found that he had suffered inhuman and degrading treatment.[263] The idea of 'defencelessness' was used in a case against Russia, where armed men had dragged a physically disabled man out of his home in the middle of a cold night in only an undergarment.[264] While these terms – precariousness and defencelessness – are rarely used by the Court, it appears that they are used as synonyms of vulnerability in this context.

c. Risk of Abuse by Other Detainees

A further cause of vulnerability in detention stems from traits or behaviours that make detainees more prone to abuse by other inmates. This includes individuals who have cooperated with the authorities as informants,[265] who are less

[259] *Semenova v Russia* App no 11788/16, Judgment of 3 October 2017, para 4.

[260] *Kondrulin v Russia* App no 12987/15, Judgment of 20 September 2016, paras 21 and 23–24.

[261] *Maylenskiy v Russia* App no 12646/15, Judgment of 4 October 2016, paras 15, 19 and 22.

[262] *Klimov v Russia* App no 54436/14, Judgment of 4 October 2016, paras 22–31.

[263] *Archip v Romania* App no 49608/08, Judgment of 27 September 2011, paras 57–59.

[264] *Aliyeva v Russia* App no 1901/05, Judgment of 18 February 2010, para 87.

[265] *J.L. v Latvia* App no 23893/06, Judgment of 17 April 2012, para 87; *D.F. v Latvia* App no 11160/07, Judgment of 29 October 2013, para 92.

able than average to control their emotions,[266] who identify as members of the LGBTQI community,[267] or who are related to prison guards or who have previously worked as police officers and private security guards,[268] along with those who have committed crimes of a sexual nature against children.[269] The Court has also established vulnerability based on specific contexts, for example of Serbs who had been convicted of war crimes against Bosniacs and who were kept in a largely Bosniac prison.[270] In addition, states have an obligation to protect detainees from fellow inmates with an increased propensity to violence, for example psychopathic cellmates.[271]

The Court has held in this regard that states are under an obligation to 'take all steps reasonably expected to prevent real and immediate risks to prisoners' physical integrity, of which the authorities had or ought to have had knowledge'.[272] This means keeping at-risk individuals in separate cells.[273] However, it is not sufficient to comply with this obligation by moving vulnerable prisoners from cell to cell nearly constantly, and 'any transfers of vulnerable prisoners should form part of a carefully designed strategy for dealing with inter-prisoner violence'.[274]

Notably, it is not decisive whether at-risk prisoners have brought about the risk of abuse by their own actions. This is consistent with the Court's case law under Article 3 writ large, given that the protection afforded by an absolute prohibition cannot be 'lost' by victims.[275] For example, in the case of a young detainee with no experience of the criminal justice system who suffered 'systematic abuse' by other prisoners, the Court held that his distress in detention may have caused his provocative behaviour. The authorities should have known that this would render the applicant more vulnerable to abuse, and should have reacted at least to his visible injuries.[276]

However, conflicts with other inmates must reach a certain seriousness and likelihood in order to render a detainee vulnerable. In one case against Latvia, the Court held that an applicant, who alleged that he had cooperated with law enforcement and was therefore at risk of abuse by other inmates, could not be

[266] *Premininy v Russia* App no 44973/04, Judgment of 10 February 2011, paras 73 and 86.

[267] *Korpachyova-Hofbauer v Bulgaria* App no 56668/12, Decision of 1 September 2015, para 35, citing *Stasi v France* App no 25001/07, Judgment of 20 October 2011, para 91.

[268] *Korpachyova-Hofbauer* (n 267), para 35, citing *Aleksejeva v Latvia* App no 21780/07, Judgment of 3 July 2012, para 34; *Totolici v Romania* App no 26576/10, Judgment of 14 January 2014, paras 6, 48–49; *Starovoitovs v Latvia* App no 27343/05, Decision of 27 November 2012, paras 35–38; *Belyayev v Russia* App no 43852/12, Judgment of 15 January 2019, para 38.

[269] *Korpachyova-Hofbauer* (n 267), para 35, citing *M.C.* (n 52), para 90.

[270] *Rodić and Others v Bosnia and Herzegovina* App no 22893/05, Judgment of 27 May 2008, paras 69–70.

[271] *Korpachyova-Hofbauer* (n 267), para 35.

[272] *D.F.* (n 265), para 84.

[273] *Belyayev* (n 268), para 38.

[274] Ibid, paras 86–87 and 92.

[275] Compare, for example, *V. v United Kingdom* (n 91), para 69.

[276] *Premininy* (n 266), paras 73, 81 and 86.

considered vulnerable given that he had also – contradictorily – submitted that he had *not* cooperated with the authorities.[277] The Court thus stopped short of rendering vulnerability contingent on a detainee's reputation or alleged reputation within an institution.

In the same case, the Court also held that the applicant's mental health issues did not create a sufficient potential for conflict with other inmates, given that his mental health had been stable for a decade.[278] In other words, the Court held, mental illness per se does not place inmates at risk of violence from others. This stands in contrast to the Court's broad-brush approach to vulnerability and mental illness in other cases, and its finding that persons who suffer from mental illness are less likely and able to complain of ill-treatment.

This indicates a perception that detainees must be cowed and defenceless before being considered vulnerable to violence in detention. This perception emerges even more clearly elsewhere, for example in the separate opinion of Judge Kūris in the *Kardišauskas* case. He emphasised the applicant's record of poor behaviour in prison and argued that 'the applicant could hardly be considered a genuinely vulnerable type of prisoner'.[279] This approach is exceedingly problematic. Making vulnerability conditional on the 'innocence' or likeability of an applicant is not only extremely subjective, but it also ignores a fundamental tenet of human rights law, namely that human dignity and the human rights protection to which it entitles its bearers are universal and characteristic of all human individuals. In addition, the protection of Article 3 cannot be waived or lost. An objective risk of abuse in prison should – and, in the Court's case law, usually does – entitle an individual to the protection associated with this vulnerability, independently of the person's likability, innocence, or responsibility for creating the risk of abuse.

One other case – albeit decided under another provision of the Convention, the right to liberty and security under Article 5 ECHR – bears mentioning in the context of protecting detainees from violence. In 2016, the Court examined an application against Hungary concerning the detention of an asylum-seeker who claimed to have fled his home state, Iran, because he faced prosecution and potentially severe penalties there due to his 'homosexuality'.[280] In Hungary, the applicant was placed in detention among other asylum-seekers. The Court held that, in detaining asylum-seekers who claim to belong to a vulnerable group in their home state, the authorities 'should exercise particular care in order to avoid situations which may reproduce the plight that forced these persons to flee in the first place'.[281] In other words, states must avoid revictimising or further exposing these individuals to ill-treatment. In the case concerned, the authorities had

[277] *Kostjučenkovs v Latvia* App no 19826/04, Decision of 8 March 2011, para 49.

[278] Ibid.

[279] *Kardišauskas v Lithuania* App no 62304/12, Judgment of 7 July 2015, Concurring Opinion of Judge Kūris, para 3.

[280] *O.M. v Hungary* App no 9912/15, Judgment of 5 July 2016, para 8.

[281] Ibid, para 53.

failed in this duty by not considering whether LGBTQI people like the applicant 'were safe or unsafe in custody among other detained persons, many of whom had come from countries with widespread cultural or religious prejudice against such persons'.[282] This reasoning complements the developments under Article 3 regarding the detention of those who are vulnerable to abuse or ill-treatment from co-detainees, and as indicated previously in this chapter the idea of preventing revictimisation is one that seems to be developing – albeit perhaps less explicitly – also under the Court's Article 3 case law.[283]

d. Risk of Abuse by Persons in Positions of Authority

The risk of abuse in detention does not only stem, of course, from other inmates, but can come from prison employees and other persons in positions of authority.

When it comes to how vulnerable to abuse detainees feel, the Court has found that feelings of vulnerability can be particularly acute for those detained alone.[284] Isolation in detention can exacerbate physical and mental pain or suffering,[285] and detainees' mental state can deteriorate if they are exposed to long stretches of isolation, which can cause chronic stress and emotional and social isolation that, in turn, render the individual concerned particularly vulnerable.[286] Due to this vulnerability, additional pressure on them – for example, refusing to allow one detainee under such circumstances to change his urine-soaked clothes – may violate Article 3.[287] However, the mere fact of isolation does not always suffice to consider an applicant vulnerable: the Court has also rejected the argument of vulnerability made by an applicant who showed no signs of 'typical symptoms'.[288]

In addition to this psychological element, i.e. concerning the feeling of vulnerability, the Court considers that the risk of abuse and ill-treatment in detention is particularly acute where applicants are detained alone, illegally and in secret.[289] In *Dikme v Turkey*, the Court held that the applicant – who had been detained for 16 days without access to a lawyer, doctor, relatives or friends, or a court – 'was left entirely vulnerable … to the reprehensible conduct of his custodians and the police officers responsible for questioning him, and, even more seriously, to acts of physical torture'.[290] The Court went on to find that the applicant had been beaten,

[282] Ibid.
[283] *M.G.C.* (n 55), paras 70–75.
[284] *Stepuleac v Republic of Moldova* App no 8207/06, Judgment of 6 November 2007, para 65.
[285] *Dikme* (n 199), para 91.
[286] *Öcalan v Turkey (No 2)* App no 24069/03, 197/04, 6201/06 and 10464/07, Judgment of 18 March 2014, para 122; *Cirino and Renne v Italy* App no 2539/13 and 4705/13, Judgment of 26 October 2017, para 80.
[287] *Burlya and Others v Ukraine* App no 3289/10, Judgment of 6 November 2018, para 83.
[288] *Hansen v Norway* App no 48852/17, Judgment of 29 May 2018, para 151.
[289] *Otamendi Egiguren v Spain* App no 47303/08, Judgment of 16 October 2012, para 41; *Dikme* (n 199), paras 82 and 91; *Lyapin v Russia* App no 46956/09, Judgment of 24 July 2014, para 119.
[290] *Dikme* (n 199), para 82.

and that the physical and mental pain and suffering that he had experienced was 'likely to arouse in him feelings of fear, anxiety and vulnerability likely to humiliate and debase him and break his resistance and will'.[291]

Given the Court's understanding of vulnerability in detention as dependence-based, it is unsurprising that it considers isolated, secret, or incommunicado detention, which entails the removal of all safeguards against ill-treatment, to make individuals more vulnerable.[292] Persons accused of a crime are exposed to a legal power imbalance,[293] and cutting them off from the resources and sources of resilience that the world outside the prison has to offer intensifies that imbalance. The less able prisoners are to communicate with the outside world and to complain about their treatment, the more vulnerable they are to abuse by persons in a position of authority.[294] This especially concerns limitations on access to lawyers, doctors, and family members who may draw attention to the detained person's plight, but it depends on the circumstances of each case, and for example may also require access to an interpreter.[295]

The detention period in question must not be particularly long in order for this case law to apply. In 2016, regarding an applicant who was held in incommunicado detention for six hours, the Court found that 'such detention, applied in violation of all laws and in the absence of all procedural guarantees, cannot but increase the vulnerability of the applicant and constitute a factor that favours ill-treatment'.[296]

The type of crime in question may also make a difference. Certain types of crimes may make detainees more vulnerable to violence by law-enforcement officers. In one case, for example, an applicant was considered particularly vulnerable in this regard because he was being interrogated in connection with the murder of a police driver. Here, the Court insinuated that the applicant's account of the violence that he had suffered was particularly believable because the officers in question may have been enraged by the murder of one of their own.[297] There is little analogous case law about identities that make detainees more vulnerable, but one example could be where a detainee identifies or is perceived as 'a homosexual', and is therefore subjected to violence.[298]

e. Strip-Searching and 'Helplessness'

A curiosity of the Court's approach to the particular vulnerability of certain detainees concerns strip-searches. In this regard, the Court has established – in

[291] Ibid, para 91.
[292] *Leonid Petrov v Russia* App no 52783/08, Judgment of 11 October 2016, paras 54 and 65; *L.G. v Belgium* App no 38759/14, Judgment of 18 September 2018, para 99.
[293] *Kovalchuk v Ukraine* App no 21958/05, Judgment of 4 November 2010, paras 60–61.
[294] *Beortegui Martinez v Spain* App no 36286/14, Judgment of 31 May 2016, para 46.
[295] *Razzakov v Russia* App no 57519/09, Judgment of 2 February 2015, para 54.
[296] *Oleynik v Russia* App no 23559/07, Judgment of 21 June 2016, para 58, translation by the author.
[297] *Sergey Ryabov v Russia* App no 2674/07, Judgment of 17 July 2018, not reported, para 41.
[298] *Zontul v Greece* App no 12294/07, Judgment of 17 January 2012, para 88.

case law not related to vulnerability – that systematic full-body strip-searching violates Article 3 unless justified on specific security-related grounds.[299] The same goes for inappropriately conducted, insulting, or unhygienic searches, including searches conducted by a person of the opposite sex.[300]

Mentioning this jurisprudence is relevant here because of a further condition that is occasionally imposed. That strand of judgments concerns strip-searches that comply with the requirements outlined above. In order for the suffering evoked by such a search to surpass the threshold of Article 3, applicants must not only be in a vulnerable position – as they will always be while in detention – but they must also be 'in a particularly helpless situation'.[301]

The helplessness requirement stems from a judgment concerning the strip-searching of a handcuffed and allegedly blindfolded detainee. There, the Court found that the applicant's helplessness rendered the strip-search in question degrading.[302] The Court has taken that finding and turned it into an additional requirement on strip searches. Whether helplessness and particular vulnerability are synonymous has, however, not been made clear, although it would certainly seem that the two concepts are related. Either way, the fact that a detainee is physically restrained is an additional factor to be considered here, arguably as a source of particular vulnerability, and the Court has 'condemned the practice of gratuitously imposing potentially debasing measures' on these vulnerable applicants.[303]

Two cases from 2018 further underscore the close connection between helplessness and vulnerability. In *Abu Zubaydah v Lithuania* and *Al Nashiri v Romania*, the Court dealt with applications from persons detained by the CIA.[304] At the time, it was the CIA's stated policy that 'captured terrorists' could be exposed to 'a wide range of legally sanctioned techniques … designed to psychologically "dislocate" the detainee, maximize his feeling of vulnerability and helplessness, and reduce or eliminate his will to resist'.[305] The measures applied included, as a matter of standard procedure, the blindfolding and hooding of detainees, the removal of their hair upon arrival in detention, leg shackling, incommunicado and solitary confinement, and exposure to continuous loud noise and light. These cases indicate that vulnerability and helplessness, which Article 3 protects against and which the CIA had sought to maximise, are the core business of detainees' Article 3 rights.

[299] *Van der Ven v Netherlands* App no 50901/99, Judgment of 4 February 2003, Reports 2003-II, paras 58–63; *Lorsé and Others v Netherlands* App no 52750/99, Judgment of 4 February 2003, paras 70–74.

[300] *Valašinas v Lithuania* App no 44558/98, Judgment of 24 July 2001, Reports 2001-VIII, paras 114–18; *Iwańczuk v Poland* App no 25196/94, Judgment of 15 November 2001, paras 58–59.

[301] *Jaeger v Estonia* App no 1574/13, Judgment of 31 July 2014, para 42, or *Julin v Estonia* App nos 16563/08 …, Judgment of 29 May 2012, para 189.

[302] *Wieser v Austria* App no 2293/03, Judgment of 22 February 2007, para 40.

[303] Ibid; *Orłowski v Poland* App no 18877/12, Judgment of 6 November 2018, para 83.

[304] *Abu Zubaydah v Lithuania* App no 46454/11, Judgment of 31 May 2018, para 653; *Al Nashiri v Romania* App no 33234/12, Judgment of 31 May 2018, para 670.

[305] Ibid, paras 40 and 42, respectively.

f. Comments

The context of detention is perhaps the first that comes to mind when one thinks of torture. The conventional image of ill-treatment as something that is applied in detention in order to extract information or a confession from the victim certainly illustrates the ease with which the authorities can impact the physical and psychological integrity of an individual who is cut off from the outside world by prison walls. However, beyond the intentional infliction of suffering through torture, detainees are also exposed to other threats to their physical and psychological integrity. They depend on the state to not only protect them from ill-treatment aimed at extracting information, but also to ensure that they are adequately housed, fed, clean, and cared for. Because the state assumes responsibility for the persons detained in its prisons and institutions, it thus bears obligations to ensure adequate conditions of detention for those individuals.

To date, the Court has found in numerous instances that states have failed their obligations to vulnerable detainees under Article 3. However, the Court's jurisprudence has not always been this way: the Court was once much more reluctant to evaluate domestic policy decisions regarding incarceration, and hesitated to make findings that would impose cost burdens on states.[306] Today, a more proactive Court relies on vulnerability and external standards and findings, such as those of the CPT, to engage more closely with cases.[307]

The detention context highlights the different tiers of protection created by the Court's vulnerability reasoning. While the special relationship of dependence between detainees and the state creates a degree of vulnerability in all persons deprived of their liberty, certain detainees receive special protection because they are even more vulnerable given the intersection of detention and other factors, such as mental health issues or physical disability. The Court has been proactive in creating positive state obligations to ensure adequate detention conditions and in finding that Article 3 has been violated in the context of detention. From ensuring adequate hygiene and medical care to providing protection to individuals who are at risk of violence in detention, the Court requires states to ensure that the human dignity of detainees is preserved and that they do not undergo suffering or humiliation amounting to ill-treatment. While the flood of applications from certain countries shows that detention conditions in many states remain below the standard required by the ECtHR,[308] the Court's vulnerability reasoning has

[306] Steve Foster, 'The Effective Supervision of European Prison Conditions' in Francesca Ippolito and Sara Iglesias Sánchez (eds), *Protecting Vulnerable Groups: The European Human Rights Framework* (Hart, 2015) 381–400, 384–85; *Reed v United Kingdom* App no 7630/76, Decision of 6 December 1979, DR 19, 113, para 35, where prison conditions were considered 'unsatisfactory' but nonetheless failed to meet the threshold of severity.

[307] *Abu Zubaydah* (n 304), paras 350–54; Foster (n 306), 387–88.

[308] Some examples being detention conditions in Bulgarian (*Neshkov and Others* (n 255)) and Russian prisons (*Zayev v Russia* App no 36552/05, Judgment of 16 April 2015; *Razzakov* (n 295)).

prepared the foundations for a context-sensitive engagement with the Article 3 rights of detainees. In doing so, it underscores the fact that human dignity and the right to be free from ill-treatment, suffering and humiliation cannot be limited along with the right to liberty of detainees, but remain very much applicable in the detention context.

B. Military Conscripts

Like detainees, conscripted military personnel find themselves vulnerable because they are under the control of the authorities, and the state likewise has an Article 3 obligation to protect their physical wellbeing.[309] This requires states to take reasonable steps to protect conscripts from ill-treatment of which the authorities had or ought to have had knowledge.[310]

While all conscripts are, given this case law, considered to be in a vulnerable position analogous to that of detainees, some conscripts may be particularly vulnerable. For example, conscripts who suffer from psychosocial disabilities may experience particular stress and anxiety if subjected to military life, and their suffering may therefore go 'beyond that of any regular conscript in normal military service'.[311] If conscripts display this kind of vulnerability, states are required to ensure that they can perform their military service in a manner compatible with Article 3, which includes detecting and reacting to their vulnerability in a timely manner.[312]

This is one more example of the types of situations in which vulnerability reasoning can shift the Court's perspective and bring it closer to the context underlying an application. Persons who are drafted into military service are, often at a very young age, thrust suddenly into military life. Instead of subscribing to the archetype of the strong and unfazed soldier, and deferring to states' competence for organising their armed forces, the Court has – quite rightly – recognised that conscripts find themselves in a challenging situation, particularly if they suffer from psychological problems. Here, the vulnerability heuristic serves to facilitate a shift in perspective and promotes genuine understanding for the situation and power structure in which these individuals find themselves.

C. Persons in State Institutions

Like detainees and military conscripts, persons who are deprived of their liberty in other contexts are also vulnerable, given that they are equally under the state's exclusive control. The Court has recognised this similarity, finding that vulnerability

[309] *Denis Vasilyev v Russia* App no 32704/04, Judgment of 17 December 2009, para 115; *Premininy* (n 266), para 73; *Placì* (n 16), para 49.
[310] *Placì* (n 16), para 49.
[311] Ibid, para 58.
[312] Ibid, para 59.

arises not only when individuals are under exclusive state control in a penitentiary or military conscription context, but in any situation where individuals find themselves in the state's sole authority.

For example, in its 2012 *Stanev v Bulgaria* judgment, the Court considered the case of an individual suffering from schizophrenia who had been placed in a social care home for people with mental disorders under crowded, unhygienic, demeaning, and generally poor conditions. In examining the case, the Court held that Article 3 applies to 'anyone in the care of the authorities' and 'to all forms of deprivation of liberty'.[313] In another judgment, in 2015, the Court built on this, citing the 'position of inferiority and powerlessness which is typical of patients confined in psychiatric hospitals' as requiring more stringent review of whether a given treatment or punishment is compatible with Article 3.[314]

The Court's case law shows that vulnerability in the institutional setting arises regardless of the duration of time during which an individual is in the state's custody, and is present from the very beginning of an applicant's deprivation of liberty, even if it only lasts one hour.[315] As this jurisprudence relates vulnerability to state control, it can be expected that this case law would also apply to those who have voluntarily entered an institution and but cannot freely leave it, or those who have been placed there by a legal guardian.

IV. Vulnerability Due to Victimisation

The chapter so far has covered various ways in which the situations or characteristics of applicants preceding an alleged Convention violation can render them vulnerable. In addition to this, the Court has also found that a Convention violation may, in and of itself, render someone vulnerable.[316] This reasoning – the recognition of victimisation as a source of vulnerability – may seem circular at first. However, when considering the types of cases concerned and the destructive psychological effect that ill-treatment has on its victims,[317] the Court's approach is, in fact, rather straightforward.

Victims' rights have, in the last decades, increasingly gained international recognition, with a focus on access to legal proceedings and on providing reparation.[318] In the Council of Europe, the Committee of Ministers has for example

[313] *Stanev v Bulgaria* App no 36760/06, Judgment (GC) of 17 January 2012, Reports 2012, para 206.

[314] *M.S. (No 2)* (n 175), para 98.

[315] *Ilievska v former Yugoslav Republic of Macedonia* App no 20136/11, Judgment of 7 May 2015, paras 60–61.

[316] *N. and M. v Russia* App nos 39496/14 and 39727/14, Decision of 26 April 2016, para 60.

[317] Margi Laird McCue, *Domestic Violence: A Reference Handbook*, 2nd edn (ABC-CLIO 2008), 79; Katie M Edwards et al, 'Rape Myths: History, Individual and Institutional-Level Presence, and Implications for Change' (2011) 65(11) *Sex Roles* 761–73, esp 765–66.

[318] UN GA, Basic Principles and Guidelines on the Right to a Remedy and Reparation for Victims of Gross Violations of International Human Rights Law and Serious Violations of International

enjoined states to ensure that '[crime] victims who are particularly vulnerable, either through their personal characteristics or through the circumstances of the crime, can benefit from special measures best suited to their situation.'[319]

At the same time, certain types of crimes have received particular attention in the sense of states' obligations to combat them. When it comes to gender-based violence, for example, the Council of Europe has created the Istanbul Convention, which places states under an obligation to fully address gender-based violence in all its forms, including by taking measures to prevent such violence, to protect victims, and to prosecute perpetrators, for example through the criminalisation of various types of violence.[320]

The creation of positive obligations, particularly investigative ones, under Article 3 ECHR transforms these developments into a tangible improvement for victims' access to justice in Strasbourg.[321] The following will explore how the Court utilises vulnerability to respond to three particular contexts of victimisation: domestic and sexual violence, victims of a violation of Article 3, and applicants who experience what is called a 'sense of vulnerability'. At the same time, it should be noted at the outset that the reception of human rights-based duties to deploy the criminal law has been critical in the scholarly literature.[322]

A. Victims of Domestic and Sexual Violence

The present section groups together cases concerning all victims of sexual violence, as well as those who, due to victimisation, experience a sense of vulnerability reaching the threshold of Article 3. This conglomeration of cases is based on the fact that, while the Court does discuss domestic and gender-based violence as a problem of gender discrimination under Article 14 ECHR,[323] this is not reflected in its approach to Article 3. Victims of sexual violence can have any gender, and when it comes to domestic violence as a form of ill-treatment, the Court takes an inclusive approach to the types of violence concerned and to the gender of possible victims.[324] This approach allows it to capture various types of violence against

Humanitarian Law, UNGA Res 60/147 of 16 December 2005, paras 2(a), 3(d), 10, 11(a)–(c), 13, 15–23; Council of Europe, European Convention on the Compensation of Victims of Violent Crimes of 24 November 1983, ETS 116, in force since 1 February 1988, 26 states parties.

[319] Council of Europe Committee of Ministers, Recommendation Rec(2006)8 of the Committee of Ministers to Member States on Assistance to Crime Victims, 14 June 2006, para 3.4.

[320] Council of Europe, Convention on Preventing and Combating Violence against Women and Domestic Violence, 11 May 2011, CETS No 210, entered into force 1 August 2014, 34 states parties.

[321] For more on the recognition of victims' rights on the international plane, see Cherif M Bassiouni, 'International Recognition of Victims' Rights' (2006) 6(2) *Human Rights Law Review* 203–79.

[322] Laurens Lavrysen and Natasa Mavronicola, *Coercive Human Rights: Positive Duties to Mobilise the Criminal Law under the ECHR* (Hart, 2020), and the discussions therein; Mattia Pinto, 'Historical Trends of Human Rights Gone Criminal' (2020) 41(4) *Human Rights Quarterly*, 729–61.

[323] *Volodina* (n 33).

[324] Ibid, para 71.

victims of any gender, including child victims.[325] This does not mean, that the Court does not engage with the gendered nature of many forms of especially domestic violence, but that this largely falls under Article 14. In that context, the Court has recently displayed a turn to a gender-sensitive approach of its interpretation of the ECHR.[326]

i. *Rape and Sexual Violence*

Sexual violence against minors is a well-explored source of vulnerability in the Court's case law, as discussed previously in this chapter. When it comes to adult victims of sexual violence, its case law is more scarce, and its acknowledgement of victims' vulnerability is less forthcoming.

Regarding sexual violence perpetrated by state actors, the Court has clearly acknowledged that the context of detention gives rise to vulnerability. In 1997, it held that the treatment suffered by the applicant in *Aydin v Turkey* – a 17-year-old who had suffered rape in detention – would have created in her in an 'overall sense of vulnerability', and that she had therefore suffered torture.[327] Since then, the Court has recognised the dependency and powerlessness of victims who suffer sexual violence in detention as regards obtaining justice, and held that they are in a vulnerable position when it comes to questions of proof.[328] Today, the rape of detainees by state officials has been recognised as 'an especially grave and abhorrent form of ill-treatment given the ease with which the offender can exploit the vulnerability and weakened resistance of his victim'.[329]

However, vulnerability to and arising from sexual violence is not limited to situations of detention, as the Court has also recognised. Faced with 'defendable' claims of such acts, whether perpetrated by state actors or private parties, states are therefore under an obligation to conduct an investigation capable of identifying the perpetrators and holding them accountable even when the victim is not under their exclusive control. This applies particularly to vulnerable individuals, including children and intellectually disabled persons, who should benefit from additional protection in light of their inability or lack of willingness to report abuse.[330] In the absence of an appropriate response, the Court has held, the authorities risk producing 'a background of impunity' that may violate Article 3.[331]

[325] *Opuz* (n 32), para 132.
[326] *Volodina* (n 33).
[327] *Aydin* (n 24), para 84.
[328] *Zeynep Avci v Turkey* App no 37021/97, Judgment of 6 February 2003, para 65.
[329] *Maslova and Nalbandov v Russia* App no 839/02, Judgment of 24 January 2008, para 107; *Zontul* (n 298), para 88.
[330] *M.B.* (n 36), para 52.
[331] *I.C.* (n 63), para 55.

However, when it comes to sexual violence perpetrated against adult victims by private actors and absent an intersection with another ground for vulnerability (be it detention, minor age, intellectual disability, or some other ground), there is less clarity in the case law about victims' vulnerability. In the period under study, there was in fact only one relevant judgment. In that case, the Court addressed the way in which proceedings must be structured in order to provide redress to the victim, engaging with the victim's vulnerability and the effects of the authorities' response. The Court applied a standard of diligence to the authorities' approach to the case, and found that they had fallen short of Convention requirements, given the length of the domestic proceedings (which featured a preliminary investigation that lasted eight years), the victim's related uncertainty that the aggressors would be punished, and the fact that the victim was required to relive the events in question numerous times while being repeatedly questioned.[332]

It is however difficult to generalise based solely on this case. Beyond this case, ie in other non-intersecting sexual assault cases, the Court has not considered adult victims vulnerable. This implies that the victims are sufficiently able to come forward about their ordeals and to undergo the resulting proceedings. How does this compare to the Court's approach to vulnerability in other situations? It can be argued, of course, that victims of sexual violence are not homogenous: they will have varying experiences of ill-treatment and different reactions to that experience. Likewise, it can be argued that the Court can find Convention violations without considering an applicant vulnerable.[333] However, the other sources of vulnerability do not require homogeneity among victims either, and being considered vulnerable works in applicants' favour in various ways, as discussed below. In addition, the Court's current approach raises problems given the very nature of sexual violence, as – in the Court's own words – it 'leaves deep psychological scars on the victim which do not respond to the passage of time as quickly as other forms of physical and mental violence'.[334] Especially because sexual violence is an exercise of power over the victim, it could instead be argued that every victim of such violence is vulnerable, and that the state must react to the underlying imbalance of power.

ii. Domestic Abuse

One of the Court's first leading judgments regarding domestic abuse was *Opuz v Turkey*.[335] There, the Court found that Article 1 ECHR, in combination with Article 3, places states under an obligation to ensure that individuals in their jurisdiction are not ill-treated, including by private individuals. On this basis, it

[332] *S.Z.* (n 180), para 52.
[333] Heri (n 71).
[334] *Aydin* (n 24), para 83.
[335] *Opuz* (n 32).

went on to hold that vulnerable individuals are particularly – thus, especially but non-exclusively – entitled to state protection through effective deterrence of such acts.[336] The Court considered that the applicant was vulnerable inter alia due to the protracted violence she had suffered, the threat and her fear of further violence, as well as the 'vulnerable situation of women in south-east Turkey'.[337]

Subsequently, in considering the vulnerability of victims of domestic violence, the Court has referred to recognitions of this vulnerability in relevant international instruments.[338] The Court has considered victims of domestic violence to be vulnerable if they cannot physically defend themselves against a stronger aggressor[339] or if they are particularly young or of advanced age.[340] Physical injuries and a fear of further violence also indicate vulnerability and entitle victims to state protection.[341] However, such aggravating factors may not be necessary in order for the Court to recognise the vulnerability of victims of domestic abuse. For example, in 2014, the Court had regard for 'how vulnerable victims of domestic abuse usually are' in justifying the need for a *proprio motu* investigation.[342]

Given the particular vulnerability of victims of domestic violence, the Court has recognised the need for active state involvement in their protection, which entails overlapping positive obligations. This means that the domestic authorities must (a) take reasonable measures to prevent ill-treatment of which they knew or ought to have known (which entails a real and immediate risk of ill-treatment of an identified individual), (b) comply with a (procedural) obligation to conduct an effective official investigation where arguable claims of ill-treatment are raised and (c) establish and effectively apply a system punishing all domestic violence and provide sufficient safeguards to victims.[343]

A judgment from 2016 illustrates the many ways in which victims of domestic abuse are vulnerable. In that case, *M.G. v Turkey*, the Court held that it is necessary for the domestic authorities to take into account the precarious situation and particular moral, physical and/or material vulnerability of the victims of such abuse.[344] In addition, the Court referred to victims' feelings of vulnerability where no protection from abuse is provided.[345] It noted that the applicant was forced to live in hiding, fearing that – absent speedy proceedings to ensure protection for herself and her children – she would be exposed to further violence. Even though no further acts of violence took place, the Court held that 'it could not ignore the

[336] Ibid, para 159.
[337] Ibid, para 160.
[338] *E.M. v Romania* App no 43994/05, Judgment of 30 October 2012, para 58.
[339] *Eremia v Republic of Moldova* App no 3564/11, Judgment of 28 May 2013, para 61, concerning an aggressor who was 'a police officer trained to overcome any resistance.'
[340] *C.A.S. and C.S.* (n 53), para 81; *Mudric* (n 147), para 51.
[341] *Rumor v Italy* App no 72964/10, Judgment of 25 May 2014, paras 58 and 60.
[342] *T.M. and C.M. v Republic of Moldova* App no 26608/11, Judgment of 28 January 2014, para 46.
[343] *Bălșan v Romania* App no 49645/09, Judgment of 23 May 2017, para 57.
[344] *M.G. v Turkey* App no 646/10, Judgment of 22 March 2016, para 95.
[345] Ibid, para 105.

feeling of fear in which she lived – living in hiding for two and a half years – nor the impact of the violence that she suffered on her personal, social and family life, which persist even today'.[346]

In 2017, the Court took a similar approach when considering the case of a victim of domestic abuse whose child was murdered by her abuser. It held that the victim had not received effective state protection, and that the domestic authorities had failed to take into consideration the situation of 'precariousness and particular, moral, physical, and material vulnerability' facing the applicant, and offer appropriate support.[347] In cases concerning violence against women, the Court held, it is incumbent on the national authorities to take into account the situation of precariousness and particular, moral, physical and material vulnerability of the victims and to do so in the shortest time possible.[348]

A last case in this context, *Irina Smirnova v Ukraine*, concerns the ill-treatment of a female retiree by her flat's co-owners.[349] This case has already been mentioned above in the context of the vulnerability of the elderly, but the abuse aspect merits revisiting here. In this case, the Court noted the importance of taking measures to protect vulnerable people, and argued for a holistic assessment of situations of potential abuse and sensitivity to the psychological effects on the victim, stating that '[w]here an individual makes a credible assertion of having been subjected to repeated acts of domestic violence or other types of harassment, however trivial the isolated incidents might be, it falls on the domestic authorities to assess the situation in its entirety, including the risk that similar incidents would continue'.[350] It went on to provide concrete guidance for what this assessment should look like, arguing that it should 'take due account of the psychological effect that the risk of repeated harassment, intimidation and violence may have on the victim's everyday life' and react to the systematic nature of abuse.[351] Thus, the Court argued that the state response, which ultimately took 12 years to impose prison sentences on the applicant's harassers, had been insufficient given the lack of a 'swift intervention' by the authorities and the misrecognition of the systematic and on-going nature of her ill-treatment.[352]

iii. A Victim-Oriented Approach

The vulnerability of victims of domestic and sexual violence works in two ways in the Court's jurisprudence. First, it addresses the likelihood that someone will

[346] Ibid, para 104, translation by the author.
[347] *Talpis* (n 70), para 115.
[348] Ibid, para 130.
[349] *Irina Smirnova* (n 148), paras 9–18.
[350] Ibid, para 71.
[351] Ibid.
[352] Ibid, para 77.

become a victim. Secondly, vulnerability also addresses the likelihood that someone will be able to complain about and prove their alleged victimisation. Together, at their best, these two branches of the Court's vulnerability reasoning show that the Strasbourg judges seek a contextual and reality-based understanding of how domestic and sexual violence work – namely, that these sorts of transgressions are dramatically underreported by victims and, even where they are reported, difficulties of proof as well as the shame and fear of stigmatisation experienced by the victim can mean that help is not available and the perpetrators are not brought to justice.[353]

Sexual and domestic violence are expressions of power and control over the victim,[354] and inflict particularly intense forms of trauma from a psychological standpoint.[355] Failing to recognise the suffering of the victims of sexual and domestic violence or engaging in a stigmatising response – such as, for example, the perpetuation of so-called 'rape myths' – represents a secondary victimisation or 'revictimisation' of the victims by the legal system.[356] The Court's vulnerability jurisprudence allows it to respond to the particular psychology of victims and has the potential to, by shifting attention to the perspective of the victim, prevent revictimisation in future cases.

Before moving on, it should be noted that the Court has remained silent on the vulnerability of victims of human trafficking under Article 3. This runs counter to the work of other international instances,[357] and to the fact that the situation of these individuals is, in a number of ways, comparable to that of victims of abuse or of violations of Article 3. Human trafficking, too, is a particularly traumatic experience, and one that involves elements of power, control, domination, and the lack of options for escape, as well as, often, sexual violence. Where these cases are brought under Article 3, vulnerability reasoning has not played a role in the Court's jurisprudence to date, even though the Court has not lacked opportunities to address this matter.[358] By comparison, when cases are instead brought under the prohibition of slavery and forced labour in Article 4 ECHR, reference to vulnerability has been made in recent case law.[359] This could trickle down into the Article 3 jurisprudence in the future.

[353] McCue (n 317), 79. See also, on rape myths, Edwards et al (n 317).

[354] McCue (n 317), 80, 88.

[355] Ask Elklit and Dorte M Christiansen, 'ASD and PTSD in Rape Victims' (2010) 25(8) *Journal of Interpersonal Violence* 1470–88.

[356] Joanne Hattendorf and Toni R Tollerud, 'Domestic Violence: Counseling Strategies that Minimize the Impact of Secondary Victimization' (1997) 33(1) *Perspectives in Psychiatric Care* 14–23; Edwards et al (n 317).

[357] See, for example, CEDAW Committee, Concluding Observations on the Combined Fourth and Fifth Periodic Reports of Myanmar, UN Doc CEDAW/C/MMR/CO/4–5, 25 July 2016, para 44f.

[358] *M. and Others* (n 50), para 105. See also *G.J. v Spain* App no 59172/12, Decision of 21 June 2016, para 52, where the Court's main concern was to distinguish the *Valentin Câmpeanu* case (n 22).

[359] *V.C.L. and A.N. v the United Kingdom* App nos 77587/12 and 74603/12, Judgment of 16 February 2021, paras 149 and 159.

B. Victims of a Violation of Article 3

In a small but noteworthy number of cases beyond the contexts discussed above (ie, unrelated to domestic or sexual violence), the Court has also considered the vulnerability of victims of a violation of Article 3.[360] States likewise bear an obligation to these vulnerable individuals to conduct an in-depth and effective investigation under Article 3 and under the right to an effective remedy in Article 13 ECHR.[361]

The fact that victims of ill-treatment are less willing to report their experiences means that states must investigate potential ill-treatment as soon as there is a sufficient indication – thus, a 'credible assertion' – that it has taken place.[362] In this regard, the Court has held even if applicants fail to comply with their duty of diligence to make a timely application to the Court, this is not decisive if either a) the state is aware that ill-treatment may have occurred or b) the applicant is particularly vulnerable. The latter depends on 'the complexity of the case and the nature of the alleged human rights violations at stake, and [whether] it was reasonable for the applicant to wait for developments that could have resolved crucial factual or legal issues'.[363]

The Court's reasoning as concerns the vulnerability of victims of ill-treatment appears, to a certain extent, to contradict the Court's selective model of vulnerability as described above. If any victim of an Article 3 violation is vulnerable, then vulnerability under Article 3 describes every applicant alleging a violation of his or her rights under that provision. Because anyone can be a victim of such a violation, this potentially applies to every human individual. However, while there are undoubtedly many advantages to a recognition of universal human vulnerability, such a recognition does not seem to be the Court's intention. Instead, while this particular strand of jurisprudence opens up the concept of vulnerability in order to provide a broader, more inclusive umbrella of protection, it does so by attaching it to a particular effect. The relevant jurisprudence ties into the Court's approach to victims of domestic and sexual violence, and seeks to counteract the underreporting and intimidation that characterises instances of ill-treatment that do not fall under those two categories but evoke similar effects. This helps the Court to mount an adequate response to the particular psychology of certain

[360] *Gisayev v Russia* App no 14811/04, Judgment of 20 January 2011, para 116; *Members of the Gldani Congregation of Jehovah's Witnesses and Others v Georgia* App no 71156/01, Judgment of 3 May 2007; *Buzilo* (n 18), para 29; *Ilhan v Turkey* App no 22277/93, Judgment (GC) of 27 June 2000, Reports 2000-VII, paras 61 and 92.

[361] *Stanimirovic v Serbia* App no 26088/06, Judgment of 18 October 2011, para 39.

[362] Ibid, para 39; *Ilhan* (n 360), paras 61 and 92; *Otašević v Serbia* App no 32198/07, Judgment of 5 February 2013, para 30.

[363] *Mocanu and Others v Romania* App nos 10865/09 …, Judgment (GC) of 17 September 2014, Reports 2014 (extracts), para 265; *Ismogulov v Russia* App no 60890/08, Decision of 27 March 2018, para 31.

victims and thereby to isolate cases in which applicants are less able to obtain justice.[364]

The Court's approach to the vulnerability of victims of an Article 3 violation seems to have a predominantly procedural utility. This reflects a broader discussion on the need to facilitate access to justice for victims of ill-treatment. Extensive work is being done on this, for example, by national and international organisations on counselling and assisting victims of torture in particular.[365] This work is motivated by the recognition that because torture – and to a lesser extent also inhuman and degrading treatment – breaks the will of victims and dehumanises them, it can disintegrate the individual personality, destroy social, intimate, and family ties, and destabilise entire communities.[366] Torture in particular reduces individuals to positions of extreme distress and helplessness and can have lasting cognitive, emotional and behavioural consequences.[367] In this regard, the Istanbul Protocol, which provides a manual on how to investigate and document ill-treatment, recommends that experts should

> attempt to relate to mental suffering in the context of the individual's beliefs and cultural norms … Ideally, this attitude will communicate to the victim that his or her complaints and suffering are being recognized as real and expectable under the circumstances. In this sense, a sensitive empathic attitude may offer the victim some relief from the experience of alienation.[368]

Certainly, this will depend on the circumstances of the ill-treatment in question and on its severity. Where the Court's vulnerability reasoning means recognition of the suffering of victims of ill-treatment, it may be doing as the Istanbul Protocol recommends by allowing individuals to experience procedural justice even where the outcome of their application may not be favourable.[369] Procedural justice describes the recognition that participation in the proceedings, perceived neutrality of the adjudicators, a feeling of being treated with respect by the system and trust in the decision-making authority can increase individuals' satisfaction with human rights adjudication and the perceived standing of the Court.[370] Experiencing proceedings as just may also be a step on the road to recovery from the feeling of powerlessness associated with acts of torture or other ill-treatment.[371]

[364] OHCHR, 'Istanbul Protocol: Manual on the Effective Investigation and Documentation of Torture and Other Cruel, Inhuman or Degrading Treatment or Punishment' (revised edn, 2004) HR/P/PT/8/Rev.1, www.ohchr.org/Documents/Publications/training8Rev1en.pdf), esp 46–47.

[365] See, for example, the organisations and bodies that participated in drafting the Istanbul Protocol (OHCHR (n 364), iii).

[366] Ibid, 45.

[367] Ibid, with further references, and 46–47.

[368] Ibid, 46.

[369] Eva Brems and Laurens Lavrysen, 'Procedural Justice in Human Rights Adjudication: The European Court of Human Rights' (2013) 35(1) *Human Rights Quarterly* 176–200.

[370] Ibid, 180–82.

[371] Ibid, 182, citing Tom R Tyler, 'Procedural Justice and the Courts' (2007) 44(1/2) *Court Review: The Journal of the American Judges Association* 26–31, 26.

C. Feelings of Vulnerability

In addition to the procedural requirements on states given the vulnerability of victims of ill-treatment, the very similarly worded 'sense or feeling of vulnerability', as experienced by individual applicants in a variety of contexts, has also been recognised as a source of vulnerability by the Court. In and of itself, this can affect applicants' procedural rights as well as the substantive findings made under Article 3 under certain circumstances.[372]

The first relevant case in this regard was again *Aydin v Turkey*, decided in 1997, where the Court held that the applicant's treatment added to her 'overall sense of vulnerability' in detention, and found that she had been tortured.[373] Today, if applicants are subjected to treatment likely to arouse feelings of vulnerability, the Court takes this into consideration along with feelings of fear and anxiety as an indicator that the individual has been humiliated and debased and that Article 3 has therefore been violated.[374]

In fact, according to the Court's current case law, it seems that if a given treatment inspires extreme feelings of vulnerability in individuals, this is not only significant but even potentially sufficient for finding a violation of Article 3.[375] In one case, the Court found that the various penalties and punishments inflicted on a conscientious objector to military service had been disproportionate and that they 'aimed more at repressing the applicant's intellectual personality, inspiring in him feelings of fear, anguish and vulnerability capable of humiliating and debasing him and breaking his resistance and will'.[376] In another case, the Court similarly held that the youth of the applicant and the fact that he had been denied access to counsel in detention would have 'inspired in him a feeling of vulnerability, of powerlessness and of fear when faced with State agents'; this would have caused him to feel 'fear, anguish and inferiority capable of humiliating him and eventually breaking down his physical or moral resistance'.[377]

Similarly, in *El-Masri*, concerning an applicant who was mistaken for an al-Qaeda operative and detained in a Macedonian hotel until he was flown to Afghanistan by a CIA 'extraordinary renditions' team, the Court held that there was

> no doubt that the applicant's solitary incarceration in the hotel intimidated him on account of his apprehension as to what would happen to him next and must have caused him emotional and psychological distress. The applicant's prolonged confinement in the

[372] For example requiring states to investigate alleged ill-treatment diligently (*Stepuleac* (n 284), para 65; compare *Keser and Kömürcü v Turkey* App no 5981/03, Judgment of 23 June 2009, para 72) or influencing the Court's findings on the admissibility of an application (*Mocanu and Others* (n 363), para 275).

[373] *Aydin* (n 24), especially para 84.

[374] *Dikme* (n 199), para 91; *Ilaşcu and Others* (n 3), para 446; *Bilen v Turkey* App no 34482/97, Judgment of 21 February 2006, para 35.

[375] *Sultan Öner and Others* (n 50), para 134; *Fahriye Çalışkan v Turkey* App no 40516/98, Judgment of 2 October 2007, paras 43–44; *Stepuleac* (n 284), para 65.

[376] *Ülke* (n 28), para 62.

[377] *Doğanay* (n 199), para 32, translation by the author.

> hotel left him entirely vulnerable. He undeniably lived in a permanent state of anxiety owing to his uncertainty about his fate.[378]

The Court generally does not require applicants to prove their feelings of vulnerability, which is understandable given that such proof may not be possible. Instead, the Court infers a sense of vulnerability – or its absence[379] – from the situation.[380]

In this context, the Court builds upon the idea that mental suffering can, in and of itself, constitute torture or ill-treatment. It thereby seems to equate vulnerability with a feeling of defencelessness against abuse, with powerlessness vis-à-vis the torment inflicted by state actors, and with humiliation at the injustice suffered. Vulnerability in this sense is slippery: it provides a highly subjective standard, one that is difficult to prove or disprove in the individual case. At the same time, this idea of a sense of vulnerability as understood by the Court may be seen as part of the very core of a violation of Article 3, as it is difficult to argue that victims of such a violation would not feel powerless, debased in their dignity and humiliated and, therefore, vulnerable.

The sense-of-vulnerability jurisprudence is indeterminate, but it can be understood as aiming to capture particular extremes in terms of fear and anguish. In fact, when read together with the jurisprudence discussed above on victims of domestic and sexual violence, the Court's understanding of the 'sense of vulnerability' becomes rather clear. From this perspective, the Strasbourg judges use it to counteract or neutralise the effects of victimisation, namely the lower rates of reporting, the problems of proof, and the psychological trauma that accompany the more severe, direct, interpersonal, and intentional forms of ill-treatment.

This case law also serves to simply recognise psychological suffering. In this regard, even if it may sometimes seem difficult to determine the added value of the sense-of-vulnerability jurisprudence beyond the fact that it explicitly names the feelings experienced by all victims of ill-treatment, the idea is significant. This type of vulnerability reasoning invites judges to reimagine the facts from the perspective of the victim and to acknowledge the suffering that he or she has undergone. Any effects for the outcome of the case aside, this is already a substantial step towards doing procedural justice.[381]

V. Vulnerability in the Context of Migration

If one aspect of the Court's vulnerability jurisprudence has received scholarly scrutiny in recent years, it is the case law concerning migration. Since the Court

[378] *El-Masri v former Yugoslav Republic of Macedonia* App no 39630/09, Judgment (GC) of 13 December 2012, Reports 2012, para 202.

[379] *Todorov* App no 51562/99, Decision of 29 September 2005.

[380] *Levinta* App no 17332/03, Judgment of 16 December 2008, para 73. See also *Rachwalski and Ferenc* (n 3), para 61.

[381] Brems and Lavrysen (n 369).

sealed the recognition of asylum-seekers as a vulnerable group in *M.S.S.*,[382] scholars including Moritz Baumgärtel, Sylvie Da Lomba, and Veronika Flegar, along with others, have discussed this topic.[383] It is in the migration context that many of the greatest strides in the Court's vulnerability case law under Article 3 have been made, but also where vulnerability and its consequences can be particularly controversial.

A. Vulnerability in the Host State

In 2011, the Grand Chamber issued perhaps its most important judgment on the vulnerability of asylum-seekers to date. That judgment was *M.S.S. v Belgium and Greece*, and it stemmed from an asylum-seeker's complaint about his return from Belgium to Greece under the EU's Dublin Regulation as well as about his living conditions in Greece.[384] In that judgment, the Court made the appealingly generalisable finding that 'the applicant, being an asylum-seeker, was particularly vulnerable because of everything he had been through during his migration and the traumatic experiences he was likely to have endured previously'.[385] Concerning the overcrowding and unhygienic conditions experienced by the applicant during his detention at a Greek holding centre, the Court found that 'taken together, the feeling of arbitrariness and the feeling of inferiority and anxiety often associated with it, as well as the profound effect such conditions of detention indubitably have on a person's dignity, constitute degrading treatment contrary to Article 3 of the Convention. In addition, the applicant's distress was accentuated by the vulnerability inherent in his situation as an asylum-seeker'.[386]

The Court went on to note the 'considerable importance' it attached to the status of the applicant as an asylum-seeker, a group that it considered 'particularly underprivileged and vulnerable' and thus in need of special protection.[387] It also examined the applicant's living conditions in Greece upon release, namely

[382] *M.S.S.* (n 7).

[383] Moritz Baumgärtel, 'Facing the Challenge of Migratory Vulnerability in the European Court of Human Rights' 38(1) *Netherlands Quarterly of Human Rights* (2020) 12–29; Sylvie Da Lomba, 'Vulnerability, International Human Rights Adjudication and Migration Governance' 10 *Inter-American and European Human Rights Journal* (2019) 3–37; Ben Hudson, 'Migrant Vulnerability and the European Court of Human Rights (ECtHR): Exposing the Limits of the Concept of Vulnerability in the Mediterranean Migration Context', 4 *Maritime Safety and Security Law Journal* (2018) 26–46; Lieneke Slingenberg, 'The Right Not to be Dominated: The Case Law of the European Court of Human Rights on Migrants' Destitution' 19(2) *Human Rights Law Review* (2019) 291–314; Veronika Flegar, 'Vulnerability and the Principle of Non-refoulement in the European Court of Human Rights: Towards an Increased Scope of Protection for Persons Fleeing from Extreme Poverty?' 8(2) *Contemporary Readings in Law and Social Justice* (2016) 148–69.

[384] Council Regulation (EC) No 343/2003 of 18 February 2003, cited in full above at n 117.

[385] *M.S.S.* (n 7), para 232.

[386] Ibid, para 233.

[387] Ibid, para 251.

the state of extreme poverty and homelessness that he experienced, given that he was not issued a work permit.[388] Specifically regarding the 'particular state of insecurity and vulnerability in which asylum-seekers are known to live in Greece', the Court found that the authorities could not simply remain passive and wait for the applicant to turn to the police for assistance.[389] It considered that the Greek authorities had failed to display due regard for the applicant's vulnerability as an asylum-seeker and that, due to this inaction, they were responsible for his living conditions, namely his homelessness and lack of access to sanitary facilities, resources, or any basic means of subsistence.[390]

As a Grand Chamber judgment, *M.S.S.* thus established a baseline for the welfare obligations that the state owes to destitute persons who depend on it entirely. Crucially for the purposes of Article 3, the Court also countered some of the relativist arguments found elsewhere in its case law. It held that, while states were at the time experiencing 'considerable difficulties in coping with the increasing influx of migrants and asylum-seekers', and while the 'burden and pressure' placed on states by these circumstances were accentuated by the effects of the financial crisis, these considerations could not absolve states of their responsibilities under Article 3, given its absolute nature.[391]

After *M.S.S.*, the Court has continually reaffirmed states' positive obligations to protect vulnerable migrants, including by providing for them materially.[392] Because migrants may be detained in the host state, their vulnerability as migrants and as detainees intersects. The relevant jurisprudence echoes that on detention in general, though the standards required regarding detained asylum-seekers may in fact be higher.[393] This includes an implicit requirement to have regard for and respond to the intersection of various sources of vulnerability,[394] including by providing adequate medical care and conditions for minors and those who are pregnant.[395]

For example, as discussed above, the Court held in *Mubilanzila Mayeka and Kaniki Mitunga v Belgium*, which concerned an unaccompanied five-year-old who entered Belgium illegally before being detained and expelled, that

> [i]n view of the absolute nature of the protection afforded by Article 3 of the Convention, it is important to bear in mind that [the applicant's vulnerability] is the decisive factor and it takes precedence over considerations relating to [her] status as an illegal immigrant. She therefore indisputably came within the class of highly vulnerable members

[388] Ibid, paras 172 and 254.

[389] Ibid, paras 254, 258 and 259.

[390] Ibid, para 263.

[391] Ibid, para 223.

[392] *Rahimi* (n 47), para 87; *Amadou v Greece* App no 37991/11, Judgment of 4 February 2016, paras 59–62.

[393] *Aden Ahmed v Malta* App no 55352/12, Judgment of 23 July 2013, para 98; *Abdi Mahamud* (n 128), especially the Partly Dissenting Opinion of Judge Sajó.

[394] *Mahamed Jama v Malta* App no 10290/13, Judgment of 26 November 2015, paras 100–01.

[395] *Aden Ahmed* (n 393), para 97.

> of society to whom the Belgian State owed a duty to take adequate measures to provide care and protection as part of its positive obligations under Article 3.[396]

This judgment, by referring to the absolute nature of Article 3, pre-empts balancing of the applicants' interests against those of the state on the basis of her extreme vulnerability, which stemmed from the fact that she was an unaccompanied child migrant. The wording of this passage is, however, unfortunate given that, by emphasising the applicant's vulnerability in this way, the Court implies that states do not owe a similar duty to provide care and protection to adult migrants, or that Article 3 does not take precedence over states' interests with regard to those who do not fall in the category of 'highly vulnerable individuals'. The Court later clarified this jurisprudence by finding that it was not so much relevant whether the migrant children were accompanied or not, but that they were young and dependent.[397]

The idea that children in immigration detention are due special protection in light of their vulnerability was further explored by the Court in a number of 2016 judgments against France, as mentioned above in the section on children, where the Court found that the immigration-related detention of very young children together with their parents could prove traumatic to the point of violating Article 3.[398] Here the Court held that, beyond a brief period and as a measure of last resort, immigration detention of young children is impermissible.[399]

Regarding adult migrants, the Court is less willing to create sweeping change by means of vulnerability reasoning. One short-lived hope for improvement here came in 2015, with a now voided judgment of the Second Section which considered the effects of the dangerous journey by sea faced by many irregular migrants and asylum-seekers when entering Europe. The Second Section found that the applicants in *Khlaifia and Others v Italy*, who were on board vessels that were intercepted by the Italian coast guard, were in a situation of vulnerability given their traumatic experience on the Mediterranean. That and their detention in appalling conditions upon arrival in Italy, it found, violated their human dignity and therefore constituted degrading treatment.[400] However, that judgment was referred to the Grand Chamber, which departed from the Chamber judgment with respect to both the vulnerability argumentation and the finding of a violation of Article 3.[401]

As concerned the vulnerability of the applicants in *Khlaifia*, the Grand Chamber narrowed the Chamber's broad approach, which seemed to globally apply to all migrants who made use of the Mediterranean route, and instead found that despite their dangerous and exhausting crossing 'the applicants, who were not

[396] *Mubilanzila Mayeka and Kaniki Mitunga* (n 110), para 55; *Muskhadzhiyeva and Others* (n 50), paras 55–56.
[397] *Kanagaratnam* (n 114), para 67; *Popov* (n 109), para 91.
[398] *A.B. and Others* (n 82), paras 110–15, esp 110, and the remaining case law in (n 82).
[399] Ibid, para 114.
[400] *Khlaifia and Others v Italy* App no 16483/12, Judgment of 1 September 2015, para 135.
[401] Ibid.

asylum-seekers, did not have the specific vulnerability inherent in that status, and did not claim to have endured traumatic experiences in their country of origin'. It also noted that 'they belonged neither to the category of elderly persons nor to that of minors' and that 'they were aged between 23 and 28 and did not claim to be suffering from any particular medical condition.' The Grand Chamber went on to unanimously find that there had been no violation of Article 3 in the case, thereby precluding recognition of the all-inclusive vulnerability of migrants who have travelled via the Mediterranean route.[402] The Court's approach to vulnerability here does not entirely convince, because it does not display any of the sensitivity to real lived experience that it otherwise seems to be the concept's purpose to provide. Instead, the Court seems to be working with rigid categories, pigeonholing applicants into two categories: vulnerable and non-vulnerable.

At other times, the Court has used vulnerability reasoning to distinguish applicants from others in the same situation, finding – sometimes not very convincingly – that detention conditions imposed on illegal migrants violate the Article 3 rights of one individual who can be described as vulnerable, and reaching the opposite conclusion regarding another individual whom it does not consider vulnerable. A prime example of this is the 2016 *Abdi Mahamud v Malta* judgment. In another, similar case decided just a few months prior, *Moxamed Ismaaciil and Abdirahman Warsame v Malta*, the Court had found that the cumulative effect of the conditions of detention facing two female Somali asylum-seekers who arrived in Malta in 2012 did not violate Article 3 because the applicants were not more vulnerable than other detained migrants.[403] The facts of *Moxamed Ismaaciil and Abdirahman Warsame* and the claims made by the applicants were almost identical to *Abdi Mahamud*, which was decided only a few months later, but its outcome was very different.[404] Both cases were decided by the same formation of judges, and the same counsel represented all three applicants.

Despite their many similarities, these cases were decided very differently as concerns Article 3. The difference between them hinged on the concept of vulnerability. In both cases, the applicants alleged a variety of somatic and psychosomatic afflictions.[405] In the latter case, the applicant was classified as 'vulnerable' under a domestic system for finding alternative accommodation for certain migrants, at the request of her doctor, and was released from detention on this basis.[406] In other words, in the earlier case, the Court found no vulnerability and thus no violation of Article 3; in the latter one, it did both, with little explanation.[407]

[402] Ibid, para 194.

[403] *Moxamed Ismaaciil and Abdirahman Warsame v Malta* App nos 52160/13 and 52165/13, Judgment of 12 January 2016, para 94.

[404] *Abdi Mahamud* (n 128), paras 20–23, and *Moxamed Ismaaciil and Abdirahman Warsame* (n 403), paras 54–65.

[405] Ibid, paras 16–19 and para 56, respectively.

[406] *Abdi Mahamud* (n 128), paras 11–15, 18, 88.

[407] Ibid.

Judge Sajó, by now a long-time critic of the Court's approach to vulnerability,[408] wrote a powerful partly dissenting opinion in the *Abdi Mahamud* case. He argued that the applicant did not display any medical symptoms that would have made her 'particularly sensitive'.[409] He also pointed out that the majority deferred to the domestic categorisation of the applicant as vulnerable without paying any attention to the divergence between the domestic meaning and the meaning of vulnerability in Strasbourg. This gives the impression that the Court is willing to use any available vulnerability arguments to bring about applicant-friendly outcomes if it can do so without issuing judgments with wide-ranging consequences. To Judge Sajó, the real question in this case was not the applicant's vulnerability, but the length of detention that the Court is willing to tolerate for the prevention of unlawful entry for any migrant.

This argument should be seen in the light of a third case, *Aden Ahmed v Malta*, which was different on the facts from *Moxamed Ismaaciil and Abdirahman Warsame* and *Abdi Mahamud* mostly because the applicant – also a young Somali woman who was in immigration detention in the same Maltese facility in 2011–12, and who was also allegedly emotionally fragile – suffered a miscarriage in detention. The applicant in this third case was not considered vulnerable for domestic purposes, but the Court nonetheless found that she was vulnerable given the fact that 'she was an irregular immigrant and because of her specific past and her personal emotional circumstances'.[410] In that case, therefore, the Court did not specify why or how one's personal circumstances make one more vulnerable in detention. Nonetheless, the Court not only found a violation of Article 3, but it also made a distinction between immigration detention and criminal justice. The former, it held, affects 'aliens who, often fearing for their lives, have fled from their own country'.[411] This factor was relevant for the Court in finding that the cumulative conditions of detention had diminished the applicant's dignity and violated her rights under Article 3. These three cases thus show three different approaches to vulnerability, applied without clear criteria under comparable conditions and leading to dramatic differences in outcomes.

To conclude this section, it is possible to offer a certain insight into the temporal and personal scope of the vulnerability of migrants. The special vulnerability of asylum-seekers, the Court has held, ends if and when their applications for asylum are favourably decided and they are granted permission to remain in the host country. At this point, they are no longer considered vulnerable and are to be, instead, treated on a par with the general population.[412] As concerns the personal scope of this type of vulnerability, cases such as *Aden Ahmed v Malta* show that

[408] *M.S.S.* (n 7), Partly Concurring and Partly Dissenting Opinion of Judge Sajó.

[409] *Abdi Mahamud* (n 128), Partly Dissenting Opinion of Judge Sajó.

[410] *Aden Ahmed* (n 393), para 97.

[411] Ibid, para 98.

[412] *Mohammed Hassan and Others v Netherlands and Italy* App nos 40524/10 …, Decision of 27 August 2013, para 179.

irregular migrants may also be considered vulnerable, though the Court's jurisprudence in this regard has lacked consistency to date.[413]

In a 2016 decision, the Court further clarified this by holding that, while individuals whose applications for asylum have been rejected lose some of the socio-economic entitlements due to them because of their vulnerability, they may nonetheless remain vulnerable and attract special positive obligations on the part of the state. It did so when considering the case of a failed Ethiopian asylum-seeker, who claimed that the deprivation of housing and care after his asylum application was rejected violated Article 3.[414] There, the Court held that the applicant's loss of his right to legal residence in the Netherlands 'did not automatically affect his vulnerability as a migrant', although noting too that his situation was different from that in *M.S.S.*[415] Thus, the Court held, while he also found himself in a situation of uncertainty, this was 'inherently different from *M.S.S.* in that it was not linked to the Netherlands authorities' assessment of his asylum request'.[416] In other words, the Court considered – given all the circumstances, in particular a grace period during which the applicant could remain in the country and benefit from state-sponsored housing and care – that the domestic authorities had not shown 'ignorance or inaction towards the applicant's situation'.[417]

B. Vulnerability, the Risk of Ill-treatment and Removal or Expulsion

The above concerns vulnerability in a host state. But what of vulnerability due to a situation or conditions in a migrant's home state? Usually, individual applicants are required to show that there is a sufficiently individualised risk of ill-treatment in order for a return to be incompatible with Article 3 and trigger non-refoulement obligations. Vulnerability, however, may amend this requirement.[418]

There is a distinction to be made here between returns a) under the European Union's Dublin system and b) those outside that system. With regard to returns under the Dublin system, ie within the EU, the Court has been reluctant to find that conditions in the receiving state are bad enough to constitute a systemic failure to provide for the needs of asylum-seekers and thus give rise to a conditional violation of Article 3.[419] For example, regarding Greece, the Court's pre-2011 position was that it could be presumed that, as a receiving Dublin state, Greece would comply with its Convention obligations and that conditions incompatible

[413] *Aden Ahmed* (n 393), para 97.
[414] *Hunde v Netherlands* App no 17931/16, Decision of 5 July 2016, paras 55–56, referring to *M.S.S.* (n 7).
[415] Ibid, para 55, referring to *M.S.S.* (n 7).
[416] Ibid, para 56.
[417] Ibid, para 56.
[418] *Samina v Sweden* App no 55463/09, Judgment of 20 October 2011, para 64.
[419] *Mohammed Hussein and Others* (n 130), para 78.

with the Convention should be taken up with the Greek authorities.[420] The *M.S.S.* judgment was ground-breaking in that it departed from this case law and found that the Belgian authorities had violated their obligations to protect the applicant from ill-treatment in Greece.[421]

Regarding returns to Italy, the Court has repeatedly found that, if the Italian authorities are aware of an applicant's vulnerability, then there is not a sufficient risk of ill-treatment in Italy to violate Article 3.[422] In this regard, the vulnerability of children also comes into play, and may help to overcome the Court's hesitation and problems of proof. For example, in the above-mentioned *Tarakhel* judgment, in 2014, the Court found that it was not compatible with Article 3 to return a family with children to Italy absent individual guarantees from the Italian authorities that they would be kept together and received in a manner adapted to the children's ages.[423] This reasoning in *Tarakhel* gave the Court a way to move away from previous jurisprudence wherein the absence of a systemic problem with reception conditions meant that returns to Italy were considered compatible with Article 3.[424] The Court now routinely takes the vulnerability of families with minor children into account as concerns returns to Italy, though this does not always guarantee applicants success.[425]

When it comes to extra-Dublin returns, the Court has been somewhat less reluctant to find that members of certain ethnic, religious, political, or other minority groups may face a real risk of ill-treatment if transferred to non-Dublin or non-Council of Europe Member States.[426] In *Salah Sheekh v Netherlands*, the Court found that the applicant belonged to a vulnerable group in his native Somalia and would likely be marginalised, isolated, ill-treated, and harassed if returned, so that returning him would violate Article 3.[427] From this starting point, the Court has taken the vulnerability of potential returnees into account when considering whether there is a risk of ill-treatment sufficient to allow it to find a conditional violation of Article 3.[428]

[420] *K.R.S. v the United Kingdom* App no 32733/08, Decision of 2 December 2008; Gina Clayton, 'Asylum-seekers in Europe: M.S.S. v Belgium and Greece' (2011) 11(4) *Human Rights Law Review* 758–73, 761–62.

[421] *M.S.S.* (n 7), paras 344–60.

[422] *Daytbegova and Magomedova v Austria* App no 6198/12, Decision of 4 June 2013, paras 68–69; *Abubeker v Austria and Italy* App no 73874/11, Decision of 18 June 2013, paras 70–71.

[423] *Tarakhel* (n 109), para 122.

[424] Contrast ibid, paras 115, 118–22 and *Mohammed Hussein and Others* (n 130), paras 78–79.

[425] *J.A. and Others v the Netherlands* App no 21459/14, Decision of 3 November 2015, para 28; *N.A. and Others v Denmark* App no 15636/16, Decision of 28 June 2016, para 26.

[426] Compare *Eshonkulov v Russia* App no 68900/13, Judgment of 15 January 2015, para 34; *F. v United Kingdom* App no 17341/03, Decision of 22 June 2004; *Dzhaksybergenov v Ukraine* App no 12343/10, Judgment of 10 February 2011, para 37; *Hirsi Jamaa and Others v Italy* App no 27765/09, Judgment (GC) of 23 February 2012, Reports 2012, paras 125 and 155; *Savriddin Dzhurayev v Russia* App no 71386/10, Judgment of 25 April 2013, Reports 2013 (extracts), paras 179 and 181; *N.A.N.S. v Sweden* App no 68411/10, Judgment of 27 June 2013, paras 32–33; *Khamrakulov v Russia* App no 68894/13, Judgment of 16 April 2015, para 66.

[427] *Salah Sheekh v Netherlands* App no 1948/04, Judgment of 11 January 2007, paras 140 and 146.

[428] *Hirsi Jamaa and Others* (n 426), para 155.

One concrete example of this concerns the vulnerable ethnic Uzbeks who risk return from Russia to Kyrgyzstan, where they stand to be prosecuted for their involvement in inter-ethnic riots, and potentially tortured.[429] That group, the Court has held, is 'systematically exposed to a practice of ill-treatment'.[430] The systematic nature of the ill-treatment in this context, the Court has held, means that applicants must only prove that they belong to the group in question, and not prove any more individualised threat, in order for the Court to consider that they are at a real risk of ill-treatment if returned.[431]

Similar findings apply to Uzbeks facing extradition to Uzbekistan, where they have been charged with crimes related to their religious or political convictions.[432] Likewise, too, the human rights situation in Turkmenistan, which the Court has described as 'alarming' given rampant discrimination against people who were not of Turkmen origin, means that expulsions there might violate Article 3.[433]

The vulnerability of members of certain religious groups is also relevant in this context. For example, in a 2013 judgment against Russia, the Court found a violation of the state's obligations under Article 3 in a case concerning the return of an applicant to Tajikistan, where he was being persecuted on account of his Muslim faith.[434] The Court has likewise held that individuals whose extradition is sought by the Tajik authorities because of religiously or politically motivated criminal charges constitute a vulnerable group, facing a real risk of ill-treatment if removed.[435] In various cases against Sweden, the Court has also examined whether it is permissible to return members of the Iraqi Christian minority, who are vulnerable in certain parts of the country 'either directly because of their faith' or because of societal perceptions about them as a group.[436] There, however, the Court reached the conclusion that the possibility of internal relocation within Iraq made it possible to return these individuals.

Another example of a vulnerable group for expulsion purposes are LGBTQI migrants who allege that, if returned to their country of origin, they would face a risk of ill-treatment on account of their sexual orientation. In this regard, the Court's vulnerability jurisprudence has proved slow to protect LGBTQI

[429] *Kadirzhanov and Mamashev v Russia* App nos 42351/13 and 47823/13, Judgment of 17 July 2014, paras 91–92; *Khamrakulov* (n 426); *Mamadaliyev v Russia* App no 5614/13, Judgment of 24 July 2014, para 62; *Tadzhibayev v Russia* App no 17724/14, Judgment of 1 December 2015, para 43; *R. v Russia* App no 11916/15, Judgment of 26 January 2016, para 56.

[430] *Khamrakulov* (n 426), para 66.

[431] *Kadirzhanov and Mamashev* (n 429), para 92.

[432] *Eshonkulov* (n 426), para 34.

[433] *Allanazarova v Russia* App no 46721/15, Judgment of 14 February 2017, para 73.

[434] *Savriddin Dzhurayev* (n 426), paras 15 and 181.

[435] *B.U. and Others v Russia* App no 59609/17, 74677/17, and 76379/17, Judgment of 22 January 2019, para 17.

[436] *N.A.N.S.* (n 426), para 32; *M.K.N. v Sweden* App no 72413/10, Judgment of 27 June 2013, paras 32 and 33; *N.M.B.* (n 2), paras 35–36, 46; *A.G.A.M. v Sweden* App no 71680/10, Judgment of 27 June 2013, para 37; *M.Y.H. and Others v Sweden* App no 50859/10, Judgment of 27 June 2013, paras 60–61; *W.H. v Sweden* App no 49341/10, Judgment of 27 March 2014, paras 63, 65 and 67.

applicants.[437] For example, in two cases concerning expulsion to Iran, the Court has held that though 'the general situation in Iran does not foster the protection of human rights and that homosexuals may be vulnerable to abuse', the applicants had failed to prove that there were substantial grounds to believe that they would experience ill-treatment.[438] By contrast, in a later case under Article 5(1), which has already been touched upon above, the Court showed more advanced engagement with and a meaningful response to the vulnerability of a similar applicant. There, it considered that detaining a 'homosexual' Iranian asylum-seeker together with other asylum-seekers who would presumably treat him in a homophobic manner did not take his vulnerability sufficiently into account.[439] And then, in 2020, it found a conditional violation of Article 3 regarding the return of a 'homosexual person' to the Gambia, albeit without reference to the concept of vulnerability.[440]

Thirdly, the risk of being subjected to female genital mutilation potentially renders applicants vulnerable for the purposes of Article 3. The Court has recently acknowledged this, albeit in a weak and roundabout way, by finding that an applicant was not to be considered vulnerable because she had not proven that she faced a risk of exposure to (in this case, repeated) female genital mutilation.[441] This makes it possible to assume that proving such a risk would entail a finding of vulnerability.

Regarding the risk of poor medical care for ill returnees to non-Dublin states, the Court has long used an extremely restrictive approach. Beginning with its judgment in *N. v United Kingdom*, the Court – although not altogether consistently – limited ill migrants' protection from being returned to a state in which they would receive poor medical care, providing such protection under Article 3 only in extreme cases.[442] An applicant's health-related vulnerability, thus, did not always suffice in order for the Court to find that expulsion to a non-Dublin state would constitute a violation of Article 3. This approach was not always well-received. For example, Judge Power-Forde, appending a powerful Dissenting Opinion to the Chamber judgment in *S.J. v Belgium*, pointed out an inconsistency in the Court's case law: if poor reception conditions suffice to render the return of suspected terrorists incompatible with Article 3, she argued, the same should have been true for the applicant in *S.J.*, an HIV-positive, 22-year-old mother of three.[443]

[437] Raoul Wieland and Edward J Alessi, 'Do the Challenges of LGBTQ Asylum Applicants Under Dublin Register with the European Court of Human Rights?' *Social and Legal Studies* (2020) 1–21.

[438] *F. v United Kingdom* (n 426), para 1; *I.I.N.* (n 2).

[439] *O.M.* (n 280), para 53.

[440] *B. and C. v Switzerland* App nos 889/19 and 43987/16, Judgment of 17 November 2020.

[441] *Sow v Belgium* App no 27081/13, Judgment of 19 January 2016, paras 56, 68.

[442] *N. v United Kingdom* App no 26565/05, Judgment (GC) of 27 May 2008, Reports 2008. This judgment came in the wake of *D. v United Kingdom* App no 30240/96, Judgment of 2 May 1997, Reports 1997-III, paras 53 and 54. See also *Sufi and Elmi* (n 178), para 303. Compare also *M.T. v Sweden* App no 1412/12, Judgment of 26 February 2015, and the Dissenting Opinion by Judge de Gaetano.

[443] *S.J. v Belgium* App no 70055/10, Judgment of 27 February 2014, Dissenting Opinion of Judge Power-Forde. This case was referred to the Grand Chamber but struck out of the list after a friendly settlement (*S.J. v Belgium* App no 70055/10, Judgment (GC) of 19 March 2015).

Judge Power-Forde's concerns are important and justified ones that speak to the heart of the lack of care with which migrants are treated in many modern societies,[444] and touch upon a delicate area of the Court's jurisprudence, namely the question of whether socio-economic factors in a receiving non-Member State can prevent an applicant's return to that state. That is something that, in the past, the Court has been inclined to allow only if an additional test of exceptionality is met.[445]

This very high threshold requires the existence of 'compelling' humanitarian reasons, and has been applied where applicants challenge their expulsion on medical or health grounds. In this regard, the Court has noted that a balancing between individual and community interests is inherent to the Convention, and that it therefore can only block an expulsion in very exceptional circumstances, so as to spare states the financial burdens of providing medical care to non-nationals.[446] There is thus a not-so-covert balancing exercise at play in such cases,[447] and one that is difficult to square with the absolute nature of Article 3, which technically does not permit any such balancing.[448]

In this regard, however, a real shift of the balance in applicants' favour – and in the favour of consistent vulnerability reasoning – came about with the 2016 Grand Chamber judgment in *Paposhvili v Belgium*.[449] This judgment largely reshaped the Court's case law on the expulsion of seriously ill applicants, perhaps in no small part due to a third-party intervention by the Ghent University Human Rights Centre, which urged the Court to reconsider its approach given the inappropriateness of balancing budgetary considerations against individual suffering under Article 3.[450] *Paposhvili* concerned a seriously ill Georgian man who faced expulsion to Georgia, and who alleged that he would face a risk of ill-treatment contrary to Article 3 if expelled. In Belgium, he was being treated for multiple serious illnesses, including leukaemia, with cutting-edge and very expensive drugs; these were not, he alleged, available to him in Georgia. The applicant died before the Grand Chamber considered the case, but the Court decided to continue the examination because of the 'special circumstances relating to respect for human

[444] To paraphrase Hannah Arendt, *The Origins of Totalitarianism*, 2nd edn (Harvest / Harcourt Inc, 1973) 297, discussed further below.

[445] *F.N. v United Kingdom* App no 3202/09, Decision of 17 September 2013, para 31.

[446] *N. v United Kingdom* (n 442), paras 42–44. See, in this regard, Kathryn Greenman, 'A Castle Built on Sand? Article 3 ECHR and the Source of Risk in Non-Refoulement Obligations in International Law' (2015) 27(2) *International Journal of Refugee Law* 264–96, 269.

[447] *Jalloh v Germany* App no 54810/00, Judgment [GC] of 11 July 2006, Reports 2006-IX, para 119; Hemme Battjes, 'In Search of a Fair Balance: The Absolute Character of the Prohibition of Refoulement under Article 3 ECHR Reassessed' (2009) 22(3) *Leiden Journal of International Law* 583–621.

[448] Stijn Smet, 'The "Absolute" Prohibition of Torture and Inhuman or Degrading Treatment in Article 3 ECHR: Truly a Question of Scope Only?' in Eva Brems and Janneke H Gerards (eds), *Shaping Rights in the ECHR: The Role of the European Court of Human Rights in Determining the Scope of Human Rights* (CUP, 2013) 273–93, 274, 289.

[449] *Paposhvili v Belgium* App no 41738/10, Judgment (GC) of 13 December 2016, Reports 2016.

[450] Ghent University Human Rights Centre, '*Paposhvili v Belgium*: Third Party Intervention', 17 July 2015, www.hrc.ugent.be/wp-content/uploads/2015/09/Paposhvili.pdf.

rights' involved.[451] The Court ultimately came to the conclusion that, had the Belgian authorities expelled Mr Paposhvili without assessing the risk to his health, they would have violated Article 3 ECHR.[452]

This finding was momentous, and it came about because, while acknowledging the state prerogative regarding aliens on their territory, the Court came to the conclusion that its application of Article 3 since *N. v United Kingdom*, ie, interpreting the provision as only blocking the expulsion of persons near death, had deprived seriously but non-critically ill applicants 'of the benefit of that provision' – ie, of their Article 3 rights.[453] The Court thereby changed its case law to mean that persons who risk 'a serious, rapid and irreversible decline in his or her state of health resulting in intense suffering or to a significant reduction in life expectancy' fall under the 'very exceptional cases' requirement and meet the threshold of Article 3.[454] Where applicants allege a risk of health-related treatment falling under Article 3, the Court held, States must 'examine the applicants' fears and … assess the risks they would face if removed to the receiving country', and submit their allegations to 'close scrutiny'.[455] This means that states must compare an applicant's state of health pre-removal to the projected evolution thereof after expulsion.[456]

Paposhvili was a leap forward from *N. v United Kingdom*. The importance of this case is that the cost of treating Mr Paposhvili was not allowed to outweigh – or, in fact, to be placed in the balance with – his potential suffering. It should be noted, however, that the Court did not go so far as to use vulnerability language, despite the fact that the applicant, respondent government, and the two third-party interveners all referred to the concept. Time will tell how the Court will deal with similar cases, but it seems that there is still a certain degree of reluctance to set an overly broad precedent in this type of case.

Regarding the expulsion of mentally ill applicants, Article 3 provides stronger protection than other provisions of the Convention, specifically Article 8. For example, under the latter provision, the Court often rather generously presumes that the receiving states will provide adequate treatment or simply examines whether the individual concerned will be stable for the duration of the transfer.[457] By contrast, the return of a mentally ill individual without assurances that he or she will receive adequate treatment in the receiving country in other cases may constitute a conditional violation of Article 3.[458] Mental illness can

[451] *Paposhvili* (n 449), para 133, referring to Art 37(1) ECHR.
[452] Ibid, operative part of the judgment, para 1.
[453] Ibid, para 181.
[454] Ibid, paras 182–83.
[455] Ibid, paras 184 and 187.
[456] Ibid, paras 188 and 205.
[457] See, in this context, the case of *Khan v Germany*, which – albeit brought under Art 8 and without reference to vulnerability – illustrates this phenomenon very well (referring to the Chamber judgment, *Khan v Germany* App no 38030/12, Judgment of 23 April 2015, para 53, as the Grand Chamber case was struck out (*Khan v Germany* App no 38030/12, Judgment (GC) of 21 September 2016 (Struck out of the List), paras 37–42)).
[458] In the context of Art 3, see *Tatar* (n 113), where Judge Lemmens, in his Partly Dissenting Opinion, argued for the recognition of the applicant's vulnerability and the need to obtain assurances.

sometimes even be the sole deciding factor for whether an applicant should (not) be returned.[459] The case law on this matter is, however, heterogeneous. In some cases, the Court applies the exceptionality test, and requires 'compelling humanitarian grounds against removal'.[460] For example, in *F.N. v United Kingdom*, the Court considered that the applicant – who had allegedly been raped in her home state, Uganda, immediately before her departure there, and who had since been suffering from depression and therefore required regular access to anti-depressant medication – had not sufficiently demonstrated such compelling humanitarian grounds against removal. The fact that the applicant had become homeless upon return to her home state and had therefore suffered renewed rape leading to the birth of a child, as well as having irregular access to her medication for financial reasons, did not change this outcome.[461]

C. Comments

The Court has developed a voluminous case law on vulnerability and migration, and the *M.S.S.* judgment cemented the recognition of asylum-seekers as a vulnerable group. However, in this context, vulnerability and its consequences can be particularly controversial.

For example, in his attached Partly Concurring and Partly Dissenting Opinion in *M.S.S.*, Judge Sajó raised a number of criticisms about vulnerability reasoning that merit further consideration here. In short, he argued against understanding asylum-seekers as a vulnerable group, and contended that 'although many asylum-seekers are vulnerable persons, they cannot be unconditionally considered as a particularly vulnerable group', because the Court's approach to vulnerable groups only applies to groups of which all members, 'due to their adverse social categorization, deserve special protection'.[462] Citing the Court's case law under Article 14, the Judge admitted that restrictions of the rights of particularly vulnerable groups entail a narrow margin of appreciation and require very weighty reasons.[463] This approach, he conceded, is merited given the lasting consequences of the prejudice to which these groups were historically subjected.[464] However, Judge Sajó reasoned that asylum-seekers could not be classified as a vulnerable group, contending that, on the one hand, they have not historically suffered prejudice with lasting consequences rendering them socially excluded – a problematic argument to make in contexts of rampant anti-migrant sentiment – and, on the other, that they cannot be considered a homogeneous group. The majority's approach,

[459] *Sufi and Elmi* (n 178), paras 303 and 312.
[460] *F.N.* (n 445), para 31.
[461] Ibid.
[462] *M.S.S.* (n 7), Partly Concurring and Partly Dissenting Opinion of Judge Sajó.
[463] Ibid.
[464] Ibid.

he argued, meant that Article 3 and 'the constitutional position of a welfare state are getting even closer' as there 'seems to be only a small step between the Court's present position and that of a general and unconditional positive obligation of the State to provide shelter and other material services to satisfy the basic needs of the "vulnerable"'.[465]

Several of these arguments require breaking down. The socio-economic obligations that Judge Sajó feared here seem to have gained traction in the Court's jurisprudence, albeit to a very modest extent. While the judge's definition of group vulnerability corresponds to the Court's Article 14 jurisprudence, he fails to recognise that the vulnerability of individuals has begun to play an equally, if not more, important role in the Court's jurisprudence. In addition, his requirement of homogeneity among the members of vulnerable groups is a seriously problematic one that would nullify individual identities and circumstances in any group. In any event, vulnerability has not led to the imposition of wide-ranging socio-economic obligations on states. The reason for this is partly that the Court is not being as principled as Judge Sajó, in his separate Opinion, expected it to be.

Judge Sajó was responding to the power of Article 3, namely the fact that it enshrines unconditional obligations given its absolute and non-derogable nature. However, the Court continues to struggle to reconcile state interests with the absolute nature of Article 3. That struggle is particularly evident in its jurisprudence on migrants and asylum-seekers. Recognising the vulnerability of these individuals means engaging with their dependency and the real consequences of return; this, in turn, potentially has some politically sensitive consequences, including high financial costs, if the Court wishes to take the absolute nature of Article 3 seriously. On the other hand, minimising harms or failing to engage with the right to dignity of migrants and asylum-seekers undermines the core values of Article 3, namely their equal entitlement to the Convention's protection and their human dignity.

In *Abdi Mahamud v Malta*, Judge Sajó wrote another relevant Separate Opinion concerning vulnerability.[466] There, the judge criticised the vagueness of the Court's approach to individual vulnerability. This case was an example of a recurring trend in Strasbourg: where the Court struggles to make findings that would have large-scale socio-economic and political consequences, it uses vulnerability to provide relief only to certain badly-off applicants. In this vein, as outlined above, it has even gone so far as to defer to the domestic determination of who is vulnerable. The problems with this are multiple: not only does the Court provide different levels of protection for applicants in objectively similar circumstances, but it also invites a variable and disjointed understanding of vulnerability. In addition, it creates an incentive for states to attempt to avoid violation judgments by using a very restrictive domestic definition of vulnerability.

[465] Ibid.
[466] *Abdi Mahamud* (n 128), Partly Dissenting Opinion of Judge Sajó.

The variability of the Court's approach is evident when comparing *Abdi Mahamud* to the *Moxamed Ismaaciil and Abdirahman Warsame*[467] and *Aden Ahmed* cases.[468] These three very similar cases, as discussed above as well, display different outcomes linked to the three different approaches to vulnerability used, with the applicants being considered (i) invulnerable by the domestic and Strasbourg authorities or (ii) vulnerable by Strasbourg *because* of a domestic assessment or (iii) vulnerable *despite* that assessment. What these three cases have in common is that all three indicate a willingness to use vulnerability to distinguish cases. *Aden Ahmed* distinguished immigration detention from imprisonment and the applicant's fragile mental and physical state from that of her co-detainees. *Moxamed Ismaaciil and Abdirahman Warsame* distinguished the applicants in that case, not considered vulnerable, from vulnerable applicants such as the one in *Aden Ahmed*. *Abdi Mahamud* used vulnerability reasoning to find a violation in circumstances almost identical to those in *Moxamed Ismaaciil and Abdirahman Warsame*, distinguishing the applicant in the former case from the latter on the basis of a domestic assessment of vulnerability.

This mixture of approaches not only creates confusion about what vulnerability means and who will be considered vulnerable in any given case, and thus affects the predictability and credibility of the Strasbourg case law. It also does nothing to address the fact that immigration detention lasting – as was the case in these judgments – for up to 18 months can have a dramatic impact on any affected person, not just those who are considered vulnerable on the domestic or Strasbourg plane. On the other hand, using vulnerability as the yardstick by which cases are distinguished is certainly an improvement over the 'compelling humanitarian grounds' test, which proves almost impossible for applicants to meet.

One further comment is necessary in this regard, namely concerning the *Hunde v the Netherlands* case. There, the Court distinguished the vulnerability of a failed asylum-seeker from that of asylum-seekers whose applications were still pending; specifically, it found that states do not owe the same obligations regarding housing and care to failed asylum-seekers as they do to applicants such as the one in the *M.S.S.* case.[469] While the outcome of this case was consistent with the Court's general approach to expulsions, cases such as this one present a conceptual problem. Thus, if asylum-seekers are vulnerable because of everything they have been through during their migration and the traumatic experiences that they are likely to have endured, as the Court held in *M.S.S.*,[470] as well as their dependence on the state, then it is not clear why a failed asylum-seeker should not be considered equally vulnerable, as the failure of one's asylum application is unlikely to reverse one's migration-related trauma or one's dependence on a host state. Of course, failed asylum-seekers have, by definition, been shown to lack the risks of

[467] *Moxamed Ismaaciil and Abdirahman Warsame* (n 403).
[468] *Aden Ahmed* (n 393).
[469] *Hunde* (n 414), para 55, referring to *M.S.S.* (n 7).
[470] *M.S.S.* (n 7), para 232.

persecution or ill-treatment that those whose applications are pending may have claimed. However, the vulnerability framework provided by the Court to date does not create a convincing basis for distinguishing these two categories from each other, except for – as the Court itself argues – via the need to balance individual and general interests, an argument which has little or no place under the absolute prohibition enshrined in Article 3.[471]

VI. Vulnerability Due to Discrimination and Marginalisation

In the past, the Court has taken the vulnerability of members of religious, ethnic, political, and other minorities into consideration when evaluating whether these individuals face a risk of ill-treatment abroad. However, the Court's understanding of the vulnerability of these minorities, along with other groups who face discrimination, such as LGBTQI persons and those living with HIV/AIDS, also applies beyond the migration context.

The Court's case law regarding vulnerable minorities under Article 3 revolves around the recognition of specific groups who have – historically or recently – been exposed to discrimination as a group. This part of the Court's vulnerability jurisprudence under Article 3 most strongly evokes its approach to vulnerability under Article 14. In other words, this is a way to render certain situations suspect because they concern a member of a particular minority. In these cases, the Court recognises that the general situation of these groups – the usual conditions of their interaction with members of the majority or with the authorities – is particularly difficult and rife with discriminatory attitudes.

A. Vulnerable Ethnic Minorities

The first and foremost group recognised by the Court in this context – and the only one that has been recognised as a 'vulnerable group' in the Court's sense of the term – are Roma people and Travellers. Since 2001, the Court has repeatedly referred to the vulnerability of Roma and Travellers under Article 3.[472] These cases generally involve targeted discriminatory treatment inflicted by either state or private actors.

For one, the Court held that the Roma are in a particularly vulnerable situation in their interactions with police.[473] Other state actors may also perpetrate discriminatory violence against Roma: in *I.G. and Others v Slovakia*, the Court held that

[471] *Hunde* (n 414), para 54.
[472] *Smith v United Kingdom* App no 34334/96, Decision of 3 May 2001.
[473] *Sashov and Others v Bulgaria* App no 14383/03, Judgment of 7 January 2010, para 55.

the non-consensual sterilisation of young Roma women constituted a violation of Article 3, and in doing so took into consideration the vulnerability of the population group to which they belonged and also the importance of female fertility in that group's culture.[474] Elsewhere, it found that, because of 'their turbulent history and constant uprooting, the Roma have become a specific type of disadvantaged and vulnerable minority', meaning that they require special protection and that the state must vigorously investigate offences against them, also where committed by private actors.[475] In 2018, the Court found that the Russian authorities, who failed to protect Roma applicants from a 'pogrom' and simply advised them to leave before their homes were ransacked by a mob, had subjected them to degrading treatment, given their vulnerability.[476]

The second ethnic group repeatedly considered vulnerable by the Court in its Article 3 jurisprudence concerns situations in non-member states. This situation has been discussed above, and for example concerns ethnic Uzbeks who risk being returned to Kyrgyzstan, where they stand to be prosecuted for their involvement in inter-ethnic riots and potentially subjected to torture or ill-treatment.[477]

B. Vulnerable Religious Minorities

Religious minorities may also be vulnerable for the purposes of Article 3. These cases largely concern the state obligation to protect against violence by private parties. For example, in a judgment against Serbia concerning the violence inflicted on a leading member of the Hare Krishna community by private individuals, the Court held that after various incidents 'it should have been obvious to the police that the applicant, who was a member of a vulnerable religious minority … was being systematically targeted and that future attacks were very likely to follow'.[478] As the police failed to take sufficient preventive measures, the Court found a violation of Article 3. Similarly, in *Begheluri and Others v Georgia*, the Court examined the response of the authorities to the religiously motivated violence and aggression inflicted on a group of Jehovah's Witnesses by private parties and by police. The Court found that, given the applicants' helplessness, the vulnerability of their situation, and the indifference they experienced when seeking the assistance of the authorities, they had likewise suffered a violation of Article 3.[479]

[474] *I.G. and Others v Slovakia* App no 15966/04, Judgment of 13 November 2012, paras 125, and also – in the context of Art 14–160.

[475] *Balázs v Hungary* App no 15529/12, Judgment of 20 October 2015, para 53.

[476] *A.N. and Others v Russia* App nos 61689/16, 20421/17, 23188/17 …, Judgment of 23 October 2018; para 134.

[477] *Kadirzhanov and Mamashev* (n 429), paras 91–92; *Mamadaliyev* (n 429), para 62; *Khamrakulov* (n 426), paras 65–66.

[478] *Milanović v Serbia* App no 44614/07, Judgment of 14 December 2010, para 89.

[479] *Begheluri and Others v Georgia* App no 28490/02, Judgment of 7 October 2014, para 113.

As noted above, the vulnerability of religious groups is also relevant in the migration context: it may be incompatible with Article 3 to return individuals to a state where they will face persecution on account of their religion.[480] This relates to violence not only by the state, but also by private parties.[481]

C. Vulnerable LGBTQI+ People

As concerns the vulnerability of members of the LGBTQI+ community, the Court to date has mostly considered this in the context of migration, as discussed above.

Beyond this, there have also been two Article 3 cases that relate to vulnerability in detention and – real or presumed – LGBTQI identity. However, in both cases, the Court focused on the applicants' vulnerability as detainees, and not on their LGBTQI identity. In one case, the Court considered whether the state had complied with Article 3 in subjecting a 'homosexual' inmate to solitary confinement after he alleged that he had been sexually abused.[482] In that case, the Court found no violation of Article 3, stating that the provision should not impose excessive burdens on the authorities.[483] In another case, the Court heard an Article 3 complaint concerning the rape of an inmate by state officials who (mistakenly) presumed that he was 'a homosexual'. There, too, the vulnerability analysis concerned not the applicant's presumed sexual orientation, but his detention.[484]

The dearth of case law in this regard does not mean that LGBTQI identity does not, in a number of Member States, expose individuals to an acute risk of abuse and violence, both by state and non-state actors.[485] Recently, the Court had an opportunity to consider this type of vulnerability in depth under Article 3 taken together with Article 14 ECHR. The case was *Identoba and Others v Georgia*, and it concerned violence against persons participating in a march organised by members of the LGBTQI community. In its judgment, the Court held that states have an obligation, albeit not an absolute one, to 'take all reasonable steps to unmask possible discriminatory motives' for ill-treatment.[486] This, the Court acknowledged, is a 'difficult task' and one that does not require a particular result, but simply requires states' 'best endeavours'.[487] However, it also held, '[t]reating violence and brutality with a discriminatory intent on an equal footing with cases that have no such overtones would be turning a blind eye to the specific nature of acts that are

[480] *Savriddin Dzhurayev* (n 426), paras 15 and 181.
[481] *N.A.N.S.* (n 426), paras 32 and 33; *M.K.N.* (n 436), paras 32 and 33.
[482] *Stasi* (n 267), para 91.
[483] Ibid, paras 78, 91.
[484] *Zontul* (n 298), paras 16, 79, 88.
[485] *Identoba and Others v Georgia* App no 73235/12, Judgment of 12 May 2015, paras 68, 72; PACE, Resolution 1728(2010) of the Parliamentary Assembly on Discrimination on the Basis of Sexual Orientation and Gender Identity, 29 April 2010, esp paras 3–8.
[486] *Identoba and Others* (n 485), para 67.
[487] Ibid.

particularly destructive of fundamental rights'.[488] Given the 'precarious position' of LGBTQI individuals in Georgia and the prevalence of negative opinions against them, the Court held that 'the discriminatory overtones of [the violent incident in question] and the level of vulnerability of the applicants, who publicly positioned themselves with the target group of the sexual prejudice, are particularly apparent'.[489] Given the fact that the march's organisers had requested protection in advance and also given 'the history of public hostility towards the LGBT community in Georgia', the Court held that the authorities knew or ought to have known about the risks, and were obligated to provide heightened protection.[490] The Court underlined the necessity of meaningful inquiry into the discriminatory motives behind the attack on the march in light of the hostile climate in Georgia and the homophobic hate speech uttered by the assailants. It held that, otherwise, 'prejudice-motivated crimes would unavoidably be treated on an equal footing with ordinary cases without such overtones, and the resultant indifference would be tantamount to official acquiescence to or even connivance with hate crimes.'[491] In addition to this investigative obligation, it held, the authorities were under 'a compelling positive obligation to protect the demonstrators'.[492]

The reasoning in *Identoba* repeatedly invoked the concept of vulnerability, and shows engagement with the realities of homophobic violence and the need for the authorities to respond to these types of societal attitudes where they put discriminated-against people at risk. However, situations in the various Member States vary greatly. In a 2016 case against Romania, the Court indicated that it may not be entirely ready to classify all LGBTQI individuals as vulnerable. In that judgment, which involved violence by private actors against members of the LGBTQI community after a march, the Court acknowledged that 'the LGBTI community in the respondent State finds itself in a precarious situation, being subject to negative attitudes towards its members'.[493] As a result, it found that the homophobic violence suffered by the applicants 'was directed at their identity and must necessarily have aroused in them feelings of fear, anguish and insecurity'.[494] However, vulnerability language did not enter into the Court's reasoning under Article 3, meaning that it did not describe the Romanian LGBTQI community as vulnerable.

Nevertheless, the recent recognition of the vulnerability of the LGBTQI community in at least one Member State with a culture of entrenched homophobia illustrates the potential to use the vulnerability of certain groups to create positive state obligations to protect them. *Identoba* provides much-needed recognition of the risks associated with a particular sexual orientation or gender identity in

[488] Ibid.
[489] Ibid, para 68.
[490] Ibid, para 72.
[491] Ibid, para 77.
[492] Ibid, para 80.
[493] *M.C. and A.C. v Romania* App no 12060/12, Judgment of 12 April 2016, para 118.
[494] Ibid, para 119.

certain countries. This approach may continue to develop in different directions, including potentially into a recognition that discriminatory treatment as such may constitute an affront to human dignity that meets the standard of degrading treatment.[495] This could also mean that discriminatory intent suffices to raise ill-treatment to the level of torture, or that the Court will have to engage with violence against LGBTQI people also in countries without violent and dominating discourses of homophobia and transphobia. However, today, engagement with the vulnerability of LGBTQI people still appears to be in its nascent stages.

D. HIV/AIDS

Except for in the context of detention, as discussed above, and in the very specific circumstances of terminally ill cancer patients seeking access to an experimental medicine,[496] physical illness has not been generally recognised by the Court as a ground for vulnerability under Article 3.[497] There is one potential exception to this rule, however, and that is the case of people living with HIV/AIDS. The Court has established that these individuals constitute a vulnerable group for the purposes of Article 14 ECHR.[498] When it comes to Article 3, like most other physical illnesses, the Court has mostly dealt with the vulnerability brought about by HIV/AIDS in the detention context, but the fact that this group faces stigma and discrimination in ways comparable to the groups discussed above means that this case law could have broader implications.

Most of the relevant cases here do concern the obligation to provide adequate medical care to detainees. Thus, when detaining persons living with HIV/AIDS, states must have regard to their fragile state of health, and must monitor their illness and provide medical care.[499] The fragile state of health of seropositive people is an 'aggravating factor' regarding ill-treatment inflicted on these individuals, and intensifies the obligation of the State to justify that treatment.[500]

In an expulsion context, returning an HIV-positive migrant to a country where he or she will not receive adequate health care can amount to a death sentence.[501] However, the Court was, for a long time, generally unwilling to accept arguments that an applicant's medical condition and the alleged inability to obtain adequate

[495] *Karaahmed v Bulgaria* App no 30587/13, Judgment of 24 February 2015, para 73, citing *Begheluri and Others* (n 479), para 100.

[496] *Hristozov and Others* (n 19), para 122.

[497] Compare *Karaahmed* (n 495), para 76, where the Court held that the applicant's poor eyesight did not make him vulnerable.

[498] *Kiyutin* (n 5), paras 64 and 68.

[499] *Kozhokar v Russia* App no 33099/08, Judgment of 16 December 2010, para 111; *Khudobin v Russia* App no 59696/00, Judgment of 26 October 2006, Reports 2006-XII (extracts), paras 89 and 96.

[500] *Taïs* (n 238), paras 8 and 89.

[501] PACE, Resolution 1997 (2014), 'Migrants and Refugees and the Fight against AIDS' adopted by the Standing Committee on 23 May 2014, para 7.

care upon removal justified finding a Convention violation.[502] In *N. v United Kingdom*, discussed above, the Court found that there would be no violation of Article 3 if an HIV-positive applicant were to be returned to Uganda. The Court was only willing to protect against the most extreme cases of ill migrants being returned to face a breakdown of their medical treatment.[503] Later cases equally refused to appreciate how an applicant's health would evolve after expulsion or whether they would have practical access to required medication.[504] Fortunately, recent case law on expelling very ill non-nationals indicates that this jurisprudence may have changed in applicants' favour.[505] Nevertheless, it remains to be seen how the vulnerability of applicants who depend on permission to remain in a host country to continue to access adequate medical care for their HIV/AIDS-related medical issues will be recognised in the Court's future case law.

Beyond this, however, there is not much case law on the vulnerability of persons living with HIV/AIDS and Article 3. This stands in contrast to the Court's progressive jurisprudence under Article 14, whereby persons living with HIV/AIDS have been recognised as a vulnerable group.[506] Through this case law, the Court has pushed back against discrimination against these persons by requiring particularly weighty reasons to justify discriminatory treatment.[507] Discrimination on the basis of seropositivity intersects with stigma against LGBTQI individuals, those living in poverty, intravenous drug users, and foreign nationals.[508] The Court's Article 14 case law provides, or can provide, a corrective to this. By finding that 'people living with HIV are a vulnerable group with a history of prejudice and stigmatisation', the Court has refused to accept exclusionary rules based on the generalisation that these individuals behave unsafely,[509] which it described as lacking a factual basis and failing 'to take into account the individual.'[510]

[502] This jurisprudence revolves around the judgment in *N. v United Kingdom* (n 442) and has been subject to intense criticism (François Julien-Laferrière, 'L'éloignement des étrangers malades: Faut-il préférer les réalités budgétaires aux préoccupations humanitaires?' (2009) 77 *Revue trimestrielle des droits de l'homme* 261–77, 263; Sylvie Da Lomba, 'Vulnerability, Irregular Migrants' Health-Related Rights and the European Court of Human Rights' (2014) 21(4) *European Journal of Health* Law 339–64). For an exception to the rule, see *D. v United Kingdom* (n 442).

[503] *N. v United Kingdom* (n 442).

[504] *S.J.* (n 443), para 125, referred to the Grand Chamber but struck out of the list after a friendly settlement.

[505] *Paposhvili* (n 449).

[506] *I.B.* (n 9), para 81; *Novruk and Others v Russia* App nos 31039/11 …, Judgment of 15 March 2016, para 100.

[507] *Kiyutin* (n 5), paras 63–64.

[508] Richard Parker and Peter Aggleton, 'HIV and AIDS-Related Stigma and Discrimination: A Conceptual Framework and Implications for Action' (2003) 57 *Social Science & Medicine* 13–24, 15; *Kiyutin* (n 5), especially at paras 66–74.

[509] *Kiyutin* (n 5), paras 64, 68, 71.

[510] Ibid, para 68. On this case, see also Lourdes Peroni and Alexandra Timmer, 'Vulnerable Groups: The Promise of an Emerging Concept in European Human Rights Convention Law' (2013) 11(4) *International Journal of Constitutional Law* 1056–85, 1067.

VII. Vulnerability, Pregnancy and Precarious Reproductive Health

While sex is one of the prohibited grounds for different treatment contained in the prohibition of discrimination in Article 14 ECHR, the Court does not consider women vulnerable as such. Instead, its case law shows that female(-identifying) applicants may be considered vulnerable due to a particular situation in which they find themselves. This may be due to an experience of victimisation, for example in the form of gender-based violence, or due to various contexts that particularly affect women. One such ground for vulnerability relates particularly to those who are pregnant and their needs and the needs of their unborn children during pregnancy.

This requires some clarification before turning to the case law. Given that not all women are able to become pregnant, and cisgender women are not the only ones who experience pregnancy, or the vulnerability associated with it, the Court's approach is a sensible one. From this perspective, it is good news that the Court separates vulnerability due to pregnancy (which it recognises under certain circumstances) from the idea of vulnerability based on gender (which it does not recognise as a source of vulnerability absent other factors). However, at the same time, stereotypes and discrimination related to gender may be linked to the ways in which pregnancy-related healthcare is denied: these will be discussed further on in this section. In addition, it should be noted that the Court does not display any terminological awareness of the fact that non-female-identifying people can become pregnant, and references to 'women' below draw from that case law without seeking to imply definitions of womanhood. In general, it can be noted that the vulnerability of those who are pregnant, particularly those in precarious situations of reproductive health, represents a special case of vulnerability that can be linked to dependency and State control.

The Court's case law on vulnerability in pregnancy began with the 2004 *Bati and Others v Turkey* judgment, discussed above, wherein the Court considered an adult applicant to be vulnerable because she was pregnant at the time of her ill-treatment in police custody. While the judgment does not indicate whether the applicant was considered vulnerable in her own right or whether the vulnerability in question was that of her unborn child,[511] it did represent the beginning of the Court's recognition of the vulnerability of women who are pregnant or giving birth under Article 3.[512]

The vulnerability that arises during pregnancy creates special positive obligations on the part of the state. For example, in 2016, the Court found that the

[511] Although the Court's recognition of the rights of the unborn child as such has been hesitant, see *Vo v France* App no 53924/00, Judgment (GC) of 8 July 2004, Reports 2004-VIII.

[512] *Bati and Others* (n 49), para 122. Compare, for a later example, *Nechiporuk and Yonkalo v Ukraine* App no 42310/04, Judgment of 21 April 2011, para 156.

Russian authorities, in expelling a pregnant woman and her four minor children from Russian territory but then leaving them stranded in an unfamiliar city during winter, had violated their positive obligations under Article 3. The applicant and her children were described, in the judgment, as being in a 'very vulnerable position'.[513] In other words, here it was not the pregnancy itself, but the situation into which the pregnant applicant was thrust by the state that rendered her and her children vulnerable.

In the context of medical treatment, the vulnerability that arises during pregnancy seems to relate to uncertainty about the health of the foetus and the health of pregnant applicants themselves. In *R.R. v Poland*, for example, the applicant – who suspected a genetic malformation in her unborn child – was refused access to genetic testing by doctors opposed to abortion. When she finally obtained genetic testing – after the expiration of the legal time limit for access to an abortion – her suspicions were confirmed. In considering whether there had been a violation of Article 3, the Court found that the applicant was 'in a situation of great vulnerability', for '[l]ike any other pregnant woman in her situation, she was deeply distressed by information that the foetus could be affected with some malformation'. The doctors' 'procrastination' had exposed her to 'weeks of painful uncertainty concerning the health of the foetus, her own and her family's future and the prospect of raising a child suffering from an incurable ailment'.[514]

The *R.R.* case indicates that, to a certain extent, the vulnerability of women as concerns their reproductive health is a function of state interference in their independent decision-making regarding these matters. This is reflected in other cases, as well. For example, where rape results in pregnancy – as it did in *P. and S. v Poland* – states must not frustrate and humiliate victims seeking to undergo an abortion. In this context, the Court has enjoined states to have regard to the vulnerability, age, views and feelings of the victim.[515] Regarding the non-consensual sterilisation of young Roma women during childbirth, the Court has used similar arguments to classify this as degrading treatment.[516]

In the context of detention, which entails a significant loss of autonomy regarding decision-making on prenatal care, the Court has held that the state must provide a minimum level of support to pregnant detainees. For example, in the 2013 case of a detained irregular migrant who had a miscarriage in detention, the Court held that she was doubly vulnerable due to, on the one hand, her general background as a migrant and her circumstances and, on the other, her fragile health. Given the fact that she was pregnant, the Court held that the state was required to take

[513] *Shioshvili and Others v Russia* App no 19356/07, Judgment of 20 December 2016, paras 83 and 86.
[514] *R.R. v Poland* App no 27617/04, Judgment of 26 May 2011, Reports 2011 (extracts), para 159.
[515] *P. and S.* (n 54), paras 162–66.
[516] *I.G. and Others* (n 474), para 123.

special measures, which should have included providing 'adequate surroundings' and 'an appropriate and varied diet'.[517]

This vulnerability, like all vulnerability, is contextual. The vulnerability that arises during pregnancy, the case law now indicates, is not simply a derivative of the vulnerability of an unborn child or an expression of a pregnant person's own physical fragility, but also considers their position of powerlessness and dependence vis-à-vis state institutions. This includes the position of those who are pregnant regarding healthcare providers, on whom they may depend for information about the health of their foetus and access to certain care and services. The Court's vulnerability reasoning in this context serves to recognise the essential nature of access to appropriate care during pregnancy, and to give this interest primacy over state interests. Vulnerability reasoning also allows the Court to emphasise the importance of protecting a person's own decision-making about reproduction free of state interference.

In this context, however, there is still work to be done. For example, the UN Human Rights Committee has outpaced the ECtHR as concerns the recognition that denial of access to abortion services, at least as concerns potentially problematic pregnancies, constitutes a violation of the prohibition of torture and inhuman and degrading treatment.[518] The Court generally considers these cases under Article 8 ECHR[519] or declares them inadmissible.[520]

As noted at the outset of this section, this case law has, so far, been about the rights of cisgender women. However, the intersection of pregnancy with transgender or non-binary identity would likely generate particularly acute vulnerabilities. This case law could also have potential implications for cisgender men. For example, involuntary and medically unnecessary sterilisation of people of any gender could potentially be found to be a violation of Article 3. In a similar regard, under Article 8 (but with reference to Article 3), the Court has made great strides in recent years concerning the requirement of sterilisation for legal recognition of trans people's gender identity.[521] Last but not least, and to complete the picture, there is no reason why the Court could not find, in future cases, find that the Article 3 rights of non-pregnant parents-to-be may also be violated given prolonged uncertainty regarding the health of their foetus. In this regard, vulnerability reasoning can assist the user – here, the Court – in taking the suffering of any affected applicants more fully into account.

[517] *Aden Ahmed* (n 393), para 97.

[518] HRC, *Amanda Jane Mellet v Ireland*, Communication No 2324/2013, UN Doc. CCPR/C/116/D/2324/2013, Views of 31 March 2016, para 7.8. Vulnerability language also came into play in this case, see para 7.4.

[519] *A., B. and C. v Ireland* App no 25579/05, Judgment (GC) of 16 December 2010, Reports 2010, starting at para 212.

[520] *D. v Ireland* App no 26499/02, Decision of 27 June 2006, paras 86–104, concerning the exhaustion of domestic remedies.

[521] *A.P., Garçon and Nicot v France* App nos 79885/12 …, Judgment of 6 April 2017, Reports 2017.

VIII. Vulnerability Due to the Espousal of Unpopular Views

In the typology outlined at the beginning of this chapter, Alexandra Timmer recognised the vulnerability of demonstrators, dissidents, and journalists to ill-treatment by state actors due to the espousal of unpopular views as a significant source of vulnerability under the Convention writ large.[522] This type of vulnerability stems from the Court's freedom of expression jurisprudence, and as a result it has remained somewhat marginal under Article 3.

In the context of Article 3, relevant cases here often concern expulsion, for example the return of political dissidents from Russia to their countries of origin. As mentioned above, for example, the Court has recognised ethnic Uzbeks suspected of participating in inter-racial riots in Kyrgyzstan as vulnerable in the context of returns.[523] The same goes for the political opposition in Kazakhstan[524] and 'individuals whose extradition was sought by either Uzbek or Tajik authorities on charges of religiously or politically motivated crimes'.[525] In addition, the Court has considered the 'precariousness' of the situation of dissidents and perceived dissidents in Sudan, finding it incompatible with the Convention to return registered political opponents of the regime to the country.[526]

In other words, where an extradition request shows that an applicant stands accused of religiously and politically motivated crimes, the Court considers this sufficient to demonstrate that the applicant is a member of the vulnerable group in question.[527] This case law does not, however, block the return of any person accused of a crime in these destination countries: those whose extradition is sought for offences that are 'neither politically nor religiously motivated' are not members of the vulnerable group in question.[528]

Outside of the expulsion context, in 2015, the Court explored a particular facet of demonstrators' vulnerability to police violence. In *Cestaro v Italy*, the Fourth Section found that the beating of a 62-year-old demonstrator by security forces had constituted torture. The blows inflicted by the authorities caused multiple fractures, from which the applicant never fully recovered. The Court held that the victim – who was sitting against a wall with his hands up when beaten – was in a situation of vulnerability due to his age, and also noted that police cannot

[522] Alexandra Timmer, 'A Quiet Revolution: Vulnerability in the European Court of Human Rights' in Martha Albertson Fineman and Anna Grear (eds), *Vulnerability: Reflections on a New Ethical Foundation for Law and Politics* (Ashgate, 2013) 147–70, 157–58, and the case law cited therein.

[523] *Khamrakulov* (n 426), para 66; *U.N. v Russia* App no 14348/15, Judgment of 26 July 2016, paras 39–40.

[524] *Dzhaksybergenov* (n 426), para 37.

[525] *Golubyatnikov and Zhuchkov v Russia* App no 49869/06 and 44822/06, Judgment of 9 October 2018, para 17.

[526] *A.A. v Switzerland* App no 58802/12, Judgment of 7 January 2014, para 40.

[527] *T.M. and Others v Russia* App nos 31189/15 …, Judgment of 7 November 2017, para 20.

[528] *B.T. v Russia* App no 40755/16, Decision of 5 December 2017, para 28.

be indifferent to the physical vulnerability of demonstrators due to their age or gender, nor to signs of capitulation.[529] To some extent, this case also evokes the risks of violence by private parties or receiving states faced by those demonstrating for LGBTQI rights.[530] However, the case law here is too sparse to make any findings about what vulnerability means to the Court in these circumstances.

IX. Intersecting Vulnerabilities

The above has discussed instances in which individuals simultaneously exhibit multiple traits that render them vulnerable – they may, for example, be detained, suffer from a mental illness, and be of Roma ethnicity. Cumulatively, the interaction between these traits marginalises individuals, places them in complex situations of vulnerability and influences their social reality and experiences.[531] Termed intersectionality in the non-discrimination context, and based on a concept originated by Kimberlé Crenshaw in the field of critical race theory,[532] this interplay of various grounds for vulnerability places the affected individuals in positions of particularly acute defencelessness to ill-treatment. In other words, the sum of various vulnerabilities is greater than its parts.

The Court has recognised that particular issues arise when various grounds for vulnerability intersect, although not in as many words. In the *B.S. v Spain* case, for example, the Court found a violation of Article 14 in conjunction with Article 3 in its procedural aspect given the fact that the domestic courts' decisions 'failed to take account of the applicant's particular vulnerability inherent in her position as an African woman working as a prostitute'.[533] This finding came after two third-party interveners invited the Court to engage with the intersectionality of the grounds for the applicant's vulnerability. The first intervener, the European Social Research Unit at the University of Barcelona, pointed out that 'taking account of only one of the grounds [for discrimination] was approximate and failed to reflect the reality of the situation'.[534] The second intervener, the AIRE Centre, 'invited the Court to recognize the phenomenon of intersectional discrimination, which required a multiple-grounds approach that did not examine each factor separately'.[535] The Court's judgment supports the conclusion that, while not explicitly acknowledging the intersection of the applicant's ethnicity, foreign origin, gender and engagement in the sex trade or exploring this concept, and seemingly unwilling to use the term 'intersectionality', the Court took the third party interventions into

[529] *Cestaro* (n 146), para 180.
[530] *Identoba and Others* (n 485), paras 68–70; *Karaahmed* (n 495), paras 11–25.
[531] Kimberlé Crenshaw, 'Mapping the Margins: Intersectionality, Identity Politics, and Violence Against Women of Color' (1991) 43(1241) *Stanford Law Review* 1241–99, 1244–45.
[532] Ibid; Crenshaw (n 13).
[533] *B.S.* (n 14), para 62.
[534] Ibid, para 56.
[535] Ibid, para 57.

account, and is at least willing to display some awareness about the harms suffered at the intersection of various grounds for vulnerability.[536]

Though the facts of *B.S.* provide one of the most explicit examples of intersectionality under Article 3, it does not stand alone. The Court has considered a number of applications brought by individuals who fall into multiple vulnerability-related categories. For example, *Mubilanzila Mayeka and Kaniki Mitunga v Belgium* concerned an applicant who was a minor, an illegal immigrant, and unaccompanied by her family.[537] The applicants in *I.G. and Others v Slovakia* were of Roma ethnicity, minors, and pregnant.[538] The applicant on whose behalf the *Centre for Legal Resources on behalf of Valentin Câmpeanu v Romania* case was brought was young, deprived of his liberty, of Roma ethnicity, suffered from a profound intellectual disability, and had been diagnosed with HIV as a child.[539] In other words, intersectional cases can and frequently do come before the Court. In addition, the intersection of grounds for vulnerability is extremely common in the Court's case law concerning vulnerability in detention. For example, as discussed above, the Court has frequently held that persons who are both detained and suffer from mental health issues are particularly vulnerable, as they may experience particular feelings of distress, fear and anguish while deprived of their liberty.[540]

While the Court's case law thus shows some recognition of the accrued and unique vulnerabilities that arise with the accumulation of relevant traits, the Court does not explicitly explore the sum of vulnerabilities concerned, their specific effects, and the ways in which the individuals concerned are especially marginalised or resilient. In other words, it fails to engage with the concept of intersectionality. Instead, the Court tends to list the various grounds for vulnerability one after another and then, without further discussion, conclude that, given the applicant's resulting – albeit sometimes termed particular or extreme[541] – vulnerability, Article 3 has been violated.[542] Where the Court's recognition of intersectionality in these cases is implied or missing, it remains unclear whether all of the factors that give rise to vulnerability were taken into consideration, and to what effect, or whether there has been real appreciation for the applicant's position inside structures of oppression, discrimination, and vulnerability.

The way in which the Court goes about responding to cases where grounds for vulnerability intersect depends on the circumstances. In the context of detention, the Court has set up special protections that apply in such cases, lowering the threshold of suffering and anguish that must be reached in order to find a violation of Article 3 and explicitly acknowledging the heightened terror and

[536] Ibid, para 62.
[537] *Mubilanzila Mayeka and Kaniki Mitunga* (n 110), para 55.
[538] *I.G. and Others* (n 474), paras 6, 123, 143.
[539] *CLR on behalf of Valentin Câmpeanu* (n 22), paras 104, 108 and 143.
[540] For example in *Kudła* (n 173), para 99.
[541] *CLR on behalf of Valentin Câmpeanu* (n 22), para 108.
[542] For example, *P. and S.* (n 54), paras 161, 162 and 166.

humiliation experienced by vulnerable victims.[543] In the context of expulsion and removal cases, the intersection between poor conditions in the receiving State and another ground for vulnerability, for example childhood age, can make the difference for finding a conditional violation of Article 3.[544] In the past, the Court has also attended to the 'cumulative risks of reprisals' faced by applicants for various reasons in the receiving State.[545] Where young age and sexual victimisation intersect, too, the Court has recognised the special vulnerability of those who find themselves at this intersection and required States to attach sufficient weight to the 'special psychological factors' at play.[546]

However, the Court's implicit acknowledgment of intersectional vulnerability has its limits. For example, in *A.S. v Switzerland*, the Court considered the possibility of returning an individual who was an asylum-seeker, a victim of torture, and suffered from mental health issues to Italy. The Court's judgment tested the limits of *Tarakhel*, with the Court finding that though it was possible that 'a significant number of asylum-seekers might be left without accommodation or accommodated in overcrowded facilities without any privacy, or even in insalubrious or violent conditions', as the applicant was not critically ill and both the speed with which his condition would deteriorate upon removal and his access to medical treatment in Italy involved 'a certain degree of speculation', removal would not violate Article 3.[547]

The thought behind the restrictiveness of the Court's vulnerability and intersectionality jurisprudence in the context of asylum and expulsion may be similar to the one behind its failure to recognise the exclusions that arise from the intersection of poverty and other grounds for vulnerability. The disenfranchising power of poverty has not been recognised in the Court's Article 3 vulnerability case law, perhaps because of fears that such recognition would give rise to a wide-ranging obligation to provide financial support to the indigent – in other words, that it would open the floodgates of socio-economic support obligations. Situations of extreme material poverty have been regarded as a violation of Article 3 under certain circumstances, namely when they affect particularly vulnerable individuals who are dependent on the state.[548] However, poverty in itself – thus particularly, but not only, where it intersects with a disadvantaged ethnicity, mental illness, or another of the traits discussed above – may effectively prevent individuals from claiming their rights.

In this regard, a group of Strasbourg judges, writing for a seminar, once remarked that while the Convention does not protect a 'right not to be poor', situations of extreme poverty may breach the Convention and limit those affected

[543] *Kudła* (n 173), para 99; *Aydin* (n 24), paras 83–84.
[544] *Tarakhel* (n 109), paras 118–22.
[545] *Samina* (n 418), para 64.
[546] *M.C.* (n 52), para 183.
[547] *A.S. v Switzerland* App no 39350/13, Judgment of 30 June 2015, para 36.
[548] *M.S.S.* (n 7), paras 172 and 254.

in their ability to avail themselves of their rights.[549] The judges pointed out that, according to the Court's 1978 *Airey* judgment, complaints about entirely insufficient pension sums and other social benefits could in principle raise issues under Article 3.[550]

In this same vein, the Court has found that a lack of resources cannot justify the failure to secure Convention rights and freedoms, including under Article 3.[551] Poverty affects a wide range of human rights, and it often affects those who are already vulnerable for another reason. The floodgate argument – the fear that the Court would create a financially untenable welfare state by recognising conditions of extreme material poverty in those who depend on the state for survival as a Convention violation – does not change the fact that conditions of extreme material poverty can entail a level of suffering and deprivation that should be recognised as meeting the threshold of Article 3.

One laudable development in this context was the 2021 judgment in *Lacatus v Switzerland*, where the Court recognised the existence of a human right to beg as part of Article 8 ECHR, referring at various times to the applicant's vulnerability as an illiterate and destitute young Roma woman.[552] However, while the Court invoked the concept of human dignity here, it neither considered Article 3, nor seemed willing to go beyond a recognition of the fact that prohibiting someone from ensuring their own survival through begging was impermissible, as opposed to making a finding about the effects of poverty on human dignity more generally, or about the specific vulnerability that comes from poverty or the intersection of various sources of vulnerability.

X. Underexplored Sources of Vulnerability

The grounds for vulnerability that the Court has recognised to date are likely not final. Its approach to the concept has undergone gradual evolution, and the Court has progressively identified vulnerable groups and individuals as its case law has developed. The present chapter has shed some light on why certain groups and individuals are recognised as vulnerable. This is often based on the discrimination or inequality faced by a group and the individuals who belong to it, or on a situation of dependency, including the inability of individuals to claim their rights. As will be argued below, this comes down to a denial of basic human dignity and the

[549] Julia Laffranque, Guido Raimondi, Ledi Bianku, Angelika Nußberger and Linos-Alexander Sicilianos, 'Implementing the European Convention on Human Rights in Times of Economic Crisis', *Seminar Background Paper* (25 January 2013), www.echr.coe.int/Documents/Seminar_background_paper_2013_ENG.pdf, 1.

[550] Ibid, 2, citing *Airey v Ireland* App no 6289/73, Judgment of 9 October 1979, Series A32, para 26.

[551] Laffranque et al (n 549), 4, citing *Poltoratskiy v Ukraine* App no 38812/97, Judgment of 29 April 2003, Reports 2003-V, para 148 and *Orchowski v Poland* App no 17885/04, Judgment of 22 October 2009, para 153.

[552] *Lacatus v Switzerland* App no 14065/15, Judgment of 19 January 2021.

capabilities that human individuals need in order to live a life that ensures their dignity. On this basis, it is possible to suggest some further groups and individuals who face inequality, discrimination or dependency, and who could therefore arguably also fall under the Court's approach to vulnerability.

Recognition of some of these further sources of vulnerability appears to be gaining traction in the Court's Article 3 case law. For example, it seems that the Court has made some headway towards more solid recognition of the vulnerability of the LGBTQI community or of the elderly. Regarding other factors, however, the Court displays reluctance.

Especially in the migration context, a number of harms are thereby ignored or 'privatised' by the Court – an argument that will be explored below. This is true, for example, of the risk of exposure to female genital mutilation or the risks based on gender inequality in a receiving State. Outside of the migration context, too, there are further possible examples: two that come to mind are the fate of those suffering from drug addiction[553] and homeless persons who are not asylum-seekers. Perhaps the most flagrant example of all, however, is that of vulnerability due to extreme poverty, which was touched upon above and will be explored further in chapter five.

[553] See, *mutatis mutandis*, *Miah v United Kingdom* App no 53080/07, Decision of 27 April 2010, para 14.

4

The Growth and Impact of Vulnerability Reasoning

Chapter Summary

The preceding chapter has explored the reasons why the Court may identify an applicant or group as vulnerable. The following will expand on this, and discuss not only the distribution and pervasiveness of references to vulnerability in the Article 3 case law, but also the various types of effects that vulnerability reasoning can trigger. It will show that the concept of vulnerability can affect the life of an application in Strasbourg from start to finish, from its categorisation under the Court's priority policy, to the admissibility requirements and issues of proof, to shaping states' material and procedural obligations and affecting awards made in terms of just satisfaction and consequential orders.

Keywords: effects of vulnerability; interim protection; admissibility; burden of proof; remedies; positive obligations; quantitative analysis.

I. A Quantitative Analysis of Vulnerability under Article 3

This volume is based on a systematic analysis of the vulnerability case law under Article 3 until early 2019. This allows for a quantitative evaluation of the Court's vulnerability case law to complement the qualitative analysis in the preceding chapter.

To begin with, it is possible to note that, for a number of years, the use of vulnerability in the Court's case law increased dramatically. In the early 1980s to the early 1990s, the concept was not used under Article 3 ECHR, and throughout the 1990s, references were exceedingly scarce. This stands in stark contrast to the pervasive use of vulnerability in the new millennium. However, the number of references is currently declining. Figure 4.1 shows the number of times the Court has relied on vulnerability reasoning in the decade from 2009.

The figure clearly shows that the number of references to vulnerability made by the Court in its Article 3 case law peaked in 2016, when 76 such references were made, and has steadily declined since. To understand why this is the case,

Figure 4.1 Number of References to Vulnerability by the Court under Article 3 (2009–beginning of 2019)

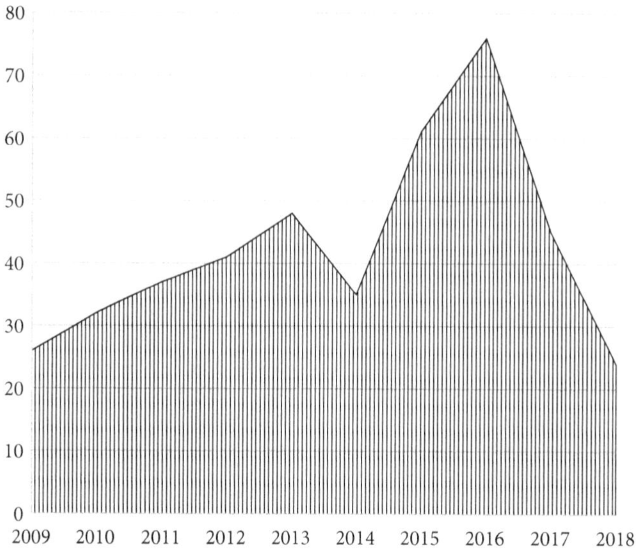

it is helpful to put the Court's vulnerability reasoning into the perspective of its case law on Article 3 as a whole. By doing so, it emerges that, while vulnerability reasoning was, at least for a time, increasingly pervasive under Article 3, the general increase in the number of violation judgments regarding the provision kept pace with this development until 2016. In other words, vulnerability may not necessarily or not only have become more prevalent over time, but its use seems to some extent to have increased in proportion with the ever more productive output of the Court. Figure 4.2 tracks this development as concerns the violation judgments issued by the Court under Article 3, providing both an overview of this synchronised increase and of the relative prevalence of the concept.

Figure 4.2 also shows that the abovementioned *decrease* in the number of references to vulnerability is also evident when looking only at violation judgments. This invites speculation that vulnerability reasoning is used not in cases where established case law allows for a straightforward violation finding, but in more activist judgments. It should be noted, too, that the relevance of the concept is not – or at least not necessarily – decreasing along with the quantity of references made in this regard. As shown in the preceding chapter and as noted above, the concept has served to amend the approach to Article 3 in a number of regards. That case law remains, and the Court continues to rely on it and build upon it. This allows for two observations.

First, the work done by vulnerability reasoning is here to stay. While the Court's decision not to refer to vulnerability explicitly in some cases makes the

Figure 4.2 Violation of Article 3 Judgments Using Vulnerability, and Overall, as of 1 January 2019, by Year

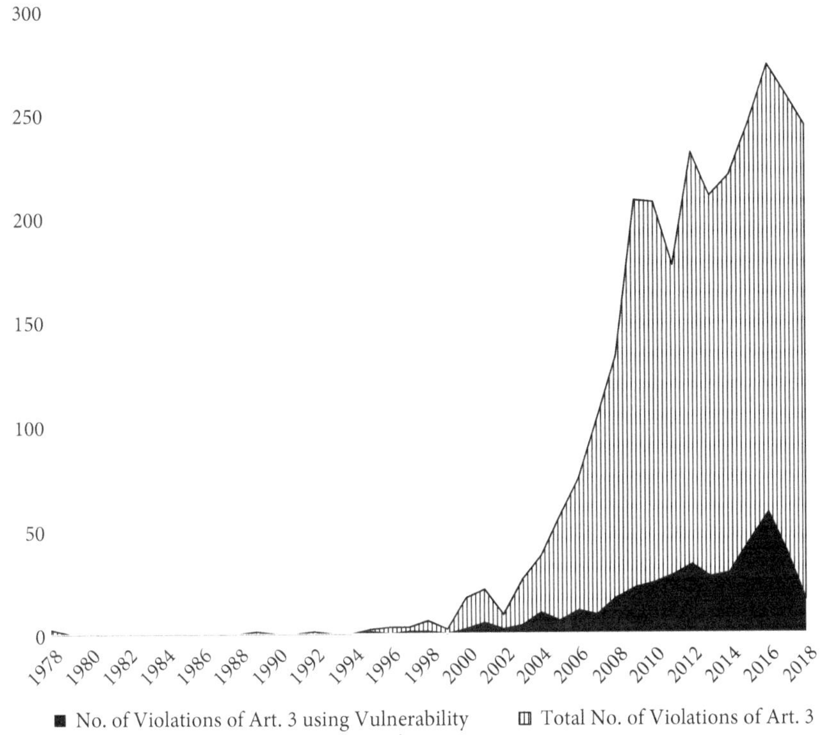

relevant case law harder to find systematically, the Court is implicitly continuing many of the same approaches as those facilitated by vulnerability. Thus, in recent cases it has for example reflected on an applicant's disability, the particular needs and hardships associated with it, and the ways in which this requires a State response and tailors the standards under Article 3, all without explicitly referring to vulnerability.[1]

Again, it is not clear what the reasons for the decrease in references to vulnerability are: there has been no statement of principle by the Court in this regard, and relevant cases continue to come before it. Based on the above, it seems that, during the last 10 years, the Court has used vulnerability to achieve agreement among judges about expanding the scope of Article 3. Now having done so, and having both established a more inclusive case law in various respects and entered a period

[1] See for example *Tsarpelas v Greece* App no 74884/13, Judgment of 26 April 2018, where no reference to vulnerability was made, although the case was later cited by the Court as one concerning vulnerability (in *SH.D. and Others v Greece, Austria, Croatia, Hungary, Northern Macedonia, Serbia and Slovenia* App no 14165/16, Judgment of 13 June 2019, para 48).

of deference or even 'walking back',[2] it may no longer be as necessary to deploy vulnerability reasoning in as many cases, as the Court can now rely on existing vulnerability case law to justify making similar findings.

Lastly, it is interesting to note that the data indicates that references to vulnerability are present in the Article 3 jurisprudence of all five Sections of the Court and – though, given the smaller number of its judgments and decisions, to a lesser extent – of the Grand Chamber. Though the composition of the Sections changes over time, and that of the Grand Chamber changes on a case-by-case basis, this does provide some indication of the pervasiveness of the concept. Of course, judicial formations change over time, and they are fluid in the sense that the Grand Chamber judges also sit in the Chamber and in the Committees, but this provides a sense that vulnerability reasoning is not merely the pet issue of a select few judges, but a pervasive concept.

Lastly, it is possible to disaggregate the types of violations of Article 3 that the Court finds by relying on vulnerability. As outlined previously, these various types of violations – torture, inhuman treatment and punishment, and degrading treatment and punishment – are in a hierarchical relationship, with torture being the most severe type of violation of Article 3. The Court has used vulnerability reasoning to find a violation of Article 3 by an explicitly recognised act of torture in 37 cases to date; the remaining 496 violations of Article 3 found under reference to vulnerability involved inhuman or degrading treatment or punishment (426 total cases) and/or purely procedural (39 cases) or conditional (31 cases) violations of Article 3, though the Court sometimes fails to specify which type of violation of Article 3 it is dealing with.[3]

In short, it appears that vulnerability reasoning under Article 3 is firmly entrenched in the Court's jurisprudence across a variety of grounds, across time, across all sections of the Court and across the various aspects of Article 3. However, this does not mean that vulnerability permeates or defines all of the Court's jurisprudence under the provision. The Court's reliance on vulnerability remains, outside of the specific contexts in which it is best-developed, the exception rather than the rule. This will be discussed in more detail in the following section.

II. The Effects of Vulnerability under Article 3 ECHR

Vulnerability reasoning permeates the Court's case law and applies to a range of situations and traits. But what does vulnerability actually *do*? The present section discusses the various types of impacts and effects that vulnerability reasoning can have on the Court's approach to a case.

[2] Laurence Helfer and Erik Voeten, 'Walking Back Human Rights in Europe?', 31(3) *European Journal of International Law* (2020) 797–827.

[3] *Serce v Romania* App no 35049/08, Judgment of 30 June 2015, paras 48–49; *Andrișcă v Romania* App no 65804/09, Judgment of 3 February 2015, para 74.

A. The Court's Priority Policy

One of the first things that happens when a case arrives in Strasbourg is that it is assigned a category under the Court's priority policy. That policy explicitly mentions the concept of vulnerability, stating that the highest-priority category is reserved for 'urgent cases concerning vulnerable applicants'.[4] These cases are thereby expedited and receive the highest priority treatment, even higher than other Article 3 cases, which generally fall into the third category (out of seven). Cases falling under the top three priority categories are destined to be examined by the Chamber or Grand Chamber, meaning that they are more likely to be considered in detail by the Court. However, it is not clear how the Court determines whether an applicant is vulnerable for the purposes of the priority policy, without having examined the case on the merits. This is presumably a simplified assessment, and one based on recognitions of vulnerability in previous case law.

B. Admissibility *ratione personae*

Tightening the admissibility criteria for applications before the Court is a commonly proposed way to reduce the Court's workload, albeit one that is undeniably harmful to applicants. In this context, vulnerability reasoning under Article 3 ECHR can be used to loosen the requirements on the *ratione personae* admissibility of applications. There are two main areas of relevance here: the possibility of bringing a case on behalf of a victim, and the loss of victim status by the victim him- or herself because of the availability of domestic redress and compensation.

i. Cases Brought on Behalf of Victims

When it comes to cases brought on behalf of victims, an illustrative example here is the *Ilhan v Turkey* case. The applicant in *Ilhan* was permitted to bring a case on behalf of his vulnerable brother, who had been subjected to ill-treatment and had suffered a brain injury. The Court held that it must apply the rules on the admissibility of applications with some flexibility and without undue formalism, and that those rules, along with the ECHR as a whole, have to be interpreted so as to make Convention rights practical and effective.[5] Finding that the applicant's brother was vulnerable, the Court held that the applicant had validly introduced the application in Strasbourg on his behalf.[6]

[4] ECtHR, 'The Court's Priority Policy', www.echr.coe.int/documents/priority_policy_eng.pdf, as amended on 22 May 2017.

[5] *Ilhan v Turkey* App no 22277/93, Judgment (GC) of 27 June 2000, Reports 2000-VII, para 51.

[6] Ibid, para 55.

There have been other similar cases before the Court.[7] Of these, the most notable is *Centre for Legal Resources on behalf of Valentin Câmpeanu v Romania*, which concerned post-mortem proceedings brought by an NGO on behalf of a particularly vulnerable individual. The Court permitted the applicant NGO to represent the deceased applicant, because the opposite conclusion would mean risking that 'the respondent State might escape accountability under the Convention'.[8] In his separate opinion, Judge Pinto de Albuquerque summarised the intention underlying the judgment by maintaining that '[d]ifferent situations must be treated differently. Thus, the right of access to court for extremely vulnerable persons warrants positive discrimination in favour of these persons'.[9]

While the Court emphasised the exceptional nature of the *Valentin Câmpeanu* case, at the time, the idea of positive discrimination underlying the judgment seemed to indicate a new willingness of the Court to introduce a more flexible application of the admissibility criteria concerning vulnerable individuals and groups. As the judges of the First Section put it in one 2015 decision, it seemed that the Court was ready to display 'reasonable flexibility in ensuring that formal criteria related to admissibility and representation do not result in unjustified exclusion of the most vulnerable victims from the protection guaranteed by the Convention'.[10]

However, the finding made in *Valentin Câmpeanu* is in constant tension with the Court's need to reduce its case load and the impetus to emphasise formal rules to this end. As a result, the rule created in that judgment may have been rather severely undermined by two later developments: first, the amendment of the Rules of Court to require a strike-out where an applicant has not provided a signature authorising proceedings on his behalf by a legal representative,[11] and secondly, certain decisions rendered by the Court, namely *N. and M. v Russia, G.J. v Spain* and *Bulgarian Helsinki Committee v Bulgaria*, which were communicated before those rules took effect.[12]

In *N. and M.*, which was brought by the applicants' lawyer after her clients had allegedly been subjected to enforced disappearance from Russia to Uzbekistan in violation of interim measures indicated by the Court, the Strasbourg judges

[7] See *Y.F. v Turkey* App no 24209/94, Judgment of 22 July 2003, Reports 2003-IX, brought on behalf of the applicant's vulnerable wife (paras 31–36), and *Association for the Defence of Human Rights in Romania – Helsinki Committee on behalf of Ionel Garcea v Romania* App no 2959/11, Judgment of 24 March 2015, paras 39–46 (brought by a human rights NGO).

[8] *CLR on behalf of Valentin Câmpeanu v Romania* App no 47848/08, Judgment (GC) of 17 July 2014, Reports 2014, para 112.

[9] Ibid, Concurring Opinion of Judge Pinto de Albuquerque, para 9.

[10] *Tagayeva and Others v Russia* App nos 26562/07 …, Decision of 9 June 2015, para 473, which primarily concerns Art 2 ECHR but makes a general restatement of principle.

[11] r 47.1.c. of the Rules of the European Court of Human Rights of 14 November 2016, www.echr.coe.int/Documents/Rules_Court_ENG.pdf.

[12] *N. and M. v Russia* App nos 39496/14 and 39727/14, Decision of 26 April 2016, paras 60–63; *G.J. v Spain* App no 59172/12, Decision of 21 June 2016, paras 45–53; *Bulgarian Helsinki Committee v Bulgaria* App nos 35653/12 and 66172/12, Decision of 28 June 2016, paras 50–61.

declared the application inadmissible. In doing so, they held that the applicants' interests could just as well have been protected if their relatives had brought applications on their behalf in Uzbekistan. This decision created a major tear in the protection of vulnerable individuals, given that the facts of the case indicated a flagrant case of enforced disappearance and that the applicants' family members were resident in a non-Member State of the Council of Europe where they, too, feared persecution.[13] This judgment in effect privatises the burden of protecting the most fundamental human rights, namely the right to life and the right to be free from torture and IDT, by forcing the family members of vulnerable individuals to choose between bringing an application in Strasbourg and their own safety.

Another nail in the coffin of the promise held by *Valentin Câmpeanu* came with the decision in *G.J. v Spain*.[14] That case was brought by an NGO on behalf of a pregnant woman who alleged that she had been the victim of trafficking, had been forced into prostitution and that, if she were returned to Nigeria, she would run the risk of being recaptured by her traffickers. Despite these claims, the applicant was returned to Nigeria by the Spanish authorities, in an exceedingly problematic way[15] and before she had issued a written authority to the NGO in question, Women's Links Worldwide. Obtaining such an authorisation later allegedly became impossible because, as feared, the victim was recaptured by her traffickers.[16] Regardless, the domestic instances and the Court both ultimately found that Women's Links Worldwide did not have legal standing to bring a complaint on behalf of the applicant.[17] The Court reasoned that the case was distinguishable from *Valentin Câmpeanu* on a number of grounds: first, in that case, the Romanian authorities had not objected to the representation of Mr Câmpeanu by the NGO, secondly, Mr Câmpeanu would manifestly have been unable to initiate proceedings domestically on his own, and thirdly, he had not been provided with legal counsel.[18]

The third nail in the coffin of the *Valentin Câmpeanu* judgment came with the decision in *Bulgarian Helsinki Committee v Bulgaria*.[19] There, the Court considered an application brought by an NGO on behalf of two mentally disabled adolescent girls who died in a care home. The NGO became aware of the fate of the two girls after they had already died, and initiated a series of proceedings on their behalf. In this case, the Court considered that the *Valentin Câmpeanu* jurisprudence is

[13] *N. and M.* (n 12), paras 20–26, 30 and throughout.

[14] *G.J.* (n 12).

[15] From the perspective of the Council of Europe Convention on Action against Trafficking in Human Beings, CETS No 197, Warsaw, 16 May 2005, in force since 1 February 2008, ratified by Spain on 2 April 2009, especially Art 10 (identification of the victims), Art 13 (recovery and reflection period) and Art 16 para 2 (repatriation and return of victims).

[16] *G.J.* (n 12), paras 34, 36, 41.

[17] Ibid, para 53.

[18] Ibid, para 52.

[19] *Bulgarian Helsinki Committee* (n 12), paras 50–61.

only applicable if a cumulative and rather long list of criteria is met. These criteria, it argued, are (1) the vulnerability of the direct victim, which must have made it impossible for him or her to bring a complaint while alive; (2) the significance of the allegations at stake; (3) the absence of heirs or legal representatives who may bring an application to the Court; (4) the existence of contact between the applicant association and the victim while the latter was alive; (5) intervention by the applicant association in the post-mortem domestic proceedings; as well as (6) the recognition of the applicant association's legal standing by the domestic authorities. In its decision, the Court noted that the applicant association had intervened on behalf of the girls only years after their deaths and had thus never had contact with them, and that the domestic authorities did not acknowledge their legal standing.[20] It therefore declared the case inadmissible.

In *Bulgarian Helsinki Committee*, the Court noted that its decision was 'limited to the circumstances of the case before it, and that its conclusions therefore should not be interpreted as a misrecognition of the contribution by civil society in the proceedings concerned to the protection of persons who are extremely vulnerable'. It went on to commend the 'active and vigilant role of the applicant association, which alerted the competent institutions and cooperated with them during the proceedings and investigations that were conducted.' It also 'noted with satisfaction that the Bulgarian authorities seriously took into consideration the reports of the applicant association, even absent a formal status thereof in the domestic proceedings'.[21]

By making this statement, as an ostensible obiter dictum, the Court seems to be seeking to pre-empt possible backlash against its decision and the application of its long and prohibitive list of criteria. Indeed, the role of NGOs in ensuring protection of individual rights should not be underestimated. The hopelessness of the situation of applicants such as Mr Câmpeanu is a testament to this. Even if that was not the Court's intention, the result reached in all three of these decisions – two of which were brought by reputable NGOs, and the third of which was brought by a known human rights advocate – has the potential to undermine human rights defenders' important contribution to the protection of the rights of the vulnerable. The criteria now imposed effectively mean that the Court will almost never examine these types of cases, despite the fact that the examples discussed here all concern credible allegations of severe human rights violations. This is all the more shocking because, at least in two of the cases, the decisive procedural hurdle to a substantive examination is simply the presence or absence of a signature on the application form to the Court.

The formalism displayed by the Court in this context is certainly surprising in the wake of *Valentin Câmpeanu*, which is a Grand Chamber judgment, whereas a Chamber formation decided the later three cases. The latter three decisions cannot

[20] Ibid, paras 56–58.
[21] Ibid, para 60, translation by the author.

be referred to the Grand Chamber, given that inadmissibility decisions are final. Nonetheless, it is not inconceivable that a future Grand Chamber judgment will revise the trend begun with these unfortunate decisions. For now, however, it seems that the Court is only willing to apply *Câmpeanu* to the narrowest sliver of applicants, namely those who have no living relatives and no legal capacity, and regarding whose representation by a third party before the Court the domestic authorities have no objection. This effectively renders *Câmpeanu* inapplicable to all but a fringe number of cases, and continues to leave those applicants who are vulnerable, but 'not vulnerable enough', unprotected.

ii. Loss of Victim Status

When it comes to the loss of victim status under Article 34 ECHR, which may take place if an applicant has received adequate redress and compensation on the domestic plane, vulnerability can also play a role. For example, concerning one applicant who had received compensation for a violation of Article 3 domestically, the Court took his vulnerability into account in order to find that he had nonetheless retained victim status.[22] In other cases, too, the Court has mentioned vulnerability when it came to the question of victim status.

For example, to overcome a possible loss of victim status, the Court has recalled the inability of certain vulnerable applicants to complain to the domestic authorities and seek redress. In one such case, it referred to the inability of an applicant who was detained and suffered from schizophrenia to coherently complain of his ill-treatment.[23] More generally, it has referred to the vulnerability of detainees to find that 'the fact that an applicant has been awarded a sum of money in compensation in the domestic proceedings is not decisive'.[24] To determine whether domestic redress has led to a loss of victim status, the Court held, it instead had to examine all the circumstances and determine whether the amount of compensation awarded was sufficient to compensate for the Convention violation at stake.[25]

On this basis, the Court has recognised victim status in several cases. Even where the respondent state has acknowledged the underlying breach of the Convention and compensated the applicants, the Court has found – relying again on vulnerability – that this is not decisive.[26] Similarly, regarding the failure of the domestic authorities to provide timely protection to a mentally ill minor who had been subjected to prostitution and rape, the Court found that – as the state had not compensated her for the period during which she was vulnerable and awaiting protection measures – she had not lost her victim status.[27]

[22] *Abdulkadyrov and Dakhtayev v Russia* App no 35061/04, Judgment of 10 July 2018, para 24.
[23] *Gömi v Turkey* App no 38704/11, Judgment of 19 February 2019, para 61.
[24] *Oleksa v Poland* App no 47580/13, Judgment of 12 July 2018, not reported, para 24.
[25] Ibid, paras 24–27.
[26] *Budnik v Poland* App no 61928/13, Judgment of 7 September 2017, para 21.
[27] *V.C. v Italy* App no 54227/14, Judgment of 1 February 2018, para 61.

C. Granting of Interim Protection

The Court has granted interim protection under rule 39 of the Rules of Court[28] in certain Article 3 cases specifically in light of applicants' vulnerability. For example, in the 2012 *Yordanova* judgment, the Court provided rule 39 protection in order to stall the applicants' eviction until arrangements could be made to ensure housing for the vulnerable among them.[29] Similarly, in *Hossein Kheel v Netherlands*, the Court granted interim protection because of the 'plentiful information on the vulnerable situation of single women in Afghanistan'.[30]

While it is difficult to determine with any certainty whether the Court is more likely to grant interim protection to vulnerable applicants, it should be noted that the relevant Practice Direction states that the Court will make such an order where 'it considers that the applicant faces a real risk of serious, irreversible harm if the measure is not applied'.[31] This idea of proving 'real risk' seems, at least by analogy, similar to the requirement of proof of real risk of exposure to ill-treatment in expulsion cases, where vulnerability does facilitate matters of proof for applicants. Given that little is known about the grounds for the interim protection orders made by the Court, it is not clear whether and to what extent it has regard for the vulnerability of applicants here. However, what is clear is that, as the Court's former President, Jean-Paul Costa, stated in 2011, 'the application of Rule 39 has preserved the physical integrity, the liberty and even the lives of many people who by definition are vulnerable'.[32]

D. Requirement to Use and Exhaust Domestic Remedies (Applicant's Duty of Diligence)

The Court's case law has indicated that an identification as vulnerable may exempt applicants from the obligation to diligently use and exhaust available domestic remedies before taking their case to Strasbourg.

For example, when it comes to the obligation to exhaust all available domestic remedies, the Court has exempted applicants from using specific remedies in

[28] r 39 (interim measures) of the Rules of the ECtHR of 1 January 2020, www.echr.coe.int/documents/rules_court_eng.pdf.

[29] *Yordanova and Others v Bulgaria* App no 25446/06, Judgment of 24 April 2012, para 49.

[30] ECtHR Press Unit, *Factsheet: Interim Measures*, September 2016, www.echr.coe.int/Documents/FS_Interim_measures_ENG.pdf, 4, referring to *Hossein Kheel v Netherlands* App no 34583/08, Decision of 16 December 2008.

[31] Practice direction on requests for interim measures issued by the President of the Court in accordance with r 32 of the Rules of Court on 5 March 2003 and amended on 16 October 2009 and on 7 July 2011, www.echr.coe.int/Documents/Rules_Court_ENG.pdf, 52–53.

[32] Speech by Mr Jean-Paul Costa on the occasion of the opening of the judicial year, 28 January 2011, reproduced in the Annual Report of the ECtHR for 2011, www.echr.coe.int/Documents/Annual_report_2011_ENG.pdf, 35–46, 40.

light of their mental illness.[33] As concerns the duty of due diligence in promptly applying to the domestic authorities, its response depends on the circumstances of the case. The Court has held that a delay in lodging a complaint domestically is not decisive where the authorities 'ought to have been aware that an individual could have been subjected to ill-treatment'.[34] That conclusion, originally reached in *Mocanu*, accepts that a delay in using domestic remedies does not preclude the admissibility of an application 'where the applicant was in a particularly vulnerable situation, having regard to the complexity of the case and the nature of the alleged human rights violations at stake, and where it was reasonable for the applicant to wait for developments that could have resolved crucial factual or legal issues'.[35]

Since *Mocanu*, the Court has repeated its finding that, as concerns applicants' duty of diligence to promptly contact the domestic authorities, not every delay will negatively impact the admissibility of applications brought by 'particularly vulnerable' applicants.[36] This finding is linked to the Court's consistent case law concerning states' obligation to investigate possible ill-treatment even absent an express complaint.[37] In any event, the authorities must act immediately after an official complaint is lodged, and must take into account the particular vulnerability of victims and their reduced readiness or willingness to make a complaint at all.[38]

When it comes to time limits for the use of domestic remedies, the Court has held that, in the case of continuous rights violations vis-à-vis vulnerable applicants, rigid time limits may place an 'unreasonable procedural burden' on these individuals.[39] Regarding prisoners detained under inadequate conditions, this type of approach ignores their vulnerability and the fact that their main concern is their daily struggle to meet their own basic needs and to maintain their health, dignity, and safety.[40]

While such findings remain the exception, these cases do show that the Court is potentially willing to waive the exhaustion of domestic remedies requirement and the duty of diligence for vulnerable applicants under certain circumstances.[41]

E. The Six-Month Rule

Vulnerability also comes into play concerning the application of the six-month rule – ie the rule in Article 35 § 1 ECHR that applications must be filed in Strasbourg

[33] *M.S. v Croatia (No. 2)* App no 75450/12, Judgment of 19 February 2015, para 123.

[34] *Mocanu and Others v Romania* App nos 10865/09 …, Judgment (GC) of 17 September 2014, Reports 2014 (extracts), para 265.

[35] Ibid.

[36] *Melnichuk and Others v Romania* App nos 35279/10 and 34782/10, Judgment of 5 May 2015, para 81.

[37] *Krsmanović v Serbia* App no 19796/14, Judgment of 19 December 2017, para 64, citing *Velev v Bulgaria* App no 43531/08, Judgment of 16 April 2013, paras 59–60.

[38] Ibid, para 73.

[39] *Nikitin and Others v Estonia* App nos 23226/16 …, Judgment of 29 January 2019, para 141.

[40] Ibid.

[41] *Dorneau v Romania* App no 55089/13, Judgment of 28 November 2017, para 99.

no later than six months after a final domestic decision, which will be reduced to four months by Protocol No 15 to the ECHR. The previous section concerned the diligence required of applicants in initiating domestic proceedings, and the fact that vulnerability has been seen as mitigating the consequences of a failure to do so. As concerns applicants' 'second duty of diligence', namely to speedily apply to the Court, vulnerability has helped applicants to overcome the consequences of bringing an application out of time.[42]

In cases where the domestic proceedings continue fruitlessly for years or even decades, the Court requires applicants to bring their applications to Strasbourg within six months of the moment in which they became aware, or should have become aware, that there would be no final decision in their case. The application of this rule, which raises more challenging issues than the simple calculation from the time of a final domestic decision as envisioned in Article 35 § 1 ECHR,[43] can respond to the vulnerability and feeling of powerlessness of an applicant.

For example, in *Mocanu*, the Court considered not only the applicant's failure to bring domestic proceedings in good time, but also his delay in applying to the Court. The Court held that such a delay does not preclude the admissibility of an application in exceptional cases where applicants are in a situation of particularly vulnerability. It concluded that the vulnerability and feeling of powerlessness of the applicant plausibly explained his failure to begin proceedings for over 10 years, given that 'it was not unreasonable for him to wait for developments that could have resolved crucial factual or legal issues'.[44] It held, therefore, that 'the applicant's vulnerability and his feeling of powerlessness … amount[ed] to a plausible and acceptable explanation for his inactivity'.[45]

F. The Burden of Proof

In the Court's jurisprudence, vulnerability can also affect the application of the *affirmanti incumbit probatio* principle in an applicant's favour.[46] Vulnerability thus affects the distribution of the burden of proof, and the Court considers the nature of the allegations made and the circumstances of a given case – including the vulnerability of the applicant – in order to determine whether that onus is on the applicant or on the state.[47]

In this context, the Court has for example held that, regarding persons in the state's exclusive authority, it is for the authorities to refute allegations of ill-treatment.[48] This includes proving that, when persons with a disability are

[42] Ibid, paras 82, 85–90.
[43] *Melnichuk and Others* (n 36), para 82.
[44] *Mocanu and Others* (n 34), para 275.
[45] Ibid.
[46] *Ersin Erkuş and Others v Turkey* App no 40952/07, Judgment of 31 May 2016, para 60.
[47] *Zamferesko v Ukraine* App no 30075/06, Judgment of 15 November 2012, para 47.
[48] Ibid, para 47.

placed in detention, measures are taken to ensure that their needs are met.[49] The further a person is removed from outside control – for example when they are detained unlawfully, without a record of their detention being drawn up –, the more favourably the Court views the affected individual's version of the facts.[50]

The same goes for the submission of documentary evidence. In one 2016 case, the Court found that the Russian government's failure to submit legible and complete medical records regarding an ill applicant who was vulnerable in light of his detention meant that it could 'draw inferences as to the well-foundness [*sic*] of the applicant's allegations and the Government's conduct'.[51] It went on to find a violation of Article 3 because of the inadequate medical care provided.

In addition, when states make preliminary objections alleging that applicants failed to exhaust available domestic remedies, the Court has required the state to prove that these remedies were effective if the applicants were vulnerable, for example because they were placed in a mental health facility.[52]

This approach to the burden of proof may benefit vulnerable applicants, but it works to the disadvantage of those who are *not* considered vulnerable. In this regard, the Court has found that non-vulnerable applicants cannot be absolved from the duty to substantiate an alleged Convention violation.[53] The issue of non-vulnerability is discussed more in depth in later chapters.

G. Positive Obligations

Vulnerability reasoning has also been instrumental for the continuing development of the positive obligations derived from Article 3 in combination with Article 1 ECHR.[54] These positive obligations mean that states must 'take measures designed to ensure that individuals within their jurisdiction are not subjected to ill-treatment, including ill-treatment administered by private individuals'.[55]

Regarding vulnerable individuals, states have three separate positive obligations, namely to (a) take reasonable measures to prevent ill-treatment of which they knew or ought to have known (which entails a real and immediate risk of ill-treatment of an identified individual), (b) comply with a (procedural) obligation to conduct an effective official investigation where arguable claims of ill-treatment

[49] *Z.H. v Hungary* App no 28973/11, Judgment of 8 November 2012, paras 29 and 31.

[50] *L.G. v Belgium* App no 38759/14, Judgment of 18 September 2018, para 99.

[51] *Makshakov v Russia* App no 52526/07, Judgment of 24 May 2016, paras 24, 96–97 and 101.

[52] *M. v Ukraine* App no 2452/04, Judgment of 19 April 2012, para 83.

[53] *S.N. and T.D. v Latvia* App no 5794/13, Decision of 6 December 2016, para 68.

[54] Lourdes Peroni and Alexandra Timmer, 'Vulnerable Groups: The Promise of an Emerging Concept in European Human Rights Convention Law' (2013) 11(4) *International Journal of Constitutional Law* 1056–85.

[55] *M.P. and Others v Bulgaria* App no 22457/08, Judgment of 15 November 2011, para 108; Lavrysen Laurens, 'The Scope of Rights and the Scope of Obligations: Positive Obligations' in Eva Brems and Janneke H. Gerards (eds), *Shaping Rights in the ECHR: The Role of the European Court of Human Rights in Determining the Scope of Human Rights* (CUP, 2013) 162–82, 79–80, 109–10.

are raised and, under certain circumstances, (c) establish and effectively apply a system punishing the ill-treatment and providing sufficient safeguards to victims.[56]

In this context, vulnerability provides a minimum content to states' positive obligations. One example of this is *O'Keeffe v Ireland*, where the Court refined the positive obligation to 'provide effective protection of vulnerable persons'.[57] In this case, regarding a child victim of sexual assault, it held that the positive obligation to protect should not 'impose an excessive burden on the authorities, bearing in mind, in particular, the unpredictability of human conduct and operational choices which must be made in terms of priorities and resources', meaning that not every risk of ill-treatment triggers the protective obligation.[58] However, it held, states should '*at least*, provide effective protection in particular of children and other vulnerable persons and should include reasonable steps to prevent ill-treatment of which the authorities had or ought to have had knowledge'.[59]

Positive obligations under Article 3 also require states to ensure protection from ill-treatment by private parties, which includes effective protection of identified individuals from criminal acts by third parties, 'as well as reasonable steps to prevent ill-treatment of which the authorities knew or ought to have known'. This was the finding made in *Rumor v Italy*, a case that concerned a victim of domestic violence, and where the Court held that '[c]hildren and other vulnerable individuals, in particular, are entitled to State protection, in the form of effective deterrence, against such serious breaches of personal integrity'.[60]

Article 3 also entails a positive obligation to investigate alleged violations of the provision. In *Ribitsch v Austria*, one of the very first cases in which the Court had regard to individual vulnerability in the context of Article 3, it also laid the groundwork for this investigative obligation. The Court has since held that, where there are sufficiently clear indications that ill-treatment has taken place, the authorities must investigate even where no official complaint has been made. This was justified by 'the particularly vulnerable situation of victims and the fact that people who have been subjected to serious ill-treatment will often be less ready or willing to make a complaint'.[61] Article 3 also requires 'vigorous investigation' of alleged offences against members of vulnerable groups.[62]

The Court has laid down special requirements for what that investigation should look like. For example, in a case concerning the alleged sexual assault of a minor, the Court held that the domestic authorities had violated their positive obligations

[56] *Bălşan v Romania* App no 49645/09, Judgment of 23 May 2017, para 57.

[57] *P. v United Kingdom* App no 1529/10, Decision of 12 November 2013, para 68.

[58] *O'Keeffe v Ireland* App no 35810/09, Judgment (GC) of 28 January 2014, Reports 2014 (extracts), para 144.

[59] Ibid, emphasis added.

[60] *Rumor v Italy* App no 72964/10, Judgment of 25 May 2014, para 58.

[61] *Stanimirovic v Serbia* App no 26088/06, Judgment of 18 October 2011, para 39. Compare also the similar findings in *Buzilo v Republic of Moldova* App no 52643/07, Judgment of 21 February 2012, para 29, and *Mocanu and Others* (n 34), para 275.

[62] *Balázs v Hungary* App no 15529/12, Judgment of 20 October 2015, para 53.

under Articles 3 and 8 ECHR by 'having attached little weight to the particular vulnerability of young persons and the special psychological factors involved in cases concerning the sexual assault of children'.[63] Similarly, in a case concerning the rape of a mentally disabled fifteen-year-old, the Court paid special attention to the vulnerability of the applicant when it held that the domestic authorities should have shown 'increased diligence in analysing the applicant's statements' as well as paying 'particular attention' to 'the validity of the applicant's consent to the sexual acts in the light of her intellectual capacity'.[64] It did so in light of its finding that 'failure to properly investigate or provide appropriate judicial response to complaints of sexual abuse against children or other vulnerable persons such as persons with intellectual disabilities creates a background of impunity'.[65]

In that latter case, the Court found that the domestic authorities had failed to comply with their positive obligations in multiple ways. For one, they had not taken any of the applicant's personal circumstances, including 'her age and her mental and physical development or the circumstances in which the incident took place', into account.[66] Furthermore, the Court also found that the respondent State had failed in its 'positive obligations to apply effectively a criminal-law system punishing all forms of rape and sexual abuse'.[67] In other words, Article 3 requires states to deploy the criminal law vis-à-vis certain violations of the provision. As noted above in the section concerning the sexual abuse of minors, the deterrence limb of Article 3 requires the authorities to prevent sexual abuse of minors where they have at least imputed knowledge of a corresponding risk of abuse; this includes a 'coercive obligation' to deploy the criminal law.[68]

Known vulnerability may contribute to imputing knowledge of a risk of ill-treatment to the state, which then triggers the state's positive obligations to protect certain groups or individuals.[69] In certain situations, the Court has therefore held that the state must have been aware of certain risks, for example of 'the level of sexual crime by adults against minors', and should have taken adequate measures in response.[70]

In some cases, states have positive obligations to provide care and material support to vulnerable applicants. In *Mubilanzila Mayeka and Kaniki Mitunga*, concerning an unaccompanied minor migrant, the Court held that the domestic

[63] *M. and C. v Romania* App no 29032/04, Judgment of 27 September 2011, para 119.
[64] *I.C. v Romania* App no 36934/08, Judgment of 24 May 2016, para 56.
[65] Ibid, para 55.
[66] Ibid, para 56.
[67] Ibid, para 60.
[68] Natasa Mavronicola, 'Taking Life and Liberty Seriously: Reconsidering Criminal Liability Under Article 2 of the ECHR', 80 *Modern Law Review* (2017), 1026–51; Liora Lazarus, 'Positive Obligations and Criminal Justice: Duties to Protect or Coerce?', in Lucia Zedner and Julian V Roberts (eds), *Principles and Values in Criminal Law and Criminal Justice: Essays in Honour of Andrew Ashworth* (OUP, 2012), 135–55.
[69] *O'Keeffe* (n 58), paras 144–46, 162, 168.
[70] Ibid, para 162.

authorities had violated the five-year-old applicant's rights under Article 3 when they subjected her to migration detention and expulsion. It did so by finding that the applicant, as an unaccompanied minor, 'indisputably came within the class of highly vulnerable members of society to whom the Belgian State owed a duty to take adequate measures to provide care and protection'.[71] Similarly, in *Shioshvili and Others v Russia*, the Court found that the Russian authorities, who left a pregnant woman and her four minor children stranded in an unfamiliar city during winter, had violated their positive obligations under Article 3. Because the authorities had failed to provide any form of support to the applicants after forcing them into a vulnerable situation, they had violated their duty to provide material support.[72]

In short, vulnerability and positive obligations, taken together, mean that Article 3 requires states to become responsive – in other words, to demonstrate 'active State involvement'[73] – in order to prevent and address breaches of vulnerable individuals' rights. In doing so, states must, inter alia, take the specifics of an applicant's vulnerability – such as child-specific psychology or the impaired ability of a mentally disabled person to give valid consent to a sexual act – into consideration. They must take measures that are specifically tailored to protecting the Article 3 rights of the most vulnerable members of society before, while, and after they are exposed to ill-treatment. In some cases, Article 3 may also require the state to deploy the criminal law in order to effectively protect vulnerable individuals.

H. Reassessment of a Domestic Finding

In some cases, the Court uses vulnerability reasoning not only to assess the quality of the domestic investigation, but also to re-examine the domestic authorities' evaluation of the facts of a case.

One example of this is *Balázs v Hungary*, which was brought by a Roma applicant who had suffered an allegedly racially motivated beating. Despite various indications to the contrary, including the alleged use of racist slurs by the perpetrator, the domestic prosecutor found that criminal responsibility for a violent hate crime could not be established 'beyond any doubt', and therefore discontinued the proceedings.[74] When it examined this case, the Court's starting point was that alleged offences against vulnerable individuals require 'vigorous investigation'.[75]

[71] *Mubilanzila Mayeka and Kaniki Mitunga v Belgium* App no 13178/03, Judgment of 12 October 2006, Reports 2006-XI, para 55.

[72] Ibid, para 86.

[73] *M. and M. v Croatia* App no 10161/13, Judgment of 3 September 2015, Reports 2015 (extracts), paras 135–36.

[74] *Balázs* (n 62), paras 10, 11, 74.

[75] Ibid, para 53.

The failure of the domestic authorities to see any relevance in the perpetrator's racist social media posts and their insistence on a purely racist motivation to find that a hate crime had been committed, the Court held, had led to a 'manifestly unreasonable assessment of the circumstances of the case' and a violation of Article 14 in conjunction with Article 3 ECHR.[76]

The Court also uses vulnerability to allow itself to re-examine domestic assessments in expulsion cases.[77] There, the Court has occasionally re-evaluated whether an applicant faces a real risk of harm upon expulsion by conducting its own assessment in light of the vulnerability of the applicant or the group to which he or she belongs. Although vulnerability does not always yield a favourable result for the applicants concerned in the Court's expulsion case law,[78] it has regularly led the Court to depart from the findings of the domestic authorities.[79]

I. Minimum Level of Severity

Vulnerability under Article 3 can affect the minimum level of severity that ill-treatment must attain in order to fall within the scope of the provision. In other words, vulnerability reasoning broadens the scope of Article 3.[80] As discussed above, the minimum level of severity required under this provision has long been considered relative by the Court, so this context-responsiveness is not new in itself. The Court has consistently considered that the assessment of this minimum 'depends on all the circumstances of the case', which includes applicants' vulnerability.[81]

The Court frequently finds that the nature, duration, and severity of a given instance of ill-treatment have violated Article 3 given the facts of a case as a whole, the circumstances, and the vulnerability of the applicant.[82] This applies

[76] Ibid, paras 75–76.

[77] Compare *Samina v Sweden*, where the Court held regarding the applicant's expulsion from Sweden that it did not need to re-examine the assessment made by the domestic authorities because the applicant had not proved that she was vulnerable (*Samina v Sweden* App no 55463/09, Judgment of 20 October 2011, para 64).

[78] See, for example, *Sow v Belgium* App no 27081/13, Judgment of 19 January 2016, para 56, where the applicant was not considered particularly vulnerable to female genital mutilation; *G.J.* (n 12); *A.M.E. v Netherlands* App no 51428/10, Decision of 13 January 2015, para 32.

[79] *U.N. v Russia* App no 14348/15, Judgment of 26 July 2016, paras 39–40; *Khamrakulov v Russia* App no 68894/13, Judgment of 16 April 2015, para 66; *Hirsi Jamaa and Others v Italy* App no 27765/09, Judgment (GC) of 23 February 2012, Reports 2012, paras 125 and 155.

[80] *Gjini* App no 1128/16, Judgment of 15 January 2019, para 82.

[81] *Tarakhel v Switzerland* App no 29217/12, Judgment (GC) of 4 November 2014, Reports 2014 (extracts), paras 118–119; *Khlaifia and Others v Italy* App no 16483/12, Judgment (GC) of 15 December 2016, Reports 2016 (extracts), para 160.

[82] See, for example, *Grzywaczewski v Poland* App no 18364/06, Judgment of 31 May 2012, para 102; *Wenerski (No 2)* App no 38719/09, Judgment of 24 July 2012, paras 56 and 59; *I.G. and Others v Slovakia* App no 15966/04, Judgment of 13 November 2012, para 123. See also *Zarzycki v Poland* App no 15351/03, Judgment of 12 March 2013, where the Court held that *even though* the applicant was vulnerable, the threshold of severity had not been met (para 125).

to individuals belonging to a recognised 'vulnerable group' – individuals with disabilities,[83] asylum-seekers[84] and Roma,[85] to be specific – but also to individuals recognised simply as 'vulnerable'.[86]

For example, the Court has taken the special vulnerability of detainees who are in poor health into account, finding that poor detention conditions exacerbate the feelings of distress of these vulnerable persons.[87] When it comes to states' positive obligations, a failure to take into account the specific needs and extreme vulnerability of applicants can raise treatment up past the threshold of severity.[88] In *R.R. v Poland*, for example, the Court found that the domestic authorities' failure to provide timely information to the applicant about the health of her foetus meant that she was exposed to 'weeks of painful uncertainty' and 'acute anguish'; given that she was in a 'situation of great vulnerability', this meant that the threshold under Article 3 had been met.[89]

The *R.R. v Poland* judgment also touches upon another interesting aspect of the Court's vulnerability jurisprudence, namely the fact – as discussed above – that a sense of vulnerability can in and of itself be humiliating and meet the threshold of severity required under Article 3.[90] In other words, the severity of a feeling of humiliation can suffice to meet the threshold of severity required under Article 3.

J. The Intent and Purpose Requirements of Torture

The Court takes vulnerability into account when determining whether a given treatment constitutes torture, as opposed to inhuman or degrading treatment. This is particularly true in cases concerning detainees (especially those in unrecorded detention) who are ill-treated by the authorities in order to extract information.[91] While the intent and purpose requirements are usually also discussed in these cases – although the Court has admitted that it is not always straightforward to link ill-treatment to the aim of extracting a confession[92] – vulnerability argumentation serves to underscore the utter denial of rights and dignity that occurs in these situations.[93]

[83] *Z.H.* (n 49), paras 29–31.

[84] *Tarakhel* (n 81), paras 118–19; *M.S.S. v Belgium and Greece* App no 30696/09, Judgment (GC) of 21 January 2011, Reports 2011, paras 232–33, 251, 263.

[85] *I.G. and Others* (n 82), para 123.

[86] *Menesheva v Russia* App no 59261/00, Judgment of 9 March 2006, Reports 2006-III, para 61; *Wenerski (No 2)* (n 82), paras 56 and 59.

[87] *Wenerski (No 2)* (n 82), para 56.

[88] *Tarakhel* (n 81), para 119.

[89] *R.R. v Poland* App no 27617/04, Judgment of 26 May 2011, Reports 2011 (extracts), paras 159, 161.

[90] *Rachwalski and Ferenc v Poland* App no 47709/99, Judgment of 28 July 2009, para 61.

[91] *Razzakov v Russia* App no 57519/09, Judgment of 2 February 2015, para 54; *Lykova v Russia* App no 68736/11, Judgment of 22 December 2015.

[92] *Kaverzin v Ukraine* App no 23893/03, Judgment of 15 May 2012, para 174.

[93] *Razzakov* (n 91), para 54.

In some cases, even in detention, ill-treatment cannot be linked to the purpose of extracting a confession. In one case against Greece, the Court considered the rape of a male detainee by a guard. There was no discussion of a proscribed purpose here, and instead the Court focused on whether the treatment was intentional and the fact that it was 'a particularly serious and reprehensible form of ill-treatment given the ease with which the perpetrator could abuse the vulnerability and fragility of the victim.'[94] Focusing on the particular cruelty of the act and the intentionality of the guard's behaviour, the Court found that it had constituted torture.[95]

Similarly, the applicants in *Cirino and Renne v Italy*, who complained about the conditions of their detention and the gratuitous and repeated acts of violence they suffered in prison, were both described as vulnerable and found to have been tortured. This finding was based on the deliberate, premeditated, and organised nature of their ill-treatment, the routine nature of ill-treating 'problematic' detainees at the facility in question, and the fact that the treatment served to punish and discipline them.[96] The purposive element was applied very loosely here, and it should be noted that much ill-treatment of this severity, if not administered at random, could be described as a form of punishment, discipline, or intimidation, which the Court has also recognised as proscribed purposes.[97]

There are other cases in which the elements of purpose and intent take a back seat in the Court's understanding of what constitutes torture. For example, in *Cestaro v Italy*, violence perpetrated by police against a vulnerable elderly man sitting with his arms up and his back against a wall led the Court to make a finding of torture.[98] Here, the Court did note that there are two elements to defining torture: severity and purpose.[99] It went on to discuss various reasons why the treatment suffered constituted torture, but did so while focusing largely on the gratuitous, unmerited, and excessive nature of the violence inflicted, and not on its purpose.

In this regard, it is remarkable that there have been no cases to date in which the ill-treatment inflicted by private parties was characterised as torture by the Court. In other words, the Court seems to continue to see torture as something that only state actors can perpetrate, which is a somewhat questionable approach, especially given the level to which state acquiescence or toleration can facilitate or even encourage private ill-treatment.[100] In addition, specifically in a vulnerability context, it is relevant to recall that the UNCAT lists discrimination as a

[94] *Zontul v Greece* App no 12294/07, Judgment of 17 January 2012, para 88, translated from the original French by the author.
[95] Ibid, para 92.
[96] *Cirino and Renne v Italy* App no 2539/13 and 4705/13, Judgment of 26 October 2017, paras 78–87.
[97] *Gäfgen v Germany* App no 22978/05, Judgment (GC) of 1 June 2010, Reports 2010, paras 89–90.
[98] *Cestaro v Italy* App no 6884/11, Judgment of 7 April 2015, paras 176, 178, 190.
[99] Ibid, para 171.
[100] *Volodina v Russia* App no 41261/17, Judgment of 9 July 2019, regarding the authorities' toleration of domestic violence.

proscribed purpose that can qualify treatment as torture. For example, when it comes to gender-based or homophobic violence, it could be argued that failing to recognise ill-treatment based on these vulnerability-related motives as torture if they are severe enough to justify doing so means 'turning a blind eye to the specific nature of acts that are particularly destructive of fundamental rights'.[101]

K. Hindrance by the State (Article 34 ECHR)

Under Article 34 ECHR, which concerns the right to individual application, the Contracting States to the Convention 'undertake not to hinder in any way the effective exercise of this right'. States are thereby precluded from hindering applicants' effective communication with the Court. This requirement, too, is responsive to an applicant's vulnerability.[102] For example, in a 2015 case against Russia, the Court found that, in determining whether states have complied with Article 34, 'regard must be had to the vulnerability of the complainant and his or her susceptibility to influence exerted by the authorities'. In that case, the Court held that the applicants – who were imprisoned, barely spoke Russian, had no family or social support, and were not provided with a translator – were 'particularly at risk to unacceptable practice [*sic*]'.[103]

Article 34 also enshrines positive obligations regarding applicants in a situation of vulnerability and dependence. Regarding these individuals – including detainees – the authorities have an obligation 'to furnish all necessary facilities to make possible a proper and effective examination of applications'.[104] This includes providing applicants with stationery, stamps, and the files needed to make an application to the Court.[105] In one 2016 case, for example, the Court held that Article 34 'may impose on the State authorities an obligation to provide copies of documents to applicants who find themselves in situations of particular vulnerability and dependence and are unable to obtain the documents needed for their files without State support'.[106] This obligation has been narrowed again in other cases, with the Court arguing that states are not automatically required to provide copies of any requested document.[107]

L. Just Satisfaction (Article 41 ECHR)

The vulnerability of applicants is also relevant in the context of just satisfaction claims under Article 41 ECHR. As concerns the need for applicants to submit a

[101] *M.C. and A.C. v Romania* App no 12060/12, Judgment of 12 April 2016, para 113.
[102] *Knyazev v Russia* App no 25948/05, Judgment of 8 November 2007, paras 116–19.
[103] *L.M. and Others v Russia* App nos 40081/14 …, Judgment of 15 October 2015, para 160.
[104] *Yusunova and Yusunov v Azerbaijan* App no 59620/14, Judgment of 2 June 2016, para 109.
[105] *Szemkovics v Romania* App no 27117/08, Decision of 17 December 2013, paras 27–31, esp 30.
[106] *Savchenko v Ukraine* App no 1574/06, Judgment of 22 September 2016, para 214.
[107] *Tymchenko v Ukraine* App no 47351/06, Judgment of 13 October 2016, para 104.

corresponding claim for damages, in one 2015 judgment, an applicant – who had suffered a violation of Article 3 on account of his conditions of detention – failed to make a claim for just satisfaction. The Court noted that the individual concerned 'must have suffered considerably' under the detention regime in question, as he was missing a hand and had committed acts of self-harm.[108] Under Article 41 ECHR, the Court ruled that he would have been entitled to EUR 23,250 in just satisfaction had he made a corresponding claim. The Court held that given that the case concerned 'a serious breach of Article 3 of the Convention suffered by a disabled and particularly vulnerable applicant, it would be unduly harsh fully to reject his claim in respect of non-pecuniary damage', therefore awarding him half of the amount to which he would have been entitled, so EUR 11,625.[109] This is a curious result, given that the Court seems to have been uncomfortable both with not providing just satisfaction at all, and with making a full award, and seems to have relied on vulnerability to create a compromise, perhaps as a way of reaching an equitable medium between different judges' opposing opinions.

In addition to the above, vulnerability may also play a role when it comes to determining the *amount* of just satisfaction awarded by the Court, or its decision to award any amount at all.[110] Here, too, the case law is spotty and there is not much clarity about when, why, or how vulnerability will play a role.

In 2017, the Grand Chamber had an opportunity to address this issue in *Nagmetov v Russia*. It found that it can occasionally and exceptionally make awards even where applicants have not made a 'specific claim' for just satisfaction.[111] This was an Article 2 case, and the majority did not address the issue of vulnerability, but the three dissenters did refer to the concept, which indicates that it may have been discussed by the majority as well.[112] Arguably, covert vulnerability analysis could be part of *Nagmetov*'s regard for the overall context of a Convention violation, or part of establishing the particular gravity and impact of a violation. Future case law will have to show what the role of vulnerability is in this regard.

M. Consequential Orders (Article 46 ECHR)

Consequential orders are made by the Court in selected violation judgments to indicate the measures that states must take to end a rights-violating situation and fulfil their obligations under Article 46 ECHR.[113] Nesa Zimmermann has argued that vulnerability may make the Court more likely to order individual or general

[108] *Neshkov and Others v Bulgaria* App nos 36925/10 …, Judgment of 27 January 2015, paras 69 and 302.
[109] Ibid, para 302.
[110] *Ilgiz Khalikov v Russia* App no 48724/15, Judgment of 15 January 2019, para 107.
[111] *Nagmetov v Russia* App no 35589/08, Judgment (GC) of 30 March 2017, paras 69 and 71.
[112] Ibid, Joint Dissenting Opinion of Judges Raimondi, O'Leary, and Ranzoni, para 42.
[113] *Stanev v Bulgaria* App no 36760/06, Judgment (GC) of 17 January 2012, Reports 2012, para 255, citing *Broniowski v Poland* App no 31443/96, Judgment (GC) of 22 June 2004, Reports 2004-V, para 194.

measures.[114] She supports her argument by referring to *Yordanova and Others v Bulgaria*.[115] Although the Court has been vague in this regard, some other judgments support her conclusion.

When it comes to general measures encouraged by or linked to vulnerability, there are a number of examples from the Article 3 case law. For example, in *Savriddin Dzhurayev v Russia*, the Court held that 'in view of their particularly vulnerable situation, applicants in respect of whom the Court has indicated interim measures must be granted effective protection by the State not only in law, but also in practice'. It then went on to order a general measure requiring the domestic authorities to implement an 'appropriate mechanism, tasked with both preventative and protective functions' to tackle kidnapping and irregular removal from Russia.[116]

Another example of this came about in *Sławomir Musiał v Poland*, where, considering serious and structural problems with conditions in Polish prisons, the Court required the respondent state to rapidly take 'necessary legislative and administrative measures … in order to secure appropriate conditions of detention of detained persons, in particular, adequate conditions and medical treatment for prisoners, who, like the applicant, need special care owing to their state of health'.[117] In yet another case, the Court had regard to the vulnerability of criminal suspects in requiring urgent specific reforms to the national legal system.[118]

Vulnerability may also lead to an order of specific measures. For example, in *Neshkov and Others v Bulgaria*, concerning a particularly vulnerable applicant facing harsh detention conditions, the Court ordered that, to 'redress the effects of the breach of his rights under Article 3 of the Convention, the authorities must, if he so wishes, urgently transfer him to another correctional facility'.[119]

There does thus seem to be some willingness on the part of the Court to indicate general and individual vulnerability-related measures. When it comes particularly to general measures, these may provide an avenue for addressing broader systems of disadvantage and marginalisation. It is difficult to make general conclusions in this context, however, given that the Court's reasons for ordering general measures under Article 46 ECHR are varied and complex, and depend on the nature and circumstances of the case, the urgency of providing redress and the question of whether legislative changes are necessary to address the issue, for instance.[120]

[114] Nesa Zimmermann, 'Legislating for the Vulnerable? Special Duties under the European Convention on Human Rights' (2015) 25(4) *Swiss Review of International and European Law (Schweizerische Zeitschrift für internationales und europäisches Recht)* 539–62, 562.

[115] Ibid, 561, referring to *Yordanova and Others* (n 29), para 166.

[116] *Savriddin Dzhurayev v Russia* App no 71386/10, Judgment of 25 April 2013, Reports 2013 (extracts), para 262.

[117] *Sławomir Musiał v Poland* App no 28300/06, Judgment of 20 January 2009, para 107.

[118] *Kaverzin* (n 92), paras 174 and 182.

[119] *Neshkov and Others* (n 108), para 292.

[120] See Helen Keller and Cedric Marti, 'Reconceptualizing Implementation: The Judicialization of the Execution of the European Court of Human Rights' Judgments' (2015) 26(4) *European Journal of International Law* 829–50, 843.

5

Evaluation of the Court's Approach in Practice

Chapter Summary

This chapter provides an interim evaluation of the Court's approach to vulnerability in practice and a roadmap of the key topics covered in the following chapters. It summarises the Court's approach to vulnerability as one that allows it to respond to individual needs and experiences as well as structures of oppression and systems of discrimination and powerlessness. While the concept is revolutionary in this sense, it has been introduced hesitantly and selectively by the Court. This selectivity, which is likely a pragmatic response to political realities and the Court's case load crisis, has resulted in a concept calibrated to render vulnerability the exception, rather than the rule.

Keywords: judicial activism; judicial deference; universal vulnerability; selective vulnerability; backlash; the ECtHR's case load.

I. Vulnerability as a Vehicle of Exclusion and Inclusion

The mapping exercise conducted above has shown that the Court takes a diversified approach to vulnerability. Taken all together, the many grounds for vulnerability recognised by the Court thus far create a patchwork that covers significant parts of every human individual's life span, and of some lives in particular. In other words, we all begin our lives as children, many of us grow dependent in our old age, and, over the course of our lives, a significant number of us experience hospitalisation, mental health issues, detention, pregnancy, victimisation, migration, or a host of other factors that can make us vulnerable. Seeing the Court's approach in this way, namely as a patchwork that loosely covers all human individuals at one stage of life or another, aids the recognition that dependence and physical fragility are natural characteristics of human life, and universal.

This does not, however, seem to be the approach intended by the Court. Instead, vulnerability primarily seems to allow the Court to respond to particular contexts, albeit a wide range of them.[1] Looking at cases in which the Court found that the applicants were not vulnerable,[2] and the many more in which vulnerability did not come into play at all, vulnerability under Article 3 no longer looks like a panacea for evoking context-sensitivity and a more responsive Court, or at least it becomes clear that it only works in this way for selected applicants.

Granted, vulnerability allows the Court to provide targeted and tailored attention to the persons who particularly require this given their dependency, marginalisation, or inability to stand up for their own rights. The Court thereby engages with the structural disadvantages facing particular groups and individuals, and levels the playing field for them. Nonetheless, many applicants will not reap the benefits of this type of vulnerability reasoning. Indeed, many aspects of the Court's tactic seem calibrated to render vulnerability the exception rather than the rule. This approach is most evident when examining the Court's jurisprudence in migration-related cases.[3]

In applying vulnerability selectively and as a vehicle for exceptional findings, the Court seems to assume that able-bodied members of a nation's ethnic, political, and religious majority who are cisgender, heterosexual, and who are neither under state control, victimised, pregnant, mentally ill, or disabled, nor migrating, and who fall in an age range between 18 and 65, are not only the norm, but are also invulnerable, rational, and independent. These individuals therefore stand to be distinguished from the vulnerable, who now emerge as fundamentally different and removed from the non-vulnerable. Those considered vulnerable thereby become framed as an out-group of others whom it is easy to ill-treat, easy to get away with ill-treating or easy to rationalise ill-treating because of their disadvantaged or dependent position.

At the same time, this approach frames a certain group, those not considered vulnerable, as invulnerable. This is problematic because invulnerable subjects do not need the protection offered by human rights, and in fact human rights law has no invulnerable subjects. Applying the Court's current approach, which singles out particular aspects of life and particular lives for protection under the concept of vulnerability, is counter-productive in this sense, as it may reduce individuals to their vulnerability, potentially alienates different classes of applicants, and reinforces social divisions. This approach also does not correspond to lived human

[1] Jonathan Herring, 'Vulnerability, Children and the Law' in Michael Freeman (ed), *Law and Childhood Studies*, vol 14 (OUP, 2012) 243–63, 256, from 258.

[2] *Kanlibas v Turkey* App no 32444/96, Decision of 28 April 2005; *Barbu Anghelescu v Romania (No 2)* App no 2871/02, Decision of 26 February 2008; *Miah v United Kingdom* App no 53080/07, Decision of 27 April 2010, para 14; *Kostjučenkovs v Latvia* App no 19826/04, Decision of 8 March 2011, para 49; *S.S. v United Kingdom* App no 12096/10, Decision of 24 January 2012, para 74; *Shakurov v Russia* App no 55822/10, Judgment of 5 June 2012, para 137; *Valiulienė v Lithuania* App no 33234/07, Judgment of 26 March 2013, para 69 (where the Court found that the applicant was not vulnerable by virtue of her gender, and then failed to examine whether she was vulnerable as a victim of domestic violence).

[3] Compare, for example, *Abdi Mahamud v Malta* App no 56796/13, Judgment of 3 May 2016, and *Moxamed Ismaaciil and Abdirahman Warsame v Malta* App nos 52160/13 and 52165/13, Judgment of 12 January 2016, discussed above at 161).

reality. Human beings are by their very nature interdependent, even if they fail to fall under the Court's understanding of vulnerability.[4] The idea of a self-reliant and invulnerable human rights subject – the archetype of the rational liberal subject, in other words – is a fallacy that the Court should work to overcome.

Following this reasoning, and as discussed below, vulnerability theorists have argued that the concept of special, selective vulnerability should be jettisoned in favour of an approach that embraces the universal vulnerability of all beings embodied in fragile human physical form.[5] However, from a practice-oriented perspective it is possible to argue that neither approach – that offering protection only to a few, in the sense of singling out the vulnerable, or that offering undifferentiated protection to all, in the sense of negating particular vulnerability – is wholly satisfactory.

II. Reticence, Selectivity and the 'Floodgates' Problem

In this regard, it is helpful to draw on the arguments made in the context of minority rights. There, it is widely acknowledged that minority rights protection is not complete without two pillars: first, the equal application of rights to all legal subjects, and secondly the protection of 'special' rights granted only to members of minorities.[6] In the present context, too, it could therefore be argued that the Court need not choose between the two alternatives – namely paying attention to either universal or exceptional vulnerability – but can instead combine the two. The Court's vulnerability reasoning as described above would fall under or even constitute the second pillar, with universal human vulnerability being protected implicitly in the first pillar through the application of the Convention to all. Both of these pillars are, in other words, necessary for full human rights protection.

The problem in applying this two-pillar reasoning to the vulnerability context, however, is that who gets to benefit from the 'special' rights, or how far these rights go, is not very clearly defined. Indeed, the Court has been cryptic about how it defines vulnerability, and reluctant to grant broad application to the special protections recognised for the vulnerable. The selectivity of the Court's approach is likely a pragmatic response to the political realities facing it today.

[4] Herring (n 1), 255–56.

[5] Martha Albertson Fineman, 'The Vulnerable Subject: Anchoring Equality in the Human Condition' (2008) 20(1) *Yale Journal of Law and Feminism* 1–23; Lauren B Wilcox, *Bodies of Violence: Theorizing Embodied Subjects in International Relations* (OUP, 2015); Anna Grear, *Redirecting Human Rights: Facing the Challenge of Corporate Legal Humanity* (Palgrave Macmillan, 2010), from 115.

[6] Kristin Henrard, 'Equal Rights versus Special Rights? Minority Protection and the Prohibition of Discrimination' (European Commission 2007), 14–15.

While the Court has not developed an explicit overarching theory of vulnerability – likely partly by design,[7] and partly because of the individual application-based nature of its work – its vulnerability approach allows it to distinguish certain cases from the mass of applications before it. Concern about the 'floodgates' argument – the idea that a judgment in one applicant's favour will cause similar applications to pour in to the Court's Registry, which will both overstretch the Court's capacities and force it to create broad obligations on states that, if applied to all human rights subjects, will be financially and politically untenable – is voiced particularly where a case has socio-economic implications. At the same time, focusing overly on the floodgates problem can lead to indefensible protection failures. The Court's fear of its own success, in this sense, is one that should not be imposed on the interpretation of rights without at least a degree of critical reflection and evidence of a truly untenable result.[8]

While the Court is reluctant to make findings entailing economic consequences for states, it has also held that, in principle, it cannot accept the absence of financial resources as a defence against alleged Convention violations.[9] The argument that protecting the rights of the individual should be avoided because it might require the protection of the rights of many more individuals is not a good one, and it is indeed a very difficult one to make where absolute rights such as Article 3 are concerned. However, of course, the situation facing the Court is complicated by the fact that it is engaged in the long-term dynamic interpretation of a controversial human rights instrument, and depends on the cooperation of states for the enforcement of its judgments. In a post-Brexit world, with voices in certain states clamouring ever louder for a denunciation of the ECHR, these concerns are certainly not without foundation.

Given these realities, actors within the Court may see vulnerability as a way out: it allows the Court to avoid floodgates risks by rendering cases exceptional, at least to a degree. This means that they cannot be relied on[10] by individuals who are not deemed (as) vulnerable. However, this binary approach serves neither those who are deemed vulnerable nor those who are not, given the exclusions that

[7] Michael O'Boyle, 'The Notion of "Vulnerable Groups" in the Case Law of the European Court of Human Rights', Venice Commission, Doc CDL-LA(2016)003, 12 February 2016, 3.

[8] *N. v United Kingdom* App no 26565/05, Judgment (GC) of 27 May 2008, Reports 2008, Joint Dissenting Opinion of Judges Tulkens, Bonello and Spielmann, para 8.

[9] Julia Laffranque, Guido Raimondi, Ledi Bianku, Angelika Nußberger and Linos-Alexander Sicilianos, 'Implementing the European Convention on Human Rights in Times of Economic Crisis', *Seminar Background Paper* (25 January 2013), www.echr.coe.int/Documents/Seminar_background_paper_2013_ENG.pdf, 4, citing *Poltoratskiy v Ukraine* App no 38812/97, Judgment of 29 April 2003, Reports 2003-V, para 148 and *Orchowski v Poland* App no 17885/04, Judgment of 22 October 2009.

[10] While the Court is not formally bound by a system of precedent, of course, its authority is only convincing if it decides cases in a consistent manner. Its case law is thus not binding *erga omnes*, but does constitute *res interpretata* vis-à-vis the respondent state, and thus predicts how the Court will respond to similar complaints from other states (Oddný Mjöll Arnardóttir, 'Res Interpretata, Erga Omnes Effect and the Role of the Margin of Appreciation in Giving Domestic Effect to the Judgments of the ECtHR', 28(3) *European Journal of International Law* (2017) 819–43).

it potentially generates. As will be argued below, it is both more useful and less harmful to conceive of vulnerability as part of a spectrum, opposite its pendant of resilience, on which every individual falls.

What is certain is that the concept of vulnerability cannot, on its own, be expected to bring about a more activist jurisprudence on behalf of some or all human rights subjects: such a revolution requires the Court to stand up to the political pressures that dictate otherwise. What the Court needs is not less or more narrow reliance on vulnerability, but more and broader emphasis on it. Vulnerability, as a proxy for engagement with human suffering, the realities of human existence, and the exigencies of a life in human dignity, can help build a better, more responsive and nuanced jurisprudence under Article 3. As will be discussed below, this requires an explicit discussion of why and how the vulnerability of certain applicants is considered relevant in a given case.

While vulnerability has elsewhere been described as a 'quiet revolution' in the Court's jurisprudence,[11] the present analysis provides a slightly different account of the concept: while it has certainly been introduced quietly, it has also been applied hesitantly and selectively. Certainly, vulnerability may well come into play in borderline cases. It can lend particular weight to the interests of individuals who have been historically discriminated against or who have difficulty voicing their complaints, for example. But it should not be lauded as a mechanism that will automatically liberate human rights bearers from the ill-fitting archetype of the traditional liberal subject. Why this is the case will be explored in more depth in Part III of this volume, which integrates a theoretical approach into the Court's case law.

[11] Alexandra Timmer, 'A Quiet Revolution: Vulnerability in the European Court of Human Rights' in Martha Albertson Fineman and Anna Grear (eds), *Vulnerability: Reflections on a New Ethical Foundation for Law and Politics* (Ashgate, 2013) 147–70.

PART III

Contextualising and Critiquing the Court's Approach

6

Situating Vulnerability Reasoning in a Broader Context

Chapter Summary

The present chapter provides context for understanding the Court's approach to vulnerability. It does so in three main ways. First, it refers briefly to trends in the work of other human rights bodies, showing that the Court is not alone in deploying this concept. Secondly, it looks at minority protection, showing that vulnerability reasoning evolved in parallel to key moments relating to the protection of minorities, and discusses how a turn to vulnerability fits into the Council of Europe's approach to minority rights. Thirdly, it looks at another key area in which the ECtHR applies vulnerability reasoning, namely its non-discrimination case law under Article 14 ECHR.

Keywords: minority rights; non-discrimination; Article 14 ECHR; comparative perspective; margin of appreciation.

I. Vulnerability and Other Human Rights Bodies

As noted in the introduction to this volume, the Court is not alone in using the concept of vulnerability, or in using it as it does, namely to describe specific situations and groups that require particular attention without providing a clear definition of the concept. A number of human rights bodies have taken the same approach, including the UN Committee on Economic, Social and Cultural Rights (CESCR),[1] the UN Human Rights Committee (HRC), in its documents but not its Views,[2] the European Committee for the Prevention of Torture and

[1] Audrey R Chapman and Benjamin Carbonetti, 'Human Rights Protections for Vulnerable and Disadvantaged Groups: The Contributions of the UN Committee on Economic Social and Cultural Rights' (2011) 33(3) *Human Rights Quarterly* 682–732, 683–85.

[2] HRC, 'General Comment No 21 on Article 10 (humane treatment of persons deprived of their liberty)', UN Doc HRI/GEN/1/Rev 9 (Vol I), 202–04, adopted on 10 April 1992, para 3.

Inhuman or Degrading Treatment or Punishment (CPT),[3] the Committee on the Rights of the Child,[4] the Committee on the Elimination of Discrimination against Women (CEDAW),[5] the European Committee of Social Rights,[6] the Inter-American Court of Human Rights,[7] and the European Committee against Racism and Intolerance (ECRI),[8] to name a few. The concept is also an integral part of the EU legal framework applicable to asylum-seekers and refugees.[9]

This is one part of the context of the Court's vulnerability reasoning, although a somewhat remote one in the sense that the Court usually does not refer to these other bodies in finding that someone is vulnerable; its reasoning in this regard is mostly self-contained.[10] In other words, the approaches of these bodies do not provide much insight into the Court's approach beyond indicating that the Court is not alone in using this concept and in using it selectively, ie not in the sense of universal vulnerability. In addition, the fact that so many bodies use this concept may be an indication that regard for vulnerability is considered an intrinsic or underlying element of human rights guarantees.

Next to this source of context, however, there is another one, namely the context of how the concept came to be within the Council of Europe system. The following will explore the evolution of minority protection internationally and within the Council of Europe and suggest that vulnerability came about, at least in part, as a response to the limping along of efforts to provide minority protection.

[3] CPT, CPT Standards, CPT/Inf/E (2002) 1, Rev 2015, January 2015, www.cpt.coe.int/en/documents/eng-standards.pdf, 45–46.

[4] Kirsten Sandberg, 'The Convention on the Rights of the Child and the Vulnerability of Children' (2015) 84(2) *Nordic Journal of International Law* 221–47, 223.

[5] CEDAW Committee, General Recommendation No 19: Violence against Women, UN Doc A/47/38, 1992, para 15.

[6] European Committee of Social Rights, Conclusions 2015 (Andorra), Doc 2015/def/AND/17/2/EN, 4 December 2015.

[7] IACtHR, *Ximenes Lopes v Brazil*, Judgment of 4 July 2006, Series C-149, para 103; IACtHR, *González et al ('Cotton Field') v Mexico*, Judgment of 16 November 2009, Series C-205, paras 282 and 284; Rosmerlin Estupiñan-Silva, 'La vulnerabilidad en la jurisprudencia de la Corte interamericana de derechos humanos: Esbozo de una tipología', *Derechos Humanos y Políticas Públicas: Manual* (Red Derechos Humanos y Educación Superior, 2014), 193–231, 197.

[8] ECRI, General Policy Recommendation no 3 on Combating Racism and Intolerance against Roma/Gypsies, 6 March 1998, www.coe.int/t/dghl/monitoring/ecri/activities/GPR/EN/Recommendation_N3/Rec03en.pdf, 4.

[9] See, for example, Directive 2013/33/EU of the European Parliament and of the Council of 26 June 2013 laying down standards for the reception of applicants for international protection (recast), [2013] OJ L180/96–116, Art 2k. Overall, see Joanna Pétin, 'Exploring the Role of Vulnerability in Immigration Detention' (2016) 35 *Refugee Survey Quarterly* 91–108, 93, with supporting references.

[10] Although there are exceptions. See *Khlaifia and Others v Italy* App no 16483/12, Judgment (GC) of 15 December 2016, Reports 2016 (extracts), paras 46–47, referring to the International Law Commission (ILC)'s 'Draft articles on the expulsion of aliens', UNGA Res A/RES/69/119 (10 December 2014).

II. Vulnerability and the Context of Minority Rights

A. Attention to Minority Rights in the 1980s and 1990s

The creation of minority-specific international legal protections did not take off until the late 1980s.[11] This era saw the conclusion of numerous bilateral treaties concerning minority rights between individual states,[12] which, however, were often characterised by ambiguousness, 'escape clauses' and guarantees of territorial integrity.[13] In Europe, the development of strong minority protections did not really take off until the early 1990s, when the Conference on Security and Co-operation in Europe (CSCE), now the Organization for Security and Co-operation in Europe (OSCE), adopted a series of non-binding minority rights instruments.[14] In 1992, the UN joined in, adopting its Declaration on the Rights of Persons Belonging to National or Ethnic, Religious and Linguistic Minorities[15] One year later, in 1993, it held the Second World Conference on Human Rights in Vienna.[16]

To understand who falls under the protection of these instruments, it is helpful to clarify what constitutes a minority group. That definition, like the definition of the concept of vulnerability, has been the source of controversy in the course of drafting the relevant international instruments, reflecting a lack of international consensus.[17] An early definition was provided by UN Special Rapporteur Francesco Capotorti in 1979, who defined a minority as:

> A group numerically inferior to the rest of the population of a State, in a non-dominant position, whose members – being nationals of the State – possess ethnic, religious or linguistic characteristics differing from those of the rest of the population and show, if only implicitly, a sense of solidarity, directed towards preserving their culture, traditions, religion or language.[18]

[11] Rainer Hofmann, 'Minorities, European Protection' in Rüdiger Wolfrum (ed), *Max Planck Encyclopedia of International Law* vol II (OUP, 2012), 240–53, 241, para 2.

[12] For examples, see Arie Bloed and Pieter Van Dijk (eds), *Protection of Minority Rights Through Bilateral Treaties: The Case of Central and Eastern Europe* (Kluwer Law International, 1999). In all, see Hofmann (n 11), 241, para 2.

[13] Kristin Henrard, 'Minorities, International Protection' in Rüdiger Wolfrum (ed), *Max Planck Encyclopedia of International Law* vol VII (OUP, 2012) 254–70, 264–65, para 63.

[14] Document of the Second Meeting of the Conference on the Human Dimension of the CSCE, Copenhagen, 29 June 1990, www.osce.org/node/14307; 'The Challenges of Change,' Document of the Summit of the CSCE, Helsinki, 9–10 July 1992, from 8.

[15] UN Declaration on the Rights of Persons Belonging to National or Ethnic, Religious and Linguistic Minorities, Doc A/RES/47/135, 18 December 1992.

[16] IACtHR, *Ximenes Lopes v Brazil* (n 7), Separate Opinion of Judge Antônio Augusto Cançado Trindade, para 42, with further references.

[17] Henrard (n 13), 254, para 1.

[18] Francesco Capotorti, 'Study on the Rights of Persons Belonging to Ethnic, Religious and Linguistic Minorities' (1979) UN Doc E/CN 4/Sub 2/384/Rev 1, para 568; OHCHR, 'Minority Rights: International Standards and Guidance for Implementation' (Geneva 2010) HR/PUB/10/3, www.ohchr.org/Documents/Publications/MinorityRights_en.pdf, 2.

This definition has been criticised because of its requirements of numerical inferiority and of nationality.[19] Commentators have also suggested that the definition should be widened to allow the recognition of groups that did not originally meet its criteria as 'minorities', for example persons with disabilities, certain political groupings or LGBTQI people.[20] Capotorti's definition has, however, gained general acceptance regarding the objective elements it contains, namely that a particular trait distinguishes a minority from the majority, that minorities are non-dominant in the general population, and its subjective trait, namely that they share the will to maintain this trait.[21]

How do these developments relate to the Court's vulnerability jurisprudence? Modern-day attention to the human rights of the vulnerable may be part of the legacy of the 1993 Vienna World Conference, which is at least illustrative of a turn towards vulnerability. The Conference's agenda concerned 'all human rights of women and men, including those of persons belonging to vulnerable groups'.[22] Its final outcome document called for 'promotion and protection of the human rights of persons belonging to groups which have been rendered vulnerable' and for 'the promotion and protection of the rights of persons in vulnerable sectors of [states'] populations'.[23] While it did not explicitly mention vulnerability, the Vienna Declaration itself contained an appendix on combating xenophobia, racism and discrimination, as well as another on the rights of national minorities.[24] This may all have fed into the work of the Council of Europe, where, after 1992, the number of references to vulnerability increased perceptibly in the work of various actors, including the Committee of Ministers and the Secretary-General.[25] The Court's vulnerability jurisprudence, which began to materialise as the World Conference was being prepared,[26] also emerged full-force after the Conference's conclusion.[27]

Today, as touched upon above, minority protection is based on two pillars: first, the general protection of human rights as they apply to members of minorities

[19] OHCHR (n 18), 2–3.

[20] Ibid, 3.

[21] Hofmann (n 11), 241, para 4.

[22] World Conference on Human Rights, Provisional Agenda: Note by the Secretary-General, UN Doc A/CONF 157/1, 18 May 1993, para 11.

[23] World Conference on Human Rights, Vienna Declaration and Programme of Action of 25 June 1993, UN Doc A/CONF 157/23, 12 July 1993, para I.24.

[24] Council of Europe, Vienna Summit, Final Declaration, 9 October 1993, Appendixes II and III, https://rm.coe.int/CoERMPublicCommonSearchServices/DisplayDCTMContent?documentId=0900001680536c83.

[25] See for example the Report to the Committee of Ministers of the European Population Conference held in Geneva on 23–26 March 1993 (CM(93)146, 6 August 1993, 44, 46, 52 and 53).

[26] *Tomasi v France* App no 12850/87, Report (Commission) of 11 December 1990, paras 104–05; *Olsson v Sweden (No 2)* App no 13441/87, Judgment (Chamber) of 27 November 1992, Series A250, para 87.

[27] *Ribitsch v Austria* App no 18896/91, Report (Commission) of 4 July 1994, para 115; *Aksoy* App no 21987/93, Decision (Commission) of 19 October 1994, 70; *S.P., D.P. and A.T. v United Kingdom* App no 23715/94, Decision (Commission) of 20 May 1996.

as human individuals, and secondly, the more specific provisions of minority protection aimed specifically at protecting these groups.[28] To Kristin Henrard, minority rights are 'actually just one of several sets of category-specific human rights, namely special rights for persons belonging to vulnerable groups'.[29] Other examples of these 'special rights', she argues, can be found in group-specific human rights instruments such as the CRC.[30] The two pillars of general and group-specific human rights protection complement each other, and minority-specific protections supplement lacunae in the protection afforded by more general human rights instruments.[31]

If these two pillars are related, then understanding specific minority rights is essential for understanding the concept of vulnerability as it relates to universal rights. The following will in particular explore the protection of minorities in under the auspices of the Council of Europe. This will transition into an examination of the way in which minority protection-related arguments have flowed into the development of vulnerability reasoning under Article 14 ECHR, which in turn informs the vulnerability heuristic employed under Article 3 ECHR.

B. Minority Protection in the Council of Europe

The two-pillar approach to minority protection can also be observed in the Council of Europe. After the Second World War, the Council of Europe provided some degree of minority protection with Article 14 ECHR's 'accessory' protection of non-discrimination, which was later supplemented by a non-accessory prohibition of discrimination in Protocol No 12 to the Convention.[32] Beyond this, the ECHR contains no further specific protection of minority rights, although of course the universal rights in the Convention also apply to members of minorities.[33]

In 1992, when the UN and other actors were adopting their own minority protections, the Council of Europe adopted a legally binding instrument by creating the European Charter for Regional or Minority Languages.[34] In 1994, these efforts were followed by the adoption of the Framework Convention for the Protection of National Minorities (FCNM).[35] The groundwork for this treaty, as well as for the

[28] Henrard (n 13), 258, para 28.
[29] Ibid, 258, para 27.
[30] Ibid.
[31] Ibid, 259, para 29, and 261, paras 43–44.
[32] Hofmann (n 11), 240–41, para 1; Protocol No 12 to the ECHR, ETS 177, Rome, 4 November 2000, in force since 1 March 2005, 20 states parties.
[33] Ibid; Henrard (n 13), 261, para 44.
[34] European Charter for Regional or Minority Languages, ETS 148, Strasbourg, 5 November 1992, in force since 1 March 1998, 25 states parties.
[35] Framework Convention for the Protection of National Minorities (FCNM), ETS 157, Strasbourg, 1 February 1995, in force since 1 February 1998, 39 states parties, preamble, 10th recital, referring to the Document of the Copenhagen Meeting of the Conference on the Human Dimension of the CSCE, cited above at n 14.

establishment of the permanent ECtHR and the creation of ECRI, was thus being laid at the same time as the Vienna Declaration was being prepared.

Today, the effectiveness of minority rights protection in Europe can be separated into three tiers: (i) the strong, binding judicial system of the ECHR, (ii) the legally non-binding one provided by the OSCE or the Council of Europe's ECRI, and (iii) the intermediate, quasi-judicial system under the FCNM, with its Advisory Committee's non-binding opinions, which form the basis of corresponding binding decisions by the Committee of Ministers.[36] Although the ECHR, in structural terms, offers the strongest system of minority rights protection in Europe, its relevance in this area is limited because it lacks minority-specific guarantees and because the Court has, historically, been reticent in addressing such issues.[37]

The entry into force of Protocol No 12 to the ECHR, which introduces a non-accessory prohibition of discrimination, was seen as a potential step towards strengthening the role of the Court in this area, but the Protocol has only been ratified by 20 states to date and the Court has issued only a handful of relevant judgments.[38] An Additional Protocol on the protection of national minorities was suggested in the 1990s, but was not pursued in light of a failure to agree on the content of such an instrument.[39] Attempts to draft a new proposal for such an Additional Protocol in 2011 have been accompanied by expressions of regret about the low number of ratifications of Protocol No. 12, the FCNM and the Language Charter, and the 'numerous shortcomings' in their implementation.[40]

Despite – or perhaps because of – these lacunae, the ECtHR has gradually moved from a restrictive, formal take on equality with a focus on the state margin of appreciation to an approach that recognises and incorporates the need to protect minorities, including from indirect discrimination.[41] In 1999, the Court found that a democracy, which it considers to be characterised by 'pluralism, tolerance and broadmindedness', is not simple majority rule: 'a balance must be achieved which ensures the fair and proper treatment of minorities'.[42] The Court went on to find that measures restricting the rights of a minority must be not merely 'useful' or 'desirable' but 'necessary'.[43] This approach was further developed two years later

[36] Hofmann (n 11), 245–46, paras 18–20. See also Council of Europe Committee of Ministers, Resolution Res(2002)8 on the Statute of the European Commission against Racism and Intolerance, 13 June 2002.

[37] Hofmann (n 11), 245, para. 17. See also, instead of many, the *Belgian Linguistics* Case App nos 1474/62 …, Judgment of 23 July 1968, Series A6.

[38] Hofmann (n 11), 245, para 17, referring to Protocol No 12 to the ECHR (n 32).

[39] Henrard (n 13), 263, para 51, and PACE, Committee on Legal Affairs and Human Rights, Report on an Additional Protocol to the European Convention on Human Rights on National Minorities, AS/Jur(2011)46, 8 November 2011, 9–10, paras 30–35.

[40] PACE (n 39), especially 1, paras 2 and 3.

[41] Henrard (n 13), 266, paras 73–74, 76–77; *Thlimmenos v Greece* App no 34369/97, Judgment (GC) of 6 April 2000, Reports 2000-IV, paras 46–47; *D.H. and Others v Czech Republic* App no 57325/00, Judgment (GC) of 13 November 2007, Reports 2007-IV, from 175, esp para 183.

[42] *Chassagnou and Others v France* App nos 25088/94 …, Judgment (GC) of 29 April 1999, Reports 1999-III, para 112.

[43] Ibid.

in *Chapman v United Kingdom*, where the Court observed an emerging consensus 'recognising the special needs of minorities and an obligation to protect their security, identity and lifestyle'.[44]

This case indicates how lacunae in minority rights protection may have brought about the turn to vulnerability. In *Chapman*, the Court held that, though it was unable to find a consensus on minority protection that was concrete enough to allow it to identify clear standards, and though its own role was a 'strictly supervisory one',[45] there *was* a standard by which it could judge the actions of the government: the affected group's vulnerability. In this regard, the Court stated that 'the vulnerable position of Gypsies as a minority' required 'some special consideration' of their needs and their lifestyle regarding the decisions both on a regulatory plane and in adjudicating individual cases.[46] It accordingly found that the state bore a positive obligation under Article 8 ECHR 'to facilitate the Gypsy way of life'.[47] This finding by the Court, in one of its most important judgments concerning the vulnerability of Travellers, provides an indication that the concepts of vulnerability and minority protection are, at least originally, closely interlinked.

The minority in *Chapman* took the vulnerability argument a step further. In their joint dissenting opinion, seven of the judges disagreed with the Court's interpretation of its own role as strictly supervisory. The judges argued against the majority's reluctance to take an activist role given 'the clearly recognized need of Gypsies for protection', arguing that such reluctance perpetuated their 'vulnerability as a minority whose needs and values differ from those of the general community'.[48] The minority took a more invasive (and, from today's perspective, contemporary) approach by arguing for the application of a 'compelling reasons' test when the lifestyle of the group's members is limited.[49]

In *Chapman* and like cases, the reference to vulnerability eliminated the need to wait for the development of a European consensus on the standards of minority protection. The Court's reference to vulnerability thus allowed it to fill a significant gap in the protection afforded to minorities. The judges, in applying this approach, also circumvented the need to create a definition of minorities and replaced any such categorisation with vulnerability or, in the words of the minority, 'the clearly recognized need of Gypsies for protection'.[50] Using the vulnerability of minority groups, the Court thus narrowed the state margin of appreciation regarding measures concerning them.

[44] *Chapman v United Kingdom* App no 27238/95, Judgment (GC) of 18 January 2001, Reports 2001-I, para 93.

[45] Ibid, para 94.

[46] Ibid, para 96.

[47] Ibid.

[48] Ibid, Joint Dissenting Opinion of Judges Pastor Ridruejo, Bonello, Tulkens, Strážnická, Lorenzen, Fischbach and Casadevall, para 3.

[49] Ibid.

[50] Ibid.

III. Vulnerability in the Court's Non-Discrimination Jurisprudence

The way in which the Court used vulnerability in *Chapman* has become commonplace in later jurisprudence under Article 14 ECHR, the Convention's accessory prohibition of discrimination. Article 14 protects against differences in treatment that are 'based on an identifiable characteristic, or "status"' that cannot be justified reasonably and objectively.[51] Discrimination can either arise directly, when a person is treated less favourably than another on the basis of a prohibited ground, or indirectly, when seemingly 'neutral' treatment disproportionately impacts the members of a group on the basis of a prohibited ground.[52]

When a prima facie case of discrimination has been established, it may be possible to justify the relevant difference in treatment.[53] In this regard, the Member States of the Council of Europe have a certain margin of appreciation in determining what treatment constitutes discrimination, and in balancing the interests at stake.[54] The Court, in determining the extent of this margin, has regard to whether there is 'common ground' among states. Where there is no such consensus, national authorities have more discretion in determining whether a difference in treatment is justified.[55] This latter, watered-down version of the justification test is often applied where states have regulated a given matter in different ways or where there are scientifically, legally, morally, or socially complex issues at play.[56] States also have a wide margin of appreciation regarding general economic or social strategy. Given that the national authorities are better placed to make decisions in this context, the Court will generally respect domestic policy choices unless they are 'manifestly without reasonable foundation'.[57]

The state margin of appreciation has, conversely, also been limited in certain instances. So, when an individual is a member of a certain group, distinctions are subject to a stricter justification test, namely the requirement

[51] *Stummer v Austria* App no 37452/02, Judgment (GC) of 7 July 2011, Reports 2011, para 87; Aalt Willem Heringa and Fried van Hoof, 'Prohibition of Discrimination (Article 14)' in Pieter van Dijk, Fried van Hoof, Arjen van Rijn and Leo Zwaak (eds), *Theory and Practice of the European Convention on Human Rights*, 4th edn (Intersentia, 2006) 1027–51, 1034–35, citing the judgment of the Court in *Koua Poirrez v France* App no 40892/98, Judgment of 30 September 2003, Reports 2003-X, para 46, and 1043.

[52] Moeckli Daniel, 'Equality and Non-Discrimination' in Daniel Moeckli, Sangeeta Shah and Sandesh Sivakumaran (eds), *International Human Rights Law*, 2nd edn (OUP, 2014) 157–73, 165–66. On direct discrimination, see *Marckx v Belgium* App no 6833/74, Judgment of 13 June 1979, Series A31, paras 38–43. On indirect discrimination, see *D.H. and Others* (n 41), paras 183 and 184; *Di Trizio v Switzerland* App no 7186/09, Judgment of 2 February 2016, paras 80–90.

[53] *Di Trizio* (n 52), paras 91–102. For more, see Moeckli (n 52), 167–69.

[54] Heringa and van Hoof (n 51), 1034–35, citing *Koua Poirrez* (n 51), paras 46 and 1043.

[55] Heringa and van Hoof (n 51), 1044.

[56] *Sheffield and Horsham v United Kingdom* App nos 22985/93 and 23390/94, Judgment (GC) of 30 July 1998, Reports 1998-V, paras 60–61, 76–77. In all, see Heringa and van Hoof (n 51), 1044.

[57] *Stummer* (n 51), para 89.

of 'very weighty reasons'.[58] A distinction has even been found to be a priori unjustifiable when it is based on race and, in the past, on religion.[59] The 'very weighty reasons' test is applied, inter alia, to distinctions on the basis of sexual orientation and gender,[60] nationality,[61] birth in or out of wedlock,[62] and ethnicity.[63]

In addition, and to tie the above into the subject of the present volume, the weighty or serious reasons test has been implemented in the context of cases concerning groups that the Court has labelled as vulnerable. The state only has a limited margin of appreciation regarding alleged discrimination against members of such groups.[64] The Court has justified this by referring to the social exclusion that results from lasting historical prejudice, which may entail legislative stereotyping and thereby preclude an individualised evaluation of a person's capacities and needs.[65]

The relevant case law identifies a number of groups that are vulnerable on the basis of gender, sexual orientation, race or ethnicity, intellectual disability, or HIV/AIDS infection.[66] Though the determination of the groups that can be considered 'most vulnerable' in this context may not be complete, the case law on Article 14 clearly delineates the content of that concept, and its effect: the margin of appreciation afforded to the national authorities under Article 14 is limited if an individual belongs to a group that has historically suffered 'prejudice with lasting consequences' that led to its 'social exclusion'.[67]

While this jurisprudence, which has been discussed elsewhere and taken up by the Court in later judgments, concerns Article 14 ECHR, it provides some insight into how the Court came by the still-undefined concept of vulnerability under Article 3.[68] The relevance of non-discrimination rules for the present analysis lies not only in the fact that the humiliation that can constitute degrading treatment

[58] *Konstantin Markin v. Russia* App no 30078/06, Judgment (GC) of 22 March 2012, Reports 2012 (extracts), para 127. In all, see Heringa and van Hoof (n 51), 1046.

[59] Contrasting *Hoffmann v Austria* App no 12875/87, Judgment of 23 June 1993, Series A255-C, para 36) with *Eweida and Others v United Kingdom* App nos 48420/10 , Judgment of 15 January 2013, Reports 2013 (extracts)) shows that the Court has backed down from this position. On race, see *D.H. and Others* (n 41), para 196.

[60] *Konstantin Markin* (n 58) para 127; *X. and Others v Austria* App no 19010/07, Judgment (GC) of 19 February 2013, Reports 2013, para 99; and *Vallianatos and Others v Greece* App nos 29381/09 and 32684/09, Judgment (GC) of 7 November 2013, Reports 2013 (extracts), para 77.

[61] *Gaygusuz v. Austria* App no 17371/90, Judgment of 16 September 1996, Reports 1996-IV, para 42; *Koua Poirrez* (n 51), para 46; *Ponomaryovi v Bulgaria* App no 5335/05, Judgment of 21 June 2011, Reports 2011, para 52.

[62] *Mazurek v France* App no 34406/97, Judgment of 1 February 2000, Reports 2000-II, para 49; *Sahin v Germany* App no 30943/96, Judgment (GC) of 8 July 2003, Reports 2003-VIII, para 94.

[63] *Oršuš and Others v Croatia* App no 15766/03, Judgment (GC) of 16 March 2010, Reports 2010, para 149.

[64] *Alajos Kiss v Hungary* App no 38832/06, Judgment of 20 May 2010, para 42, with references.

[65] Ibid, para 42, with references.

[66] *Kiyutin v Russia* App no 2700/10, Judgment of 10 March 2011, Reports 2011, para 63, referring to *Alajos Kiss* (n 64), para 42.

[67] *Alajos Kiss* (n 64), para 42, with references.

[68] *I.B. v Greece* App no 552/10, Judgment of 3 October 2013, Reports 2013, para 79. For more, see Alexandra Timmer, 'A Quiet Revolution: Vulnerability in the European Court of Human Rights' in

may result from 'discrimination on various grounds, such as ethnic, national, or social origin, color, gender, religion, sexual orientation, disability, or age'.[69] The Court's non-discrimination case law is also relevant because it can be considered the origin, or at least part of the origin, of its understanding of vulnerability. The two continue to overlap in some regard, as well, for – as the remainder of this volume will show – a vulnerability-based approach to Article 3 can help to ensure substantive equality between applicants.

Martha Albertson Fineman and Anna Grear (eds), *Vulnerability: Reflections on a New Ethical Foundation for Law and Politics* (Ashgate, 2013) 147–70.

[69] Manfred Nowak, 'What Practices Constitute Torture?: US and UN Standards' (2006) 28(4) *Human Rights Quarterly* 809–41, 840.

7

Vulnerability Deciphered – Human Dignity, Substantive Equality and Judicial Empathy

Chapter Summary

The concept of vulnerability relates to a number of other core concepts of the Court's jurisprudence, especially the ideas of human dignity and of equality. The present chapter will take up these ideas and deepen the analysis of vulnerability in light of these underlying themes. It will also invoke interrelated concepts, such as a capabilities approach and the idea of judicial empathy. This discussion fits the Court's practical approach to vulnerability into the theoretical debates that underpin and surround it, and explores the significance of vulnerability in relation to and in light of these concepts. It is argued that vulnerability is inseparable from ideas of human dignity and substantive equality. It is, in fact, related to the very foundations of the ECHR, and can revitalise debates about the meaning of justice. This strengthens the idea of a responsive state that is evoked by a vulnerability approach.

Keywords: human dignity; substantive equality; social justice under the ECHR; judicial empathy; judicial emotion; foundations of human rights; capabilities approach.

I. On Human Dignity and Vulnerability

To determine whether a given treatment is compatible with Article 3 ECHR, the Court often uses compatibility with human dignity as a metric. In other words, both vulnerability and human dignity inform the Court's evaluation of ill-treatment cases. These two concepts also inform each other: the principles ensconced in human dignity – the intrinsic value of every individual human being and the importance of respect and support for the autonomy of the individual – are important for any cogent account of vulnerability.[1] However, while vulnerability

[1] Luís Roberto Barroso, 'Here, There, and Everywhere: Human Dignity in Contemporary Law and in the Transnational Discourse' (2012) 35(2) *Boston College International and Comparative Law Review* 331–93, 334.

is used by the Court to indirectly address the impact on human dignity generated by particular scenarios and traits, reference to human dignity directly entails a universalist approach.

The following will explore the meaning of human dignity, first in a general sense and then in the context of the Court's case law. It will contrast the idea of dignity as an objective and universal metric for ill-treatment with the special protection granted to vulnerable applicants by the Court.

A. Main Principles of Human Dignity

The concept of dignity is both a pervasive and an evasive one under international human rights law. It is not mentioned in the text of the ECHR, although Protocol No 13 to the Convention mentions 'the inherent dignity of all human beings' in its preamble.[2] The ICCPR, ICESCR and UDHR all contain numerous mentions of the concept,[3] and it also features in the American Convention on Human Rights[4] and the African Charter on Human and Peoples' Rights.[5]

The concept of human dignity did not end up in these instruments by accident. Instead, the concept has a long history as a hierarchical or official status akin to 'worthiness' and as a term for the worth accorded to humans by virtue of being human, beginning in Roman law.[6] A religious idea of dignity arose during the Middle Ages, when the idea of the 'inherent dignity of man' came to mean that humanity, having been created in God's image, was different from beast.[7] Pre-Enlightenment thinkers, including Pico della Mirandola, cemented the idea of dignity as a characteristic of all humanity and linked it with the possession of reason.[8] In the late 1700s, Immanuel Kant formulated his famed and secular idea of dignity when he argued that, given their human dignity, individuals should be treated as ends, and not as means to an end.[9] Dignity later became the rallying

[2] Protocol No 13 to the Convention for the Protection of Human Rights and Fundamental Freedoms concerning the abolition of the death penalty in all circumstances, adopted on 3 May 2002, CETS 187, in force since 1 July 2003, ratified by 44 Member States, preamble, first recital.

[3] Preamble and Art 10 of the ICCPR; preamble and Art 13 of the ICESCR; Arts 1, 22 and 23 UDHR.

[4] American Convention on Human Rights, adopted on 22 November 1969, entered into force on 18 July 1978, OAS Treaty Series No 36, 1144 UNTS 123, 25 States parties, Arts 5, 6, 11.

[5] Organization of African Unity, African Charter on Human and Peoples' Rights, 27 June 1981, entered into force on 21 October 1986, CAB/LEG/67/3 rev 5 (1982) 21(1) *International Legal Materials* 58–68, 53 states parties, Art 5.

[6] Christopher McCrudden, 'Human Dignity and Judicial Interpretation of Human Rights' (2008) 19(4) *European Journal of International Law* 655–724, 656–57, with further references.

[7] Ibid, 658.

[8] Ibid, 659, citing Giovanni Pico della Mirandola, *On the Dignity of Man* (Charles Glenn Wallis, Paul JW Miller and Douglas Carmichael trs, Hackett Publishing Company, 1998), 5.

[9] Ibid, citing Immanuel Kant, *Metaphysics of Morals* (Mary J Gregor tr, CUP, 1996), section 38 of Part II. See also Roberto Adorno, 'Human Dignity and Human Rights as Common Grounds for Global Bioethics' (2009) 34(3) *Journal of Medicine and Philosophy* 223–40, 230–31.

cry for a variety of movements seeking social reform, for example in the fight for women's suffrage and for the abolition of slavery.[10]

The concept also has its critics. Arthur Schopenhauer, for example, argued that the idea of human dignity, 'once it was uttered by Kant, became the shibboleth of all perplexed and empty-headed moralists. For behind that imposing formula they concealed their lack, not to say, of a real ethical basis, but of any basis at all which was possessed of an intelligible meaning'.[11] Others have qualified the concept of dignity as a merely rhetorical one or as a placeholder for the rationale behind human rights.[12]

Despite criticism, references to the concept of human dignity continued to grow on the national and international plane. After the fall of the Third Reich, the concept of innate human dignity found entrance into many of the national constitutions of countries that are now Member States of the Council of Europe. In the international arena, two particular developments stimulated the inclusion of human dignity in a multitude of human rights instruments. First, the UN General Assembly's 1986 guidelines for new human rights instruments recommended that such instruments be 'of fundamental character and derive from the inherent dignity and worth of the human person'.[13] Since then, the major UN human rights instruments have referred to human dignity.[14] Secondly, the 1993 Vienna World Conference on Human Rights adopted dignity as its central organising principle.[15] The Vienna World Conference, which was discussed above in light of its emphasis on the protection of the vulnerable, recognised and affirmed that 'all human rights derive from the dignity and worth inherent in the human person'.[16]

Despite this plethora of references to the concept, the exact definition of human dignity remains elusive. Christopher McCrudden has interpreted this to mean that human dignity allowed the drafters of human rights instruments to proceed on the basis of their agreement that human rights norms are necessary despite their 'embarrassing' inability to agree on one theoretical foundation for human rights. As he puts it, '[dignity's] utility was to enable those participating in the debate to insert their own theory. Everyone could agree that human dignity was central, but not why or how'.[17] However, though it serves as a placeholder, he argues, dignity is not devoid of its own content: it 'carried an enormous amount of content, but different content for different people'.[18] McCrudden identifies three aspects of a

[10] McCrudden (n 6), 660–61, with further references.

[11] Arthur Schopenhauer, *The Basis of Morality* 2nd edn (Arthur Brodrick Bullock tr, Dover Publications, 2005), 51; McCrudden (n 6), 661.

[12] McCrudden (n 6), 675–77, 722.

[13] General Assembly Resolution A/RES/41/120 of 4 December 1986 on setting international standards in the field of human rights, Art 3 para 4 lit b; McCrudden (n 6), 669, with further references.

[14] Compare, for example, the preambles of the CRC (first and second recital) and the UNCAT (second recital).

[15] McCrudden (n 6), 670.

[16] World Conference on Human Rights, Vienna Declaration and Programme of Action of 25 June 1993, UN Doc A/CONF.157/23, 12 July 1993, preamble, second recital.

[17] McCrudden (n 6), 678.

[18] Ibid.

minimum core of dignity: (i) the intrinsic worth every human possesses in light of his or her humanity, (ii) the need for recognition and respect of this intrinsic worth by others and (iii) the idea of a limited state that exists for the sake of human individuals, and not vice versa.[19]

The placeholder aspect of human dignity denotes the vacuum left by the move away from religious or natural law considerations as the underpinning values of rights. Taken as an innate condition of the human that pre-exists authority, and thus in the sense of 'human dignity as empowerment', human dignity gives individuals the right to have rights and frees them to pursue the goals that they autonomously choose.[20] Human rights as understood today can thus be understood as entitlements that protect the underlying, fundamental value that is human dignity – as opposed to understanding the right to dignity as a human right.[21]

Even if not strictly understood as a right, the concept of human dignity guarantees an equal moral status to all members of the human race.[22] While human dignity, like humanity, cannot be lost – at least not by a living[23] human being – it is in itself a vulnerable ideal in that it can be subjected to harms.

B. Dignity and the ECtHR

Human dignity can be understood as a 'thick' or as a 'thin' concept. A thin understanding of dignity sees the concept as synonymous with a human rights catalogue, meaning that it does not assist in the interpretation of that catalogue, while a thick understanding of dignity gives the concept independent meaning and uses it as an interpretative tool for identifying the content of human rights.[24] In the context of the ECtHR, dignity has both 'thick' and 'thin' connotations. However, the ECtHR does not understand dignity as an independent, justiciable, and enforceable human right – at least not directly. Instead, human dignity has garnered a place in the Court's evolutive interpretive technique as a guiding principle underlying the Convention.

As indicated above, one notable effect of the concept, and one that is of particular relevance to the present analysis, is that it has helped the Court to clarify and expand the reach of Article 3 ECHR. This began in 1973, in the *East African Asians*

[19] Ibid, 679.

[20] Beyleveld Deryck and Brownsword Roger, *Human Dignity in Bioethics and Biolaw* (OUP, 2001), 1–28; Adorno (n 9), 232.

[21] Nikolaidis Charilaos, *The Right to Equality in European Human Rights Law: The Quest for Substance in the Jurisprudence of the European Courts* (Routledge, 2015), 12, with further references.

[22] Natasa Mavronicola, 'Torture and Othering', in Benjamin Goold and Liora Lazarus (eds), *Security and Human Rights*, 2nd edn (Hart, 2019), 42–43.

[23] The question of posthumous dignity is more challenging: in the Strasbourg case law, it 'enjoys only temporary protection' (*Jäggi v Switzerland* App no 58757/00, Judgment of 13 July 2006, Reports 2006-X, para 41).

[24] McCrudden (n 6), 680–81.

case, when the Commission adopted the applicants' definition of degrading treatment as that which lowers the sufferer in 'rank, position, reputation or character, whether in his own eyes or in the eyes of other people', albeit narrowing that definition to 'interferences with the dignity of man of a particularly serious nature' by introducing the threshold of severity.[25]

Four years later, in addressing the merits of the Article 3 complaint concerning corporal punishment in *Tyrer v United Kingdom*, the Court held that the applicant's punishment '– whereby he was treated as an object in the power of the authorities – constituted an assault on precisely *that which it is one of the main purposes of Article 3 … to protect, namely a person's dignity and physical integrity*'.[26] This equates dignity with psychological or mental integrity, and therefore frames it as an antonym of suffering and a complement of pain, which describes attacks on *physical* integrity.[27]

Since the late 1970s, the Court has occasionally seemed to conflate dignity and the scope of Article 3.[28] For example, regarding detainees, the Court has held that 'any recourse to physical force which has not been made strictly necessary by [their] own conduct diminishes human dignity and is *in principle* an infringement of the right set forth in Article 3'.[29] The meaning of dignity – and of the words 'in principle' here – became even clearer with the 2015 *Bouyid v Belgium* judgment.[30] There, the Court included a section on dignity – along with a section on the vulnerability of minors – in its comparative materials, and emphasised the strong ties between human dignity and the essence of the ECHR, as well as Article 3 and degrading treatment or punishment in particular.[31] The Court stated that ill-treatment reaching the threshold of severity for a violation of Article 3 need not necessarily involve 'actual bodily injury or intense physical or mental suffering'. Where these aspects are absent, but an individual is nonetheless treated in a humiliating or debasing manner showing 'a lack of respect for or diminishing his or her human dignity, or [that] arouses feelings of fear, anguish or inferiority capable of breaking an individual's moral and physical resistance', this can constitute degrading treatment, whereby humiliation in the victim's own eyes suffices.[32]

[25] *East African Asians (British Protected Persons) v United Kingdom* App nos 4403/70 …, Report (Commission) of 14 December 1973, para 189.

[26] *Tyrer v United Kingdom* App no 5856/72, Judgment of 25 April 1978, Series A26, para 33, emphasis added.

[27] Bryan S Turner, *Vulnerability and Human Rights* (Pennsylvania State University Press, 2006), 27 and 35.

[28] *Kudła v Poland* App no 30210/96, Judgment (GC) of 26 October 2000, Reports 2000-XI, para 94; *Svinarenko and Slyadnev v Russia* App nos 32541/08 and 43441/08, Judgment (GC) of 17 July 2014, Reports 2014 (extracts), para 138.

[29] *Ribitsch v Austria* App no 18896/91, Judgment of 4 December 1995, Series A336, para 38, emphasis added.

[30] *Bouyid v Belgium* App no 23380/09, Judgment (GC) of 28 September 2015, Reports 2015; Natasa Mavronicola, 'Bouyid v Belgium: The "Minimum Level of Severity" and Human Dignity's Role in Article 3 ECHR' (2020) 1(1) *The European Convention on Human Rights Law Review* 105–24.

[31] Ibid, paras 45–47, 81, and 87–90.

[32] Ibid, para 87.

The words 'in principle', the Court held in *Bouyid*, need not indicate that some interferences with dignity fall below Article 3's threshold of severity. In other words: '[a]ny interference with human dignity strikes at the very essence of the Convention', meaning that '*any* conduct by law-enforcement officers *vis-à-vis* an individual which diminishes human dignity constitutes a violation of Article 3 of the Convention. That applies in particular to their use of physical force against an individual where it is not made strictly necessary by his conduct, *whatever the impact on the person in question*.'[33]

This controversial finding, which was strongly criticised in particular by three minority judges,[34] equates protection of human dignity and the scope of Article 3. This, as the minority judges point out, represents a change in the Court's case law. In *Ireland v United Kingdom*, the Court accepted that there could be 'violence which is to be condemned both on moral grounds … but which does not fall within Article 3'.[35] The Court's finding in *Bouyid* accordingly shows an evolution in the Court's understanding of the relationship between dignity and Article 3.

The *Bouyid* judgment, although using dignity in a novel way, was not entirely unprecedented. In *Svinarenko and Slyadnev v Russia*, for example, the Court had previously recognised objective incompatibility with human dignity as a violation of Article 3. There, the Court held that 'the very essence of the Convention is respect for human dignity'.[36] It had regard to the 'objectively degrading nature' of holding the applicants in metal cages during trial, 'which is incompatible with the standards of civilized behaviour that are the hallmark of a democratic society – an affront to human dignity in breach of Article 3'.[37]

In short, it emerges from cases like *Bouyid* and *Svinarenko and Slyadnev* that Article 3 is violated whenever judges consider that a given treatment disrespects the innate dignity of an applicant as a human being endowed with intrinsic value. The account of *Bouyid* – and of dignity in the Article 3 case law more widely – offered by Natasa Mavronicola is a rather convincing one in this context. She argues that the harm addressed by the Court in *Bouyid* is the harm of being treated like an object: the provision, she argues, 'is not there purely to protect human beings from suffering certain forms of harm – rather, it proscribes certain forms of absolute wrongs, including but not isolated to wrongs which result in significant human suffering and other forms of harm'.[38]

At the same time, concerns remain. First, there is the idea that, like suffering, wrongs may be to some degree subjective, context-dependent or socially constructed. Then, too, there is the argument that – if dignity is the foundation of

[33] Ibid, para 101, emphases added.

[34] Ibid, Joint Partly Dissenting Opinion of Judges de Gaetano, Lemmens and Mahoney.

[35] Ibid, para 5, citing *Ireland v United Kingdom* App no 5310/71, Judgment of 18 January 1978, Series A, No 25, para 167.

[36] *Svinarenko and Slyadnev* (n 28), para 138, emphasis added.

[37] Ibid.

[38] Natasa Mavronicola (n 30).

all human rights[39] – an Article 3 that protects against all violations of dignity would leave little or no room for the application of other ECHR rights and turn Article 3 into a catch-all. This would undermine the article's ability to adequately capture and sanction the very worst abuses, or in fact any abuses at all. Dignity-related harms, for example the use of racial slurs, would then either fall under Article 3, thereby extending the provision's scope, or would not fall under the provision, thereby implying that they are compatible with human dignity and therefore legitimising them. In other words, Article 3 is likely not a panacea for all dignity-related harms, and references to dignity as an explanation for finding violations of Article 3 without further discussion of the nature of state and especially police power may be problematic in the long run.

A further and related matter of concern is the unspecified content of dignity. In this regard, Christopher McCrudden's understanding of human dignity as a placeholder carries some truth. Dignity serves as a rallying cry for rights protection, but it is also very evident from the Court's judgments – *Bouyid* in particular[40] – that it is not willing to clarify the content of that concept. This may be due to a lack of agreement within the Court, or to the leeway that vagueness leaves the Court for future decisions. In *Bouyid*, this vagueness – together with the Court's emphasis of the fact that the ill-treatment in question was administered to what it considers to be a particularly significant body part, namely the applicants' faces[41] – may also be strategic, to limit future reliance on the judgment. Whatever the reasons for this lack of explanation, the definition of dignity is thus left to the intuition of the user.[42]

However elusive the concept of dignity may be, an additional element of the relevant case law requires discussion. This is the fact that, in both *Svinarenko and Slyadnev* and *Bouyid*, the applicants were particularly dependent on and exposed to the state. In this context, dignity allows the Court to find a violation of Article 3 where it considers that the state has not met baseline standards for the treatment that all human beings deserve. This relates to Natasa Mavronicola's concept of 'absolute wrongs'.[43] From this perspective, dignity reasoning allows the Court to give a straightforward negative answer to questions such as whether it is permissible for police officers to hurt detainees[44] or whether persons on trial for criminal charges may be humiliated in court.[45] These findings should not be taken as an indication

[39] *Svinarenko and Slyadnev* (n 28), para 118; *Pretty v United Kingdom* App no 2346/02, Judgment of 29 April 2002, ECHR 2002-III, para 65; Jean-Paul Costa, 'Human Dignity in the Jurisprudence of the European Court of Human Rights', in Christopher McCrudden, *Understanding Human Dignity* (OUP, 2013), 393–402, 402.

[40] Ibid, Joint Partly Dissenting Opinion of Judges de Gaetano, Lemmens and Mahoney, para 4.

[41] Ibid, para 104.

[42] Schachter Oscar, 'Human Dignity as a Normative Concept' (1983) 77(4) *The American Journal of International Law* 848–54, 849.

[43] Mavronicola (n 38); Mavronicola Natasa, *Torture, Inhumanity and Degradation under Article 3 of the ECHR: Absolute Rights and Absolute Wrongs* (Hart, 2021).

[44] *Bouyid* (n 30), paras 3, 10–11, 15.

[45] *Svinarenko and Slyadnev* (n 28), paras 48–49.

that just any modicum of humiliation or distress will violate Article 3: these cases concerned dependence and state control. In other words, there is – or at least, if these findings are to be reconciled with the preservation of an enforceable Article 3, there should be – an implicit connection to vulnerability reasoning here.

In this regard, vulnerability addresses those cases in which a unitary standard of treatment that is acceptable for human beings in an objective but abstract sense fails to adequately capture particular situations. The Court has addressed dignity reasoning as 'objective', which seems to imply that vulnerability reasoning, as its complement, is subjective. In any event, the two concepts are inextricably linked: vulnerability means ensuring equal protection of dignity, and there can be no respect for dignity without an understanding of human beings' vulnerability to dignity-related harms. The following section will delve into this to examine whether there is truly a division between objective and subjective tests for ill-treatment and, if this is the case, whether this is a workable approach.

C. The Objectivity of Assessing Ill-treatment

The human dignity standard under Article 3 allows the Court to evaluate a given form of treatment and determine whether it can be reconciled with the intrinsic worth of individuals as humans. This is independent of whether the particular individual concerned actually perceived a treatment as degrading or humiliating. In other words, it is not permissible under the ECHR for any criminal defendant to be caged in the courtroom, no matter if they are hardened criminals or they do not mind the cage, because such treatment is objectively incompatible with the standards of a civilised democratic society.[46] This is, in other words, an objectively verifiable wrong. In this sense, human dignity recognises the shared humanity that is also part of Martha Albertson Fineman's approach to universal human vulnerability.

Compared to this objectively verifiable and universal standard, the vulnerability reasoning used by the Court has the opposite effect. Instead of allowing the Court to find that a given treatment is objectively impermissible, vulnerability lets the Court take the experience of particular applicants and their conditions of life, specific traits, experience of fear or subjugation, marginalisation and dependency into consideration. Consequently, an adult's experience of a given treatment – for example, immigration detention – may not constitute a violation of Article 3, whereas a young child's experience of the same treatment may violate that provision.[47] This relates to the relativity of Article 3's threshold of severity and its dependence on all the circumstances of the case.[48]

[46] Ibid, para 138.

[47] *Mubilanzila Mayeka and Kaniki Mitunga v Belgium* App no 13178/03, Judgment of 12 October 2006, Reports 2006-XI, esp paras 55 and 58.

[48] *Ireland* (n 35), para 162.

Given that the human dignity approach is considered an objective one by the Court, vulnerability considerations could be considered to be a pendant to this, and a more subjective test. In this regard, an analogy to former ECtHR judge Françoise Tulkens's statement that '[e]quality and non-discrimination are subjective rights which must remain under the control of those who are entitled to benefit from them' is possible.[49] This recognises the importance of taking the views and experiences of the marginalised and discriminated into account. However, the process of establishing a human rights violation, particularly one as grave as a violation of Article 3 ECHR, should be described as subjective only with caution. Such language may imply that the violation in question is not particularly grave or somehow justifiable or relative.

Dignity and vulnerability-based approaches can certainly be used in a complementary manner, as the Court's combination of the two concepts in past cases has shown.[50] *Bouyid* was a prime example of this. However, in that judgment, separate paragraphs concerning each of these concepts led to a somewhat disjointed result.[51] It may ultimately not be clear from the text of a judgment whether human dignity considerations, vulnerability, both, or other factors led to the finding of a violation of Article 3. This ambiguity may do more harm than good, with the Court appearing to throw a wide array of possible arguments into a judgment in order to reach the desired result. This 'everything but the kitchen sink' style of argumentation may result from a lack of agreement among judges, the struggle to unite various strains of case law, or a push by a particular judge to have a pet issue incorporated into a judgment. The unfortunate result is that it is not possible for the reader – and thus the scholar, the national judge, the domestic authorities executing the judgment, or the potential applicant – to know which particular arguments led to the final outcome in a case.

In order to harmonise these approaches in theory and, subsequently, in practice, it can be contended that vulnerability reasoning explores certain structural causes of dignity harms. If human dignity is a universal claim to respect for 'the intrinsic importance of human life', meaning that 'people never be treated in a way that denies the distinct importance of their own lives',[52] then it serves to distinguish the human from the non-human. That which is identified as human is consequently seen as deserving of protection. At the same time, there is not only one way of being human and thus no standard-issue archetype of human possessed of dignity.

[49] *Leyla Şahin v Turkey* App no 44774/98, Judgment (GC) of 10 November 2005, Reports 2005-XI, Dissenting Opinion of Judge Tulkens, para 12.

[50] *Bouyid* (n 30), esp paras 45–47, 52–53, 83, 87–90, 100–03, 107, 109–11, where both human dignity and vulnerability reasoning entered into play.

[51] Ibid, contrasting paras 45–47 and 52–53; see also paras 81–113, where the relation of the two concepts goes unexplained as they never appear in the same paragraph.

[52] Ronald M Dworkin, *Life's Dominion: An Argument About Abortion, Euthanasia and Individual Freedom* (Random House, 1994), 236; Adorno (n 9), 231.

Vulnerability, taken in this context, can refine the understanding of any one human's dignity by taking other identity-relevant traits into account, such as age, gender, race, belief, ethnic background, sexual orientation, gender expression, experiences of victimisation and dependency, and so forth. This would respond to the fact that, while humanness creates a blanket dignity-based entitlement to rights protection, not all human individuals experience humanness in the same way; vulnerability therefore creates specific entitlements linked to specific variations on humanness. In other words, those who experience dependency or a particular risk of or exposure to ill-treatment require special protection so that their human dignity is protected to the same extent as that of other individuals who do not experience this type of vulnerability to the same extent. This can be rationalised via the equality component of human dignity: every human is, by nature of being human, endowed with an equal right to respect for human dignity, but not every human individual can live out that dignity in the same ways. Ensuring equal, practical and effective respect for dignity means counteracting, to the extent that this is possible, the structural limitations caused by the traits or situations that cause vulnerability.

This informs how the description of vulnerability as a 'subjective' standard must be understood. Vulnerability should not – and, for practical reasons, cannot – mean that Article 3 is violated whenever a person risks any morally impermissible treatment or feels humiliated. This should also not mean that any violation of Article 3 can ever be considered trivial or justifiable.

Focusing on vulnerability as a manner of tailoring the threshold of severity without thereby abolishing or necessarily lowering it may help to assuage concerns about a subjective Article 3. The threshold of severity's responsiveness to concrete situations is only logical if we consider the diversity that exists among the people protected by Article 3: for example, children need particular care, discriminated minorities face difficulties in accessing remedies, and people who are dependent on others for their wellbeing need certain safeguards to prevent abuse. When the Court finds a violation of Article 3 in one of these contexts, it thereby finds that special attention and care are required in order to ensure equal protection.

In the context of the Convention in general, Alexandra Timmer has argued that '[b]y underpinning dignity with vulnerability considerations, the Court creates a holistic picture of the sufferings of the applicant: a picture that includes contextual factors such as embodiment, location, mental state and material realities.'[53] Certainly, the Court uses vulnerability to understand the mental and material realities of certain applicants. However, the Court's approach to vulnerability, at least in the Article 3 context, is much too selective to be seen as addressing all of the diverse realities of human embodiment and experience.

[53] Alexandra Timmer, 'A Quiet Revolution: Vulnerability in the European Court of Human Rights' in Martha Albertson Fineman and Anna Grear (eds), *Vulnerability: Reflections on a New Ethical Foundation for Law and Politics* (Ashgate, 2013) 147–70, 166.

D. Formulating an Account of Vulnerability and Dignity

Vulnerability can be seen as both a complement and an antonym to human dignity. In the latter sense, and to paraphrase Hannah Arendt, it can be understood as a manner of describing those who are deprived of human dignity: still technically human, but stripped of all of the associated qualities and protections, they are vulnerable to horrific treatment.[54]

Vulnerability here addresses constellations in which individuals are othered because they are perceived to differ from the majority in some way, and therefore lose – in the eyes of that majority – their human dignity and the protections associated with it.[55] Recognition of universal human dignity serves to prevent such othering and dehumanisation, and thus ensures a sort of formal baseline equality among all humans. However, as the below will argue, the reach of this type of equality is limited, and it fails to address systemic disadvantages that compromise the freedom, agency, and integrity that human dignity arguably entails.

Given the existence of a universal guarantee of human dignity in the ECHR system, there is limited value to understanding vulnerability as the absence of dignity as per the Arendtian understanding. Here, the concept does something different: it fine-tunes protections based on human dignity by facilitating special consideration that compensates for particular disadvantages. So, while respect for human dignity protects 'the right to have rights', respect for human vulnerability in some sense protects the right to effectively enjoy rights in practice. Understood in this way, vulnerability can be used to identify elements of individuals' identities and situations that entitle them to special protection so as to ensure substantive equality and preserve their human dignity. In this regard, and despite the Court's tendency to consider them separately,[56] vulnerability and dignity are inextricably linked.

The above has mapped the response that dignity and vulnerability evoke before the Court, which uses vulnerability as a tool allowing it to identify specific instances where the equal application of general rules may result in an unfair or unrealistic result for particular individuals. However, the 'subjective' standard incarnated by the vulnerability heuristic need not mean that the Court's judges are partial or biased when deciding cases. The subjectivity described here does not mean that their decisions are subject to their own personal tastes and whims, but describes the attention paid to the particular situation and characteristics of a given applicant. Perhaps a better way to express this would be to leave the language of objectivity and subjectivity aside entirely, and to consider the human dignity standard an abstract test and the vulnerability heuristic a more concrete one.

[54] Hannah Arendt, *The Origins of Totalitarianism*, 2nd edn (Harvest/Harcourt, 1973), 297. See also Jeffrey C Isaac, 'A New Guarantee on Earth: Hannah Arendt on Human Dignity and the Politics of Human Rights' (1996) 90(1) *The American Political Science Review* 61–73, 64.

[55] Mavronicola (n 22), for example at 34.

[56] See the approach taken in *Bouyid* (n 30), comparing paras 87–90, 100–03 and 111 (concerning dignity) with paras 83, 107, 109–10 (concerning vulnerability).

II. On Vulnerability, Justice and Equality

Vulnerability reasoning has been lauded as a mechanism for advancing equality under the ECHR.[57] This appears self-evident when the concept is applied under Article 14 ECHR, which guarantees freedom from discrimination on the basis of a list of proscribed grounds.[58] Under Article 3 ECHR, it is perhaps less directly evident how the concept of vulnerability can contribute to equality. However, and as indicated in the previous section, there is in fact a strong connection here.

The universality of human dignity – the idea that we all equally crave and deserve societal recognition of our intrinsic worth as individuals – provides a strong basis for fighting inequality, and a foundation for formal equality.[59] In addition, it is argued below that the Court's vulnerability reasoning may promote a certain vision of justice. This, in turn, may help to trouble or disturb the idea of the independent liberal legal subject.

A. The Demands of Equality

i. Theoretical Beginnings of Equality Theory

Equality and inequality are complex concepts, and are best understood as a system of principles that, together, provide a theory of social justice.[60] For millennia, beginning with the Aristotelian conception of equality, these concepts have been seen as interrelated. In simple terms, Aristotelian equality means treating like cases alike and unlike cases not alike; where these principles are respected, the outcome will be perceived as just.[61] In other words, unjustified unequal treatment is incompatible with justice.

From this starting point, with its formal take on equality, understandings of equality and its counterpart, non-discrimination,[62] have evolved over time. Thus, while the equality theories of antiquity did not take issue with societies which distributed wealth, freedoms, rights, and power heterogeneously among their members – understanding this disparity as the just deserts of the inferior – the

[57] Lourdes Peroni and Alexandra Timmer, 'Vulnerable Groups: The Promise of an Emerging Concept in European Human Rights Convention Law' (2013) 11(4) *International Journal of Constitutional Law* 1056–85, esp 1074–76, 1079–80; Samantha Besson, 'La vulnerabilité et la structure des droits de l'homme: L'exemple de la jurisprudence de la Cour européenne des droits de l'homme', in Laurence Burgorgue-Larsen (ed), *La vulnérabilité saisie par les juges en Europe* (Editions Pedone, 2014), 63.

[58] Peroni and Timmer (n 57), 1080–82.

[59] Nikolaidis (n 21), 12–13.

[60] Stefan Gosepath, 'Equality' in Edward N Zalta (ed), *The Stanford Encyclopedia of Philosophy* (Stanford University, 2011).

[61] Aristotle, *Aristotle's Nicomachean Ethics* (Robert C Bartlett and Susan D Collins trs, University of Chicago Press, 2012), Book V.3.

[62] Oddný Mjöll Arnardóttir, *Equality and Non-Discrimination Under the European Convention on Human Rights* (Martinus Nijhoff, 2003), 6–9.

modern idea of universal human dignity created a minimum standard of treatment that is deserved equally by all humans.[63] Consequently, equality today means that individuals are entitled to be treated equivalently with regard to certain conditions of life, even if they are not identical, because, despite their differences, all humans are alike in certain fundamental respects.[64] In other words, because we all crave societal recognition of our intrinsic worth (and thus, of our human dignity), we must all be entitled to the same respect.[65]

ii. Substantive Equality, Binaries and the Liberal Legal Subject

Moving away from the Aristotelian understanding of formal equality, it has today been widely recognised that a formal take on equality alone does not suffice to guarantee justice. Diversity between individuals, the difficulty of ensuring comparability, and the need to address structural disadvantage mean that a formal take on equality must be supplemented by a substantive one to even come close to providing equality.[66] Or, in the sense of Ronald Dworkin's theory, all individuals deserve to be treated with equal concern and respect.[67] Put differently, although absolute equality may not be practicable, the idea of justice-as-fairness-as-impartiality requires that individuals are not treated differently on the basis of their immutable personal traits or elementary choices in life.[68]

A guarantee of substantive equality may require action in order to compensate the disadvantaged for the impacts of unfavourable societal dynamics.[69] Substantive equality can mean a reaction to context in order to engage with asymmetrical power structures.[70] Beyond the lowest common denominator of equality – the principle of granting equal treatment in equal situations – it is thus necessary to ensure equality in substance in order to address 'the most invidious form of inequality; the one that results from social norms and attitudes'.[71] In this regard, equality is inextricable from ideas of human dignity and autonomy, and represents an end in itself.[72]

To Catharine MacKinnon, Aristotelian equality is really 'no equality rule at all', given the abstractions it entails in practice.[73] She has made an eloquent plea for

[63] Gosepath (n 60), 2.3. On the development of the concept of human dignity, see in this chapter.
[64] Nagel Thomas, *Equality and Partiality* (OUP, 1995), *passim*, and esp at 64–65 and 105.
[65] Nikolaidis (n 21), 10–12.
[66] Arnardóttir (n 62), 23.
[67] Ronald M Dworkin, *Taking Rights Seriously* (Harvard University Press, 1978), xii, 227, 229, 355–56, 370; Gosepath (n 60), 2.3.
[68] Nikolaidis (n 21), 2–3, 9, 11.
[69] Ibid, 15.
[70] Arnardóttir (n 62), 23.
[71] Nikolaidis (n 21), 3.
[72] Ibid, 4–5, 13.
[73] Catharine A MacKinnon, 'Substantive Equality: A Perspective' (2011) 96 *Minnesota Law Review* 1–27, 2–3, 5.

substantive equality regarding gender discrimination, arguing for recognition of the 'realities' that impede certain people from being full and equal citizens.[74] In doing so, she has railed against conventional approaches to gender equality on the premise that 'because sex is conceived as a difference, and equality is understood as based on sameness in the Aristotelian approach of "likes alike, unlikes unalike", the worse the inequality gets, the more disparate its social reality becomes, the less this legal approach can do about it'.[75] Substantive equality's core insight, she argues, is that inequality entails a social relationship that orders groups or categories by rank, including 'better and worse, clean and dirty, served and serving, appropriately rich and appropriately poor, superior and inferior, dominant and subordinate, justly forceful and rightly violated or victimized'.[76] However, justifying inequality by means of these binaries is an error, because no social group is more valuable than another.[77]

MacKinnon's arguments concern the binary approach to gender, where the male side of the binary entails advantages. A critique of maleness and femaleness as monolithic, disparate categories that inherently justify the exclusion of women from full legal subjectivity is represented in the writings of other feminist scholars, as well. For example, Simone de Beauvoir's *The Second Sex* argues that women are othered because they are objectified and attributed an otherness that legitimates their oppression.[78] A related but opposite concept is Luce Irigaray's idea of 'saming', which 'denies the objectified other the right to her difference', ie the right to be recognised as an equal despite failing to fit a predominant and oppressive archetype.[79]

In short, these feminist accounts recognise the need to re-evaluate the exclusions of the liberal legal subject and its binary categorisations. This is, in other words, a claim for substantive equality. By contrast, formal equality requires a comparison, and when that comparator is an exclusionary one – for example, as it often is, the liberal legal subject, which represents an abstracted, decontextualised, and disembodied 'everyman' who is considered rational over all else[80] – then it follows that many concrete and contextualised human individuals are conceived as 'other' or as deviant or, thus, as 'unlikes'.[81]

Of course, however, the male-female binary is not the only dichotomy that needs to be challenged in this context. A wide variety of traits are ordered into

[74] Ibid, 22.
[75] Ibid, 6.
[76] Ibid, 11–12.
[77] Ibid, 12.
[78] Simone De Beauvoir, *The Second Sex* (Constance Borde and Sheila Malovany-Chevallier trs, Random House, 2011) as explored in Naomi Schor, *Bad Objects: Essays Popular and Unpopular* (Duke University Press, 1995), 51.
[79] Schor (n 78), 51, referring to Luce Irigaray, *Speculum of the Other Woman* (Gillian C Gill tr, Cornell University Press, 1985), 118–20.
[80] Anna Grear, *Redirecting Human Rights: Facing the Challenge of Corporate Legal Humanity* (Palgrave Macmillan, 2010), 43–44.
[81] Sandra Fredman, *Discrimination Law*, 2nd edn (OUP, 2011), 3.

an oversimplified binary model, including traits that cause discrimination – for example, the distinction between whiteness and non-whiteness, autonomy and dependency, ability and disability, straightness and queerness, and cisgender and transgender individuals.

Beyond the idea of an in-group and an out-group, the idea of binaries made up of two monolithic categories underlies the structure of (neo-)liberalism: the binary distinctions between public and private and between reason and emotion are emblematic of the liberal order that shapes capitalistic, patriarchal and hierarchical modern Western European societies.[82] While none of these binaries reflect the complex, interconnected, and diverse nature of human life and experience, they have become more set with the passage of time, and as a result they structure our perception of reality even if they do not reflect that reality.[83] Often these binaries are interlinked, with the suggestion being that the female, emotional, physical, and private sides are connected, as are the male, rational, mental, and public ones. As these groupings suggest, such dichotomies entail an attribution of value and can entail exclusions from full subjectivity.[84]

The fact that women were once considered unfit for political life because of the nature of their female brains and because of their emotionality helps to understand the nature and harmful effect of these binaries.[85] Such expectations may, to a certain extent, be self-perpetuating, by preventing women from accessing education, through the workings of confirmation bias, and by bringing out negatively valued traits in the face of disrespect, but – needless to say – they are by no means grounded in reality. Nevertheless, given the binary understanding of gender, it was long accepted that women were so different from men that they existed outside of the idealised legal subject.

Substantive equality, in this context, means ensuring equal subjectivity and thus the equality of opportunities to live a life of agency and dignity. This does not mean extending the fiction of the liberal legal subject, but doing away with it entirely. Taken against this background, it is possible to identify four separate claims of substantive equality. These are the claim to *recognition* of equal universal human dignity, the claim to *redistribution* in order to remedy social disadvantages,

[82] Roberta G Sands and Kathleen Nuccio, 'Postmodern Feminist Theory and Social Work' (1992) 37(6) *Social Work* 489–94; Andrew Edgar and Peter Sedgwick, *Cultural Theory: The Key Concepts*, 2nd edn (Routledge, 2008), 27–28.

[83] Edgar and Sedgwick (n 82), 27–28.

[84] Martha Albertson Fineman, 'Beyond Identities: The Limits of an Anti-Discrimination Approach to Equality' (2012) 92 *Boston University Law Review* 1713–70, 1751; Catriona Mackenzie, Wendy Rogers and Susan Dodds, 'Introduction: What is Vulnerability and Why Does It Matter for Moral Theory?' in Catriona Mackenzie, Wendy Rogers and Susan Dodds (eds), *Vulnerability: New Essays in Ethics and Feminist Philosophy* (OUP, 2014) 1–29, 5–6.

[85] Compare, on this, Georg Wilhelm Friedrich Hegel, *Elements of the Philosophy of Right* (Allen W. Wood ed, HB Nisbet trs, CUP, 1991), 207, para 166, who wrote that '[w]omen may well be educated, but they are not made for the higher sciences, for philosophy and certain artistic productions which require a universal element … When women are in charge of government, the state is in danger, for their actions are based not on the demands of universality but on contingent inclination and opinion.'

the claim to *participation* in political decision-making, and the claim to *transformation* into a society that is accepting and accommodating of diversity.[86] A vulnerability approach can facilitate all four of these claims.

iii. Advancing Equality through Vulnerability Reasoning

In her work on vulnerability, Martha Albertson Fineman has argued that pure sameness of treatment does not suffice to address 'persistent forms of subordination and domination'.[87] Writing from the United States context, Fineman accordingly finds it 'perplexing' when a non-discrimination rule 'ignores existing inequalities of circumstances and presumes an equivalence of position and possibilities'.[88] Fineman's work calls for an enrichment of this understanding of equality by departing from the liberal legal subject that underpins it. Like Luce Irigaray, who argues for the reversal of 'saming' by injecting the feminine into legal subjectivity,[89] Fineman thus argues for the injection of *vulnerability*. Because the liberal subject is decontextualised and disembodied, and therefore in some sense invulnerable, the vulnerable subject seems like a more realistic alternative.[90] By focusing on our shared vulnerable embodiment, we can transcend binary and exclusionary models of subjectivity that generate modern inequalities, and transcend the public-private divide and assumptions about the 'deservedness' of poorer treatment.[91]

To some extent, Fineman's arguments concern the libertarian tendencies present in United States politics. However, her approach to equality-through-vulnerability is salient beyond that context, including to address the binaries that plague liberalism, like the one that overly prizes autonomy and devalues dependency and care.[92] The most fundamental binary for present purposes is the one between vulnerability and invulnerability. Often, when reference is made to vulnerability in law and politics, it serves as a method for identifying victimhood and dependency. This implies that invulnerability is a separate condition, and placed at the more highly valued side of a binary.[93] In other words, this leaves the stigmatising idea of vulnerability-as-other intact. However, if vulnerability is understood not as a form of deviance but as a trait inherent to human embodiment and thus to human life, it can serve

[86] Carolina Yoko Furusho, 'Uncovering the Human Rights of the Vulnerable Subject and Correlated State Duties under Liberalism' (2016) 5(1) *UCL Journal of Law and Jurisprudence* 175–205, 183.

[87] Martha Albertson Fineman, 'The Vulnerable Subject: Anchoring Equality in the Human Condition' (2008) 20(1) *Yale Journal of Law and Feminism* 1–23, 3.

[88] Martha Albertson Fineman, 'The Vulnerable Subject and the Responsive State' (2010) 60(2) *Emory Law Journal*, 251.

[89] Irigaray (n 79), beginning at 13.

[90] Fineman (n 87), 2, 10–12; Wilcox Lauren B., *Bodies of Violence: Theorizing Embodied Subjects in International Relations* (OUP, 2015), 32; Grear (n 80), 97; Furusho (n 86), 178–80. See also Dianne Otto, 'Lost in Translation: Re-Scripting the Sexed Subjects of International Human Rights Law' in Anne Orford (ed), *International Law and Its Others* (CUP 2006) 318–56, esp 331, 341, 347–48.

[91] MacKinnon (n 73), 11–12; see also Fineman (n 88), 251.

[92] Fineman (n 87), 17.

[93] Furusho (n 86), 184–85.

as a lens through which these binaries and resulting stigmas can be examined and inequality addressed. This allows for a re-examination of the demands of equality – as well as autonomy, dignity, and the foundation of human rights in general – in order to counteract the ossified binaries that affect their application.[94]

Recognising our universal vulnerability does not in itself represent a substantive approach to equality, however. It does not account for the fact that some lives are more precarious than others. While we are all equally vulnerable, in short, we are all also differently vulnerable, and the diversity of human experiences necessarily means that the specific forms, sources and expressions of vulnerability faced by each human individual vary. Vulnerability, if taken as a heuristic device serving the purpose of identifying inequalities, is a tool for context-sensitivity and for responding to the various manifestations of disadvantage.[95] It is, in other words, a way to consider the specific exclusions generated by the various axes of a person's identity in order to fully address systems of oppression.

To ensure substantive equality, attention to the vulnerable subject must have regard for the specific issues generated where various sources of disadvantage intersect. Intersectionality is a concept coined by critical race scholar Kimberlé Crenshaw, and it means that the experiences of those who are situated at the juncture of two or more grounds for marginalisation or discrimination are different from those of people who fall under one of these traits.[96] Crenshaw's intersectionality concept requires the user to 'look beneath the surface and beyond the prevailing norm paradigm that leaves various synergetic vulnerabilities unnoticed in the margins'.[97] Only by taking all sources of privilege and disadvantage into account, including intersectional ones, can the demands of substantive equality be met.

While social justice theories have moral and philosophical appeal, they are also informative for human rights purposes because they relate not just to the foundational principle of equality, but also to human dignity, to the equality of all before the law and to the prohibition of arbitrariness.[98] But what, precisely, is the relevance of equality and social justice for understanding the Court's approach to vulnerability under Article 3 ECHR? This lies in the fact that vulnerability addresses an equality problem – a problem that states, if they are to display equal concern for all individuals in their territory, must address. While the Court's approach to Article 3 is to some extent already informed by equality considerations, vulnerability reasoning enhances this by incorporating regard for applicants' context,

[94] Ibid, 184, 186–87.

[95] Ibid, 185–86.

[96] Kimberlé Crenshaw, 'Mapping the Margins: Intersectionality, Identity Politics, and Violence Against Women of Color' (1991) 43(1241) *Stanford Law Review* 1241–99, *passim* and esp at 1244–45.

[97] Oddný Mjöll Arnardóttir, 'Multidimensional Equality from Within: Themes from the European Convention on Human Rights' in Dagmar Schiek and Victoria Chege (eds), *European Union Non-Discrimination Law: Comparative Perspectives on Multidimensional Equality Law* (Routledge-Cavendish, 2009) 53–71, 55.

[98] Nikolaidis (n 21), 14–15.

ie realities of dependence and disadvantage, and the power structures that reinforce these situations.[99]

By using Article 3 to address certain disadvantages facing applicants because of their vulnerability – such as a child's difficulty in being understood and believed when making allegations of rape, a disabled prisoner's problems in bringing timely submissions to Strasbourg, or the issues facing a Roma person when interacting with the police – the Court is building on this case law. Using vulnerability like this can open up the Court's reasoning to context-sensitivity, drawing on the lived disadvantages facing applicants. In this way, Article 3 develops the potential to acknowledge and deal with some of the inequalities that affect individual and group wellbeing by addressing certain of the factors that accentuate the precariousness of human existence.[100]

B. Imagining a Socially Just Polity

The preceding sections have referred to various social justice theories. In fact, vulnerability theory itself represents a theory of justice. But what, then, do these theories – or does justice – require? For present purposes, a particularly relevant concept is the idea of substantive equality as an equal ability to exercise certain fundamental human 'capabilities', which together allow the autonomous pursuit of a life in dignity. This capabilities approach, which builds upon ideas of what a just society should look like and has had a profound impact in the development context, has been the subject of extensive work by Amartya Sen in the field of economics and Martha C Nussbaum in the philosophical context.[101] The following prefaces an analysis of the capabilities theory and of the ways in which the Court's Article 3 jurisprudence could bring the Strasbourg case law closer to the relevant understandings of justice and equality.

i. A Primer on Social Justice Theories

Much has been written about what a just polity would look like. Ideas about equality, advantage, and distributive and social justice mark the work of some of modern legal philosophy's most eminent thinkers. Ideas of social justice build on the concept of equality, and can be understood as addressing 'issues of equity,

[99] Arnardóttir (n 97), 63.

[100] On poverty, precariousness and precarity, see Judith Butler, *Precarious Life: The Powers of Mourning and Violence* (Verso, 2004).

[101] Amartya Sen, *Inequality Reexamined* (OUP, 1992); Amartya Sen, *Development as Freedom* (OUP, 1999); Martha C Nussbaum, 'Capabilities as Fundamental Entitlements: Sen and Social Justice' (2003) 9(2–3) *Feminist Economics* 33–59; Martha C Nussbaum, *Creating Capabilities: The Human Development Approach* (Belknap Press, 2011); Rosalind Dixon and Martha C Nussbaum, 'Children's Rights and a Capabilities Approach: The Question of Special Priority' (2012) 97(3) *Cornell Law Review* 549–94.

power relations, and institutionalized oppression' and as seeking to 'establish a more equitable distribution of power and resources, so that all people can live with dignity, self-determination, and physical and psychological safety'.[102] This focuses on a number of specific goods or, more precisely, capabilities – such as the right to be free from prejudice and stereotyping and to have one's differences reasonably accommodated.[103] It also specifies a minimum of wellbeing as the just deserts of all human individuals. Ultimately, it aims to address the differences between individuals that affect their equal ability to pursue their conceptions of a good life and individual happiness.[104] This can include conceptions of socio-economic or distributive and global justice. In short, these approaches focus on holistically describing the injustice presented by inequality, and on ways of overcoming that injustice.

In order to understand some of the claims made by social justice theories today, it is helpful to take a look at the theory of justice posited by John Rawls. His work aims to identify the minimal structure of a morally just hypothetical society, and has been reimagined to fit a more nuanced equality argumentation by Martha Nussbaum.[105] Rawls theorised an alternative to utilitarianism that showed inequality and poverty to be irreconcilable with the greater good.[106] To hypothesise a just polity, Rawls tried to identify the rules that the future members of that polity would choose if they were unaware of their own societal position in that society. This aims to identify the societal structures that individuals would design from behind a 'veil of ignorance'.[107]

Social inequality can also be illustrated in an ultimately rather similar way through a thought experiment designed by Ronald Dworkin. Dworkin, who conceived of equality as equal welfare for all,[108] was committed to the idea that polities must have equal concern and respect for all of their members, famously arguing that '[e]qual concern is the sovereign virtue of political community'.[109] He postulated, via an anecdote about the survivors of a shipwreck who find themselves on a desert island, that if the stranded survivors divide up the island's resources among themselves, that division would not be equal if any of the survivors would have preferred another bundle of resources than the one they received.[110]

Although neither of these two experiments leads to a full-fledged theory of socio-economic and global justice, both Rawls's veil of ignorance and the

[102] Diane J Goodman, *Promoting Diversity and Social Justice: Educating People from Privileged Groups*, 2nd edn (Routledge, 2011), 4.
[103] Nikolaidis (n 21), 5, 10.
[104] Sen, *Inequality Reexamined* (n 101), 2–6 and throughout.
[105] Ibid.
[106] John Rawls, *A Theory of Justice*, revd edn (Belknap Press, 1999).
[107] Ibid, 53, 130–31.
[108] Ronald M Dworkin, *Sovereign Virtue: The Theory and Practice of Equality* (Harvard University Press, 2002).
[109] Ibid, 1.
[110] Ibid, 66–71.

Dworkinian desert island scenario represent starting points for identifying the injustice of inequality.[111] Rawls in particular does not exclude the existence of certain socio-economic inequalities, gives liberty priority,[112] and has received his fair share of criticism in this and other regards[113] What is relevant here is that Rawls's theory relates to egalitarian principles,[114] arguing that the measure of equality is an assessment of whether individuals can enjoy certain primary social goods – including basic freedom and property rights and a social basis of self-respect – which allow them to pursue their own ends.[115]

At the same time, Rawls allows variations between individuals – thus, diversity in the distribution of abilities and talents according to what he describes as the 'natural lottery' – to result in 'natural inequalities'.[116] Indeed, Rawls's theory was meant to focus on 'the relative position of individuals with standard needs and endowments'.[117] This excludes, for example, people living with a disability. Still, some scholars have argued in favour of Rawls's experiment because individuals in the original position would presumably address the inequalities arising from disability.[118] Others have questioned whether these inequalities can be considered 'natural', and have instead recast them as social constructs.[119]

The Rawlsian model is a product of its time in various ways.[120] At the same time, a modernised approach to Rawls's work can help to push back against some of the harms and deprivations that plague the current political era,[121] and his theory provides a jumping-off point for the capabilities theory set out below.

ii. Casting Vulnerability as a Matter of Justice

The Rawlsian exercise can be used to trigger a discussion about the requirements for ensuring justice in the face of vulnerability. Perhaps those behind the veil of ignorance would design a utopian polity in which variation in innate traits, health,

[111] Charles R Beitz, *Political Theory and International Relations*, revd edn (Princeton University Press, 1999), 126–76.

[112] Rawls (n 106), 53, 130–31.

[113] See, for example, Amartya Sen, 'Equality of What?' (Tanner Lecture on Human Values, Stanford University, 22 May 1979), http://tannerlectures.utah.edu/_documents/a-to-z/s/sen80.pdf, 201.

[114] John Rawls, *Justice as Fairness: A Restatement* (Erin Kelly ed, Belknap Press, 2001), 124, 129–30.

[115] Ibid, 58–61. See also Ingrid Robeyns and Harry Brighouse, 'Introduction: Social Primary Goods and Capabilities as Metrics of Justice' in Harry Brighouse and Ingrid Robeyns (eds), *Measuring Justice: Primary Goods and Capabilities* (CUP, 2010) 1–13, 1–2.

[116] Lorella Terzi, 'What Metric of Justice for Disabled People?: Capability and Disability' in Harry Brighouse and Ingrid Robeyns (eds), *Measuring Justice: Primary Goods and Capabilities* (CUP, 2010) 150–73, 153.

[117] Ibid, 153. See also Rawls (n 106), 64–65, 89.

[118] Thomas W Pogge, *Realizing Rawls* (Cornell University Press, 1989), 44–47.

[119] Kasper Lippert-Rasmussen, 'Are Some Inequalities More Unequal than Others? Nature, Nurture and Equality' (2004) 16(2) *Utilitas* 193–219.

[120] Katrina Forrester, *In the Shadow of Justice: Postwar Liberalism and the Remaking of Liberal Philosophy* (Princeton University Press, 2019), 279.

[121] Ibid.

or situation in society would not exclude anyone from legal subjectivity. However, for present purposes, this exercise has some significant, but illuminating, flaws. First of all, the utopian result described here is not necessarily what Rawls – given his acceptance of 'natural inequality' – would have predicted. In addition, focusing on purely distributional questions does not necessarily entail a critical examination of the societal structures that cause discrimination, nor trigger a shift to an inclusive society or to community-based models. In addition, this experiment tempts the veiled designers to create a polity in which traits linked to disadvantage simply do not exist. This issue is hard to overstate here: also in the context of vulnerability, the relevant traits and situations should not be seen as pejorative in and of themselves, because doing so reiterates the dehumanisation and othering that underlie them and negates not only the fact that these traits are constitutive of identity and culture, but also the legitimate and equal worth of the individuals currently bearing them. In other words, the experiment cannot and must not be a eugenic one. Instead, it should be about ensuring equal real-world enjoyment of dignity and agency. Thus, if this experiment serves any purpose here, it is to test for and mediate the disadvantage or inequality that vulnerability-related traits entail as constructs that affect life in society.

It can be argued that the existence of vulnerability is not an injustice in and of itself, for it is an inextricable element of human life. Instead, the injustice lies in the fact that differences in vulnerabilities entail differences in the quality and autonomy of individual lives. Examined in this way, the traits that give rise to vulnerability can be seen as connected to limitations on the ability to pursue one's own and unique conception of the good life[122] that are imposed or reinforced by society. The above experiments may not be indispensable for finding that disadvantage exists or for deeming it morally problematic. However, they highlight the ways in which trait-dependent variations in the distribution of access to resources and opportunities constitute structural disadvantages and place individuals in unequal positions. This discussion may also be helpful in overcoming 'pluralism anxiety'[123] and the cognitive barriers that obstruct less vulnerable individuals from recognising the existence of the systems that accord them this status.

This perspective also helps to clarify the inadequacy of the rational liberal subject, tying into the work of Martha Albertson Fineman. Fineman's two-part vulnerability paradigm emphasises the universality of vulnerability by virtue of human embodiment as well as the differences among individuals that arise from embodiment's various manifestations and social structures.[124] This sort of thinking

[122] Variation in the conception of the good life is one aspect of human diversity that is, in fact, taken into account by Rawls to some extent (John Rawls, *Political Liberalism*, expanded edn (Columbia University Press, 2005), 184, 186–87); Terzi (n 116), 153.

[123] Yoshino Kenji, 'The New Equal Protection' (2011) 124(3) *Harvard Law Review* 747–803, as discussed in Timmer (n 53), 168.

[124] Martha Albertson Fineman, 'Equality and Difference: The Restrained State' (2015) 66(3) *Alabama Law Review* 609–26, 613–14, 618–19.

about vulnerability reinterprets the Rawlsian original position by – instead of imagining that we might be vulnerable once the veil is lifted – lifting the veil and showing us that we are in fact already vulnerable.

Both Fineman's responsiveness to vulnerability as described here and Rawls's access to primary social goods are, in the end, metrics for injustice. However, neither of these two approaches seems to generate genuine care for the other, as they both relate to warding off risks to oneself (or persons close to oneself). Neither approach means that the particularly vulnerable deserve special protection in their own right; instead, they mean protecting everyone to the same standard – even if that takes a variety of measures tailored to differences among us – because we all face more or less the same risks in the course of our lives. In this sense, both approaches are based on the needy self and the risks to which it is exposed. Genuine empathy and care for the other is, of course, something else altogether, and will be explored later on in this chapter.

First, however, the following section will continue the exploration of vulnerability as a question of injustice by exploring an alternative to Rawls's primary social goods. This alternate account provides a different metric for justice, namely whether individuals have the 'capabilities' to exercise particular real 'functionings' in the world.[125]

iii. *Understanding the Capabilities Approach*

Rawls's idea of justice as fairness is, ultimately, a social contract-based construction that is removed from real-world context. It assumes that the individuals concerned are rational adults possessed of moral faculties and fully aware of their own need for material things, as Amartya Sen and Martha Nussbaum accurately identified[126] and Rawls himself acknowledged to a degree.[127] In addition, for such experiments to translate into real-world equality for the hypothetical participants, it would be necessary for these individuals to have an understanding of the evolution of their own needs over the entire course of their life span.

Building on criticisms of the just world theories outlined above and based on Amartya Sen's critique of the incompleteness of a Rawlsian approach to equality,[128] Martha Nussbaum has poignantly argued that Rawlsian equality ignores the realities of many extremely dependent individuals, and in fact cannot be reconciled with the existence of people with cognitive disabilities.[129] She argues that a liberal

[125] Nussbaum, *Creating Capabilities* (n 101), 24–25.

[126] Sen (n 113), 215–17; Nussbaum, *Fundamental Entitlements* (n 101), 51.

[127] John Rawls, 'Kantian Constructivism in Moral Theory' (1980) 77(9) *The Journal of Philosophy* 515–72, 546, as mentioned in Nussbaum, *Fundamental Entitlements* (n 101), 53, and noting that his theory relates to those who are 'directly or indirectly associated together throughout a complete life,' whereas the situations of those who do not meet these criteria must be left aside until a polity has been constituted and can address them.

[128] Sen (n 113), 217–19.

[129] Martha C Nussbaum, *Frontiers of Justice: Disability, Nationality, Species Membership* (Belknap Press, 2007), 135.

emphasis on freedom and autonomy fails to respect plurality in the conceptions of the good life and to recognise that not only autonomous lives are worthwhile.[130]

In other words, Nussbaum integrates the realities of care and dependence – and thus also the realities of diverse vulnerability – into theories about what a just world should look like. Nussbaum's capabilities approach can thus be understood as a critique of moral theory as not taking human vulnerability sufficiently into account. She understands human dignity as enmeshed with vulnerability, arguing that the 'dignity of the human being is the dignity of a needy enmattered being'.[131] Indeed, our dignity is the 'animal sort of dignity, and that very sort of dignity could not be possessed by a being who was not mortal and vulnerable'.[132] She thus takes her argument back to the Kantian distinction between personhood and animality, which she describes as deeply problematic.[133] She argues that it suggests that 'the core of our personality is self-sufficient rather than needy, and purely active rather than also passive'.[134] She identifies this as the source of a negation of our own vulnerability, which makes us wrongly imagine our dignity as atemporal and not susceptible to the growth and decline that accompany human life, with its periods of dependency.[135]

The resulting capabilities approach – as created by Sen and developed by Nussbaum – responds to realities of dependence by focusing on a list of specific capabilities needed to ensure that individuals are able to live in a manner conforming to human dignity.[136] Nussbaum has described capabilities as 'the answers to the question "[w]hat is this person able to do and to be?"'.[137] Sen has similarly described them as what gives one 'the freedom to achieve actual livings that one can have reason to value'.[138]

These capabilities can be divided into three categories: basic, internal and combined capabilities. These describe, by turn, a person's innate faculties, the traits and abilities that they train or develop through interaction with their environment, and the 'substantial freedoms' made up of their internal capabilities and their socio-political and economic conditions, which together allow for an understanding of their opportunities for choice and action in their specific situation.[139] Nussbaum has also been more specific about what the required capabilities could look like in a particular context. For example, together with Rosalind Dixon, she has written regarding children that their physical, emotional and cognitive

[130] Nussbaum, *Fundamental Entitlements* (n 101), 49–50.
[131] Nussbaum (n 129), 278.
[132] See both Nussbaum, *Fundamental Entitlements* (n 101), 51–52, and Nussbaum (n 129), 132.
[133] Nussbaum (n 129), 131–33.
[134] Ibid, 132.
[135] Ibid, 132–33.
[136] Martha C Nussbaum, *Women and Human Development: The Capabilities Approach* (CUP, 2001); Nussbaum (n 129), esp at 155–57; Dixon and Nussbaum (n 101), from 552. See also Sen (n 113).
[137] Nussbaum, *Creating Capabilities* (n 101), 20.
[138] Sen, *Development as Freedom* (n 101), 73, discussed in Robeyns and Brighouse (n 115), 2.
[139] Nussbaum, *Creating Capabilities* (n 101), 20–24.

immaturity and their reduced agency mean that the state has a special responsibility to ensure that they enjoy certain capabilities which are essential for a life in human dignity.[140] In other words, instead of imagining what individuals – in this particular case, children – would demand of the polity if they were the rational, sentient actors behind the veil of ignorance, Nussbaum herself takes on this role and creates a minimum list of capabilities – such as health, bodily integrity, self-respect and the ability to design one's own conception of the good life – that must non-negotiably and cross-culturally be guaranteed to all human individuals in order to guarantee the equal ability to enjoy a life in dignity.[141]

In a sense, Nussbaum thereby creates her own catalogue of fundamental human rights. She argues that a just society should treat every person as an end, and ensure universal enjoyment of a minimum threshold level of each relevant capability.[142] Although Nussbaum acknowledges that her list of capabilities may not be final,[143] any unitary and Western understanding of capabilities should be subjected to critical analysis, and the risk of essentialism is certainly present here, the idea of capabilities has been employed plentifully in the development context, with numerous actors – notably the UN – utilising the approach.[144]

iv. Interlacing Vulnerability and Capabilities

The question now, of course, is to determine the use of a capabilities approach for practical and theoretical approaches to vulnerability. First, it should be noted that a capabilities approach fosters a context-responsive understanding of autonomy – understood as 'the capacity to lead a self-determining life and the status of being recognised as an autonomous agent by others'[145] – and thus bolsters a theory of vulnerability with a much-needed understanding of the 'freedom to choose'.[146] It sheds light on the demands of substantive equality for real human individuals

[140] These central capabilities are (i) life, (ii) bodily health, (iii) bodily integrity, (iv) senses, imagination, and thought, (v) emotions, (vi) practical reason, which means the ability to design one's own conception of the good and reflect critically about one's life, (vii) affiliation, which contains both elements of being able to live with and toward others and empathy towards others as well as living with self-respect and without humiliation, (viii) living with concern for and in relation to animals, plants, and the world of nature, (ix) play and recreation, and (x) political and material control over one's environment. For more detail, see Nussbaum, *Fundamental Entitlements* (n 101), 41–42; Dixon and Nussbaum (n 101), 558, fn 37.

[141] Nussbaum, *Fundamental Entitlements* (n 101), 48.

[142] Nussbaum, *Creating Capabilities* (n 101), 33–40; Nussbaum, *Fundamental Entitlements* (n 101), 40; Catriona Mackenzie, 'The Importance of Relational Autonomy and Capabilities for an Ethics of Vulnerability', in Catriona Mackenzie, Wendy Rogers and Susan Dodds (eds), Vulnerability: New Essays in Ethics and Feminist Philosophy (OUP, 2014) 33–59, 50.

[143] Nussbaum, *Fundamental Entitlements* (n 101), 41.

[144] Robeyns and Brighouse (n 115), 2; OHCHR, 'Human Rights and Poverty Reduction: A Conceptual Framework', 2004, HR/PUB/04/1, 3, 6–8.

[145] MacKenzie (142), 41.

[146] Ibid, 51–52; Mackenzie, Rogers and Dodds (n 84), 9.

engaged in relationships of giving and receiving care, whose dignity is constant even as their level of vulnerability varies and evolves. In some sense, an emphasis on capabilities also answers the controversial question concerning the 'equality of what?' that substantive equality demands.[147]

Martha Albertson Fineman considers Martha Nussbaum's capabilities approach dangerous, given what she sees as a focus on the 'base level of human worth', which in turn facilitates definitions of 'what does and does not constitute a valuable life'.[148] Indeed, it is inherently problematic to list what capabilities should be important to all people. However, Nussbaum's capabilities are not about forcing or expecting any one individual to do any one particular thing. Thus, to take a relatively innocuous example, 'lying peacefully in the grass' is a 'functioning', according to Nussbaum,[149] and its enjoyment is therefore dependent on a range of capabilities that put individuals in a situation to choose to lie down and be able to enjoy nature. However, this does not mean that all individuals should be forced to spend any particular time in the grass, nor that they will all enjoy this activity. The essential element here, as Nussbaum herself has argued, is the freedom to choose.[150]

This emphasis of the freedom to choose is, of course, evocative of the independence and autonomy of the liberal legal subject, and not all that different from the conception of the good life pursued by the unveiled citizens of Rawls's utopian polity. But it can also be understood differently, as a question of ensuring individual agency. Nussbaum's ideas about capabilities offer an alternative to the liberal subject especially when read alongside vulnerability theory and its universalising force. Capabilities-related thinking thus enriches the understanding of universal vulnerability by drawing attention to the effects of particular individual sources of vulnerability, including social, economic, legal and political structures, as well as interpersonal and social relationships.[151] In this sense, it highlights not only the vulnerabilities that arise from physical embodiment, but provides a way of addressing the deprivation of capabilities and autonomy that results from all types and sources of vulnerability.[152]

Capabilities theory – which, when contrasted to the Rawlsian vision of justice as the distribution of a standardised, homogeneous package of resources – is responsive to variations in individuals' needs, abilities and situations, in a manner comparable to vulnerability theory.[153] In other words, as Elizabeth Anderson has

[147] MacKenzie (n 142), 48; Sen (n 113).
[148] Fineman (n 87), 14, fn 39.
[149] Nussbaum, *Creating Capabilities* (n 101), 25.
[150] Ibid.
[151] MacKenzie (n 142), 38.
[152] Ibid, 37–38.
[153] Elizabeth Anderson, 'Justifying the Capabilities Approach to Justice' in Harry Brighouse and Ingrid Robeyns (eds), *Measuring Justice: Primary Goods and Capabilities* (CUP, 2010) 81–100, 87.

argued, if capabilities are understood to create a 'sufficientiarian' standard, or one that 'provide[s], to each person, access to a package of resources adjusted to that person's ability',[154] then the capabilities approach becomes one that incorporates and responds to vulnerability.

This sufficientiarian approach means, for example, that persons with physical disabilities are entitled to public assistance, ranging from wheelchair ramps to support in obtaining appropriate employment or accommodation; individuals who do not speak the local language are entitled to translations of vital public documents; and women who suffer domestic abuse are entitled to access counselling and safe-houses.[155] By providing each individual with a tailored package of resources, equal and effective access to a life in dignity is guaranteed; while this does not per se guarantee the functionings of a life in dignity, and must be dynamic as needs change, it nonetheless gives all individuals equal standing to pursue such a life.[156]

From this perspective, the responsive state evoked by a vulnerability heuristic and the support required under a capabilities approach are, to a certain extent, two ways of bringing about the same or at least a similar result. In the words of Carolina Yoko Furusho, 'convergences between vulnerability and capability theories stem from their common understanding of human beings as subjects who build resilience over time, in a context-sensitive approach that rejects the understanding of the liberal legal subject as *a priori* invulnerable'.[157] As a result of this common understanding, the responsibility for addressing harms is shifted from those who suffer them to the entity that is best able to address them – the state.[158]

These two theories are, in other words, not only similar: they also inform and improve each other. An emphasis on the universality of human vulnerability may improve the foundational account of human rights under the capabilities approach.[159] Furthermore, the identification of the various types and forms of vulnerability builds on the various ways in which individuals need support in order to compensate for their 'capability deficits'. If a just society eradicates 'compounded capability deficits or corrosive disadvantage', this also means addressing the flawed social policies that fail to respond to vulnerability and simultaneously cause capability failures.[160] Lastly but very importantly, capability theory can improve a vulnerability-based approach in that it compensates for some of its failures, including the propensity for paternalism that it can entail.[161]

[154] Ibid.
[155] Ibid, 92–93, as interpreted in MacKenzie (n 142), 53.
[156] MacKenzie (n 142), 53.
[157] Furusho (n 86), 193.
[158] Ibid, 195.
[159] Ibid, 193–95.
[160] MacKenzie (n 142), 54.
[161] Ibid, 55–56.

Ensuring that all human rights subjects benefit from equal opportunities to live a life of agency and dignity goes beyond mere recognition of equality and the possibility of equal participation, but also entails a degree of redistribution to make that participation effectively possible as well as a transformation of society.[162] Thus, achieving substantive equality in the exercise of civil and political rights may require measures that more typically fall under the socio-economic heading, including material support, education and ensuring an adequate standard of living. For the purposes of the ECHR, combatting inequality requires effective protection of every person's basic human dignity by ensuring that all individuals have a minimum level of certain capabilities; this includes socio-economic measures.

At the same time, this does not necessarily mean that Article 3 ECHR should be used to protect every capability related to human functioning. Vulnerability reasoning, like 'sufficientiarian' capabilities-based demands, is based on identifying specific problem areas and fundamental deprivations of the building blocks of autonomy and dignity. In this regard, vulnerability has been described as a 'limiting rather than a limitless principle'.[163] While vulnerability does sieve cases and may thus have a limiting function, however, the interdependence of different human rights means that vulnerability and capabilities theories can transform the application not just of a particular provision, but of the human rights framework as a whole.

Under Article 3 specifically, a combined vulnerability-capabilities approach allows for a normative conclusion, namely that extremes of suffering, degradation and ill-treatment should continue to be captured by the Court, but in a manner that does not try to force variable human vulnerability into a monolithic standard. Here, too, agency – in the sense of an equal ability to exercise capabilities[164] – must be a guiding principle. While vulnerability alone can emphasise the victimhood of applicants, a capabilities approach shifts the focus to building resilience.

Understanding variable but universal human vulnerability is essential for creating a system that can be described as ensuring substantive equality. An appropriate ethical-legal imperative thus requires the recognition that human beings are 'essentially social, relational, and interdependent' and that their 'ability to exercise freedom and agency cannot be conceived apart from socio-material reality'; in order for all humans to be able to lead self-guided meaningful lives and flourish equally, a certain institutional environment is needed.[165] Employing a vulnerability-based approach thus not only makes socio-economic obligations more plausible under Article 3 and other Convention provisions, but helps to develop the positive obligations of states.[166]

[162] Furusho (n 86), 183, citing Fredman (n 81), 25–33.
[163] Peroni and Timmer (n 57), 1084.
[164] Furusho (n 86), 190.
[165] Ibid, 185, 189 and 191.
[166] Ibid, 204; Timmer (n 53), 165–67.

III. On the Court's 'Legitimacy' and Judicial Empathy

At some level, it can be argued that vulnerability is a placeholder for the level of empathy that the Strasbourg judges – and, by association, Member State governments and European societies overall – are willing to exercise vis-à-vis individual human rights subjects. That is because, when considering whether an applicant experienced sufficient suffering to violate Article 3, the Strasbourg judges often use vulnerability to select those cases in which they engage in depth with applicants' feelings and experiences. On the surface, this does not seem fair to those applicants who are deemed not vulnerable, and it also does not provide the Court with a methodologically sound approach for consistently identifying the cases where suffering was particularly acute. However, the utility of vulnerability from a cognitive standpoint is that it reframes the questions facing the Strasbourg judges: it permits them to reinterpret the facts of the case and the applicable rules under the Convention in a manner that nudges both the judges and those who read and implement their judgments towards a certain outcome.

Ultimately, the utility of vulnerability in the Court's jurisprudence lies in its role as an equaliser. It compensates for shortcomings in individuals' abilities to complain about violations of their rights, provides recognition for particular ways in which they suffer and helps draw attention to the ways in which state authorities fail to respond to their special needs. It does this by causing a shift from a presumably neutral perspective to a victim-based one. In doing so, when it comes to the applicants considered vulnerable by the Court, helps to identify the stereotypes or expectations that disadvantage vulnerable individuals in claiming their rights and having their voices heard, and replaces them with others that, albeit likely still stereotyping those concerned, provide advantages from a substantive and procedural point of view.

Vulnerability reasoning, applied in this way, can be portrayed as relying on empathy with the situation of victims to overcome the Court's tendency to see individual cases as part of the huge and seemingly endless mass of present and future applications before it. Vulnerability reasoning thereby allows the Court to overcome its fears of opening the floodgates to an unmanageable number of applications or setting a precedent[167] with unintended consequences, at least in the individual case. In some way, therefore, it helps the Court do what it was set up to do – assess compliance with its interpretation of the ECHR without caving to political and societal pressures – albeit not optimally. This idea, of vulnerability as a vehicle for empathy, is explored in the following sections.

[167] In the sense of a *res judicata* or *res interpretata*, although not a binding precedent (Oddný Mjöll Arnardóttir, 'Res Interpretata, Erga Omnes Effect and the Role of the Margin of Appreciation in Giving Domestic Effect to the Judgments of the ECtHR', 28(3) *European Journal of International Law* (2017) 819–43).

A. Challenges to the Court's 'Legitimacy'

Any theory that potentially entails tangible socio-economic dictates for states is generally met with resistance under international human rights law. In this regard, it must be noted that, while the Court's vulnerability heuristic helps to identify injustice, it has also been part of progressive judgments in controversial areas. In such instances, the Court exposes itself to challenges regarding its legitimacy to impose on domestic decision-making. How, then, can the Court respond to the moral and philosophical demands of equality-through-vulnerability under the consent-based ECHR system?

Dimitris Xenos, in an early analysis of the Court's vulnerability jurisprudence, noted the importance of the Court's subsidiarity when it comes to requiring the Member States to take measures to protect vulnerable people, especially when this concerns material assistance.[168] He argued that there is a 'democratic limit on the Convention in relation to issues that can potentially put an unnecessary and impossible burden on the limited resources of the state'.[169] The Court has indeed shown a lack of willingness to impose a burden on finite state resources.[170] In some cases, too, the Court takes a utilitarian and conservative approach by applying its European consensus jurisprudence: it allows the majority of states to determine the standard of human rights protection to be applied.[171] By contrast, the vulnerability and human dignity argumentation strategies it has employed in other cases allow it to emphasise the humanity, suffering and need for protection of the agency of applicants and to thus make findings contrary to that majority opinion.

It could be argued that – given its role as a human rights adjudicator tasked with interpreting and applying a vitally important human rights treaty – the Court should take the latter approach in all cases. In this vein, former ECtHR judge David Thór Björgvinsson has rightly criticised the deference exhibited in certain areas by the Strasbourg jurisprudence, arguing that it is 'highly questionable if a human rights court can hide behind the moral preferences of the majority in one country in its understanding of rights of individuals holding different moral views. This may appease some of the Court's critics, but it also puts the Court's "moral capital" at risk in the long run.'[172] That moral capital, he argues, is safeguarded by

[168] Dimitris Xenos, 'The Human Rights of the Vulnerable' (2009) 13(4) *International Journal of Human Rights* 591–614, 605.

[169] Ibid, 610.

[170] *N. v United Kingdom* App no 26565/05, Judgment (GC) of 27 May 2008, Reports 2008, paras 44–45.

[171] Under Art 3, this effect can for example be seen, albeit implicitly in the *Tyrer* case (*Tyrer* (n 26), paras 31 and 38), where the Court relied on the fact that a majority of Member States prohibit birching as a form of punishment.

[172] David Thór Björgvinsson, 'The Role of Judges of the ECtHR as Guardians of Fundamental Rights of the Individual', in Martin Scheinin, Helle Krunke and Marina Aksenova (eds), *Judges as Guardians of Constitutionalism and Human Rights* (Edward Elgar, 2016), 329–51.

coherent, cogent argumentation and a Court that holds fast to its progressive case law despite criticism.[173]

Björgvinsson's approach evokes – and, in fact, bases on – the theory of interpretation advanced by George Letsas.[174] This account argues that the Court's 'living instrument' doctrine jettisons traditional forms of treaty interpretation, including the opinion of the Convention's drafters and the public and authorities in the Member States,[175] and instead searches for the 'truth' of Convention rights.[176] Letsas considers a moral reading of the ECHR indispensable if the Court is to perform its function of protecting the human rights that the citizens of the Council of Europe Member States 'really' have (as opposed to the ones that states consider them to have).[177]

Protection of individuals' human rights is the Court's core function. Nevertheless, its progressive interpretation of the ECHR exposes it to criticism, particularly from states.[178] In this regard, and although the present volume is reluctant to describe the Court as vulnerable, as other commentators have done,[179] it is possible to argue that the Court, like certain types of applicants considered in the previous chapter, exhibits a dependency that constrains its agency. The reluctance to describe the Court as vulnerable here stems from the fact that this use of the term does not relate to the effects of embodiment, which it lacks, or to its marginalisation or powerlessness, but simply to the fact that it, like any system, is not unassailable. While this is quite different from the imbalances of power and privilege that characterise human vulnerability, in any event, it is certainly true that the Court depends on the continued collaboration and goodwill of states.

Strong arguments have been made for the Court's democratic legitimacy as an institution and its functional legitimacy as an influence on domestic law.[180] Among other things, it has been noted that courts are counter-majoritarian by nature and that the process of electing the Strasbourg judges involves democratically chosen parliamentarians.[181] Regarding the 'legitimacy' of the Court's interpretative ethic, in contrast to its institutional legitimacy, Article 32(1) ECHR designates the ECtHR as the master of the Convention's interpretation. As such,

[173] Ibid.

[174] See George Letsas, *A Theory of Interpretation of the European Convention on Human Rights* (OUP, 2007), as discussed in chapter one of this volume.

[175] George Letsas, 'The ECHR as a Living Instrument: Its Meaning and Legitimacy' in Andreas Føllesdal, Birgit Peters and Geir Ulfstein (eds), *Constituting Europe: The European Court of Human Rights in a National, European and Global Context* (CUP, 2013) 106–41, 123.

[176] Letsas (n 174), from 74, esp 75.

[177] Letsas (n 175), 124.

[178] See, for example, the response in the United Kingdom to the judgment in *Hirst v United Kingdom (No 2)* App no 74025/01, Judgment (GC) of 6 October 2005, Reports 2005-IX.

[179] Timmer (n 53), 167–69.

[180] Michael O'Boyle, 'The Future of the European Court of Human Rights' (2011) 12(10) *German Law Journal* 1862–77, esp 1866–67; Robert Spano, 'Universality or Diversity of Human Rights? Strasbourg in the Age of Subsidiarity' (2014) 14(3) *Human Rights Law Review* 487–502, 488, with further references.

[181] Spano (n 180), 488.

it is 'the falsest of false dawns' to imagine replacing the Court's creativity and its occasionally quasi-legislative character with a mechanical application of rules that will not conflict with decisions made in the domestic sphere.[182] Nonetheless, its judgments overall will certainly have more traction and garner less criticism and better results regarding implementation if they are well-reasoned and coherent.

For his part, former Judge Pinto de Albuquerque has criticised the Court for failing to offer legal certainty to states or clear guidance to potential vulnerable applicants. He criticises the exceptionalism currently practiced by the Court in this area, arguing that

> By not providing clear and general criteria, and by linking its finding to the 'extraordinary circumstances' of the case, the [Court] not only weakens the authority of its reasoning and restricts the scope of its findings and their interpretative value, but also provides less guidance, or no guidance at all, to States Parties and interested institutions and persons who might be willing to intervene in favour of helpless, vulnerable victims of human rights violations.[183]

Certainly, it is not enough for the Court to reach 'the right results by unconvincing, awkward means'.[184] While Judge Pinto de Albuquerque criticises the lack of guidance provided by the Court – justifiably, given that states cannot prevent violations of standards that they do not understand – this lack of clarity may be a method of self-preservation. In a political climate of backlash and reform, the Court may be protecting itself via its demure approach to progressive interpretation. Still, it remains debatable whether this approach is the right one.

While some of the judgments issued in the vulnerability context may be utilised by those who criticise the Court's 'judicial activism', there is also a strong case to be made for the legitimacy of a principled case law that uses vulnerability not to trigger an automatic violation judgment but instead as a factor that encourages the allocation of scarce state resources where they are needed most.[185] There are also some steps that the Court can take to limit critiques of its vulnerability heuristic. This would mean that, in addition to the issue of predictability, the Court should concern itself with the consistency and inclusiveness of its vulnerability case law. The above has described in detail how the Court has interpreted and applied vulnerability in a number of Article 3 cases, across a variety of procedural and substantive points.

To display the consistency that will cement vulnerability's role in the case law, the concept should guarantee substantive equality among all applicants, and thus be mainstreamed consistently into the Strasbourg jurisprudence. In short, the Court needs to determine how and why each and every applicant is vulnerable or resilient. In this vein, for example, the Court seems inconsistent if it finds that

[182] See Richard A Posner, *How Judges Think* (Harvard University Press, 2010), 15.

[183] *CLR on behalf of Valentin Câmpeanu v Romania* App no 47848/08, Judgment (GC) of 17 July 2014, Reports 2014, Concurring Opinion of Judge Pinto de Albuquerque, para 11.

[184] Ibid, para 16.

[185] Peroni and Timmer (n 57), 1084.

Roma applicants are vulnerable in one judgment and not in the next,[186] or if it offers special protection to one marginalised group but not another – for example if it protects those who are disadvantaged because of their dependency on provision by the state in detention but not those who find themselves in situations of extreme poverty. In addition, to ensure that it does not reduce applicants to their vulnerability, the Court should recognise not only their vulnerability, but also their resilience.[187] In this regard, a degree of self-awareness – thus, the recognition that the Court itself is part of the liberal order – would be indicated.[188]

There should be limits to the kinds of pressures that the Court is willing to accommodate in its case law. In particular, it should stop short of catering to the 'us-against-them' idea voiced by some critics.[189] Criticism of human rights in the current socio-political climate also means rejection of increased attention to vulnerable groups and individuals and their rights.[190] Described by Kenji Yoshino as 'pluralism anxiety', a fear-based reaction to the plurality and diversity of 'new' or 'newly visible' sorts of people is not uncommon.[191] Courts shying away from equality-based claims on the basis of pluralism anxiety may try to compensate by emphasising liberty, and polities may experience 'impatience with the seemingly endless proliferation of identities and identity politics'.[192]

Yoshino has considered the use of argumentation that relies on general rules – for example, emphasising the right of all adults to marry the consenting adult of their choosing, as opposed to promoting same-sex marriage specifically – as a way to make equality-based claims more convincing. This appeals to the cognitive longing for simplicity, and is also an appeal to empathy.[193] These strategies could potentially have salience as concerns the reception of the Court's jurisprudence, as well. So, if vulnerability were to be presented as a universal human trait instead of way to accord special treatment to some, it might retain its current effects with broader appeal. At the same time, there is a risk of erasure implicit in this style of argument.

B. Understanding Empathy and Otherisation

Human vulnerability is inextricably linked with human emotion. Only an invulnerable being has no reason to fear, to feel anger or to suffer.[194] Vulnerability can

[186] See, for example, *Balogh v Hungary* App no 47940/99, Judgment of 20 July 2004, where no mention of vulnerability is made, presumably because of the absence of a submission to that effect. See also *Boacă v Romania* App no 40355/11, Judgment of 12 January 2016.

[187] On resilience, see Fineman (n 87), 13–15; see also Peroni and Timmer (n 57), 1074.

[188] Timmer (n 53), 169.

[189] Ibid, 168, for more details.

[190] Ibid.

[191] Yoshino (n 123), as discussed in ibid.

[192] Ibid, 750–52.

[193] Ibid, 793–94.

[194] Martha C Nussbaum, *Hiding from Humanity: Disgust, Shame, and the Law* (Princeton University Press, 2004), 6.

also evoke disgust and shame by reminding us of our animalistic defencelessness and mortality.[195] However, it likewise reminds us that all humans share this defencelessness and a mortal form, and can stimulate empathy and create communities of compassion.[196] As Bryan Turner has written, vulnerability gives rise to a collective sympathy and a range of rights.[197] Our 'collectively held recognition of individual frailty' thereby provides human rights with emotive force as a 'system of mutual protection'.[198] The importance of sympathy has been subject to philosophical studies that see in this concept the antidote to the 'bourgeois coldness' that made the Holocaust possible[199] or as a necessary element of morality and driver of solidarity.[200]

As the jurisprudence of the Court summarised in this volume shows, vulnerability as pure emotion is also relevant for the purposes of the case law under Article 3 ECHR, and indeed its presence makes a convincing case for finding a violation of that provision.[201] In this regard, the Court increasingly gives vulnerable applicants the space to describe how they felt under given circumstances, displays understanding for the psychological effects of marginalisation and trauma, and even presumes the presence of anguish and fear in specific cases. It also seems that – by responding to the circumstances of individual lives, recognising advantage and disadvantage and having regard to the lived experience of applicants – the ECtHR's judges demonstrate a significant degree of empathy with vulnerable individuals' struggles.[202] In this sense, there seems to be some link between the idea of vulnerability and emotion, both on the part of the victim of an ECHR violation and of the adjudicator tasked with determining whether there has been such a violation.

The idea of judicial emotionality seems, at first view, difficult to reconcile with judicial impartiality and the principle of legal foreseeability, and describing judging as empathetic evokes an air of illogicality or sentimentality. Indeed, arguing for the moral 'legitimacy' of the Court's judgments on the basis of their emotional appeal threatens to open a Pandora's box of criticisms and problems, including the issue of privileging emotions over facts. On the other hand, of course, individual judges are human individuals who are shaped by their backgrounds, context and

[195] Ibid, 89–90, 94.

[196] Ibid, 50; Furusho (n 86), 197.

[197] Turner (n 27), 9; Bryan S. Turner, 'Outline of a Theory of Human Rights' (1993) 27(3) *Sociology* 489–512, 502.

[198] Turner (n 27), 507.

[199] Theodor W Adorno, 'Erziehung nach Auschwitz 1966', in Gerd Kadelbach (ed), *Erziehung zur Mündigkeit: Vorträge und Gespräche mit Hellmuth Becker 1959–1969* (Suhrkamp, 1970) 92–109 from 106.

[200] Compare the interpretation of the work of Max Horkheimer in José Manuel Barreto, 'Ethics of Emotions as Ethics of Human Rights: A Jurisprudence of Sympathy in Adorno, Horkheimer and Rorty' (2006) 17(1) *Law and Critique* 73–106, from 93.

[201] See *Govedarski v Bulgaria* App no 34957/12, Judgment of 16 February 2016, para 62; *Nasr and Ghali v Italy* App no 44883/09, Judgment of 23 February 2016, para 286.

[202] The term empathy has been used here – as opposed to sympathy – because the emotion in question relates to judges imagining themselves in the position of applicants.

audience, and who display the same cognitive responses to stimuli as any other person; an emotionless judge is thus illusory.[203] In this regard, it is possible to understand emotional engagement – and particularly empathy – as an antonym of judicial apathy, and as a necessary vehicle for context-engagement. Emotion in general and empathy in particular are by no means alien to adjudication: the question is rather whether and to what extent they should explicitly inform the outcomes of cases. The following will explore the proper role of emotion in judging in more detail, and then turn to the meaning of empathy for vulnerability reasoning. This serves, first of all, to examine and ultimately debunk the idea that judicial empathy is necessarily incompatible with impartial judging, and, secondly, to preempt criticisms of the Court's approach to vulnerability-based and empathy-based judging.

i. The Place of Emotion in Legal Reasoning

The desire to recognise vulnerability, as well as resistance to this same recognition, can both be described as emotion-based reactions: one based on empathy, and one on fear.[204] As noted above, emotions and the law may seem, at first sight, incompatible: emotions are easily labelled as biased, erratic or irrational, while the law should aspire to neutrality, rationality and impartiality. This reflects the entrenched dichotomy between reason and emotion, and touches on the debate concerning the appropriateness of emotional elements in the context of morality. The idea that emotion is irrational can be traced to the Stoic philosophers, who advocated the end of emotion – that is to say, the abolishment of ties to the world – in the pursuit of rationality and invulnerable self-sufficiency.[205] According to Immanuel Kant, too, emotions taint moral thinking,[206] and Thomas Hobbes argued that the ideal judge should be 'able in judgement to divest himself of all fear, anger, hatred, love, and compassion'.[207]

Nevertheless, the idea that the law can and should operate without ties to the real world is a strikingly problematic one. It is difficult to conceive of a judge's mind as pure reason free from human emotions, including such basic functions as anger, trust and pity. This inability to set aside emotion is part of the reason why

[203] For more in this area, see among others Posner (n 182), 111–12, 106, 174; Adam N Glynn and Maya Sen, 'Identifying Judicial Empathy: Does Having Daughters Cause Judges to Rule for Women's Issues?' (2015) 59(1) *American Journal of Political Science* 37–54.

[204] Yoshino (n 123), 751–59.

[205] Compare the work of Martha Nussbaum, who has traced the rationalist approach through history and seeks to vindicate emotions, at least in part, from the realm of irrationality (Martha C Nussbaum, 'Beyond the Social Contract: Capabilities and Global Justice – An Olaf Palme Lecture, Delivered in Oxford on 19 June 2003' (2004) 32(1) *Oxford Development Studies* 3–18, 6–7 and *passim*).

[206] Immanuel Kant, *Anthropology from a Pragmatic Point of View* (Mary J Gregor tr, Martinus Nijhoff 1974), *passim* and particularly at 118, 121, 133–34, 138–39.

[207] Thomas Hobbes, *Leviathan: Parts I and II* (Aloysius P Martinich ed, Broadview, 2005), 210, para 28, referred to in Terry A Maroney, 'The Persistent Cultural Script of Judicial Dispassion' (2011) 99(2) *California Law Review* 629–81, 630–31.

judges in all kinds of jurisdictions must recuse themselves if they have a particular emotional attachment or involvement in a case. Like all of the dichotomies discussed above, the rationality-emotion binary is easily exposed as an oversimplification that artificially splits interconnected categories into monolithic concepts.[208] Under the right circumstances, emotions are a non-negligible element of the law. In fact, the study of law and emotion is emerging as its own discipline, with scholars seeing emotions as 'engagements with the world, not mere reactions or instincts',[209] and disaggregating emotions in order to study them individually.[210] That does not mean, of course, that all emotions are equal or equally constructive, or should be attributed equal significance, or that emotions should be given free reign.[211] It simply means that law is unthinkable without emotion, to which it must appeal and which it must take into account.[212]

In this regard, Martha Nussbaum has indicated that emotion and vulnerability together are the very reason for certain legal protections, arguing that '[w]ithout appeal to a roughly shared conception of what violations are outrageous, what losses give rise to a profound grief, what vulnerable human beings have reason to fear – it is very hard to understand why we devote the attention we do, in law, to certain types of harm and damage'.[213] In her analysis, emotions represent a natural consequence of vulnerability in that they represent a response to actual, potential or fortunately avoided damage.[214]

In this regard, it is interesting to conduct a short excursus into the United States context, where the place of empathy in the courtroom has been the subject of protracted discussion. That debate began when former President Barack Obama declared his intention to nominate judges on the basis of their empathy, stating even before his election that he would select individuals who had 'the heart, the empathy, to recognize what it's like to be a young teenage mom, the empathy to understand what it's like to be poor, or African-American, or gay, or disabled, or old'.[215] Statements like this stirred an academic debate on the place of empathy in judging, with proponents of the President's approach lauding the merits of responsiveness to inequality and bias, and opponents arguing that the idea of empathy in judging in itself constitutes bias and a cover for liberal activism that threatens the impartiality of the courts.[216] The partisan debate that resulted, described by

[208] Emily Kidd White, 'Till Human Voices Wake Us: The Role of Emotions in the Adjudication of Dignity Claims' (2014) 3 *Journal of Law, Religion and State* 201–39, 204–05.

[209] Robert C Solomon, *The Passions: Emotions and the Meaning of Life* (Hackett, 1993), ix.

[210] White Emily Kidd (n 208), 205.

[211] Solomon (n 209), x.

[212] Nussbaum (n 194), 6.

[213] Ibid, 6.

[214] Ibid.

[215] As reported in Whelan Edward, 'Obama's Constitution: The Rhetoric and the Reality' (*Weekly Standard*, 17 March 2008), www.weeklystandard.com/obamas-constitution/article/15945.

[216] Lithwick Dahlia, 'Once More, Without Feeling: The GOP's Misguided and Confused Campaign Against Judicial Empathy' *Slate* (11 May 2009), www.slate.com/articles/news_and_politics/jurisprudence/2009/05/once_more_without_feeling.html.

one commentator as the 'empathy wars', presented an image of conservatives as impartial and progressives as biased and activist.[217]

Variation in the way judges decide cases is, of course, inevitable: this stems from the existence of judicial discretion, differences between cases and the fact that judges do not mechanically apply absolutely clear-cut rules to absolutely proven facts.[218] In addition, it may also have something to do with the traits of the individual judge: proponents of judicial diversity – both as gender and as race are concerned – see variations in the backgrounds and experiences of judges as a way to enrich judging and to tackle problems created by what has been described as the 'myth' of judicial impartiality.[219] At the same time, the idea of emotional judgments based on the feelings of a particular judge at a particular time evoke concerns about partiality and arbitrariness.

Research on the impact of the emotions, especially empathy, on adjudication has identified them as a source of guidance that anchors judicial interpretation, and not as the enemy of reason.[220] This research has disaggregated emotions from momentary moods and subjective feelings, and has begun to see them instead as a method for understanding evaluative legal concepts, such as dignity, cruelty or the best interests of the child.[221] Empathy, in particular, has been identified as important for understanding human dignity.[222] Law and emotion scholars understand emotion as a way of focusing on individual cases and fastening on to those where intervention is required.[223] Judicial empathy has also been advanced as a manner by which judges can, in discrimination-related cases, see a treatment or harm from the perspective of a 'reasonable member' of the affected group, and identify subtle inequalities.[224] In other words, it may allow judges to transcend a majoritarian perspective that reflects and reproduces entrenched discrimination and imbalances of power.

Even so, the idea of judicial empathy continues to ring alarm bells. For example, there is a risk that empathy as an openness to understanding individuals' struggles will turn into a blind emotional preference for some applicants, and mean that justice is not done for less likable individuals. In this regard, researchers have shown a link between particular experiences and empathy with certain types

[217] Mary Anne Franks, 'Lies, Damned Lies, and Judicial Empathy' (2011) 51(1) *Washburn Law Journal* 61–72, 62.

[218] Posner (n 182), 5.

[219] Sherrilyn A Ifill, 'Racial Diversity on the Bench: Beyond Role Models and Public Confidence' (2000) 57(2) *Washington and Lee Law Review* 405–95, 405, 457; Feenan Dermot, 'Women Judges: Gendering Judging, Justifying Diversity' (2008) 35(4) *Journal of Law and Society* 490–519. For the international plane, see Freya Baetens (ed) *Identity and Diversity on the International Bench: Who is the Judge?* (OUP, 2021).

[220] Emily Kidd White (n 208), 204–06.

[221] Ibid, 205, fn 15.

[222] Ibid, 207–209.

[223] Sherman Nancy, 'The Place of Emotions in Kantian Morality' in Alix Cohen (ed), *Kant on Emotion and Value* (Palgrave Macmillan, 2014) 11–32, 12.

[224] Godsil Rachel D, 'Expressivism, Empathy and Equality' (2003) 36(2) *University of Michigan Journal of Law Reform* 247–304.

of claims. In particular, researchers in the United States have found that conservative male judges who have daughters are more likely to decide cases in favour of women's rights and equality than those who do not, arguably because the fact of having daughters – and thus only that fact – causes the judges to learn and care about women's issues.[225] There is also a risk that empathy is finite, that compassion will be exhausted and that judges will no longer be able to understand and respond to the situation of individual applicants. In the sense of such 'compassion fatigue', Hannah Arendt has argued against compassion and empathy in judging, considering that these emotions are 'innermost motives which are not for public display' and which are corrupted in the public sphere.[226]

Given these risks, and in order to render it a usable concept in adjudication, judicial empathy should be separated from the idea of compassion or pity. It should be understood not as a fleeting feeling, but as a consistent willingness of judges to treat individuals whose life experiences and situations are different from their own with the same level of understanding, tolerance and – to evoke Dworkin[227] – equal concern. In other words, as one commentator so pithily put it, '[e]mpathy in a judge does not mean stopping midtrial to tenderly clutch the defendant to your heart and weep'.[228] Instead, it is useful to understand empathy as an antonym of apathy[229] and as a tool for seeing humans as means and not as ends.[230] In other words, it recognises that applicants feel the same feelings as a judge, and thereby humanises applicants and can be one of a number of factors that judges take into account in the process of interpreting and applying the law.[231]

Empathy, when reserved to those who are most like one's self, can certainly lead to bias. However, empathy as described above is more of a general and constant mind-set than an emotion, and represents an openness to understanding the effects of disadvantage, marginalisation and inequality in any human individual, including those who are unlike one or not particularly sympathetic. Thus understood, empathy permits the recognition that inequality-based 'extreme disadvantages, loss of agency and deprivation of necessary resources' are unacceptable.[232]

ii. Empathy and the ECtHR's Vulnerability Case Law

A succinct instrument like the ECHR requires interpretation, and the application of various interpretative techniques and approaches necessarily leaves a certain

[225] Glynn and Sen (n 203).
[226] Hannah Arendt, *On Revolution* (Viking Press, 1963), 91.
[227] Dworkin (n 67), 227, 355.
[228] Lithwick (n 216).
[229] Paul Gordon Lauren, *The Evolution of International Human Rights: Visions Seen*, 3rd edn (University of Pennsylvania Press, 2011), 40.
[230] Alluding here to the Kantian imperative not to use people as mere means to one's ends (Immanuel Kant, *Practical Philosophy* (Mary J Gregor tr, CUP, 1996)), 80, 4:430).
[231] Posner (n 182), 19.
[232] Furusho (n 86), 197.

discretion to the interpreting judge. It could be argued that the Court uses vulnerability to interpret the Convention and to respond with empathy – as an antonym of apathy – to the particular plight of specific applicants. If this is the case, it is not necessarily clear that an empathetic response is misplaced in the Court's approach.

Interpretation necessarily means that the interpreting judge's life experience and understanding of morality enter into play. This includes the degree to which the judge identifies with or has understanding for the predicament of the applicant in a given case. In the context of the Convention, the judges' degree of empathy with the perspective of the applicants, with their particular reaction to trauma or with their difficulty in dealing with the authorities could potentially make a difference regarding whether they find that an application is well-founded, that there has been an interference with the invoked provisions or even, in extreme cases, that the application constitutes an abuse of the right of individual petition under Article 35§3(a) ECHR; all of these aspects of a case – along with many others – depend to no uncertain extent on the judges' appraisal of the situation.

Certain cases from the Article 3 context show that, where applicants face hurdles in bringing a case to Strasbourg, empathy can help ensure effective individual access to the Court. For example, in *Neshkov and Others v Bulgaria*, one applicant's claim for just satisfaction was only declared admissible due to the judges' understanding for the problems caused by his physical disability and the resulting delay in filing his claim.[233] In *M.S. v Croatia (No 2)*, the Court empathised with the applicant's difficulty in exhausting the domestic remedy available before the Constitutional Court given her mental illness.[234] In this regard, empathy is less a synonym to emotionality and more an antonym to excessive formalism. Similarly, in *Mocanu*, the Court showed understanding for the feeling of powerlessness of victims of ill-treatment and thus allowed applications that may otherwise have been considered out of time.[235]

As concerns the substance of Article 3 ECHR, the willingness of the Court to find violations of that provision where an individual experiences humiliation, anxiety, or a sense of vulnerability also depends significantly on the empathy of the judges for the experiences concerned and their effects on the applicants. The idea that a sense of vulnerability can violate Article 3 means that the Strasbourg judges must explore and have some understanding for how the applicants felt in a given situation; this is far from a rote application of fixed rules. In *Aydin v Turkey*, for example, the Court delved deep into the feelings of the applicant during and after

[233] *Neshkov and Others v Bulgaria* App nos 36925/10 …, Judgment of 27 January 2015, paras 69 and 302.

[234] *M.S. v Croatia (No 2)* App no 75450/12, Judgment of 19 February 2015, para 123.

[235] *Mocanu and Others v Romania* App nos 10865/09 …, Judgment (GC) of 17 September 2014, Reports 2014 (extracts), para 275.

her rape by state officials.[236] In a series of later cases, too, the Court has extrapolated what applicants 'must have felt' given their ill-treatment.[237]

In this regard, it is useful to note that empathy with victims of ill-treatment is in fact recommended by the Manual on the Effective Investigation and Documentation of Torture and Other Cruel, Inhuman or Degrading Treatment or Punishment, also known as the Istanbul Protocol. This document recommends that experts, in responding to alleged ill-treatment, should 'attempt to relate to mental suffering in the context of the individual's beliefs and cultural norms' given that 'a sensitive empathic attitude may offer the victim some relief from the experience of alienation'.[238] This does not necessarily mean finding a violation of human rights, but it does mean engaging and showing understanding for the experiences of the victims, as this can already contribute to dismantling, to some extent, the feelings of vulnerability and powerlessness facing them.

To some extent, the concept of empathy in judging and the idea of substantive equality overlap here. Thus, the willingness and ability of judges to ensure substantive equality is dependent on the extent to which they recognise the existence and impact of the differences that engender inequality and disadvantage. In this context, at least, the Court's vulnerability paradigm is related to the idea of judicial empathy, understood as a willingness and openness to engaging with context.

However, it is clear that the idea of empathy and, in a broader sense, of emotion as influential concepts in the ECtHR's case law have their limits. In this regard, it seems apparent from the Court's previous case law that the fruits of empathy end where the Court's willingness to impose its own standards over domestic political will does. For example, the Court has shown its lack of willingness to go against the 'profound moral values' of the Irish people as concerns the topic of access to abortion.[239] A similar result can be observed where medical claims against expulsion are concerned.[240] In situations such as this, vulnerability and judicial empathy thus seem reserved to exceptional cases or at least to less-than-universal application.

Another relevant issue is the question of when empathy-based context-sensitivity ends and bias begins. Put differently, when does reliance on judicial intuition, a gut feeling or understanding for an applicant represent bias in that applicant's favour, unintentional as it may be? It is important, in answering this second question, to recall that vulnerability is per se relational and subjective, but that this does

[236] *Aydin v Turkey* App no 23178/94, Judgment (GC) of 25 September 1997, Reports 1997-VI, para 83.

[237] *Aleksejeva v Latvia* App no 21780/07, Judgment of 3 July 2012, para 36; *El-Masri v former Yugoslav Republic of Macedonia* App no 39630/09, Judgment (GC) of 13 December 2012, Reports 2012, para 202; *Nalbandyan v Armenia* App no 9935/06 and 23339/06, Judgment of 31 March 2015, para 106.

[238] OHCHR, 'Istanbul Protocol: Manual on the Effective Investigation and Documentation of Torture and Other Cruel, Inhuman or Degrading Treatment or Punishment', revised edn (2004) HR/P/PT/8/Rev 1, www.ohchr.org/Documents/Publications/training8Rev1en.pdf, 46).

[239] *A., B. and C. v Ireland* App no 25579/05, Judgment (GC) of 16 December 2010, Reports 2010, as discussed in Björgvinsson (n 172), 20.

[240] *N. v United Kingdom* (n 170), paras 44–45.

not make it less helpful in focusing the authorities' and the Court's attention.[241] In addition, it is helpful to understand the Court's interpretation of the Convention as a complex process that involves a variety of factors and considerations. In this vein, it is useful to recall the theory of judging advanced by Richard Posner.[242] His research indicates that, though boxed in by textual law as well as the requirement of impartiality and the need for foreseeability, differences among the attitudes, experiences, allegiances, convictions and styles of reasoning of judges, along with other factors, may lead different judges to different outcomes in a given case.[243] Empathy for an applicant's plight – in the sense of context-sensitivity and a victim-oriented perspective – can, from this point of view, be seen as one of many elements that inform the Court's analysis. The idea of privileging the experiences and struggles of the disadvantaged over those of applicants in more advantageous positions does not, therefore, exhaust the content of the Court's approach to vulnerability: this is one of a large number of influences on the way a case is decided, and a corrective to automatism, formalism, apathy and concern about the response to a judgment.

But what, precisely, is the place of this factor in the Court's jurisprudence? In the words of Carolina Yoko Furusho, '[a]cknowledging vulnerability means stepping down from any pedestal or tower of hierarchical superiority conferred to judges and lawyers by society's institutions'.[244] In other words, the concept provokes empathy and allows the user to transcend 'it-could-have-been-me'-style reasoning, which lends itself to bias and assumptions concerning the 'deservedness' of suffering, and therefore does not guarantee effective protection of the rights of the marginalised.[245] Such reasoning ties into the just-world fallacy, which is the belief that one's environment is just, and therefore that each individual person's fate is deserved; this can lead to victim-blaming.[246]

In this sense, empathy is a way of describing the decauterisation of the other – cauterisation meaning the comprehensive exclusion of the other by legal, philosophical and political rights thinking.[247] Cauterisation brands others as inferior and rightless and deadens one's feelings for the suffering of the other.[248] The development of empathy represents a way for judges to break through this cognitive bias. It allows judges to restore the other's voice and to respond concretely to the other in order to affirm his or her life, dignity, rights and agency.[249]

[241] Joanna Pétin, 'Exploring the Role of Vulnerability in Immigration Detention' (2016) 35 *Refugee Survey Quarterly* 91–108, 97.
[242] Posner (n 182).
[243] Ibid, 13–14.
[244] Furusho Carolina Yoko, in an unpublished paper on file with the author.
[245] Hein FM Lodewijkx, Erik W de Kwaadsteniet and A Nijstad Bernard, 'That Could Be Me (or Not): Senseless Violence and the Role of Deservingness, Victim Ethnicity, Person Identification, and Position Identification' (2005) 35(7) *Journal of Applied Social Psychology* 1361–83, *passim*.
[246] Ibid, 1364.
[247] Simmons William Paul, *Human Rights Law and the Marginalized Other* (CUP, 2011), 10–13.
[248] Ibid, 11.
[249] Ibid.

Decauterising the other is particularly important in the context of Article 3, as dehumanisation and otherisation can be at the root of ill-treatment.[250] The Court's vulnerability jurisprudence allows the Strasbourg judges, by seeking to understand the experience of the affected applicants, to reverse these processes and to reincorporate affected persons into the rights dialogue. In fact, the traits recognised by the Court as engendering vulnerability are largely also those that facilitate dehumanisation and otherisation. The prison context, for example, is one that frequently leads those in a position of authority to see inmates as less than fully human.[251] Disability and mental illness can have a similar effect. Dehumanisation is also facilitated by surface differences between the self and the other, such as differences in culture, skin colour and language, or by an other perceived as threatening, such as the influx of migrants who pose a supposed risk to economic wellbeing and cultural integrity.[252]

In this context, vulnerability-as-empathy is a tool for rediscovering the humanity and individuality of applicants. In addition, judicial empathy may be a way to relativise the importance of extraneous considerations that would otherwise sway judges. Concretely, for example, focusing on the experience of the applicant may allow the Court to shift its focus away from inhibiting factors such as the anticipated response of Member States and the cost of its rulings for states' coffers, and soften the fear of opening the floodgates to an influx of applications. The Court walks a line in this sense. While it depends on states' support and must issue judgments that render rights practical and effective, meaning that considerations of states' costs and practicability do enter into play in some regard, it should not lose sight of the fact that Article 3 is an absolute right, and thus does not leave room for considerations about the preferences of government actors. Vulnerability understood as an expression of empathy can help to rebalance this equation by underscoring the importance of what is at stake in the individual case.

iii. Designing an Empathetic Approach to Vulnerability

For present purposes, the importance of empathy lies in the fact that it may lead judges to formulate criteria and an approach to adjudication that leave room – in a standardised, consistent fashion – for considering what applicants have actually experienced. In other words, it is not about bending the rules for particularly pitied applicants, but about formulating the rules in such a way that the actual experiences – fear, humiliation, helplessness, exclusion, dependency and suffering – of applicant individuals are able to enter into play in a significant way when judges

[250] Costanzo Mark A and Gerrity Ellen, 'The Effects and Effectiveness of Using Torture as an Interrogation Device: Using Research to Inform the Policy Debate' (2009) 3(1) *Social Issues and Policy Review* 179–210, especially 196–97.

[251] Ibid, 197.

[252] Ibid, 196–97.

are deciding a case. This has multiple benefits, not least that it bolsters applicants' perception of having been treated fairly, and thus of procedural justice.[253] Thus, while empathy is not an end in and of itself, it may be of significant importance in fostering a judicial culture of understanding that allows individuals to voice their complaints and issues and really be heard.

In this sense, the identification of vulnerable groups and individuals – ie the recognition that some individuals are more exposed to ill-treatment than others – provides a significant first step. Vulnerability reasoning must strike a balance between two opposing poles, namely between the universality of rights and the diversity that requires special attention for certain situations. In other words, vulnerability should not mean disregarding the fear, humiliation, helplessness, dependency or suffering of individuals who do not fall into pre-set categories. Neither can vulnerability automatically tip Strasbourg's scales in an applicant's favour in a given case: the Court's jurisprudence must maintain its respect for the principles of fairness, impartiality and coherence, which means that there can be no automatic trumps in its examination of an alleged violation of Article 3. Furthermore, the fact that an individual displays a trait that engenders vulnerability does not, in and of itself, encapsulate that individual's entire life experience, and the Court – and domestic actors – should heed the risk of essentialising the experiences of all vulnerable individuals or a subset thereof into one, and should be wary of creating additional stigma of these often already stigmatised groups. Likewise, emphasising the inability of vulnerable applicants to use and understand their rights may lead to a paternalistic result that disregards the existing capabilities of these individuals.[254]

If indeed 'the Western body is constituted through a fear of lack and loss', as one author has argued,[255] and we experience our embodiment as a flesh among flesh, then given our cognitive limitations empathetic judging may simply mean transposing one's fear of catastrophe on the other. Doing so robs the other of the opportunity to be heard and understood, in a manner that negates diversity and, in its end result, is akin to cauterisation. Ultimately, we need both universal and particular vulnerability: it is necessary to understand that while we are all vulnerable to lack, loss, and suffering, we are differently vulnerable to these calamities given our different identities, backgrounds, personalities, cultures, traits and situations. It is necessary to explain to those immunised by power that their privilege only masks their vulnerable flesh, and to counteract the effects of disadvantage

[253] See Lind E Allan and R Tyler Tom, *The Social Psychology of Procedural Justice* (Springer US, 1988); Eva Brems and Laurens Lavrysen, 'Procedural Justice in Human Rights Adjudication: The European Court of Human Rights' (2013) 35(1) *Human Rights Quarterly* 176–200, 180–82.

[254] See Peroni and Timmer (n 57), 1072–73, discussing *D.H. and Others v Czech Republic* App no 57325/00, Judgment (GC) of 13 November 2007, Reports 2007-IV, Dissenting Opinion of Judge Borrego Borrego, para 14.

[255] Lara Merlin, 'Perverse Ethics: The Body, Gender and Intersubjectivity' (2003) 4(2) *Feminist Theory* 165–78, 165–67.

where it impacts individual dignity and equal access to rights protection. Emphasis of common vulnerability on its own does not provide adequate recognition of the diversity of human experience. So, while the existence of universal European human rights protections speaks to the shared vulnerability that accompanies embodiment, focusing only on what we universally share negates diversity and exacerbates or immunises individual or group vulnerability.

IV. Interim Conclusion: Synthesising a Coherent Theory of Vulnerability

For the moral, ethical and social justice-related reasons discussed in the preceding sections, the account of a responsive State created under a vulnerability approach emerges as a strongly convincing one. As a vehicle for empathy, vulnerability provides an antidote to judicial apathy and formalism and a mechanism for context-engagement and a victim-oriented perspective. At the same time, the above has indicated a number of things that vulnerability is not, or should not be. Thus, the concept should not reduce human rights subjects to their bodily fragility, nor to a state of victimhood. It should not constitute a negation of autonomy, or represent an invitation for paternalistic interventions or coercion.[256]

Instead, a vulnerability approach should put individuals in a position to pursue their own conception of the good – in other words, it should foster their autonomy. In this regard, it is necessary to move away from the undifferentiated libertarian claim for non-intervention, which is flawed in the sense that it conflates a state that encroaches on individual rights with one that constructively engages with individuals' vulnerability in order to ensure a minimum of equal protection and equal opportunities to all.[257] That said, vulnerability is neither a panacea for all inequalities, nor a rationale for introducing a holistic welfare state. Instead, vulnerability as a trait of all human individuals serves as a force both to strengthen the foundational arguments of human rights, by highlighting the universality of both the exposure to harm and the dignity that accompany embodiment in human physical form, and by evoking empathy and solidarity through the recognition that we are all social beings inextricably embedded in complex relationships of need and care. Vulnerability in its particular form – thus, the special vulnerability that results both from certain inherent traits or from harms suffered by individuals, as well as from societal systems of misrecognition and maldistribution that disadvantage certain individuals, serves to identify and provoke a response to situations requiring particular attention in the interest of equality, dignity, and social justice.

[256] Furusho (n 86), 198–99.
[257] Ibid, 200.

8

Conclusion – A Framework for Using Vulnerability under Article 3 ECHR

Chapter Summary

This chapter connects the practical and theoretical findings that have been made about vulnerability in this volume so far. This means taking an account of vulnerability that is enriched by foundational concepts of human rights law, including human dignity, (substantive) equality and justice, as well as by ancillary ideas such as the capabilities approach and judicial empathy, and evaluating the Court's Article 3 jurisprudence on this basis. An ethical-legal imperative based on both vulnerability and respect for autonomy, as promoted through the capabilities approach, lays the groundwork for a convincing account of human rights that takes real context and various sources of marginalisation and power imbalances into account. This chapter identifies the main risks of the Court's current approach to vulnerability – its vagueness, its selectivity, and the risks of essentialising, paternalising or stereotyping vulnerable people – and seeks solutions from the theoretical perspective that was elaborated in previous chapters.

Keywords: vulnerability heuristic; sources of resilience; legitimacy; human dignity; human rights subject; legal certainty and predictability; risks of vulnerability analysis; stereotyping; judicial coherence; socio-economic rights and vulnerability.

I. Between Theory and Practice: Concerns about the Court's Approach

The Court's notion of vulnerability is autonomous, and it was introduced without explicit justification or clarification. That does not mean, however, that the Court's approach could not be improved or that it cannot learn from other approaches: after all, the Strasbourg jurisprudence is not generated in a vacuum. How, then, does the evolution of the Court's approach to vulnerability measure up to the philosophical and ethical framework surrounding that concept?

A. Universal vs Particular Vulnerability and the Problem with Vagueness

The ECtHR's former Deputy Registrar, Michael O'Boyle, has stated that the Court's vagueness on the definition of vulnerability is intentional, and that the concept should therefore be treated not as a 'doctrine', but as an intentionally open-ended approach that avoids the 'straitjacket of definition' in order to ensure future flexibility.[1] This approach sees vulnerability as an avenue for tailoring the Convention's protection to respond to real-world developments.[2]

The present volume does not share O'Boyle's level of comfort with the idea of a vague and open-ended concept. The deliberate use of a vague concept, although within the Court's power, not only impacts the predictability of its judgments and the transparency of its case law overall, but is also difficult to reconcile with ensuring equal protection of human rights.

While the Court's concept of vulnerability may originally have served as a loose hypernym for a few select marginalised groups, it has evolved to become an umbrella-style concept with various legal effects. In the Court's case law and in vulnerability theory, the concept serves as a heuristic device: it permits the user to identify hidden biases, inequalities and assumptions,[3] requires a more responsive state[4] and responds to 'the exclusions of human rights law'.[5] In the concrete context of the prohibition of torture and inhuman and degrading treatment, vulnerability permits the user to identify whether a victim was particularly impacted by a given treatment.

Martha Albertson Fineman sees vulnerability as 'detached from specific subgroups', describing it as a constant and universal part of the human condition.[6] The Court, on the other hand, singles out vulnerable populations on the basis of their disadvantage, and does not understand vulnerability as a universal human attribute or a uniting trait. In part, this may be due to the nature of the Court's role, which is, first and foremost, to determine whether human rights have been violated in an individual case before it. The Court may also consider recognition of universal human vulnerability unnecessary because this may be understood as already underlying any system of human rights protection, including the Convention. Whatever the reason, the Court's approach to vulnerability is too selective to be seen as one that explicitly addresses all of the realities of human embodiment.

[1] Michael O'Boyle, 'The Notion of "Vulnerable Groups" in the Case Law of the European Court of Human Rights', 2–4.

[2] Ibid, 4.

[3] Lourdes Peroni and Alexandra Timmer, 'Vulnerable Groups: The Promise of an Emerging Concept in European Human Rights Convention Law' (2013) 11(4) *International Journal of Constitutional Law* 1056–85, 1059, citing Martha Albertson Fineman, 'The Vulnerable Subject and the Responsive State' (2010) 60(2) *Emory Law Journal* 251–75, 266.

[4] Martha Albertson Fineman, 'The Vulnerable Subject: Anchoring Equality in the Human Condition' (2008) 20(1) *Yale Journal of Law and Feminism* 1–23, 19–22.

[5] Peroni and Timmer (n 3), 1062.

[6] Fineman (n 3), 266.

In short, the Court applies a select and flexible approach to vulnerability that allows it to choose context-sensitivity where it sees fit. In doing so, it also allows for cross-fertilisation between certain Convention articles. While there are advantages to this approach, the Court's flexibility risks muddling essential distinctions between various Convention rights. For example, when examining the Article 3 complaint made in *Z.H. v Hungary*, the Court held that interferences with the rights of vulnerable groups require 'strict scrutiny, and only very weighty reasons could justify any restriction'.[7] The Court based this on its findings in *Alajos Kiss v Hungary*, which however concerned not the application of Article 3, but the proportionality of an interference with Article 3 of Protocol No 1.[8] The problem with such cross-fertilisation is rather obvious: while states have a margin of appreciation under Article 3 of Protocol No 1, which concerns free elections, there is no such discretion under Article 3 ECHR. It is in other word impossible to justify a restriction of Article 3 rights, no matter how weighty the reasons. The Court should be aware of the risks of such muddling, which could erode the absolute nature of Article 3 far beyond the relativity that is inherent to the provision and visible, for example, in the doctrine of proportionate force.

B. The Selectivity of the Court's Vulnerability Heuristic

The Court's selective approach to vulnerability allows it to understand the mental and material realities of certain applicants and distinguish their case from others. This can trigger a number of adaptations of the Court's case law, for example justifying special state obligations under Article 3 or facilitating a relative ease of access to the Court.

A problem of some importance here is that using vulnerability to focus the Court's attention on certain applicants or groups may lead it to ignore or neglect others. Cases under Article 3 can concern the allocation of limited resources, and – where individuals considered vulnerable are given precedence in access to these resources – the theory of vulnerability as understood by the Court may adversely affect those who do not fall under that category. One example of this stems from the migration context, where the Court seems to struggle with the application of vulnerability reasoning in any general sense. For example, in *Tarakhel v Switzerland*, which concerned the return of an Afghan family to Italy under the EU's Dublin-II Regulation, the Court required assurances that the vulnerable applicants would be provided with adequate accommodation upon their return and would not be separated. Here the Court emphasised the vulnerability of the family's children,

[7] *Z.H. v Hungary* App no 28973/11, Judgment of 8 November 2012, para 29.
[8] Ibid, citing *Alajos Kiss v Hungary* App no 38832/06, Judgment of 20 May 2010, para 42.

which 'is the decisive factor and takes precedence over considerations relating to the status of illegal immigrant'.[9] Given that the Court had previously struggled with the determination of whether there was a systemic problem with reception conditions in Italy,[10] reference to the particular vulnerability of children provided a vehicle through which the Court could nonetheless find a (conditional) Convention violation here. Clearly, the Court distinguished the overall vulnerability of asylum-seekers from the 'extreme' vulnerability of children in this situation. While this judgment ensured adequate protection for the applicants concerned, it also raises questions about future applicants who are 'less' vulnerable. Given the often-limited availability of accommodation for asylum-seekers, the fact that precedence is given to particularly vulnerable individuals puts others at a heightened risk of homelessness.

It is problematic that, by applying its vulnerability approach, the Court seems to be labelling the findings made in certain cases as exceptional. The smaller the vulnerable population addressed in a given judgment, the less radical the effect of that judgment for the overall case law. This brings to mind, for example, the *D. v United Kingdom* case. There, the Court – although not using vulnerability reasoning – found that 'the very exceptional circumstances of the case' and 'compelling humanitarian considerations' meant that the removal of the applicant, who was suffering from AIDS, from the United Kingdom to St Kitts would violate Article 3.[11] This formulation was likely intended to preclude an avalanche of applications from individuals in similar circumstances. While vulnerability reasoning may have this desired effect, however, it also risks creating piecemeal and unpredictable jurisprudence. In addition, it effectively produces two groups of applicants by creating a binary distinction between the vulnerable and the invulnerable.

The existence of such a dichotomy – in other words, a rigid distinction between the vulnerable and the invulnerable – is visible when comparing the *D. v United Kingdom* with the very similar *N. v United Kingdom* judgment. *N.* has been reinterpreted recently,[12] but it nonetheless serves to illustrate this particular point. In *N.*, the Court noted that it has only the 'flexibility to prevent expulsion in very exceptional cases' to spare states the financial burdens of providing medical care to non-nationals.[13] The wording of this judgment reveals that there can be a covert balancing exercise at play in politically – or, more specifically, fiscally – delicate

[9] *Tarakhel v Switzerland* App no 29217/12, Judgment (GC) of 4 November 2014, Reports 2014 (extracts), para 99, citing *Mubilanzila Mayeka and Kaniki Mitunga v Belgium* App no 13178/03, Judgment of 12 October 2006, Reports 2006-XI, para 55.

[10] Contrast *M.S.S. v Belgium and Greece* App no 30696/09, Judgment (GC) of 21 January 2011, Reports 2011, particularly paras 249–64, and *Mohammed Hussein and Others v Netherlands and Italy* App no 27725/10, Decision of 2 April 2013, para 78.

[11] *D. v United Kingdom* App no 30240/96, Judgment of 2 May 1997, Reports 1997-III, para 54.

[12] *Paposhvili v Belgium* App no 41738/10, Judgment (GC) of 13 December 2016, Reports 2016.

[13] *N. v United Kingdom* App no 26565/05, Judgment (GC) of 27 May 2008, Reports 2008, paras. 42–44.

cases under Article 3.[14] The effect of this balancing seems to be that the interest in preventing the unwanted political or socio-economic consequences of a violation judgment is permitted to outweigh the need of the applicant concerned to obtain rights protection, except where the concerned applicant can be concerned exceptional and the consequences of the judgment thus kept in check.

While this type of balancing is, again, difficult to square with the absolute nature of Article 3,[15] a similar effect can also be observed in the context of vulnerability reasoning and Article 3. The comparison of two judgments against Malta, *Abdi Mahamud* and *Moxamed Ismaaciil and Abdirahman Warsame*, illustrates this point. These two cases, which were discussed above, are very similar on the facts. They both concern single Somali women who arrived in Malta by sea, who suffered some health-related issues and who brought the same complaints about conditions in the same migrant detention centre to Strasbourg.[16] Both cases were decided by the same composition of judges, just a few months apart. Despite the similarity of the cases, however, their outcomes were radically different. In *Abdi Mahamud*, accepting and reiterating the domestic assessment of the applicant as a vulnerable person, the Court found a violation of Article 3 ECHR.[17] As Judge Sajó noted in his separate opinion, no explanation was given for why the applicant's health made her particularly vulnerable to the combined detention conditions in question. By contrast, in *Moxamed Ismaaciil and Abdirahman Warsame*, no vulnerability and thus no violation of Article 3 was found under very similar conditions.

In this context, it appears that individual vulnerability can and does affect the Court's reasoning in applicants' favour. It could be concluded from this that, where rights are claimed by those who are arguably vulnerable, and thus distinguishable, the perceived potential impact on the underlying State interests is considered more limited and a claim under Article 3 thus more likely to succeed. Like 'exceptionality', therefore, vulnerability separates applicants into two monolithic categories made up of the vulnerable and the invulnerable. At the same time, the idea of an invulnerable human being is an oxymoron. Our physical embodiment and interaction with others in a finite physical space means that human individuals are all vulnerable and dependent.[18]

[14] See *Jalloh v Germany* App no 54810/00, Judgment [GC] of 11 July 2006, Reports 2006-IX, para 119; for more, see Hemme Battjes, 'In Search of a Fair Balance: The Absolute Character of the Prohibition of Refoulement under Article 3 ECHR Reassessed' (2009) 22(3) *Leiden Journal of International Law* 583–621.

[15] Stijn Smet, 'The "Absolute" Prohibition of Torture and Inhuman or Degrading Treatment in Article 3 ECHR: Truly a Question of Scope Only?' in Eva Brems and Janneke H Gerards (eds), *Shaping Rights in the ECHR: The Role of the European Court of Human Rights in Determining the Scope of Human Rights* (CUP, 2013) 273–93, 289.

[16] Compare *Moxamed Ismaaciil and Abdirahman Warsame v Malta* App nos 52160/13 and 52165/13, Judgment of 12 January 2016, esp paras 6–13, and *Abdi Mahamud v Malta* App no 56796/13, Judgment of 3 May 2016, paras 6–9.

[17] *Abdi Mahamud* (n 16), para 89.

[18] Fineman (n 4), 9, and Peroni and Timmer (n 3), 1058.

C. Piecemealism and the Risky Business of Vulnerability Reasoning

It would be next to impossible for the Court to comprehensively address all of the different needs and vulnerabilities and sources of resilience of all potential applicants with a general rule, not least because its judgments address particular cases and are dependent on the nature of the applications brought before it. However, it seems that the Court is more 'friendly' to some kinds of vulnerability than to others. For example, when it comes to the vulnerability stemming from detention, the Court has provided rather comprehensive guidance about states' positive and negative obligations. Of course, this is due in part to the fact that the Court has had more opportunity to refine these obligations, with cases concerning detainees being very plentiful under Article 3. In this context, the nexus to the state as the detaining authority is also more direct, which may also make a difference in the Court's willingness to impose obligations. On the other hand, regarding less straightforward issues – for example the risk of ill-treatment acceptable in expulsion cases or the often socio-economically influenced rights of Roma communities – the Court has provided much less clarity to states regarding what they must or must not do.

Beyond vagueness and the selectivity mentioned above, some authors – especially Lourdes Peroni and Alexandra Timmer – have discussed further risks associated with the Court's approach to vulnerability. They mention the risks of paternalising individuals, stigmatising or victimising them, and essentialising the experiences of many into one.[19] These dangers seem inherent in any vulnerability thesis that singles out particular individuals or groups for special protection. In order to avoid oversimplifying an applicant's circumstances, vulnerability needs to be more than a shortcut in the Court's reasoning: it must become a fleshed-out concept with real standards that are applied and tested in each individual case, and must be enhanced with an awareness of the need to bolster individual autonomy. In the particular context of Article 3, any other approach risks 'othering' vulnerable individuals. Othering, which is precisely the effect that vulnerability scholars seek to prevent by employing vulnerability theory, leads to the failure of members of the in-group to understand out-groups and to show empathy towards them; in extreme case, this leads to dehumanisation, which in turn paves the way for ill-treatment.[20] If vulnerability is to be an effective tool, it should be based on an understanding of the equal worthiness of all, and its premise should be to engage with particular setbacks that individuals face in living autonomous lives and exercising their agency.

[19] Peroni and Timmer (n 3), from 1070.

[20] Susan T Fiske, 'From Dehumanization and Objectification, to Rehumanization: Neuroimaging Studies on the Building Blocks of Empathy' (2009) 1167 *Values, Empathy, and Fairness Across Social Barriers: Annals of the New York Academy of Sciences* 31–34, 31.

An interesting case regarding the necessity of an individualised examination of vulnerability and the need to protect agency in every case is *Pretty v United Kingdom*. That case concerned a terminally ill woman who sought assurance that her husband would not be criminally prosecuted for assisting her in committing suicide. The applicant argued that the blanket domestic ban on such assistance, which aimed to protect vulnerable individuals, had exposed her to inescapable, intolerable suffering caused by her condition. Mrs Pretty argued that she was not vulnerable, and considered the government's assertion that all terminally ill and disabled individuals who contemplated suicide were vulnerable to be offensive.[21] The Court ultimately held that, in light of the Convention as a whole, particularly its Article 2, the right to life, the positive obligations under Article 3 did not cover the sanctioning of actions intended to bring about death; it thereby refused to impose a case-by-case examination of vulnerability.[22] Effectively, due to assumptions concerning the needs of vulnerable individuals, Mrs Pretty was deprived of the possibility to make an autonomous decision about the end of her life, and the state and Convention authorities deprived her of the ability to end her suffering. The pitfalls of vulnerability and the need for a case-by-case analysis become apparent when faced with individuals, like Mrs Pretty, who wish to shed the 'protections' sometimes afforded by that label.

Of course, while generalisations about the needs of applicants may not be particularly suitable for deciding individual cases, a case-by-case examination of vulnerability comes with its own risks. The above shows that the Court's jurisprudence under Article 3 can accommodate different types of vulnerability, which receive different levels of protection in its case law. As a result, the Court's vulnerability reasoning tends to appear piecemeal, selective or situational. In fact, the Court has found a violation of Article 3 in 87 per cent of the judgments in which it has employed the concept to date, indicating that perhaps vulnerability reasoning is used mainly where the Court needs to distinguish an applicant from others.[23]

Indeed, one of the main problems with the Court's approach to date – with the layers and types of vulnerability recognised – may simply be that it lacks clarity: piecemeal jurisprudence is difficult to reconcile with conceptions of equality, and may have a negative impact on the manner in which the Court's judgments are received.[24] This is problematic for reasons of legal certainty and exceptionalism.[25] If the Court – that is, a majority of judges tasked with deciding a given case – decides what it feels is intuitively 'right' for the applicant in a given case, without reaching this decision in a principled manner, it opens itself up to allegations of moral subjectivism that might detract from the universality of rights and from the

[21] *Pretty v United Kingdom* App no 2346/02, Judgment of 29 April 2002, ECHR 2002-III, paras 46, 72.

[22] Ibid, paras 55, 56 and 74.

[23] Based on the author's own research via the HUDOC database.

[24] George Letsas, *A Theory of Interpretation of the European Convention on Human Rights* (OUP, 2007), 130.

[25] *CLR on behalf of Valentin Câmpeanu v Romania* App no 47848/08, Judgment (GC) of 17 July 2014, Reports 2014, Concurring Opinion of Judge Pinto de Albuquerque, para 11.

acceptance of the Court as an institution. To borrow once again from Judge Pinto de Albuquerque, it is not enough for the Court to reach 'the right results by unconvincing, awkward means'.[26] In other words, the Court would certainly benefit from having regard to the individual circumstances in each case as well as structuring its vulnerability reasoning and applying it consistently and transparently.

D. A Roadmap for the Way Forward

In short, the Court's approach to vulnerability as it stands today does not necessarily depart from the ideal of the autonomous liberal subject. At the same time, it does not necessarily *preclude* such a departure by means of the additional recognition of universal human vulnerability. As exemplified by vulnerability in the detention context – where the Court has recognised both the general vulnerability of all detainees by virtue of detention, as well was the particular vulnerability of some detainees by virtue of, for example, a disability – the Court is willing to employ different incarnations and layers of the concept that approximate an implicit understanding of intersectionality.

The need for the Court to mould its approach to vulnerability into coherent, transparent reasoning that engages with the individual agency and dignity of every applicant is evident. At the same time, it could be argued that employing vulnerability reasoning in every single case under Article 3 is not desirable, because it will inevitably lead the Court to declare that some applicants are *not* vulnerable. Such a finding reinforces the liberal ideal of the independent legal subject and may ultimately also prove detrimental to the case of the particular applicant concerned.[27] However, that risk can be avoided if vulnerability is integrated into the Article 3 test so as to form one of several examinatory steps, and not a value judgment or a manner of determining the merit of the case as a whole. In this vein, it is essential to recognise that special consideration for an applicant's vulnerability is necessary for ensuring substantive equality.

The Court's reasoning could benefit from separating vulnerability into the grounds from which it stems. To a certain extent, the Court already determines whether an individual is dependent, or under the sole authority of the state, or a member of a group with a history of discrimination, and so on. Making such a determination in every case concerning a potentially vulnerable individual – or simply in every case – would mean that the Court could move away from using vulnerability as an argumentative shortcut, and develop it into a concept with substance and independent meaning. A willingness to engage explicitly with the factors that generate vulnerability in a particular case, and with the individual

[26] Ibid, para 16.

[27] *Miah v United Kingdom* App no 53080/07, Decision of 27 April 2010, para 14, and *Kostjučenkovs v Latvia* App no 19826/04, Decision of 8 March 2011, para 49.

circumstances of an applicant overall, would need to include engagement with the intersection of various grounds for vulnerability.

In short, the argument made here is that the Court's reasoning should weigh all of the factors of relevance, including not only those that concern the applicant's vulnerability but also those that support vulnerability's complement, namely the applicant's resilience.[28] Resilience to violations of Article 3 can take a multitude of forms, as will be explored below. The extent to which these factors actually make an individual applicant resilient to a given instance of ill-treatment will depend on the context, and must be determined in each individual case. Balancing sources of vulnerability and resilience allows for a more responsive and less harmful approach than one that juxtaposes monolithically vulnerable and monolithically non-vulnerable applicants against each other.

II. Bringing Coherence to the Court's Vulnerability Heuristic

Vulnerability before the Court is varied but selective. It has links to universal concepts like dignity and autonomy, and it can help to ensure substantive equality among applicants. But the Court's approach to the concept also lacks foreseeability. Designing a coherent approach to vulnerability means engaging with the concept as such. This requires an honest look at its effects, which here does not mean the various ways in which vulnerability affects the procedural and substantive treatment of a case,[29] but instead requires a discussion of the controversial socio-economic entitlements generated by the Convention. The Court's current approach to vulnerability can be understood as a strategy for holding back in this regard when it comes to all applicants who are not described as particularly vulnerable. However, supposed invulnerability can be harmful to affected applicants. A less damaging way of framing vulnerability would be as one part of a spectrum between vulnerability and resilience, on which all applicants fall. This, in turn, requires an examination of what resilience means.

A. Between the Protection of Dignity and a Welfare State

In his dissenting opinion in *M.S.S.*, former Judge Sajó argued that the majority's reliance on vulnerability reasoning approximated the introduction of a welfare state.[30] In general, of course, the ECHR – its Protocol No 1, with its rights to property and to education, and its Protocol No 12, including a non-accessory

[28] On resilience, see Fineman (n 4), 13–15; see also Peroni and Timmer (n 3), 1074.
[29] See chapter four of this volume.
[30] *M.S.S.* (n 10), Partly Concurring and Partly Dissenting Opinion of Judge Sajó.

prohibition of discrimination, excepted – emphasises civil and political rights over economic, social and cultural ones. However, the Court's jurisprudence has increasingly shown that the Convention can successfully be invoked in cases fitting the latter category. This includes cases on access to a court for economically disadvantaged individuals,[31] housing rights,[32] health and environmental matters[33] and questions of social security.[34] In general terms, the Court provides protection of such rights where this a precondition of respect for Convention rights, particularly Article 8 ECHR. Under Article 3 ECHR, too, some socio-economic elements have found their way into the case law. One main example of this is, of course, the *M.S.S.* case, where the Grand Chamber held Greece responsible under Article 3 for failing to provide shelter and decent living conditions to the applicant, a vulnerable asylum-seeker who was left homeless by the state's inaction.[35]

Elements of the welfare state already exist under the auspices of the Convention, to say nothing of the domestic legal systems of its Member States. However, while Judge Sajó was not wrong about the fact that the majority's judgment in *M.S.S.* introduced or at least expanded certain welfare obligations, the Court has proven exceedingly reluctant to recognise socio-economic obligations on the part of states in general terms.[36] In fact, the few clear obligations on states under Articles 2 and 3 regarding the provision of food, shelter, medical care, and other goods are generally premised on the idea that the persons concerned are particularly vulnerable given their dependence on the state, be it because they are in detention, in a social care home or seeking asylum.[37] Under Article 8, too, states have a wide margin of appreciation regarding socio-economic questions,[38] and there is no right to access a specific form of housing;[39] nor a general obligation to house the homeless.[40]

[31] Françoise Tulkens, 'The European Convention on Human Rights and the Economic Crisis: The Issue of Poverty' EUI Working Paper AEL 2013/8 (European University Institute, Academy of European Law 2013), http://cadmus.eui.eu/bitstream/handle/1814/28099/AEL_2013_08.pdf?sequence=1, 7, citing *Stankov v Bulgaria* App no 68490/01, Judgment of 12 July 2007, Reports 2001-IX, para 67.

[32] *Buckland v United Kingdom* App no 40060/08, Judgment of 18 September 2012, paras 65, 70.

[33] *Di Sarno and Others v Italy* App no 30765/08, Judgment of 10 January 2012.

[34] *Czaja v Poland* App no 5744/05, Judgment of 2 October 2012, para 66. In all, see Ingrid Leijten, *Core Socio-Economic Rights and the European Court of Human Rights* (CUP, 2018).

[35] *M.S.S.* (n 10), para 263.

[36] See, for example, *Van Volsem v Belgium* App no 14641/89, Decision of 9 May 1990, para 1; *Jazvinsky v Slovak Republic* App nos 33088/96 …, Decision of 7 September 2000; contrast with *Pancenko v Latvia* App no 40772/98, Decision of 28 October 1999, para 2. In all, see Liam Thornton, 'The European Convention on Human Rights: A Socio-Economic Rights Charter?', Suzanne Egan, Liam Thornton and Judy Walsh (eds), *Ireland and the European Convention on Human Rights: 60 Years and Beyond* (Bloomsbury, 2014), 236–38.

[37] See *Nencheva and Others v Bulgaria* App no 48609/06, Judgment of 18 June 2013 (concerning the death by neglect of children in a care home), paras 117–39; *M.S.S.* (n 10), paras 221–22, 232–33, 262–63 (concerning the conditions under which an asylum-seeker was forced to live); *Anguelova v Bulgaria* App no 38361/97, Judgment of 13 June 2002, Reports 2002-IV, paras 125–31 (concerning the delayed provision of medical care to an injured detainee, resulting in death); Thornton (n 36), 236–38.

[38] *McDonald v United Kingdom* App no 4241/12, Judgment of 20 May 2014, para 54.

[39] *Burton v United Kingdom* App no 31600/96, Decision (Commission) of 10 September 1996, para 2.

[40] *O'Rourke v United Kingdom* App no 39022/97, Decision of 26 June 2001.

While the Convention may guarantee socio-economic rights to some limited extent where they are interdependent with these and other provisions, this represents an exceedingly bare-bones framework of socio-economic obligations.[41]

In other words, the Court's jurisprudence is a far cry from creating an all-inclusive welfare state.[42] Instead, the Court is using Article 3, along with other provisions of the Convention, to require rudimentary socio-economic protections for certain categories of people. The Court is slow to do this, however: while it has for example been recognised elsewhere that extreme poverty represents a deprivation of both dignity and autonomy, and prevents individuals from effectively enjoying their human rights,[43] the Court's willingness to address this issue has been slow, and focused on removing barriers to individual subsistence instead of on providing resources.[44]

At the same time, the Court's case law under Article 3 has recognised that the failure to provide certain socio-economic assets to persons dependent on the state, such as detainees and asylum-seekers without a work permit, places these individuals in situations of suffering, humiliation and frustration that violate the Convention. It also appears that suffering associated with extremes of deprivation may, in and of itself, fall under Article 3; however, the threshold required in this regard seems to be a very high one.[45]

To a rather basic and limited but still non-negligible extent, therefore, socio-economic obligations are part and parcel of Article 3 ECHR. Building upon these arguments, it possible to imagine an interpretation of Article 3 that vindicates the rights of those who live in abject poverty. Poverty is both a source of discrimination and stigma, and a prime example of a lack of sources of resilience, as will be explored below. Given the fact that it often intersects with other grounds for marginalisation, poverty can thus be seen as both a cause and as an effect of vulnerability.[46]

The Court's current interpretation of the Convention is a far cry from requiring the large-scale redistribution of wealth from rich to poor. At the same time, and without underestimating the effect of material poverty, there may be other ways to combat some of the effects at play. So, for example, a group of Strasbourg judges have remarked that while the Convention does not protect a 'right not to be poor', situations of extreme poverty may breach the Convention.[47] Thus, poverty-related

[41] See PACE Recommendation 1415(1999) of 23 June 1999 on an Additional Protocol to the European Convention on Human Rights Concerning Fundamental Social Rights, para 13.

[42] *Salah Sheekh v Netherlands* App no 1948/04, Judgment of 11 January 2007, para 141; *Sarmina and Sarmin v Russia* App no 58830/00, Decision of 22 November 2005.

[43] European Committee of Social Rights, 'Statement of Interpretation on the Rights of Refugees under the European Social Charter', 5 October 2015, 6, para 10.

[44] *Lacatus v Switzerland* App no 14065/15, Judgment of 19 January 2021.

[45] *Pancenko* (n 36), para 2.

[46] Sandra Fredman, 'The Potential and Limits of an Equal Rights Paradigm in Addressing Poverty' (2011) 22(3) *Stellenbosch Law Review* 566–90, 567.

[47] Julia Laffranque, Guido Raimondi, Ledi Bianku, Angelika Nußberger and Linos-Alexander Sicilianos, 'Implementing the European Convention on Human Rights in Times of Economic Crisis',

vulnerability is not only about socio-economic entitlements. It can indeed be about protecting vulnerable individuals from discrimination, stigma, a lack of access to rights and varieties of ill-treatment.

In addition, as the effects of poverty can very well reach the threshold of severity required under Article 3, it would be problematic for the Court to preclude such claims. In the socio-economic context, vulnerability is often used to create a special nexus between an individual and the state, or to limit the scope of a particular finding to keep the Registry's floodgates closed. While this reluctance is understandable to some degree given the caseload crisis and the Court's political environment, there is no reason why Article 3 could not create socio-economic obligations regarding applicants living in abject conditions. If the provision can apply to the suffering caused by negligent automobile accidents[48] and to relatively minor physical injuries[49] caused by private individuals, then there is conceptually no reason why the absence of a special nexus of dependency on the state should mean that it cannot also apply here. In this regard, a more detailed and theoretically informed understanding of vulnerability may help the Court to identify those who are effectively deprived of their dignity and agency through poverty, and thereby allow it to maintain a practicable threshold of severity.

B. Emphasising Resilience

Like vulnerability, resilience – its counterpoint – is a term in common use. This means that the idea of resilience crops up in contexts as disparate as self-help books and resources about natural disasters.[50] It has been argued that many of these narratives are problematic because they blame a person's misfortune, marginalisation, or exclusion not on the underlying socio-political systems that create this situation, but on an affected person's lack of resilience. In the context of racial tensions in the United States, this has meant that 'demands for resilience have become a cleverly coded way to shame those speaking out against injustices'.[51]

For present purposes, resilience has a specific meaning: it is the counterpoint to vulnerability, and thus describes the assets that protect human individuals from harms associated with vulnerability. But what, precisely, is resilience? As per Martha Albertson Fineman's description, resilience 'comes from having some

Seminar Background Paper (25 January 2013), www.echr.coe.int/Documents/Seminar_background_paper_2013_ENG.pdf, 1.

[48] *Kraulaidis v Lithuania* App no 76805/11, Judgment of 8 November 2016, especially the Concurring Opinion of Judges Sajó, Tsotsoria, Wojtyczek and Kucsko-Stadlmayer, paras 2, 7.

[49] See *İbrahim Demirtaş v Turkey* App no 25018/10, Judgment of 28 October 2014, where an irate villager punched an official, causing a jaw fracture, paras 6 and 8. See also the Joint Dissenting Opinion of Judges Sajó and Keller, especially para 14.

[50] Sehgal Parul, 'The Profound Emptiness of "Resilience"' *New York Times Magazine* (1 December 2015).

[51] Ibid.

means with which to address and confront misfortune'.[52] Resilience is provided by the interplay of systems and institutions that help in 'lessening, ameliorating, and compensating for vulnerability'.[53] Separately and together, these institutions provide vulnerable individuals with 'assets': 'advantages, coping mechanisms, or resources that cushion us when we are facing misfortune, disaster, and violence'.[54]

Fineman identifies five types of resources that build resilience: physical, ecological or environmental, human, social and existential.[55] Physical assets are the material things that ensure physical well-being, such as shelter, food, and financial capital. Human assets are the abilities that make it easier to work and accumulate resources; they include education, knowledge and experience. Social assets are the social bonds that provide support, particularly those provided by a family, a community or an organisation to which one belongs. Ecological assets allow us to access a hospitable environment and clean water and air. Existential assets are systems of belief, religion, culture, art or politics that 'help us to understand our place within the world and allow us to see meaning and beauty in our existence'.[56]

The function of resilience is in fact much the same as that of vulnerability – it helps to paint a realistic picture of individual exposure to degradation, suffering and ill-treatment, as well as the degree of impact that this exposure has on people and their ability to prevent or counter it. Effectively empowering vulnerable individuals means responding to the inadequacy of assets and resources where these deprive them of the capability to enjoy and demand respect for Convention rights.

Resilience is, in fact, comparable to the capabilities discussed in the previous chapter.[57] A capabilities approach ensures that all human individuals enjoy a certain threshold of basic capabilities that allows them to live lives of autonomy and dignity. In the same way, ensuring that human individuals enjoy certain assets that confer resilience makes them able to exercise their rights and safeguards their dignity and autonomy.

The Court has never explicitly referred to resilience in its case law. However, the concept is to some degree implicit in the Court's analysis: the Court does not consider vulnerability in all cases, and when it does so, applicants are not always found vulnerable. When the Court fails to draw legal consequences from the vulnerability of an otherwise vulnerable applicant, or even where it finds that an applicant is not vulnerable, the Court is thus implicitly finding that vulnerability can be neutralised by other factors. These are covert resilience considerations.

In this regard, it must be made absolutely clear that none of the resources that promote resilience constitute a fail-safe against vulnerability.[58] Indeed,

[52] Fineman (n 3), 269.
[53] Fineman (n 4), 13.
[54] Ibid.
[55] Fineman (n 3), 270.
[56] Ibid, 271–72.
[57] Martha C Nussbaum, *Creating Capabilities: The Human Development Approach* (Belknap Press, 2011), 20.
[58] Fineman (n 3), 273.

emphasising resilience, where the wrong aspects are emphasised, also has its own risks. Indeed, an overemphasis of certain aspects that are understood as providing resilience can transfer responsibility for vulnerability to an applicant, unfairly 'privatising' it, or negate that vulnerability altogether. These problems are highlighted by expulsion cases concerning applicants who risk persecution or violence because of their sexual orientation if returned to their home countries. In these contexts, the Court has on occasion emphasised applicants' ability to be 'discreet'.[59] Similarly, the Court may find that women do not face a sufficiently substantiated risk of gender-related ill-treatment if returned because they have access to 'male protection networks'[60] or have received a progressive education.[61] A similar style of argumentation is visible where the Court finds that mentally ill persons could access necessary medications in their home state, without taking into account the fact that these may be financially unobtainable.[62]

Given this background, it becomes urgently necessary to understand that resilience does not necessarily exclude vulnerability, and vice versa. There are no invulnerable human individuals, and it is necessary to consider all of an individual's sources of resilience and vulnerability in determining whether a given treatment is effectively compatible with their dignity and agency or, for example, whether he or she enjoys the capability to bring a complaint in Strasbourg. To create a system that pigeon-holes applicants is to negate the autonomy of the vulnerable and the vulnerability of those deemed autonomous. It thus assumes that those presumed invulnerable – those, thus, who fit the liberal archetype – do not need the protection of the state; liberalism's others, on the other hand, receive state protection at the price of their agency and recognition of their resilience. The resulting bifurcation is obviously artificial. This demands a degree of caution or sensitivity from the Court so that it does not simply negate vulnerability with resilience-related considerations, or vice versa.

C. A Working Typology of the Sources of Resilience

If an individual's location within socio-political systems of privilege and power may compensate for or aggravate vulnerability,[63] we can begin to identify sources of resilience. In this regard, an analysis such as the present one walks a fine line. On the one hand, any attempt to list the sources of resilience is certain to be

[59] *M.E. v Sweden* App no 71398/12, Judgment of 26 June 2014, para 88. The case was later referred to the Grand Chamber, which struck the complaint out of its list without amending this finding (*M.E. v Sweden* App no 71398/12, Judgment (GC) of 8 April 2015 (Struck out of the List)).

[60] *R.H. v Sweden* App no 4601/14, Judgment of 10 September 2015, para 73.

[61] *Sow v Belgium* App no 27081/13, Judgment of 19 January 2016, para 56.

[62] *F.N. v United Kingdom* App no 3202/09, Decision of 17 September 2013, para 31.

[63] Fineman (n 4), 15–16.

incomplete, and there is a risk of overemphasising resilience in the individual case, with the effect of failing to protect vulnerable individuals. On the other hand, failing to engage with actual sources of resilience largely pre-empts any further discussion, does not address the overemphasis of certain sources of resilience in the Court's case law today, and also trivialises the abilities of those considered particularly vulnerable.[64] In addition, it is only possible to foster resilience if it is clear what is being talked about. The following will accordingly create a typology of resilience, which – although not claiming to be complete – should provide some further insight into resilience as a counterpoint to vulnerability.

A focus on the sources of resilience, as well as vulnerability, provides a much more complete picture of an individual's situation than looking solely at vulnerability. Such a picture is necessary given that, especially from an intersectional perspective, there will always be some members of a vulnerable group who are more vulnerable than others. Instead of breaking vulnerability down into endless, increasingly specific sub-categories, what is needed is a dynamic approach that balances sources of vulnerability with sources of resilience.

Given that resilience is a counterpoint to vulnerability, the following will focus on three main aspects of the latter: vulnerability as preventing individuals from claiming their rights, vulnerability through dependency, and vulnerability through marginalisation. This is different from the three types of resilience used by Martha Albertson Fineman, who emphasised physical, human and social assets.[65] Though the structure chosen differs from Fineman's, so as to make it more practically relevant to the Court's analysis, all three of Fineman's types of assets will be embedded within it.

Before turning to that typology, it is essential to recall the argument made above regarding the dangers of 'privatising' or negating vulnerability. It should be recalled, in this regard, that vulnerability is part and parcel of the human condition; as a result, no source of resilience constitutes a fail-safe or antidote against it.[66] An overemphasis of certain sources of resilience can deprive applicants of adequate protection of their rights. Examples of this can be found in the expulsion context, as argued above, where the safety of LGBTQ+ applicants may be left to their own 'discretion',[67] and that of female applicants to their male support networks[68] or their own mental faculties as developed by a progressive education.[69] In addition, it is necessary to understand resilience as a product not (only) of one's own adaptability but also of one's environment; otherwise, one moves towards the idea that 'some people simply do not have what it takes to overcome adversity, or towards

[64] Peroni and Timmer (n 3), 1074.

[65] Ibid, 14, referring to Kirby Peadar, *Vulnerability and Violence: The Impact of Globalization* (Pluto Press, 2006) 55.

[66] Fineman (n 3), 273.

[67] *M.E.* (n 59), para 88. On referral, the case was struck out by the Grand Chamber (see n 59).

[68] *R.H.* (n 60), para 73.

[69] *Sow* (n 61), para 56.

blaming those who do not possess the characteristics needed'.[70] Arguments about an applicant's resilience should thus be made with caution, as – like vulnerability – resilience is accompanied with its own series of risks.

i. Resilience as the Ability to Successfully Claim One's Rights

Multiple sources of resilience can counteract obstacles that prevent individuals from claiming their rights. Based on the findings of vulnerability made by the Court so far, as well as the relevant literature,[71] it is possible to provide examples of assets that allow vulnerable applicants to bring a timely complaint, communicate their claims, and be heard.

a. Institutional Support

One example in this context is institutional support. This could be provided by an NGO or a state instance, but also through legal aid, community support and collective action. The assets conferred by such actors can be manifold, and include support in accessing relevant information about available mechanisms and remedies, counselling, and assistance in formulating a complaint. As proceedings to claim rights generally take place before state instances, the willingness of these instances to hear, engage with and empower an individual's claims is one of the main sources of resilience to be noted here. In this regard, for example, the provision of specialised psychological support and assessment can place victims of traumatic crimes such as rape in a better position to make sure that their claims are heard.[72] In this regard, the Court has previously faulted states for failing to place alleged victims of rape in a position that would allow them to feel comfortable enough to provide a detailed account of events.[73]

One example here is the legal aid offered to needy applicants by the ECtHR, although these amounts are generally very small.[74] It is also interesting to consider an institution created in England and Wales, where an 'appropriate adult' is

[70] Marygold Walsh-Dilley, Wendy Wolford and James McCarthy, 'Rights for Resilience: Bringing Power, Rights and Agency into the Resilience Framework' Conceptual Framework (Atkinson Center for a Sustainable Future, 2013), 20.

[71] Including both Martha Albertson Fineman's work (Fineman (n 4), 15–16) and the work of other scholars cited above, including Walsh-Dilley Marygold et al (n 70).

[72] *M.G.C. v Romania* App no 61495/11, Judgment of 15 March 2016, paras 70–75.

[73] *G.U. v Turkey* App no 16143/10, Judgment of 18 October 2016, para 71.

[74] Rules of the ECtHR of 1 January 2020, rr 105–10, www.echr.coe.int/documents/rules_court_eng.pdf, referring to 'legal-aid scales'; in practice, the Court's contributions seem to max out at 850 EUR (*Đorđević v Croatia* App no 41526/10, Judgment of 24 July 2012, Reports 2012, para 175). However, there are exceptions (see *Roche v United Kingdom* App no 32555/96, Judgment (GC) of 19 October 2005, Reports 2005-X, para 185, where an applicant received EUR 3,228.72 in legal aid from the Council of Europe in complex proceedings).

assigned to vulnerable adults and minors to provide support during criminal interrogations.[75] Conceivably, appropriate adults could be specially trained legal counsel, social workers, or, in the case of a juvenile, his or her parents.[76] The appropriate adult scheme has its own problems, including the dearth of available trained volunteers, a lack of awareness in appropriate adults about the nature and extent of their role, and fears that the support of an appropriate adult will curtail some forms of abuse but not provide real access to rights.[77] However, even though the implementation of an appropriate adult scheme raises these and other concerns, the idea of assigning an independent observer to advocate for the rights of vulnerable suspects during police interrogations is a relevant example here.

In particular, the appropriate adult scheme is based on the idea that the presence of a third party can moderate othering,[78] which in turn represents an underlying cause of ill-treatment. Here, the Court could even be seen as the mediating third party. And indeed, through well-reasoned judgments, the Court help identify and provide support for sources of vulnerability. Of course, this cannot be a task for the Court alone, not least because proceedings before the Court usually come many years after a given event, and many cases will never make it that far.

Nonetheless, given that the Council of Europe, including the Court, sets standards that are greatly influential in the area of protecting the vulnerable, it can, itself, provide a resilience-conveying asset by engaging directly with vulnerable applicants and their representatives and designing empowering standards with their participation. In this regard, third-party interventions before the Court perform an important task. Yet, some vulnerable groups or individuals may be diffuse and lack a lobby, and there may thus be decreased awareness about their concrete vulnerabilities. Their voices could be strengthened, for example, through the work of the Council of Europe Commissioner for Human Rights. In particular, the former Commissioner was extensively involved in two of the Court's most influential vulnerability judgments under Article 3 to date, *M.S.S.* and *Valentin Câmpeanu*.[79] Having an advocate like the Commissioner within the Council of Europe is a potentially very powerful resilience-conveying asset.

b. Individual Assets

A number of other assets increase individuals' ability to claim their rights. These range from the education and literacy of the person concerned, including legal education, to their language skills and residence status. In this last regard, the

[75] Harriet Pierpoint, 'Taking the Protection of Vulnerable Suspects Seriously: Putting "Appropriate Adults" through their PACES' (2000) 12(3) *Practice* 49–60.

[76] Ibid, 50.

[77] Ibid, 52, 54.

[78] Helene Moglen and Sheila Namir, 'War and the Dis-Eases of Othering' (2006) 3(2) *International Journal of Applied Psychoanalytic Studies* 206–18, 212, 215–18.

[79] *M.S.S.* (n 10), para 87; *CLR on behalf of Valentin Câmpeanu* (n 25), paras 92–93 and 104–14.

deprivation of all legal status facing certain migrants, which drives them to the margins of society, can be understood as a state-imposed source of vulnerability.[80] It could also be relevant to consider whether someone enjoys socio-economic security and a degree of mental health and intellectual capacity. In this vein, Lourdes Peroni and Alexandra Timmer have pointed out that when Judge Sajó, in his separate opinion in *M.S.S.*, noted that the applicant 'had money and speaks English', he was identifying sources of resilience that tempered the applicant's vulnerability.[81]

Discussing these traits here provides another opportunity to problematise them. In other words, it bears reiteration that none of these individual-based assets necessarily compensate for vulnerability: an individualised assessment of all relevant factors is necessary in each case. Not only do individual abilities evolve throughout life, but none of these traits represents a fail-safe protection against vulnerability or ill-treatment. Thus, it is often difficult to follow the Court's argumentation and understand precisely how, for example, a woman's progressive education can protect her against female genital mutilation,[82] or how a drug addict's youth and male gender can protect him against the marginalisation that accompanies his addiction.[83]

ii. Resilience as a Counterweight to Dependency

The case law explored in this volume has shown that an individual or group may be vulnerable due to their increased exposure to ill-treatment. This type of vulnerability is often associated with dependency, including minor age, disability, or deprivation of liberty. Individuals in such situations may face difficulties in claiming their rights. They may also be more exposed to ill-treatment to begin with, given their situation and the ease with which it can be abused. In this regard, a number of assets can foster resilience.

First of all, fostering resilience in dependent individuals means understanding the ways in which their relationships of care and dependency work. This requires an awareness that resilience is not necessarily innate, but produced. It also means understanding that relationships of care and dependency create a potential for abuse, which therefore require strong safeguards. Lastly, it means designing interventions that 'aim to restore, wherever possible, the vulnerable person's sense of herself as an autonomous agent'.[84]

[80] Sara Iglesias Sánchez, 'Irregular Migrants in Europe: Deprivation of Status as a Type of State-Imposed Vulnerability' in Francesca Ippolito and Sara Iglesias Sánchez (eds), *Protecting Vulnerable Groups: The European Human Rights Framework* (Hart, 2015) 429–51, 430–31.

[81] Peroni and Timmer (n 3), 1074, referring to *M.S.S.* (n 10), Partly Concurring and Partly Dissenting Opinion of Judge Sajó, fn 8.

[82] *Sow* (n 61), para 56.

[83] *Miah* (n 27), para 14.

[84] Catriona Mackenzie, 'The Importance of Relational Autonomy and Capabilities for an Ethics of Vulnerability', in Catriona Mackenzie, Wendy Rogers and Susan Dodds (eds), *Vulnerability: New Essays in Ethics and Feminist Philosophy* (OUP, 2014) 33–59, 46.

There is certainly a link between autonomy or agency and resilience.[85] However, in some situations, for example in the detention context, the institutional environment means that vulnerable individuals can make very few meaningful choices. In contexts of severe intellectual disability, too, autonomy and agency as sources of resilience are impacted. This does not mean, however, that agency and autonomy should not be protected and fostered to the largest possible degree in these and all contexts. Indeed, it is precisely because individuals in these situations are to some extent deprived of this major source of resilience that intense scrutiny and strict safeguards are required.

Another source of resilience could lie in the possibility of accessing and obtaining social support – both in the sense of being able to contact and, if necessary, alarm outside actors, and in the sense of obtaining access to information about what one's rights and options are.[86] In this regard, visibility can be key: for example, a detainee who is particularly affluent or influential may be able to draw more attention to poor detention conditions. The same context – that of detention – also serves to clarify, however, that not all social support can be considered a source of resilience. Indeed, forcing disabled inmates to rely on the kindness of their cellmates for assistance is considered a violation of Article 3 ECHR by the Court, given the humiliation and sense of vulnerability that it entails.[87]

iii. Resilience as a Corrective for Misrecognition

Of course, some individuals are vulnerable to ill-treatment not because they are dependent, but because they belong to a group that suffers from a history of discrimination, exclusion or invisibility – an effect that has been termed 'misrecognition', and is akin to othering.[88] Here this could apply not only to the vulnerable ethnic Uzbeks who risk torture if returned from Russia to Kyrgyzstan,[89] but also to the vulnerable groups made up of persons living with HIV/AIDS,[90] asylum-seekers,[91] the Roma community,[92] and people with psycho-social disabilities.[93]

[85] Martha Albertson Fineman, 'Elderly as Vulnerable: Rethinking the Nature of Individual and Societal Responsibility' (2012) 20(2) *Elder Law Journal* 71–111, 110.

[86] MacKenzie (n 84), 46.

[87] *Kaprykowski v Poland* App no 23052/05, Judgment of 3 February 2009, para 74; *Semikhvostov v Russia* App no 2689/12, Judgment of 6 February 2014, para 84.

[88] Nancy Fraser, 'Social Justice in the Age of Identity Politics: Redistribution, Recognition and Participation' in Nancy Fraser and Axel Honneth (eds), *Redistribution or Recognition?: A Political-Philosophical Exchange* (Verso, 2003), 7–109, 29. See also Peroni and Timmer (n 3), 1065.

[89] *Kadirzhanov and Mamashev v Russia* App nos 42351/13 and 47823/13, Judgment of 17 July 2014, paras 91–92; *Khamrakulov v Russia* App no 68894/13, Judgment of 16 April 2015, para 66.

[90] *Kiyutin v Russia* App no 2700/10, Judgment of 10 March 2011, Reports 2011, para 63, para 64.

[91] *M.S.S.* (n 10), para 251.

[92] *Sashov and Others v Bulgaria* App no 14383/03, Judgment of 7 January 2010, para 55.

[93] *Alajos Kiss* (n 8), para 42.

In these cases, awareness-raising campaigns to combat negative attitudes among the general public can be an essential source of resilience.[94] The Court itself, through its case law, may be contributing to this. In the long term, correcting misrecognition may counteract vulnerability to some degree and potentially protect members of vulnerable groups from its worst effects. Similarly, as concerns LGBTQI youth, Martha Albertson Fineman has sought ways to build through education.[95]

iv. The Limits of Individual Adaptability as a Source of Resilience

Sources of resilience are not limited, of course, to the above. However, in identifying further sources of resilience, it is important these should be about tackling the reasons for and manner of responding to vulnerability-related ill-treatment, and not about making applicants able to bounce back after having been ill-treated. The focus here is not, in other words, on whether individuals can survive ill-treatment and thrive despite it.

That said, the Court does show a certain willingness to consider individual adaptability as a source of resilience in particular contexts. For example, in expulsion cases, the possibility for applicants to adapt to their situation by moving elsewhere in their home state – the so-called 'internal flight' option – is often cited as a reason for why they would not be vulnerable.[96] In such cases, in the absence of clear information about the risks concerned and the possibility of avoiding them, the Court may decide a case to an applicant's disadvantage.[97] A recent case in this regard, however, found that because a particular applicant's family – who were the source of the alleged risk in that case – was politically influential and could track her down in the home state, it was not possible to return her.[98] This development is to be welcomed given that, if adaptability is to be considered as a source of resilience, it needs to engage with the real possibility of such adaptation. In this regard, it is useful to recall the Court's *Salah Sheekh v Netherlands* judgment. There, it examined whether the applicants could be expected to integrate in a 'safe' area given local dynamics, and found that they would instead likely end up occupying a 'marginal, isolated position in society'.[99]

v. Conclusion

In the words of Martha Albertson Fineman, '[r]esilience is the essential but incomplete antidote to our vulnerability'.[100] And indeed, resilience is not a fail-safe: every

[94] Martha Albertson Fineman, 'Vulnerability, Resilience and LGBT Youth' (2014) 23(2) *Temple Political and Civil Rights Law Review* 307–329, from 325.
[95] Fineman (n 95), 328.
[96] See *Salah Sheekh* (n 42), para 141; compare also the rejection of that option in *R.D. v France* App no 34648/14, Judgment of 16 June 2016, para 43.
[97] *G.J. v Spain* App no 59172/12, Decision of 21 June 2016, paras 45–53.
[98] *R.D.* (n 96), para 43.
[99] *Salah Sheekh* (n 42), para 140.
[100] Fineman (n 95), 320.

human individual is and remains vulnerable, no matter how many resilience-bestowing assets they accumulate. To give an example, it can be noted that '[e]ven the most wealthy and resourceful asylum seeker cannot grant their own refugee status nor give themselves access in law to the host society; they are dependent on state action for this.'[101]

Resilience to vulnerability can take a variety of forms. It can be related to the individual applicant in a case – thus, concern innate, medical or psychological factors – be related to the socio-economic assets available to that person – which can be cultural, environmental, financial or educational – or be conveyed by institutions, and thus represent specific assistance and counselling, an ease of access to proceedings, and individual empowerment to claim rights. However, it is easy to overestimate the effect of some sources of resilience, and to thereby slip back into the idea of the liberal legal subject who can independently overcome or avoid ill-treatment. Applying resilience considerations in the context of ill-treatment can thus overestimate the abilities of applicants to avoid such acts, unfairly privatising the responsibility for avoiding them. While a balancing of all aspects that contribute to vulnerability and resilience should certainly be the way forward for the Court's analysis in individual cases, it should proceed with caution in this regard.

What the preceding comments have not addressed is how resilience and the capabilities approach relate to each other. In this regard, some authors have written about the need to complement vulnerability reasoning with a capabilities approach,[102] but the relationship of resilience and capabilities remains underexplored. Given the above considerations concerning resilience, and understanding capabilities according to Martha Nussbaum's theory, which sees them as the answer to the question '[w]hat is this person able to do and to be?',[103] there seems to be a close connection between the two. In other words, guaranteeing a sufficient minimum threshold of capabilities means ensuring that all human individuals enjoy the ability to live lives of autonomy and dignity. In the same way, ensuring that human individuals enjoy certain assets that confer resilience and that compensate, to some extent, for their vulnerability makes them able to exercise their rights and safeguards their dignity and autonomy. While perhaps somewhat oversimplified, this makes it possible to argue that there is a significant degree of overlap between a capabilities approach and an approach to vulnerability complemented by an understanding of the assets necessary for resilience.

[101] Gina Clayton, 'Asylum Seekers in Europe: M.S.S. v Belgium and Greece' (2011) 11(4) *Human Rights Law Review* 758–73, 769.
[102] MacKenzie (n 84).
[103] Nussbaum (n 57), 20.

III. Revolutionising the Revolution: Vulnerability Theory and its Guidance for the Court

As argued throughout this volume, the concept of vulnerability has a significant potential to affect – albeit often hesitantly or selectively – the Court's jurisprudence under Article 3. The Court's approach is by no means perfect, however, and it could be improved by taking some lessons from vulnerability theory. The following will provide recommendations for revolutionising this quiet revolution, making it a louder but also a more inclusive, sustainable, just and agency-promoting one.

A. Moving from the Invulnerability-Vulnerability Binary to a Spectrum of Vulnerability and Resilience

Developing a sound approach to vulnerability requires an explicit discussion of why and how the vulnerability of certain applicants and groups is considered relevant for the purposes of a judgment. This should replace the discussion of whether applicants are vulnerable or not. No applicant is invulnerable, or not vulnerable, because no human individual is entirely free of vulnerability. Indeed, if the Court's case law shows anything, it is that vulnerability can stem from a wide range of sources, many of which vary over a person's lifetime. Thus, the division of applicants into two categories – vulnerable and invulnerable – should be dropped entirely, and be replaced with a more nuanced approach, as outlined below.

Mainstreaming vulnerability considerations does not mean that the Court must find a violation of Article 3 in every case, given the vulnerability of every applicant. Instead, the Court should understand vulnerability as a spectrum, and take a holistic approach to both applicants' vulnerability and their resilience in order to determine where they fall on that spectrum. This allows it to determine whether there are gaps in their protection and hurdles in their access to justice for which it needs to compensate.

B. Adopting a Minimum Content of Vulnerability

The Court's approach to vulnerability, to date, has been to identify vulnerable groups and individuals in an ad hoc manner, and without defining the concept. It is perhaps true that a definition of vulnerability is not per se necessary or even productive. On the other hand, however, it is necessary to understand what the concept means – only in this way can states have some certainty about what is required of them, and individuals claim their vulnerability in Strasbourg. In this regard, it is useful to understand vulnerability as a deprivation of the capabilities and resources that allow human individuals to live autonomous lives of dignity and agency. Understanding the concept in this way ensures that it will not be abused to justify paternalistic interventions and that there is a minimum content to the concept that allows for the identification of further vulnerable groups and individuals.

C. Maintaining a Reasonable Scope for Article 3

The above has expressed unease with the idea that every offence to an individual's dignity should necessarily and automatically fall under the absolute Article 3. Similarly, the Court should build its vulnerability-related case law with care, in the knowledge that the provision does not necessarily provide the adequate forum in which to address all possible inequalities and vulnerabilities. This case law should leave a reasonable scope of application to other Convention provisions, such as Articles 8 and 14.

Of course, this should not mean that the concept or vulnerability is not relevant for the scope of Article 3. Indeed, as Manfred Nowak has argued, the very insidiousness of torture stems not (only) from the gravity of the force employed and the injuries caused, but originates primarily in the powerlessness and vulnerability of the victim.[104] The question, thus, is to assess those factors – particularly by examining the context holistically, and allowing considerations of vulnerability and resilience to inform the analysis – so as to ensure a responsive but sustainable scope for Article 3.

D. Addressing Selectivity and Promoting Inclusiveness

As concerns the particular suffering related to vulnerability, the Court should take care to display understanding or empathy only for applications who are relatable or who appear deserving of the Court's engagement. In the same vein, it should not deploy selectivity to the detriment of other applicants. Of course, the pool of potential applicants to the Court is an immensely vast one. However, if vulnerability is used to pick out some groups and individuals whose claims require special attention – say, asylum-seekers – and then to narrow this pool down further again – say, to child asylum-seekers, or even again, to unaccompanied minors – then it enhances manageability, but it does a disservice to the very salient claims that may be brought by those who do not receive priority on this hierarchy of vulnerability. Vulnerability should, accordingly, not be a way to cherry-pick those applicants whose claims are to be heard while blinkering the Court's judges about wider issues.

As far as the inclusiveness of the Court's vulnerability case law is concerned, it is highly likely that there are other reasons, beyond those identified by the Court

[104] Manfred Nowak, 'Challenges to the Absolute Nature of the Prohibition of Torture and Ill-Treatment' (2005) 23(4) *Netherlands Quarterly of Human Rights* 674–88, 677–78.

to date, to find that a group or individual is vulnerable. The present analysis has recommended some further additions to this list, including victims of trafficking and those living in poverty or homelessness, as well as a further exploration of the vulnerability of LGBTQI people and the elderly. Individual vulnerability is constantly in flux, given that it varies over the course of a human life span and is context-responsive. For this reason, it is unlikely that there will ever be a definitive list of who is vulnerable. Having a sense of what vulnerability means – a deprivation of certain capabilities, powerlessness, an inability to claim one's rights, dependency, etc – makes it easier to identify those whose vulnerability may not yet have attracted the attention of the Court or of other actors.

E. Respecting and Mainstreaming Agency

Allowing a legal concept of vulnerability to exist without any definitional contours and without an integrated understanding of the need to promote individual autonomy is risky: it means that vulnerability can be abused so as to further interests that have little to do with empowering individuals. One example is the creation of laws that discriminate against LGBTQI people on the premise of safeguarding the rights of vulnerable young people. In fact, such a use of vulnerability can be found in the Court's own case law. Namely, when considering a challenge against laws that criminalised consensual same-sex sexual contacts between adults in Northern Ireland, the Court recognised 'that one of the purposes of the legislation is to afford safeguards for vulnerable members of society, such as the young, against the consequences of homosexual practices'.[105] Other conceivable examples of this are bans on the wearing of religious symbols, notably the hijab, where this is based on argumentation concerning the protection of women as vulnerable to being pressured into wearing such an item.[106]

Using vulnerability as a blanket justification for measures that drastically affect the rights of marginalised individuals on the basis of the judgment that they are dangerous to children or lack agency, without any further evidence in this regard, is entirely unacceptable. Real arguments are needed in this regard instead of lax references to presumed vulnerability. One possible safeguard against abusive reliance on vulnerability is to emphasise agency. The measures referred to in this section are paternalistic ones, and an emphasis on agency-building and autonomy – as well as, in these specific contexts, the unacceptability of perpetuating negative stereotypes – can therefore allow for the identification of abusive vulnerability-based measures.

[105] *Dudgeon v United Kingdom* App no 7525/76, Judgment of 22 October 1981, Series A45, paras 47, 49, 60 and 62, as noted in Francesca Ippolito, '(De)Constructing Children's Vulnerability under European Law' in Francesca Ippolito and Sara Iglesias Sánchez (eds), *Protecting Vulnerable Groups: The European Human Rights Framework* (Hart, 2015) 23–47, 23.

[106] Compare the rationale for the contested ban in *S.A.S. v France* App no 43835/11, Judgment (GC) of 1 July 2014, Reports 2014, paras 17 and 42, and also PACE Recommendation 1927 (2010) of 23 June 2010 on Islam, Islamism and Islamophobia, para 3.13.

F. Providing Procedural Justice

When it comes to providing procedural justice to victims of alleged ill-treatment, this is most relevant as regards torture, which particularly reduces individuals to positions of extreme distress and helplessness and can have lasting cognitive, emotional and behavioural consequences,[107] but it is relevant for all forms of ill-treatment, and indeed for all violations of human rights. In this vein, an appropriate, empathetic and context-responsive attitude can provide victims with feelings of recognition and offer 'some relief from the experience of alienation'.[108] Where the Court's vulnerability reasoning means recognition of or at least engagement with the suffering of victims of ill-treatment, it allows individuals to experience procedural justice even where the outcome of their application may not be a 'success' in the sense of a violation finding. As noted above, being able to participate in the proceedings, the perceived neutrality of the judges involved with hearing the case, a feeling of being treated with respect by the system and of being able to trust the decision-making authority increase individuals' satisfaction with human rights adjudication and can also have a beneficial effect for the Court's acceptance.[109]

Furthermore, experiencing proceedings that are perceived as just may also be a step on the road to recovery from the feeling of powerlessness that results from an act of torture.[110] In this regard, a foreshortened vulnerability assessment that ultimately negates the vulnerability of an applicant without engaging in the arguments presented by them is not a neutral act, but a harmful and potentially re-traumatising one.

G. Awareness of the Potential for Paternalism, Stereotyping and Essentialism

Group-based approaches carry a risk of essentialising that group by flattening and standardising the experiences of its diverse members. In this regard, for example, Kirsten Sandberg has found it impossible to exclude that the approach to vulnerability of the Committee on the Rights of the Child, no matter how well thought

[107] OHCHR, 'Istanbul Protocol: Manual on the Effective Investigation and Documentation of Torture and Other Cruel, Inhuman or Degrading Treatment or Punishment' (revised edn, 2004) HR/P/PT/8/Rev 1, www.ohchr.org/Documents/Publications/training8Rev1en.pdf, 45, with further references, and 46–47.

[108] See ibid, 46.

[109] Ibid, 180–85 and throughout.

[110] Eva Brems and Laurens Lavrysen, 'Procedural Justice in Human Rights Adjudication: The European Court of Human Rights' (2013) 35(1) *Human Rights Quarterly* 176–200, 182, citing Tom R Tyler, 'Procedural Justice and the Courts' (2007) 44(1/2) *Court Review: The Journal of the American Judges Association* 26–31, 26.

out, will be transformed into punitive or paternalistic responses by States given the fact that it uses a groups-based approach at all.[111]

This can be a double-edged sword.[112] Mentioning the vulnerability of particular groups may essentialise their members while failing to mention it negates patterns of disadvantage, marginalisation, inequality and powerlessness. In this regard, the former option is preferable. Sandberg agrees: regarding the group-based approach to children, she finds that while 'the particular vulnerability of each child within such groups may vary … if the characteristics or situations that make children particularly vulnerable are not pointed out to the states, children in such situations are easily overlooked – whether by lack of awareness or by unwillingness – and so is their need for adapted measures'.[113]

Similarly, the risks of paternalism and stereotyping are difficult to eradicate from a vulnerability-based approach altogether. Certainly, emphasising dignity and agency is one corrective measure. Another is to focus on the ways in which certain specific people are rendered vulnerable, and why, instead of employing vulnerability as a label.[114] Understanding and paying due attention to the fact that vulnerability is complex, and made up of a whole range of disempowering or empowering circumstances, is another corrective.[115] In addition, it is essential to overcome the idea that 'normal' people are not vulnerable, and that only certain groups – such as asylum-seekers, detainees, etc – can be described as such. As long as this idea is permitted to persist, it will continue to stigmatise those who are vulnerable and render them other.[116] In this regard, the Court's approach should shift from one that categorises applicants as vulnerable or not vulnerable, to one that evaluates an applicant's situation more holistically and in an individualised way. The outcomes in many cases may be the same, but – for the reasons set out above – the reasoning deployed here matters as well.

IV. Final Thoughts

To conclude, it is possible to state that vulnerability has become a core concept of the Court's Article 3 ECHR case law, and that it has the potential to create closer engagement with cases – both as concerns the concrete circumstances and experiences of applicants and the underlying systems of privilege and power – by the Court. As has been argued in this volume, however, there are some lessons

[111] Kirsten Sandberg, 'The Convention on the Rights of the Child and the Vulnerability of Children' (2015) 84(2) *Nordic Journal of International Law* 221–47, 236–37.

[112] Ibid, 237.

[113] Ibid, 237.

[114] Peroni and Timmer (n 3), 1073.

[115] Ibid, 1074.

[116] Alexandra Timmer, 'A Quiet Revolution: Vulnerability in the European Court of Human Rights' in Martha Albertson Fineman and Anna Grear (eds), *Vulnerability: Reflections on a New Ethical Foundation for Law and Politics* (Ashgate, 2013) 147–70, 162.

that the Court could learn from a theoretical account of vulnerability in order to prevent a range of problems from materialising as it applies its vulnerability heuristic. In particular, it should be aware both of the fact that Article 3 should not be considered a panacea for all possible dignity-related harms, and that it is necessary to ensure that Article 3 remains applicable in practice. Neither, however, is selectivity a viable guiding principle for the concept; this only fragments the Court's case law and harms its reputation while failing to provide states with necessary guidance. One way forward would be for the Court to adopt a minimum content for its approach to vulnerability, so as to prevent abuses. This should include respect for agency and safeguards against risks such as essentialism and paternalism. By following these steps, the Court has the possibility to build a vulnerability heuristic that will continue to foster context-sensitive and human-centric judgments respectful of the core values of Article 3 ECHR: the dignity and agency of the individual.

A Note on Methodology

The present volume is based on a systematic analysis of the vulnerability jurisprudence related to Article 3 ECHR. The following explains the methodology used in obtaining, coding and analysing that case law.

This volume did not study all of the many thousands of cases examined by the Court under Article 3 to date, but only those where vulnerability explicitly played a role in the Court's decision-making. The case law to be considered was therefore filtered via the Court's own HUDOC database.[1] The data was collected by searching all document collections in both official languages, with the exception of communicated cases (where no examination of the merits has yet taken place, and it is thus not possible to derive any information about the Court's approach to vulnerability) and legal summaries (which reproduce other judgments and decisions and do not bind the Court). The search included Article 3 cases brought against any Member State, and covered judgments and decisions by all configurations of the Court on all levels of importance.

The results were narrowed to cases that included the words 'vulnerable', 'vulnerability', 'vulnérable' or 'vulnérabilité'. The Boolean wildcard symbol ('*') was used in order to include all four terms in one search, thereby avoiding overlaps, and the search term used was thus 'vuln*'. This search, which was conducted for the time span between the inception of the Court and 28 February 2019, yielded 1,147 results.

For the sake of creating a case law database that was as exhaustive as possible, a second search under the same conditions but using the terms 'precariousness', 'precarity', 'précarité' and 'précaire' was also conducted. The results overlapped almost entirely with the results found via the first search, and the Court usually reinterpreted applicants' allegations of *précarité* as a question of vulnerability[2] or used both terms together,[3] meaning that only four additional relevant cases were identified in this way.[4] This search was repeated using the term 'defenceless'; it led

[1] Which is available at http://hudoc.echr.coe.int/eng#.

[2] See *Stoyan Mitev v Bulgaria* App no 60922/00, Judgment of 7 January 2010, paras 53 and 55 as compared to para 73; *Tarakhel v Switzerland* App no 29217/12, Judgment (GC) of 4 November 2014, Reports 2014 (extracts), paras 65 and 84 (where the applicants refer to precariousness).

[3] See *M.S.S. v Belgium and Greece* App no 30696/09, Judgment (GC) of 21 January 2011, Reports 2011, contrasting para 233 ('the vulnerability inherent in his situation') and para 320 ('a state of precariousness … contrary to Article 3').

[4] *Giusto, Bornacin and v Italy* App no 38972/06, Decision of 15 May 2007; *A.A. v Switzerland* App no 58802/12, Judgment of 7 January 2014, para 40; *Archip v Romania* App no 49608/08, Judgment of 27 September 2011, para 57; *B.A.C. v Greece* App no 11981/15, Judgment of 13 October 2016, paras 32, 37, 40, 43, 46, which is not directly relevant to the present analysis because the relevant references were made under Art 8 ECHR.

to the identification of one additional case.[5] Similar searches were also conducted using the terms 'helpless', 'sans défense', 'fragilité', 'susceptible', 'susceptibility' and 'susceptibilité', but these did not lead to the identification of any additional cases relevant under Article 3.

The resulting judgments and decisions were filtered to retain only those where vulnerability had effectively been employed by the Court in its reasoning. Regarding the parts of these cases to be examined, a compromise had to be made between a 'paragraph' rule and a more comprehensive approach. On the one hand, in order to make it possible to take such a large number of cases into consideration, all of the judgments and decisions of the Court under Article 3 where vulnerability had entered into play could not be read in their entirety. It was therefore necessary to delineate which parts of the cases would be considered. On the one hand, reading all of the 1,150-odd judgments and decisions from start to finish would have been excessively labour-intensive and might have entailed conjecture regarding the attributes constituting vulnerability.[6] On the other hand, cherry-picking only the paragraphs mentioning vulnerability would have risked missing relevant information, while failing to read the facts of the case would mean that the findings on the merits could be taken out of context. A workable compromise was therefore reached by first reviewing the facts of each case and then applying an expanded paragraph rule, ie only looking systematically at the section of the merits concerning Article 3, with whole judgments being considered where deemed opportune.

Applying this methodology led to the retention of 438 cases in which vulnerability played a part in the Court's reasoning. Cases in which vulnerability was used only in its common definition, or used only in the context of other Convention rights or by third parties, were excluded. Where cases referred to the concept of vulnerability in both language versions, only the English version was counted. Where vulnerability was used by multiple configurations of the Court dealing with the same case – thus, for example, by the Commission and the Chamber, or by the Chamber and the Grand Chamber – only the final judgment or decision was counted; the findings of the other bodies were indexed as well, but separately so as to ensure that the same case was not counted twice for the purposes of the quantitative results. Where the concept of vulnerability was referred to only in a separate opinion attached to a judgment, but not in the judgment itself, the reference was included in the data for information purposes but not counted as a reference by the Court.

In order to build case law groups, the cases were coded according to – where possible – the aggregate trait or situation giving rise to the vulnerability in question. However, given that the intersection of various grounds of vulnerability

[5] *Aliyeva v Russia* App no 1901/05, Judgment of 18 February 2010, para 87.

[6] Contrast the approach taken by Audrey R Chapman and Benjamin Carbonetti, 'Human Rights Protections for Vulnerable and Disadvantaged Groups: The Contributions of the UN Committee on Economic Social and Cultural Rights' (2011) 33(3) *Human Rights Quarterly* 682–732, 703 and 705–07.

makes applicants more vulnerable than one of the individual grounds alone, it was not possible or useful to select just one of these aggregate groups for each case of intersectionality. This means that, where the Court considered that multiple traits gave rise to vulnerability, that case was coded once for each of the relevant categories. Any additional characteristics that did not play a role for the Court's finding of vulnerability – meaning that they were not explicitly or by obvious implication used as the basis for a finding of vulnerability – were not counted. However, this approach erases the intersection of the various sources of vulnerability at play. For this reason, cases of intersectional vulnerability were additionally coded as such.

Some references to very specific intersections of numerous factors could not always be added to broader categories and were more appropriately considered on their own. For example, the very specific reference to a vulnerable 'African woman working as a prostitute'[7] was flagged as a special case, as was the reference, for example, to terminally ill patients seeking access to an experimental medicine.[8]

This volume operates on the basis of case law groups built by means of the database thus created. The large number of relevant cases was thereby organised into a typology that allows conclusions to be drawn about when, how and why the Court uses vulnerability. The decision to operate on the basis of an exhaustive case law analysis was not made only because such a comprehensive examination of vulnerability-related case law was missing in the academic literature (including, but not limited to, that concerning Article 3). It was also chosen in particular because this approach facilitates tracing the evolution of the various strands of case law and the diverging approaches to vulnerability taken. In other words, it uncovers certain elements that would have gone missing in an analysis based purely on leading cases, and considers that there is added value to documenting the massive extent to which the Court uses vulnerability reasoning.

* * *

> The Council of Europe has aimed from the outset at protecting the rights of the weak, the vulnerable, the persecuted. Equality, tolerance and the acceptance of differences are its guiding principles.[9]

In 2011, the European Court of Human Rights (ECtHR) issued a landmark judgment in the case of *M.S.S. v Belgium and Greece.*[10] That judgment, which created baseline welfare obligations for certain types of applicants, concerned the prohibition of torture and inhuman and degrading treatment under Article 3 of the European Convention on Human Rights (ECHR). In this case, the Court

[7] *B.S. v Spain* App no 47159/08, Judgment of 24 July 2012, para 62.

[8] *Hristozov and Others v Bulgaria* App nos 47039/11 and 358/12, Judgment of 13 November 2012, Reports 2012 (extracts), para 122.

[9] PACE, 'Report on Gypsies in Europe', Doc. 6733, 11 January 1993, para 7.

[10] *M.S.S. v Belgium and Greece* App no 30696/09, Judgment (GC) of 21 January 2011, Reports 2011.

found that states must provide materially for people who are particularly dependent on the authorities. It did so by emphasising the special 'vulnerability' of the applicant as an asylum seeker.

Today, *M.S.S.* is part of a larger strain of case law that uses various iterations of vulnerability to tailor the Convention to context. For example, this concept has allowed the Court to create special protections for children, who fall in the 'class of highly vulnerable members of society' to whom the state must provide care and protection.[11] Children's vulnerability takes precedence over other interests, and for example means that the criteria for detaining a minor are more strict than those applicable to adult detainees. In other words, this case law recognises that identical treatment can have more intense or traumatic effects on one person than on another, depending on the circumstances. This recognition relates to the distinction between formal and substantive equality, and to the recognition that responding to context allows rights to be universal while also accommodating diversity.[12]

From a systemic perspective, the regional and international human rights framework responds to particular protection needs through 'special' human rights instruments specific to certain groups.[13] Under a universal human rights instrument such as the ECHR, vulnerability has an equivalent function: it grants special protection or a tailored response to the needs of certain groups or individuals. Vulnerability has been used in this way not just by the ECtHR, as discussed in this volume, but also by other human rights bodies. These bodies all tend to use the concept as a vague and undefined one that allows for the ad hoc protection of certain individuals or groups, which raises questions about the meaning of vulnerability and the criteria for describing someone as vulnerable. It also entails a normative question regarding what these criteria and concepts should look like.

Answers to these questions are difficult to come by. Human rights bodies often refer to vulnerability situationally, and without an explanation of the concept's definition, scope, or effects. A theoretical account of vulnerability is replaced simply with the delimitation of a list of groups and individuals considered to fall under the term in a given context, through either a 'categories approach'[14] (for example, the category of children) or a 'factor-based approach'[15] (for example, the factor of being in detention). In other words, instead of clarifying what

[11] *Mubilanzila Mayeka and Kaniki Mitunga v Belgium* App no 13178/03, Judgment of 12 October 2006, Reports 2006-XI, para 55.

[12] See Eva Brems, *Human Rights: Universality and Diversity* (Martinus Nijhoff, 2001); Antony Anghie, *Imperialism, Sovereignty and the Making of International Law* (CUP, 2004), 254–56.

[13] An example is the CRC.

[14] Chrystalla Katsapaou, 'Response to Vulnerability in Asylum: Project Report' (UNHCR, 2013), www.unhcr-centraleurope.org/pdf/what-we-do/caring-for-vulnerable-groups/response/response-to-vulnerability-in-asylum-project-report.html, 33.

[15] David Weissbrodt and Mary Rumsey, *Vulnerable and Marginalised Groups and Human Rights* (Edward Elgar, 2011); Dia Anagnostou, 'The Strasbourg Court, Democracy and the Protection of Marginalised Individuals and Minorities' in Dia Anagnostou and Evangelia Psychogiopoulou (eds), *The European Court of Human Rights and the Rights of Marginalised Individuals and Minorities in National Context* (Martinus Nijhoff, 2010), 1–26, 2.

vulnerability means and why it matters for human rights protection, human rights bodies prefer to simply state that a given individual or group is vulnerable.

For the past three decades, the ECtHR has used vulnerability reasoning in various ways to extend the scope of Convention rights. It has done so for a variety of reasons, including applicants' dependency, a risk of harm or exposure to violence, and historic oppression and marginalisation. Over time, the Court's vulnerability reasoning has acquired significance in the context of various Convention rights, including the right to life,[16] the prohibition of torture and inhuman and degrading treatment,[17] the prohibition of slavery and forced labour,[18] the right to liberty and security,[19] the right to a fair trial,[20] the right to respect for private and family life,[21] and the prohibition of discrimination.[22]

Today, references to vulnerability are most plentiful under Article 3 ECHR. In this context, the Court has developed a burgeoning case law, which spans hundreds of judgments and decisions and concerns applicants who have been considered vulnerable for a broad array of reasons. The present volume predominantly concentrates on this provision. It does so not only because vulnerability reasoning is prevalent and impactful under Article 3, but also to explore the relationship between the provision's absolute nature and its arguably relative application. Today, given the volume of vulnerability-related case law, and the various and significant effects that the concept has on Convention standards, understanding vulnerability is key to understanding the Court's approach to Article 3 ECHR and to the progressive development of its case law overall.

The Court's intentional ambiguity about the meaning of vulnerability is perplexing, especially given that vulnerability is a term in common use and not per se a legal concept. As a result, understanding the concept of vulnerability requires a closer look at *regarding whom*, *how*, and *why* the Court resorts to vulnerability reasoning.

The question of *who is vulnerable* is explored in chapter three of this volume, which maps the Court's case law under Article 3 and creates a typology of vulnerability on this basis. The bulk of references to vulnerability under Article 3 relate to dependency. This can stem from a particular need for care and support – as applies for example to children and to persons with certain disabilities –, or can be due to imprisonment, institutionalisation, or other grounds rendering a person particularly dependent on the state. However, not all references to vulnerability

[16] Art 2 ECHR; see *Salman v Turkey* App no 21986/93, Judgment (GC) of 27 June 2000, Reports 2000-VII, para 99.

[17] Art 3 ECHR; as discussed in this volume.

[18] Art 4 ECHR; see *Siliadin v France* App no 73316/01, Judgment of 26 July 2005, Reports 2005-VII, paras 126 and 143.

[19] Art 5 ECHR; see *O.M. v Hungary* App no 9912/15, Judgment of 5 July 2016, para 53.

[20] Art 6 ECHR; see *Blokhin v Russia* App no 47152/06, Judgment (GC) of 23 March 2016, Reports 2016, paras 195, 198–99.

[21] Art 8 ECHR; see *I.B. v Greece* App no 552/10, Judgment of 3 October 2013, Reports 2013, paras 79–81; *Söderman v Sweden* App no 5786/08, Judgment (GC) of 12 November 2013, Reports 2013, para 81.

[22] Art 14 ECHR; see *D.H. and Others v Czech Republic* App no 57325/00, Judgment (GC) of 13 November 2007, Reports 2007-IV, paras 181–82.

relate to dependency. Applicants may for example be vulnerable because they have experienced victimisation, including through sexual and domestic violence. They might also be vulnerable because of a context of migration, or because they belong to a marginalised group, for example certain religious and ethnic minorities or LGBTQI people. People living with a psychosocial disability or HIV/AIDS can also fall into this latter category. Situations of pregnancy and precarious reproductive health can also create vulnerabilities, as can certain political views and activities. Lastly, chapter three discusses the Court's approach to the intersection of two or more grounds of vulnerability, for example when an applicant is both a child and a member of an ethnic minority, or both a detainee and living with mental illness.

In chapter four, the volume explores *how* the Court uses vulnerability. In other words, it determines the effects of the concept. For example, the Court has relied on vulnerability to flesh out states' positive obligations to protect the wellbeing of individuals under their control[23] and to lower the threshold of severity that must be reached in order for the Court to find a violation of Article 3.[24] Beyond this, vulnerability affects many aspects of an application's life in Strasbourg – from the urgency with which it is treated, to the criteria for its admissibility, to the Court's decision on the substance of the case and even the awards made. Vulnerability can, in other words, have far-reaching effects, and it is part of the continuing strengthening or expansion of the protection afforded by Article 3, which – as part of the ECHR, a living instrument to be interpreted in light of present-day conditions – enshrines an 'increasingly high standard' that evolves with time.[25]

Lourdes Peroni and Alexandra Timmer, two of the first scholars to study the Court's vulnerability jurisprudence, have argued that vulnerability 'acts as a magnifying glass', allowing the Court to pinpoint ill-treatment and its impact on a particular applicant.[26] At the same time, even without vulnerability reasoning, the Court's assessment of whether there has been a violation of Article 3 is already context-sensitive. In other words, the minimum level of severity that must be reached in order for ill-treatment to violate Article 3 is a relative one, and dependent on all the circumstances of a case.[27] As a result, this volume asks *why* the Court nevertheless uses the concept of vulnerability. It argues that the reasons for the Court's turn to vulnerability might be found, for one, in its attempts to limit the scope of its judgments, especially where politically delicate distributive questions are at stake, while retaining the flexibility to find violations where

[23] *X. v Germany* App no 8819/79, Decision of 19 March 1981, DR 24, p 158; *Denis Vasilyev v Russia* App no 32704/04, Judgment of 17 December 2009, para 115.

[24] *Tarakhel v Switzerland* App no 29217/12, Judgment (GC) of 4 November 2014, Reports 2014 (extracts), paras 118–19.

[25] *Selmouni v France* App no 25803/94, Judgment (GC) of 28 July 1999, Reports 1999-V, para 101.

[26] Lourdes Peroni and Alexandra Timmer, 'Vulnerable Groups: The Promise of an Emerging Concept in European Human Rights Convention Law' (2013) 11(4) *International Journal of Constitutional Law* 1056–85, 1091.

[27] *Ireland v United Kingdom* App no 5310/71, Judgment of 18 January 1978, Series A no 25, para 162.

deemed necessary. Vulnerability may therefore allow for a covert balancing exercise to take place in the context of Article 3 despite the provision's absolute nature. Vulnerability narratives may also function as a consensus-building instrument in divisive cases, or they may evoke judicial empathy. At the same time, vulnerability allows for the identification of structural inequalities and disadvantages and promotes a substantively equal approach to protecting human dignity.

In this regard, the Court's approach to vulnerability relates to a well-established philosophical debate. From this perspective, vulnerability can destabilise the prevailing liberal order's concept of the legal subject as autonomous, rational and invulnerable. In these theoretical accounts, vulnerability is a mechanism for context-sensitivity and a driver for equality, justice and respect for human dignity because it represents a shared human experience linked to our embodiment in a vulnerable human form. In other words, vulnerability here is understood as a universal human experience or condition. Placing the Court's approach to vulnerability into this wider theoretical context not only sheds light on some of the pitfalls of its jurisprudence, but also potentially provides ideas for addressing them.

The present volume uses this philosophical-theoretical framework to analyse the Court's approach. This identifies a binary opposition of vulnerable applicants against those who are non-vulnerable as being deeply problematic. As an alternative, it discusses a spectrum that moves between extreme vulnerability and great resilience – ie access to resources that protect individuals against the effects of their vulnerability. Based on this approach, the volume recommends a roadmap for the Court's future case law that addresses the risks of its current selectivity.

INDEX

www.ingramcontent.com/pod-product-compliance
Lightning Source LLC
Chambersburg PA
CBHW071258180926
51613CB00001B/73
9781509941230